And I Saw the Mountain

And I Saw the Mountain
A Daily Devotional Guide

by
Kenneth E. Sullivan

Beacon Hill Press of Kansas City
Kansas City, Missouri

Copyright 1990
by Beacon Hill Press of Kansas City
ISBN: 083-411-3449

Printed in the
United States of America

Cover Photo: Pat O'Hara

Unless otherwise indicated, Scripture texts are from the KJV.

Permission to quote from the following copyrighted versions is acknowledged with appreciation:

The Holy Bible, New International Version (NIV), copyright © 1973, 1978, 1984 by the International Bible Society.

The *New King James Version* (NKJV), copyright © 1979, 1980, 1982, Thomas Nelson, Inc., Publishers.

The New Testament in the Language of the People (Williams), by Charles B. Williams. Copyrighted 1937 by Bruce Humphries, Inc., assigned 1949 to The Moody Bible Institute of Chicago.

10 9 8 7 6 5 4 3 2 1 (1990)

To
KEITH AND GAYLENE
whose own devotional book
is faith, compassion, and leadership
in action

Acknowledgments

This devotional book, *And I Saw the Mountain,* finds its setting in the everyday experiences of life as they work in and out of the routine of living. It is everybody's book as we experience the deep cry of the heart, the moments of sorrow, the times of defeat, and the enthusiasm of victory. Its thesis is that God conquers, rules, and reigns in the prepared heart and is never a disappointment. What might appear to be a divine judgment is turned into a means of grace and a source of hope.

Sometimes we go down in the dark places of the night, and into the depths of gloom; and often we find ourselves where sorrow sheds many tears, and where iniquity comes with its broken promises, and we are heard only in our cry of weakness. It is in the fabric of these human experiences that we find God dealing with something beyond what can be explained adequately in words. At the moment of our greatest insecurity He brings us to His higher places above the surrounding dangers and uncertainties.

This book began at a point of failure in one project, and by the suggestions and encouragement of Dr. Cecil Paul it rose to meet this present challenge. But even here words come ill-equipped in their proclamation of the gospel of love that is so desperately needed in our day.

To Dr. Stephen W. Nease, a close and cherished friend, whose life has been lived out in the noblest of these ideals, and who gave support and encouragement when the chips were down, I owe a debt of appreciation.

To Rev. Jerry Douds, who had a genius for simplicity that laid hold on God, and who in the unexpected places could find an oasis, I want to say, "Thank you!" It was Jerry who introduced me to *The People's Bible* by Joseph Parker, which formed the basis for the prayers, ideas, and some of the starting places for these devotional contributions.

To Bob Bollinger, whose wise counsel has touched many circumstances in the culmination of this project, I owe more than I can ever repay. And to Lucy Bollinger, whose enthusiastic response to an ordinary New England happening prompted the words, "The leaves fell off, and I saw the mountain," and provided the springboard for the title of the book, I shall be forever grateful.

To Dan Van't Kerkhoff of Baker Book House, Grand Rapids, Mich., for permission to use Joseph Parker's prayers as a source for ideas and suggestions, I owe a gratitude beyond words to express.

In those times when the pen went dry, ideas failed, and discouragement ruled the moment, my love and appreciation runs deep for the one who encouraged with the words, "Hang on. You are going to make it!"

To Him who keeps the records and followed every line that was written, discarded, and rewritten, in the good days and in the bad ones, and takes His place beside us and reveals His strength and shows us possibilities beyond our powers—to Him I owe everything.

JANUARY 1 ■

The Lord is nigh unto them that are of a broken heart; and saveth such as be of a contrite spirit.
(Ps. 34:18)

BROKENNESS! Broken vows, broken resolutions, broken hearts, broken spirits . . . a broken world! Thank God for a time and a place to mend and to begin again—on my knees, at the Cross, in His new year, for His eternity.

God's plan has a future as well as a past, and our lives are bound up in the entire scheme. His plan cannot be achieved without our will being captured and our faith being challenged. So He brings us again to a starting point, and we look at the entire year in perspective. He sees it filled with anxiety and trouble, but He also makes us aware of His forward concern.

God measures the year with His grace, and out of what we call calamity He brings consolation. Through our tears of brokenness He assures us that He will be with us. Love says we have been accepted. Heaven says the Book bears our name. The heart responds in an affirmation of love. The enemy recognizes his defeat and knows that his battle has been lost.

My brokenness has been covered by God's wholeness, and in the depths of His love the iniquity, hurt, disappointment, and bitterness have been resolved. The seal of God has been imprinted in the clay of my consecration, and my life bears the autograph of the Almighty.

All human life is related to this experience of grace, and my loving obedience will turn the severity of the year into its own security, so that my days ahead will be beatitudes of glory.

Brokenness is human; wholeness is divine. My wholeness found in His holiness!

PRAYER: *O God, in our world of sin under the power of Satan, the year has been filled with broken hearts as numerous as the sands of the sea. Often we can find no healing balm to salve the hurt of the crushing blows. Piece together the broken dreams, we pray, and let Your Holy Spirit dwell richly in the hearts of people everywhere. Amen.*

■ JANUARY 2

I speak that which I have seen with my Father: and ye do that which ye have seen.
(John 8:38)

We have been to Nazareth and have heard the declaration, "Hail, thou that art highly favoured, the Lord is with thee: blessed art thou among women" (Luke 1:28). We knelt at the manger in Bethlehem after the announcement, "For unto you is born . . . a Saviour, which is Christ the Lord" (2:11). We entered into the mystery of the Divine as we followed Him through Capernaum to Jerusalem and on to Golgotha. The events of His life overwhelmed us, rebuked us, and challenged us until we watched Him die on the Cross.

We fully expected Him to come down at the cry of the mob, but we secretly hoped that He would not. We could find no reply to His death, for we did not know that He was taking our place there. We heard His cry, "It is finished" (John 19:30), but we did not know that before our eyes stretched the whole gospel of salvation.

But this very thing was happening! However, we were not touched by the whole meaning of Calvary until the resurrection dictum, "He is not here: for he is risen, as he said" (Matt. 28:6).

Now that we have seen the Christ in whose being our own has been lost, the greatest vision of heaven will be of little consequence if we remain dumb to what we have seen and experienced.

We must speak the new message and carve a path through the jungles of heathenism and proclaim to the ends of the earth that salvation has come. The message is that God, the omnipotent One, reigns forever and forever, and His love rules supreme. Hallelujah!

PRAYER: *In You, O God, we live and move and have our being. This is our joy, because it is our strength. But it is our fear, for it is our responsibility. We lift our faces to the throne after having done our best and pray that Your mercy and love will shine upon us in abundance. Amen.*

JANUARY 3 ■

For he knoweth our frame; he remembereth that we are dust.
(Ps. 103:14)

May I have a heart-to-heart talk with You, God? Did You remember that You made me just an ordinary human being? I am not divine. I am not a superhuman. I am not almighty. Did You remember that yesterday? Have You forgotten it today?

I bruise easily, and I still cry when I am hurt. Sometimes it takes quite a while before I can get on my feet when I fall or when someone knocks me down. My feelings are hurt when I am slapped, and often it is difficult to forgive. I have told You about this before, remember? You told me that I could cast all my cares on You, for You really did care for me. I believed this, and it made me feel good. But sometimes I can't seem to find You, and when the cares are the heaviest, You seem to be the hardest to find.

I'm very shortsighted, and often the immediate looks like mountains. You told me one day about a little bit of faith that could move these difficulties away. But when I try this, the mountains grow bigger, and the contradiction mocks my dilemma.

Sometimes I get on my knees to pray, and I try to put my ideas about Your ways into big words and arguments; but it only ends up in frustration, for I get lost in Your words and reasoning.

Are You really out there looking on when I am surrounded by more demons than any human being can handle? Are You giving me a boost when I am climbing a hill too steep for my strength? Are You remembering that I am a mere speck of dust when I accuse You of expecting too much from me? Was it You who gave me life yesterday and strength today? When I fell today, was it You, God, who helped me get up again?

Thank You for supplying Your divinity to my humanity. I love You. I need YOU!

PRAYER: *May we be lost in wonder, love, and praise as we think upon this great truth of God. Open our eyes and ears so that we might see and hear Your living message. Assure us again that burdens are lifted at Calvary and that to the Cross no aching heart has ever looked in vain. Amen.*

JANUARY 4

Flee also youthful lusts: but follow righteousness, faith, charity, peace, with them that call on the Lord.
(2 Tim. 2:22)

This morning I turned on the radio and heard a man who had just returned from prison speaking to young people on the abuse of drugs and urging them to take a place of leadership in their groups. He challenged them to say to their friends, "I am not going to follow you. You follow me." Then he added, "Give them something worth following you for."

It takes stamina to be able to say, "My way is better than your way." It takes a lot of living and shaping to develop the strength for this kind of stand. But taking a stand does not necessarily destroy friendships or influence. Moral standards do not change with the times, and right is always right in whatever century we live. The enduring qualities of courage are the same yesterday, today, and forever.

There is a confirming voice in the soul of that one who dares to stand up and challenge, "You follow me." And the soul knows that Voice as the blade of grass knows the sun—and herein lies the secret of strength. Courage generally comes when we are in the company of great numbers, but the most timid of heart can find boldness in the mystery of this divine confirmation.

A friend of mine recently pinned a poster on the wall of my office depicting a very confused ape, and the caption reads, "Don't follow me, I'm lost." How great the number whose lives are caught in this confusion. Paul assured his followers of his absolute unworthiness as a person but then proceeded with the greatest challenge of his ministry: "Be ye followers of me even as I also am of Christ" (1 Cor. 11:1). This challenge can vibrate with new energy and a new passion if there can be found one who is willing to stand with the eternal in the midst of the mutable and say, "I am not going to follow you. You follow me as I follow Him!"

PRAYER: *We have been following You, O God, and Your leadership has taken us by ways that have frightened us. But Your hand has led us into the green valleys and beside the still waters of peace. Lead us on, O King Eternal, we want to follow! Amen.*

JANUARY 5 ■

Why art thou cast down, O my soul? and why art thou disquieted within me? hope thou in God.
(Ps. 42:5)

This world is reeking with disease and despair, and people everywhere are frightened. Any hope for tomorrow seems to be smothered in dread and apprehension. We have swapped our peace for pollution, and our inventions of comfort have spewed devastation on our very doorsteps. We have lost our freedom in our effort to find the larger road, the swifter progress, and the lesser burden.

Every assembly is made up of broken hearts, burdened lives, blinded eyes, and sorrow-laden souls. Every audience is a company of listeners, reaching out for words of hope and a deliverance that elude their grasp. They are not asking for a new truth, and it is too late to ask for trifles or that the laws of the universe be changed to supplant the errors of humanity.

But it is not too late to touch our world with a deeper tenderness. It is not too late to speak to them about the grace of God that can climb the marble steps of the palace or ascend the meanest staircase and talk with the same divine eloquence. It is not too late to tell them that our lives are dearer to God than any disease or dread that they contain. It is not too late to tell them that God will not be used for our selfish purposes, nor will He turn His ways into conveniences for the satisfaction of our need. But He has promised comfort for the breaking heart and can tune our ears to the whispering of heaven and give assurance for the darkest moment on earth.

We may be trembling in fear today because of what happened yesterday to our world. But our hope can extend in peace for the tomorrows because God is in control, and His purpose is above our wit or thought.

PRAYER: *We thank You, O God, for hope and confidence, and for all the voices that speak to us from above. We need these in the dark times and when the sun is shut out by the clouds of despair. This hope tells us how great is Your love, how tender Your pity, and how precious the tears of Your compassion! Amen.*

JANUARY 6

And he took a child, and set him in the midst of them.
(Mark 9:36)

God blessed our home with three precious children and poured out further glory in the gift of four grandchildren. So a big part of my life has been surrounded by the genius and innocence of the child mind. Through them I have come much closer to God's thoughts than classes of philosophy or theology could ever bring me.

In speaking of the majestic wonders of the Creator, the Psalmist observed that "from the lips of children and infants you have ordained praise" (8:2, NIV). And Jesus said that we must become like little children to qualify for entrance into His kingdom.

How wonderfully the quality of God's love is displayed in the care and concern of such small things! How wonderfully He puts on display His finest attributes! Our little children really know nothing about hatred, prejudice, grudges, defiance, or greed until we have "learned" it to them. They come to us as bundles of tenderness, forgiveness, happiness, kindness, and joy; and "of such," the Master said, "is the kingdom of heaven" (Matt. 19:14).

God places great accountability on us in the care of these little ones that He has put in our trust. And he who wantonly abuses one of these precious ones certainly must come under God's most severe judgment.

When Jesus likened the greatness of heaven to a little child, He probably taught His shortest lesson, yet as endless in suggestion and power as eternity.

Thank God for our little children and the lessons they have taught us. How often I have knelt by their bedside and prayed that I could be like them!

PRAYER: *O God, set the little child in our midst today and teach us the mystery of Your kingdom. Show us where we stand in terms of our own goodness, charity, and nobleness. May we ever learn from them whom the Master would not turn away. Amen.*

JANUARY 7 ■

And being in an agony he prayed more earnestly: and his sweat was as it were great drops of blood.
(Luke 22:42)

Prayer is much more than bending one knee, saying a few words in haste to the Lord, and then waiting for the hurried request to be put in operation by some emergency unit of heaven. Prayer is more than, "Give me, God . . . now I've got to go." Prayer is not even spending hours on my knees in patient waiting if the lock is still on the door of my heart.

God has placed conditions on all His relationships with humanity, but He has also backed up every demand with a covering promise. Consequently, there is a condition to a successful prayer, and that condition finds its involvement in the realm of love, devotion, honesty, self-surrender, agony, sacrifice, and even death. The depth of my earnestness and the expression of my desire, along with my conception of God's omnipotence, lay before Him the value lines of my devotion.

How difficult it is for us to reach this point of commitment in our ongoing relationship of ease with the Almighty God! Nevertheless, to live for His glory and in all the inspiration of His love, we must be willing to pray in earnest. Then in our identification with His purpose no pleading in words will be necessary, for our intention will be its own argument, and the eloquence of our devotion will bring persuasive powers to the throne. God will measure our demand by our sincerity, and His answer will be meted according to our readiness to receive.

We complain about unanswered prayers. But He reads our requests through the drops of our Gethsemane blood, and His ear is not deaf to the cry of the agonizing soul. The greatest prayer we could ever bring to the throne of God was uttered by Him who waits there to receive it anew from our breaking hearts. This prayer found its answer at Calvary—His Calvary. It will be answered again today at ours. "Not my will, but thine, be done" (Luke 22:42).

PRAYER: *Teach us, O God, how to pray. We could have no confidence in our prayers were we not able to breathe them at the Cross. Here is the sacred altar where man never prayed in vain. With the Cross as our altar and Christ as our Advocate we are assured of Your reply. Amen.*

■ JANUARY 8

And though I have all faith, so that I could remove mountains, and have not charity, I am nothing.
(1 Cor. 13:2)

We have been told that faith can move a mighty mountain, and it can smooth out the roughness of an angry sea in the midst of the most fierce storm. It is so powerful that even a tiny grain can change the course of nature and take charge of the universe. Jesus talked a lot about faith and seemed perturbed when He saw that impossibilities were uppermost in the thinking of the disciples. He never did give it a definition, for faith does not live in words, and it does not stoop to tell the reason why—it just keeps on working.

Faith stands at the door of the furnace and witnesses "the form of the fourth," One "like the Son of God" (Dan. 3:25).

Faith walks in the lions' den and testifies to kings of the presence of God during the dangers of the night.

Faith moves among the diseased and the infirm and enters the sickroom and says to reach out and "touch the hem of his garment" (Matt. 14:36; see 9:20-21).

Faith stands at the foot of the Cross where the mysterious communion between the soul and God takes place.

Faith does not close the door to the stranger and is not afraid to stand by the beggar or kneel by the shame of failure.

Faith turns weakness into strength, defeat into purpose, and replaces hatred with the gentle glow of love.

Faith does not shut the door or close the window to silence the sounds of youth in their laughter and song.

Faith is not selfish, demanding, or cruel, and it performs best in company with hope, love, and truth, where there is never a conflict.

Faith sings in the storm and knows the way through the darkness, saying, "Weeping may endure for a night, but joy cometh in the morning" (Ps. 30:5).

PRAYER: *We thank You, Father, for a faith that can stand in Your presence. This is our strength and our joy. It has become our song in the nighttime and our triumph in the prison, where we watch the dungeon tremble and the doors open. By faith we live and move and have our being. Amen.*

JANUARY 9 ■

And now abideth faith, hope, charity, these three; but the greatest of these is charity.
(1 Cor. 13:13)

This morning I met a lady walking down the sidewalk with a white cane—tapping, tapping, tapping! I went into the restaurant and ate my breakfast, but I kept hearing the tapping, tapping, tapping. I walked out to my car and drove to work through all the busy traffic with my unimpaired vision. But I kept hearing the tapping white cane. What were the questions that it kept asking?

Endlessly. Hauntingly. Tap. Tap. Tap.

How can I get to know the meaning of all of this? How can I put myself in the world of that tapping cane? Is it crying out to my world about cruelty and injustice? Is every tap a mark on the pavement of life for me to acknowledge and interpret—or regret? Is it trying to tell me about fears and pressures and peculiar difficulties that have never entered into my world? Is it sending out a message that can be read only by the lame, the blind, the sorrow-ridden, the infirm, and the aged? Or is it simply saying to me, "Stay out of my world—I'm afraid of yours!"

I do not know the answer—it's too big. At best "we see [only] through a glass, darkly"; and we only "know in part" (v. 12); and we only hear a faint whisper of God's magnificent whole. And as we both grope our way along, clinging to our little day we know, without really knowing how or why, that God is in control of much that He has yet to reveal to both of us.

"Then shall I know"; but for now there "abideth faith, hope, charity" (vv. 12, 13). Tap! Tap! Tap!

PRAYER: *O God, though the clouds should cover the sun, it does not mean that the sun is dead forever and that the clouds have conquered at last. If doubts arise and faith begins to waver, help us to know that, even in the darkest moments, Your face is only hidden from us for a while. Fill us with that consuming desire to continue on in this great salvation. Amen.*

■ **JANUARY 10**

But if ye forgive not men their trespasses, neither will your Father forgive your trespasses.
(Matt. 6:15)

Seventy times 7. Wow! That's 490 times—and He was talking about forgiveness? Forgive my brother nearly 500 times? Or anyone else for that matter!

Impossible! No way! That's too much forgiving.

Yet Jesus was merely touching the tip of the iceberg, for He might have said, "Peter, don't ever stop forgiving."

We can preach Christianity to others, defend the Cross with our lives, pay our tithes and go to prayer meeting every week, and even sit in our prominent place in the front pew every Sunday morning, and still ask in unbelief, "How many times did You say, Jesus?"

I suppose there is no greater attainment in Christian living for a conscientious believer than to be able to say with an honest heart, "I forgive." The demand of Jesus was for an all-out consecration, and here was the hallmark of His teaching.

How often in the frustration of the moment and the panic of the immediate our best intentions are challenged and put under the microscope. Every challenge and examination strengthens our faith and identifies for us more clearly the terms on which the Master based His doctrine. And His demands have not changed today!

Against this truth the disciples so willingly accepted 2,000 years ago, the world has placed great argument and suspicion. But the truth is established in God's eternity: Forgiveness is forever!

PRAYER: *O God, how grateful we are to know that Your forgiveness covers it all through love. It is the voice of God to the pleading of man. For that forgiving grace found at Calvary, we thank You, for by it we also share in the resurrection, the crown, and the throne. Forgiven because of Calvary! Amen.*

JANUARY 11

But of the tree of the knowledge of good and evil, thou shalt not eat of it: for in the day ... thou shalt surely die.
(Gen. 2:17)

Remember when you were a little child and the confusion that seemed to surround you with the "Do this" and "Don't do this" syndrome? Or the problems that you have imposed on your own children over the prohibitions and the possibilities you have brought to bear upon their activities? Whether we like it or not, we have been born in a world where rigid terms of right and wrong belong to everyone, and life is pretty much controlled by the direction our decisions take.

The divine injunction in the beginning was "Thou shalt not," and even in the day of our greatest temptation this must not be forgotten. The speaking Voice to our hearts is the same today, and the power to overcome the tempter has never changed. But the day of judgment is also imminent for the moment when we would eat of the forbidden.

Life is made up of continual estimations of values that arise before us every day. The arguments between penalties and rewards are difficulties with which we must grapple in our expanding growth in understanding right and wrong.

These are not mere symbols with which we can trifle, or laws that can be changed, or even questions to be argued. This is the demand of Omnipotence to every man in the Garden of Life, where standards must be raised and laws laid down to govern our decisions.

But the golden thread that extends through every Christian experience has to be, "As for me and my house, we will serve the Lord" (Josh. 24:15).

This is Christian faith! This is the Christian life!

PRAYER: *Remind us, O God, of the deceitfulness of sin, that You might also remind us of Your great mercy. "Thou God seest me"—let us live in the searchlight of this heavenly penetration and keep our hearts pure. Amen.*

JANUARY 12

Eye hath not seen, nor ear heard, neither have entered into the heart of man, the things which God hath prepared.
(1 Cor. 2:9)

One day last summer I watched a tiny ant walk across my patio, down over the edge, and across the driveway, then disappear in a small hole under some leaves. Another one came out of the same hole, retraced the steps, and disappeared on the other side. I looked up in the cloudless sky and saw the sun gleaming down from 93 million miles away, then recalled the Milky Way the night before with the billions of stars billions of miles out in space. In amazement I said, "My God made them all. How can it be?"

This is all part of the mystery of His great creation, and His omnipotence has allowed itself to be bound up in the tiny ant as well as the magnificent sun. There are no words to explain this phenomenon when I realize that the Creator's almightiness is willing to find its repose in something so insignificant and something so majestic.

There is also a mystery of grace in the arrangement, for somewhere in between the mystery of the ant and the mystery of the sun I find the mystery of myself and the deeper mystery of a personal relationship with the Creator of us all.

When I look at life in its many facets of pain, struggle, exasperation, and often its mockeries and hear Him whisper to me, "I have redeemed thee, I have called thee by thy name; thou art mine" (Isa. 43:1), then "I scarce can take it in."

Then I realize that of all the beautiful redeeming qualities of God to His creatures, none can be richer or fuller or greater than the gift of peace, along with His tender care for and communication with a human creature.

My soul sings in victory, "Oh, the wonder of it all!"

PRAYER: *Almighty God, You amaze us by the wonder of Your power, Your wisdom, and Your love. We cannot know You in all the fullness of Your being and purpose, nor can we find out the Almighty in His perfection. We know You by the small whisperings of Your love and are satisfied. Amen.*

JANUARY 13 ■

I know whom I have believed, and am persuaded that he is able to keep that which I have committed unto him against that day.
(2 Tim. 1:12)

When a little child looks up into the face of his father and says, "That's my daddy!" he does not have to give a philosophical reason for the claim. As far as he is concerned, there is no argument. The relationship has been established, and hardhearted is the father who does not beam with pride. A certainty has been established in the mind of the child that won't be denied.

A look of dismay marked the face of the interviewer when he questioned the presidential candidate on certain religious convictions. He pressed for scientific proof. He was baffled when reminded that it is possible to believe God, to love God, to obey God, and to be in communication with God without the necessity of having to construct intricate arguments to prove the fact.

Not every person is ready with a complete theory of inspiration or is able to defend a theory of scientific evidence. It is possible for a person to know that the Bible is the Word of God. At the same time that person might not be able to argue certain mysteries contained within the Book. It is possible to communicate with God and yet not be able to prove the spiritual phenomenon to the bystander. The man whom Jesus healed of blindness stood on the one thing he knew: "Whereas I was blind, now I see" (John 9:25). The fact took care of the controversy.

In order to be a Christian, it is not necessary to be able to answer every question that may come up either in ignorance or candor. The things that are praised above all else in the Bible are the broken and contrite heart, the meek and lowly spirit, and the open mind to receive God.

God takes great pride in those who bow before heaven in penitence and look up and acknowledge Him as "Abba, Father."

PRAYER: *O God, in the abundance of theories and theological arguments concerning the intricate ways of life, we pray that we will not get lost in our search for the Cross. "For God so loved the world" is the glory of all Christian service as we live under its inspiration and daily benediction. Make it so in Jesus' name. Amen.*

JANUARY 14

For the Lamb of God which is in the midst of the throne shall feed them ... and God shall wipe away all tears.
(Rev. 7:17)

The older I get, the less value and significance I place on heaven with streets of gold, walls of jasper, and gates of pearl. If these were the greatest attractions, my enthusiasm for its glitter would wane, for I have seen where this value system has led our world down here.

Redemption was placed on a much different level, and it took suffering rather than sapphires, and sacrifice instead of silver, to appease God for my salvation. John saw the redeemed coming, a crowd so vast that no man could number them, and he said, "These are they which came out of great tribulation, and have washed their robes, and made them white in the blood of the Lamb" (Rev. 7:14). It seems that the things that have eternal meaning are: tribulation and suffering; Christ and the Cross; death and immortality. These, touched by the righteousness of God, bear a far greater value in heaven than such corruptible things as silver and gold.

There will be so much humanness about us until we exchange the mortal for immortality, but the significance of earthly glitter will pale as we move nearer the eternal values. He who stands at the head of humanity said that we must bear our cross if we would follow Him. Paul would glory in nothing save the Cross and declared himself to be "crucified with Christ" (Gal. 2:20; see 6:14) that he might obtain a truer weight of glory.

My heart sings today above the glitter of the gold and the sparkle of diamonds, for the true marks of glory will be the nail-pierced hands rather than gold-plated streets.

PRAYER: *Blessed Jesus, we would know the fellowship of Your sufferings so that we may also know the power of Your resurrection. May we understand it more and more as we pass through the storms of life down here. Then show us the glory that lives in eternity. Amen.*

JANUARY 15

For whatsoever is born of God overcometh the world: and this is the victory that overcometh . . . even our faith.
(1 John 5:4)

One morning I heard a man testify in church that in his ignorance he had told God he did not need Him in his life, for he could outsmart the devil in his own human wisdom. Then he related his failure through the ingenuity of the enemy that caused his defeat. Of course, his happy conclusion was that he did need God, for his own capability was not sufficient to outwit the devil. How often we are taken in by the egotistical superiority of our own thinking and then experience the utter failure of our best efforts. It is impossible for any human cleverness to lay the elements of victorious living in the pathway of an unregenerated soul.

There is no rebuke more humbling, or any experience more blessed, than the one discovered in a face-to-face confrontation with the divine Spirit of God in that moment of his own defeat. There is no scolding in His concern, but the quiet pressure of His love speaks a language greater than the mind can grasp. It cannot be defined, but we know that the strength for our victory comes to us by the way of the Cross, with God's Spirit living in the heart and establishing himself in the very fibers of our being.

I am thankful that I heard this man's testimony, for it gave me an enlargement of imagination and a spiritual enthusiasm as I rejoiced in the openness of his honesty. God's people need to remind the world every day that His grace is sufficient for the full extent of life. I am thankful for every testimony of victory, for it is but a whisper of the great unknown and unexplored sphere of God. This is God at work. This is the glory of heavenly truth. This is man in harmony with the Infinite. This is a chain broken and a bond confirmed. This is "the righteousness which is of God by faith" (Phil. 3:9). This is my victory too—and yours!

PRAYER: *O God, the powers that rule the air and direct the world are against us. You have shown us that they that are for us are more in number and grander in quality than all that are against us. To be with You is to be in the majority, and to be in Christ is to be assured of victory. May this ever be our delight. Amen.*

JANUARY 16

Inasmuch as ye have done it unto one of the least of these my brethren, ye have done it unto me.
(Matt. 25:40)

On my way to heaven I met a man going to hell. He stopped me and asked if I would give him some help.

I said, "I'm on my way to church, and I am in a hurry." And in my hurrying I continued, "I don't have time to stop, for they are waiting for me at the church to come and pray and testify."

But I did invite him to come with me and get saved, as I continued to tell him of the grace of God and how it could change a person's life.

He said that he wasn't much into this church bit, but could I spare him a dime for some food?

Of course I knew where he would spend it, so I told him how hard I had to work for my money, and I didn't feel that I could give any of it away foolishly. Then, the people at church would be expecting to see me put my offering in the plate. But I didn't seem to be able to get through to him about the importance of the collection plate or the necessity of the church. He kept insisting that he was hungry, but I was in a hurry. I was on my way to heaven.

As I turned to leave, he caught my arm and pleaded, "Please . . . can't you help me?" I pulled away from him and went on my way to church without too much compassion for this man on his way to hell. I was busy getting to heaven.

I did get to church on time. And I smiled at my friends. And I prayed. And I cried for the lost. And I testified. And I put my offering in the collection plate. And I went home happy that everyone had a chance to hear me pray and testify and pay my way to heaven. My friend continued on his way to hell.

PRAYER: *O God, we pray for all those who are living one day at a time, hoping that peace and comfort will come tomorrow. For those who are suffering in body or mind, make the day of pain flee away in haste. Prepare their chamber so that peace and happiness may move in with the Unseen Guest to dwell with them forever. Amen.*

JANUARY 17 ■

Ye know that ye were not redeemed with corruptible things . . . but with the precious blood of Christ . . . without blemish and without spot.
(1 Pet. 1:18-19)

When you get on your knees in prayer, God does not ask how much money you have in your pocket, or how big your bank account is, or how much cash you brought along with you. He does not turn you away because you are poor or pour out abundant blessings upon you because you are rich. The abundance of salvation does not depend on your wealth, nor does He withhold His bounty until sufficient financing has been secured.

Our relationship with God does not rest on our riches; and herein lies the strength of our Christian faith. There is only one claim on Deity that ever made converts, martyrs, or saints: "Nothing in my hand I bring; / Simply to the Cross I cling." And the defense of our Christianity stands precisely at this point, and from here we are led into the deeper mysteries of salvation.

Christianity met Simon at this point, and Peter chastened him for thinking that "the gift of God may be purchased with money" (Acts 8:21). It was more than mere rhetoric when he later exhorted his readers that we "were not redeemed with corruptible things, as silver and gold . . . but with the precious blood of Christ" (1 Pet. 1:18-19).

Today I must not fasten my attention too securely on those things that are apt to prepare me for wrong purposes and motives. I know where I have been. I know where I am today. And I know the way before me that leads to victory. But I also know it is not a silver-plated pathway, nor is it lined with sapphires and diamonds. It is a way marked by the footsteps of the Man of Gethsemane, and Calvary, and the Cross.

This is also my way to God and salvation—it leads upward!

PRAYER: *O God, You have made us rich with promise, and now we pray that You will make us rich with those possessions that give freedom to the soul. Make us realize that Your riches are unsearchable and that Your wisdom is past finding out. Keep us in Your way—the heaven-bound way. Amen.*

JANUARY 18

Blessed is that man that maketh the Lord his trust.
(Ps. 40:4)

The song leader said, "Let's turn to No. 367 and continue our worship by singing 'Jesus Is All the World to Me.'" Very routine—until we began to sing, "My Life, my Joy, my All." I did not hear much more of the song. How often when great issues are involved, we are brought to close quarters with God! There is nothing unimportant to Him, nor does He want to leave anything in doubt.

"Is this really your commitment—do you want to go over it again this morning?"

"My Life." Even as the years grow into the more golden era, the call is still to lay down my life in affirmation of this truth that makes and keeps one free. All through the years the same Jesus. The same grace. The same enabling Spirit. And this morning it must be the same commitment.

"My Joy." What about the vexations, deprivations, poverty, sickness, and disappointments? My crucifixion! Oh, the miracle of redeeming love and the "nevertheless afterward" in God's economy of grace. My joy is not shackled to the immediate but to immortality, which "yieldeth the peaceable fruit of righteousness" (Heb. 12:11) and enables me to sing in the nighttime.

"My All." Or can it be one day in seven? A token of my time, talent, and tithe! Only the right hand, Lord? No! God deals in totals. No adjustments or temporary arrangements, but the whole man. The only ground on which my commitment can stand is total obedience. My All!

Not until the whole ground had been covered and all the controversies of the soul had been resolved could I continue the song, "Eternal life, eternal joy, He's my Friend!"

PRAYER: *Almighty God, You have given great peace to all those who have committed their all to You. You have become their strong Rock and Hiding Place. Continue to be our Abiding Place while the ages roll. Amen.*

JANUARY 19

Wherefore, if God so clothe the grass of the field, which to day is, and to morrow is cast into the oven, shall he not much more clothe you, O ye of little faith?
(Matt. 6:30)

One man seeking the highest office of his country, in speaking about his handling of daily activities, said, "I can't control the big pattern—I simply start at the beginning and try to handle the moment-by-moment details." The beginning of a new day has always been a challenge as well as an opportunity.

Each new day is a new revelation, a new beauty, a new experience, a new opportunity, and a new challenge. Every day God's purpose is to touch us with good things in the depth of our distress. Every day is rich with promises, and the plan from eternity is strength and wisdom. Nothing is going to happen in any day, even down to the falling of the tiny sparrow, without His knowledge.

Each new day is filled with lack of trust on the part of many people. This brings on fear, and their prayers die on the threshold of the closet in which they were uttered. They fail to see that the God who created the morning can take care of the entire day. If we could believe this, our days would, indeed, be filled with happiness.

At the beginning of each day we need to link our lives to the greatness of God's providence. God gathers up all our weaknesses and shortcomings in His omnipotence, and out of the stress of our inadequacies He brings peace and harmony.

Today is a new day, and I will draw on the almightiness of a great God. I will live and move and have my being in Him. My most insignificant affairs I will spread out before Him. I will invite Him to my table as the Giver and Sanctifier of my store.

Today, if I pass through the valley of the shadow of death, I will ask no other comfort than His rod and His staff. He does all things well. I need His moments to make up my day!

PRAYER: *O God, teach us to number our days, that we may apply our hearts unto wisdom. You have filled each one with parts, and each part is filled with Your direction from heaven. Help us to acknowledge Your providences and give heed to the divine laws. In Jesus' name. Amen.*

■ JANUARY 20

But if ye forgive not men their trespasses, neither will your Father forgive your trespasses.
(Matt. 6:15)

Probably the two greatest words ever to be spoken are "forgiven" and "forgotten." They must have come from the heart of God, and in His arrangement of things He has put "forgiven" first. This is the order in which God works when He touches man by the fullest meaning of the cross of His Son.

Paul claims that he was commissioned by God and sent to the Gentiles "that they may receive forgiveness of sins" (Acts 26:18). The second word is not unrelated, for God has promised to bury the forgiven sins in the sea of His forgetfulness to remember them against us no more forever.

Forgiven and forgotten! God says, "I forgive, and I forget." In His plan of redemption there is no room for nagging reminders of the past.

How bold then I can be before Him "in whom we have redemption through his blood, even the forgiveness of sins" (Col. 1:14; see Eph. 1:7). How bold I can be before the enemy, who can bring no accusation because God has forgotten.

This is the miracle that has made men fearless in the Kingdom and whose mighty influence has astounded the rulers of their day. These are the factors through which God's greatness becomes manifest in human flesh.

But the forgiveness that makes one strong is also His salvation that makes one tender, compassionate, loving, and kind. Is it not easier to say, "I forgive and I forget," after God has forgiven and forgotten?

Is not this my calling—to forbearance, and patience, and love, and understanding, and mercy? Forgiving because we have been forgiven. Forgetting because He has forgotten!

PRAYER: *We thank You, O God, for all of Your promises—so high in quality, yet so tender in tone and precious in all that they speak to the waiting soul. Pardon is surely the voice of God and the message of the Father. We would hear it again today. Amen.*

JANUARY 21 ■

What is man, that thou art mindful of him?
(Ps. 8:4)

Halley's Comet becomes visible in our world once every 79 years as it continues its elongated orbit in space. I think I saw it on its last voyage, as its misty stream sped very low across our horizon. At its nearest moment in distance it was millions of miles from where I stood on that hillside.

It was mind-boggling as we anticipated the wonders of creation that night. How can I believe that my few feet and inches of stature can be significant to Him who deals in millions, yea billions of miles, and comets, and stars, and universes?

That night I looked away at another Hill where stood a Cross, and I read on the outstretched arms this message: "You are great in the care and love of God."

Fear and unworthiness that had enveloped me in a shroud of darkness gave way to a glorious realization that I am part of His creation. And I stood tall, knowing that He had made me in His own image and redeemed me from destruction through His Son, Jesus Christ. I do not have to feel like a crawling, creeping creature outside His care, for I stand on firm footing in His universe.

David may never have seen Halley's Comet, but something in the heavens inspired awe and reverence in him for the Creator: "When I consider thy heavens . . . what is man, that thou art mindful of him?" (vv. 3-4). Then he places God ahead of all space and time and concludes, "How excellent is thy name in all the earth!" (v. 9).

And as He leads the comet on its orbit beyond my world, He gives me this assurance: "Have no fear, for your humanity rests on unconditional love and is held in the hand of My power." Therefore, I rest my case in the message of eternity for the ages, "For God so loved the world [my world], that he gave . . ." (John 3:16).

I will spend eternity filling in the blanks!

PRAYER: *We are fearfully and wonderfully made—how great and how little man is! You made him in Your image and in Your likeness. We lay ourselves at Your feet. We are Yours, for You know our highest usefulness. Keep us in Your care. Amen.*

JANUARY 22

Come boldly unto the throne of grace, that we may obtain mercy, and find grace to help in time of need.
(Heb. 4:16)

This morning I talked to God. Oh, mystery of mysteries. How can it be!

I probably would never be granted entrance into Buckingham Palace or gain access to the White House, but I can have audience with the Supreme Ruler of the universe.

This comes simply by accepting a divine invitation, "Come boldly unto the throne of grace, that we may obtain mercy, and find grace to help in time of need."

Such bold presumption would be a desecration and beyond human imagination were the invitation not issued from heaven. And to be able to accept it is to contradict all the programs of deceit propounded by the opposition through the ages. It is God's delight for His people to "rest in the Lord, and wait patiently for him" (Ps. 37:7).

I do not have to understand all the mysteries of godliness, for I simply begin at the Cross, where Christ worked out a doctrine of love. And from here He calls me to redemption, prayer, and communion. And my opportunities are magnified by my desire to meet Him on His terms.

When we put together the commands of Scripture, do they not speak to us of fellowship, communion, faith for the impossible, and a consciousness of freedom in the Spirit of God? And the deeper things of God are revealed only at the place of prayer and at His invitation.

The things of God may be hidden in secret places and veiled in a mystery that I cannot explain. But love unlocks the door and persuades me to come boldly before His presence.

Here is the bond of kinship that even death cannot dissolve and no other power can shake.

Through this love I can talk to Him today, and tomorrow, and the next day, and the next!

PRAYER: *Be with us, O God, for the few days and nights that we have left in Your measure of time. Help us to be better today than we were yesterday. Make our tomorrow an anticipation of Your grace and sweet presence. Keep us ever near the throne. Amen.*

JANUARY 23 ■

Ye shall not need to fight ... stand ye still, and see the salvation of the Lord with you.
(2 Chron. 20:17)

It was Sunday night, and I lay helpless in a hospital room, broken in body and anxious in spirit. The problems of my family, my church, my demolished car, my hospital bills, and the care of my people piled as high as a mountain. Visiting hours were over, and I had been sedated for the night.

The door opened, and a fellow pastor came through, sat on the edge of my bed, and said, "God sent me here to tell you to stand still, and you would see the salvation of the Lord." Then he went out into the night. My burdens lifted.

Amid the gravest problems and brokenness of heart God sends His messages in the night: "Hold steady, for God already has been working on your problems." Again from the Psalmist: "Rest in the Lord, and wait patiently for him ... and he shall give thee the desires of thine heart" (37:7, 4). Here is the rock on which the saints have stood.

Is there a person who can deny his need of help outside his own resources? Yet strength from God can become so real and vital as to make one rejoice in triumph over the tribulations, pain, and sorrow. Paul rejoiced in his hardships because they brought him closer to God. What a tribute to the sustaining power of His grace!

Life is not a matter of pain for a day, nor is it simply the distress of a night. Many prayers have encompassed burdens, details, defeats, and victories running in contradictions and affirmations that have covered a lifetime.

The great assurance of God to His people has been "Stand still and see" and "Let us not be weary in well doing" (Gal. 6:9). Length of time and weariness of spirit are God's concern, and He will not allow one to suffer beyond the reach of His love.

PRAYER: *Help us, O God, to rest patiently in You so that we will not have to know fear when it comes. Make the storms to fall in blessing upon the garden and our songs to be fresh every morning. Then our praise shall go forth to Him whose love surrounds us each day. Amen.*

■ JANUARY 24

Thy word have I hid in mine heart, that I might not sin against thee.
(Ps. 119:11)

Often we hear rebukes offered in jest on the number of Bibles we have in our homes. And it is true that many church-oriented families can count a dozen or more Bibles in various areas of the house with varying degrees of usage. In a recent missionary service the speaker talked about working with people who "do not have a Bible." Touched by the realization of their circumstances, the words haunted me: "Without a Bible!"

A garden without flowers. A furnace without fire. A bird without wings. A life without purpose. A home without love. People without God's Word.

Other religions give importance to their sacred items of wood, stone, clay, and precious metal and assign a certain superiority to each article. The things that they worship greatly affect their relationship to every other area of life including their altars and their sacrifices.

Without a Bible there can be no true conception of God, and reaching out for a Divine Being leads to superstitions, corrupt religion, and demon worship.

In our urgency for the heathen we forget the one "without a Bible" who lives on our block. God finds no sanctuary here, and the religious convictions usually do not run very deep. God's Word can never be replaced by the idols of clay or the wisdom of the world.

Maybe my calling is not to take a Bible to the heathen or knock on the neighbor's door with my excess Bibles. Would it not be a greater challenge to live out its precepts so that my neighbor would inquire about the one that I read?

PRAYER: *We thank You, O God, for giving us the Book that interprets the entanglements and riddles of life and gives them meaning. Out of its pages come assurances that the darkness is but for the moment, and great light will shine upon our path. We would stay close to the Book lest we lose our way. Amen.*

JANUARY 25 ■

God is not ashamed to be called their God: for he hath prepared for them a city.
(Heb. 11:16)

Every generation looks at the "age of martyrdom and sainthood" and extols in great detail their glorious feats and mighty acts. The faith chapter, Hebrews 11, becomes very real, and it recounts how the early people withstood the lions and gladiators; held out against emperors, kings, and rulers; and refused to recant. I have sat through sermons on the bloody details of early martyrdom, and the conclusion was always the same: "Those days are gone forever!"

How very wrong can we be!

Saints and martyrs have lived and died whom history has never recorded and who may never be identified this side of the glory land. I saw one today. No, I didn't see any blood shed, nor did I witness bloody claws tearing flesh and bone apart in a hungered frenzy. But I saw tears, and determination, and sacrifice, and courage that can never be expressed in the language of earth. I saw a heart breaking in shreds and a firm stand against surrender and read a conversation with heaven that time cannot understand. Here I saw freedom, devotion, strength, vision, and purpose—attributes that make a saint or a martyr.

The Church has moved forward by the stuff that has made them great. They were dauntless under opposition, fearless under adversity, powerful in the might of an everlasting God, and faithful unto the end.

When that mighty host moves in from the east, and the west, and the north, and the south and stands before the great throne of God with robes washed in the blood of the Lamb, I want to be there to meet the ones I have known.

And if I ever make it to heaven, it will be because one of them lived in my time!

PRAYER: *O God, our greatest aim is to live by faith, for it makes us bearers of kindness, gentleness, and love. May we be able to look at the calm of our soul and live without fear and think of death in the spirit of victory. Amen.*

JANUARY 26

The path of the just is as the shining light, that shineth more and more unto the perfect day.
(Prov. 4:18)

Gambling, drinking, superstition, and ungodliness were not uncommon in her home. She smoked her little Irish clay pipe and was never opposed to the various groups that assembled for another poker game. The whole atmosphere was charged with iniquity, and God's name was spoken only in blasphemy.

One night a change came into the home by way of an old-fashioned gospel tent meeting. She went in to mock and came out to witness to the change that had taken place in her heart at the crude mourner's bench.

When Christ comes into a life, home relationships change, details change, personalities change, concepts change, and the surrounding communities change. Lines form to unite and consolidate entire family structures or to confront opposing ideals.

In this home a deepening process went on in silence, enriched and challenged by the standards set up under the new touch of God. A home that had been full of decay and marked by the stains of iniquity was now changed into one of sacredness for the things of God, and a sense of heaven permeated the scene.

Under the transforming power of God the Christian way became her way of life, and the Bible assumed a central place in the conduct of affairs. She never tried to audit the Book but took it at face value and lived by her understanding of its demands. Fear and discouragement were giants to be slain, and her prayers were left at the door of heaven. Her mountains stepped aside, and her rivers became as dry land, for her faith was anchored in eternity.

Because she let Christ come into her home, my grandmother started a trail toward heaven that many are following even today.

PRAYER: *We thank You, O God, that in many homes today You reign supreme. Make us like children under Your care whose rest is in the perfect trust of God. And when the night gives way to day, may they be opened like pages written on by finger of God. Amen.*

JANUARY 27 ■

Enter not into the path of the wicked, and go not in the way of evil men.
(Prov. 4:14)

Honesty is supposed to be the best policy, yet some of my friends are having a very difficult time with it. In the past month two of them have missed out on good promotions in their work because they took a firm stand on matters of truth that they could not sacrifice. This morning I had breakfast with another young man whose job is in jeopardy. He could go to the top merely by trifling with a few practical bits of integrity.

The standards that this young man had set up for himself did not allow him to be true to 9 points out of 10 only. He believed that integrity and honesty cannot be broken up in small bits with varying degrees of right or wrong. He believed God's way of viewing the matter: Should anyone "offend in one point, he is guilty of all" (James 2:10).

You cannot develop a doctrine of honesty unless it is honest through and through, for God has not developed any other terms to fit the selfish interests of man's society. When He laid down the law for His people here in time, He harmonized it with the laws of eternity. To break this law is to break God's law.

The Bible is full of teaching regarding this all-important fact, and there are instructions binding upon us in the direction of rightness and truth. This world may mock the good and promote the evil, but God sees the end from the beginning and is not unaware of all the points of decisions in between.

Here is the strength of it all: "He knoweth the way that I take: when he hath tried me, I shall come forth as gold" (Job 23:10). Honesty is still the best, for it is God's way, and the final promotion is God's decision.

PRAYER: *Give us Your answers, O God, day by day, little by little as we need them. Be patient with us in our daily decisions and help us to know the truth that makes men free. Help us to look at the Cross, and pray, and wait, and say, "He is our Wisdom and our All!" Amen.*

JANUARY 28

Go ye therefore, and teach all nations ... teaching them to observe all things whatsoever I have commanded you.
(Matt. 28:19-20)

"To make a long story short." Oh, how I reject that expression! My tendency has been to spread it out and make it longer, hoping it will have more meaning. Why try to make a long story short? Why not "tell it like it is"?

The world is slow to learn this lesson in regard to God's Word, for they have rejected the Bible and are put at a disadvantage if they do try to tell their version of the story. How they have shortened it!

They have taken out all the details that don't look nice or that will cost something. They have watered it down until the effectiveness has been lost in the curtailment of its great truths. They have cut corners and filled in the valleys with the mountains until there is no challenge left. They have taken out all the dark places and disclaimed any sorrow until they do not need One to walk with them "through the valley of the shadow of death" (Ps. 23:4).

The sunshine and the homeward movement have also been removed, and they have put everything in the immediate until the long view has been wiped out. The challenge of faith has been lost, and the need for prayer and fasting has been swallowed up in short demands and quick results.

Christianity is a long story, and it cannot be shortened to take away the nights of fear or the days of anxiety. The way of the Cross is still through Gethsemane and Golgotha's hill with the nails and the piercing spear. The Resurrection morning does not come until after the black thunder has burst over the sacred events of Good Friday. And the story is still going on at the throne of God!

We can make the long story come to life by walking with Him in Emmaus again today. Our hearts will burn within us as the time flies past and every word becomes sacred!

PRAYER: *Your Word, O God, is sharp and clear to those who come within its influence. May we know it to be true because of the answering voice within that responds to its eternal message. May we know it belongs to You because of the response of love in our hearts. Amen.*

JANUARY 29 ■

I will praise thee for ever, because thou hast done it: and I will wait on thy name; for it is good before thy saints.
(Ps. 52:9)

An Exercise in Futility." No other stamp has been used with such effect. Unfortunately, much of our time is spent on those things that have no eternal value, and we put a lot of effort in things that don't count for much here on earth. Too often, after working with every fiber of nerve and energy, we are rebuffed by our dearest friends in their assessment of our accomplishment.

The story has been told that when the first steam train was about to be tested, the watching crowds cried out, "It will never run." When it went puffing down the tracks, the same disenchanted crowd continued in disbelief, "It will never stop."

One day, a young man fresh from the lumber woods left home to prepare for the ministry. His friends watched as he went on his way to college, shaking their heads, declaring, "He'll never stay." On his first sermon among his home folk one of the ladies rebuked him at the close of the service, "Boy, you preach too long!"

John the Baptist was accused of having a devil because he "came neither eating nor drinking" (Matt. 11:18). Then Jesus was severely chastised because He was discovered eating with publicans and sinners.

Too many times the only acknowledgment one gets from the world in whatever the endeavor is, is "Futility!" The mark was even stamped on the Cross: "If thou be the Son of God, come down from the cross" (Matt. 27:40).

But it was also stamped on Pilate's consent to death, the hammered nails, the soldiers' watch, the stone, the Roman seal, and the tomb. But this time God held the stamp. And the testimony to the "exercise in futility" at Calvary has been heard around the world, "Hallelujah! Christ arose!"

PRAYER: *Deliver us, O God, from those things that come to embattle our life and make us afraid of the next step. Help them to move us closer to You and not backward to that point where we first stood. Let our hands ever reach out to greater things in His name. Amen.*

■ **JANUARY 30**

Stand in awe, and sin not . . . and put your trust in the Lord.
(Ps. 4:4-5)

The little old country church at the foot of the hill was opened only for funerals and an occasional Sunday morning service. A couple of missing stones in the foundation made easy access for daring youngsters to explore the eerie sanctuary. On the pulpit was a huge Bible with a picture of God on the frontispiece. What I saw was an old man in a long, white beard and flowing hair, with a staff in one hand and lightning in the other, looking down in fierce judgment with destruction of a wicked world in mind. This formed one of my earliest impressions of God, "terrible in his doing toward the children of men" (Ps. 66:5).

Any vision of the Almighty as love and gentle forgiveness was beclouded by His thunder and awesomeness. What my young mind failed to detect was that even though destruction may have its place in divine ministries, the staff represented concern, tenderness, and care.

Are not His judgments exhibitions of His omnipotence that He might show forth His love in repentance and obedience? The call of the Almighty One is tenderness in its final appeal: "How often would I have gathered thy children together, even as a hen gathereth her chickens under her wings" (Matt. 23:37). His power has always dealt with the individual needs, while the two and three in agreement have ruled the Kingdom.

My image of God today is still one filled with omnipotence and power, but I have found a relationship to His greatness and holiness through Calvary.

And as I crawl through that broken wall again and make my way to the pulpit and open the Bible, I see a God who is almighty in love as well as in judgment. On this Rock I stand!

PRAYER: *O God, we have learned that because You are the Almighty One, You are calm and patient and hopeful even of that one who is evil and ungrateful. Thank You for this revelation through Your Son, Jesus Christ. Amen.*

JANUARY 31 ■

All power is given unto me in heaven and in earth. . . . I am with you alway, even unto the end of the world.
(Matt. 28:18, 20)

How little I knew what evil the enemy had planned for my defeat today! He got to work before I did this morning, and he knew how to place the stumbling blocks. He studied out my weaknesses and was prepared to strike me at the point where I am not very strong. He knew the people with whom I would be associated and knew about any conflicting interests that could mar our relationship. He knew the blows that had nearly crushed me yesterday, and he planned to bombard me again today with the same weapons.

But he saw me open God's Word this morning, and he was there when I knelt to pray. He was afraid when God gave me the assurance that He would not allow me to endure all the evil things that he had planned to inflict upon me. He saw the smile of victory when I learned again that God would give me sufficiency of grace for the day. When I left that place of prayer, he knew that my battles for today were in God's hands.

When my physical strength is down, and my nerves are shattered, and my hopes are darkened, the enemy moves in with clout for the final blows. But God's Spirit renews the inner man, and I find my security in my times with the Divine. And that which is hidden in my heart as an actual experience with God cannot be touched by the enemy.

While I was sleeping and the devil was planning my defeat, God was preparing for my victory. And when I prayed this morning, He said, "I am with you alway, even unto the end."

How poorly we understand God if we miss out on this great miracle of communication with heaven!

PRAYER: *O God, if our prayers were our only hope, we would be eternally lost. But we mingle them with the intercession of the One who is our Priest and trust in the mystery of His mediation. Now we are assured of heaven's reply—our victory! Amen.*

■ **FEBRUARY 1**

My confusion is continually before me, and the shame of my face hath covered me ... by reason of the enemy.
(Ps. 44:15-16)

How much does God hold us responsible for opportunities that we let go by because of fear and intimidation?

In my earlier years I worked with one of the most cynical, sarcastic, and cruel men I have ever known. On top of that he was selfish, overbearing, and rude. He gave no ground for the occupancy of good, and his language was clothed with blasphemy. He ridiculed me to tears the day he learned that I had become a Christian, and he never ceased to curse the God whom I had started to serve.

We met again after a few years. This time he was a dying man, and I was a visiting young minister. He turned on me with all his former fury and laughed to scorn the route that I had taken for my life. I sat dumb before him, overcome by the fear that had marked our previous relationship, as I listened to his diatribe of godless, sneering sarcasm. I did not talk to him about God. I did not pray with him. He died a few weeks later. My heart still hurts today.

A thousand arguments have gone through my mind to condemn and to justify my handling of this opportunity to tell a dying man of God's eternal love. How could I exclude from my mind the responsibility that had been laid upon me? Why should his blasphemous attack culminate in the defeat of the only message that could save his soul?

The only satisfying answer I can find is that I was there as a representative of Jesus Christ, and he knew it! I have to leave it with God as a message without words, spoken by the Holy Spirit to a rebelling heart, praying for a miracle in God's name.

Left in the hands of God!

PRAYER: *We thank You, O God, for the opportunities in life that open new ministries of witnessing to the needs of men. Help us to use them well to the Master's glory. Answer our cry as we pray for pardon and peace when we fail, and give us one more opportunity for obedience. Amen.*

FEBRUARY 2 ■

For his anger endureth but a moment; in his favour is life: weeping may endure for a night, but joy cometh in the morning.
(Ps. 30:5)

Decisions! Decisions! Decisions! How many times have we heard it? Yet life is made up of trying to decide and never being quite sure. How differently the course of life would have run if a different decision had been made! The problem is that we cannot look down on life from God's point of view and see how events will combine together down the road, for victory or defeat. We are always coming to crossroads—and more decisions. There are no replays down this road, and there are no dummy runs in life, nor can we ever go back.

Maybe this is best! Decisions are the stuff out of which life is made, and disappointments are often the beginnings of our most earnest prayers. Things that crush us can be among the greatest blessings of life. Instead of living in the gloom of what seemed to be a wrong decision, our lives can be touched by His presence wherever the place on the road.

Anybody can tell you what you should have done and can back it up with the assurance that "it would have been better this way." But the long road with its mysteries, disappointments, and close scrutiny of observers is an individual thing. Many of the darkest nights are lived alone.

It takes courage to say, "I'm going on," whatever the decision happened to be. The scriptural injunction is "No man, having put his hand to the plough, and looking back, is fit for the kingdom of God" (Luke 9:62). This decision carries weight with God.

Some decisions will never be justified this side of heaven, and each life has a story all its own. But God never changes in His enabling power.

A great mystery, but out of the confusion and dismay can come His assurance, "It is well!"

PRAYER: *Comfort those, we pray, Father, who do not know what to do because of the many ways before them. Some are full of temptation and others with insurmountable difficulties. Deliver them from their perplexity and lead them in the right way. Amen.*

■ **FEBRUARY 3**

> I cried unto God with my voice, even
> unto God with my voice; and he
> gave ear unto me.
> (Ps. 77:1)

How complicated we make the things that God has made so simple!

In dealing with a young man at the altar one night, I tried to point him to an acceptance of Jesus Christ by faith, in as simple a manner as possible. For I knew he had come from a background of superstition and severe religious training. He looked up at me in unbelief and said, "Reverend, there's got to be more to it than that." The devil would blanket God's simple plan of salvation with clouds of doubt, shadows of uncertainty, and the darkness of impossibilities and lies.

His world is screaming for a new theology, a new revelation, a new Book, and a new and more complicated way. God has made His way so simple that "the wayfaring men, though fools, shall not err therein" (Isa. 35:8). And when the apostle said, "I show you a more excellent way" (1 Cor. 12:31, NKJV), he was not showing the world a different way or muddying the waters. He was merely showing the value of the old.

Simon the Pharisee was confused with the simplicity of the woman washing the feet of Jesus with her tears and anointing Him with ointment.

The indignant disciples saw only waste rather than the deeper meaning of the simple act of anointing the Master.

The thief on the cross could not see the simple reason why this good Man, who had done nothing wrong, should be dying.

The man who was instructed to dip in the Jordan River seven times for his healing rebelled, saying, "I can't understand it!"

Here is the way of faith—that we simply lean on the everlasting arms, completely trust in His omnipotence, and expect the fulfillment of His promises. This is His way!

There is no more to it than that!

PRAYER: *O God, we pray for an understanding of Your truth, Your righteousness, and Your goodness. And as we understand these things, give us the faith and determination to follow after them. Then help us to understand how near You are to supply all our needs according to Your riches in glory by Christ Jesus. Amen.*

FEBRUARY 4 ■

Wait on the Lord: be of good courage, and he shall strengthen thine heart: wait, I say, on the Lord.
(Ps. 27:14)

One day while driving along the St. Lawrence Seaway, I saw a boat on its way to an overseas port with a load of grain. I could detect no movement. It was sitting idly in the water. Still? No. Almost! It was in one of the seaway lift locks, and it was rising! It was on its way to a new level so that it could bypass the rocks and rapids in the main stream. It was getting a lift in preparation for the voyage ahead.

One day I saw a saint of God sitting idly in her favorite rocker by the window in her farm kitchen. Her eyes were closed, and she was sitting still. Well, almost! Her Bible was opened on her lap, and tears had formed in drops on her cheeks. I was too young to understand, but I sensed that she was busy at the job. Later I learned that she was on her way to a distant port, and there were rocks and obstacles ahead. She was spending some time in God's lift locks for the buoyancy that would take her above the unseen dangers.

Her determination was always forward, and she never let hindrances control the journey. God's way of training has always been a challenge, but He has always proven himself by establishing and lifting. Delays are not lost time if they are spent with God, and the rush of activity is not progress if it is wasted in enemy waters.

Circumstances usually run counter to the journey, and sooner or later the obstacles control the way. But God has maintained a means of lifting above and over, and the saint of God has risen in His power.

She learned that the grace of God was equal to the obstacles and that waiting on Him is preparation.

PRAYER: *Sometimes, O God, the way is very steep, and we wish it were not so high. Sometimes we walk through great valleys, and we wish they were not so long. Sometimes we go through rough waters, and we pray for smoother ways. Keep us, wherever we are with all our ways, in Your care. Amen.*

■ **FEBRUARY 5**

The Lord is nigh unto them that are of a broken heart; and saveth such as be of a contrite spirit.
(Ps. 34:18)

The person with the greatest need in my world today is the one I will walk past and barely notice.

A friend of mine, with his new bride, moved into an apartment next door to an active church. Their lives were full of problems, and they were searching for help. Signs went up and advertising went out about special services. Each night when the saints gathered to worship and to witness, my friend and his bride would walk past the church, hoping someone would invite them to their fellowship. Nobody did! Not until he joined the navy and a drunken sailor told him that he should give his heart to the Lord did he ever hear an invitation to a better way.

How heedless we are to the needs of the one we pass by each day. When we ask the question, "How are you?" are we really wanting to know? The response is usually, "OK," or "I'm fine," when the true answer is, "Why should I tell you? I don't want to take your time."

Is it possible to keep our prayers for holy living and our unconcern in the same heart? Our walking to the other side of the problem is akin to making another heaven for God while we reserve this one for ourselves. We are substituting the God of mercy for a god who will condescend to be measured by our own selfishness.

If love means anything, it must be synonymous with concern. And that concern must encompass the cry of the one I am going to meet today.

PRAYER: *We pray, O God, for one another. Lift the pressure of the heavy burdens, that those who are weary and ill at ease may be raised up by Your gracious hand and enabled to go on with renewed hope and strength. Make all people to rejoice in the God of their salvation, and make their day a happy one. In Jesus' name. Amen.*

FEBRUARY 6

For he is our God; and we are the people of his pasture, and the sheep of his hand.
(Ps. 95:7)

One day in a hospital room I held a tiny baby in my arms and remarked to the doctor on the frailty of this bit of humanity. His response was, "Yes, I know, but God has made them to live."

God has created us with capabilities far beyond our imagination and made the impossible as the target for our highest aim. Even the weakest of us have something within that makes us mighty in God's concern.

One of the great mysteries is that out of our earthiness we have the ability to reach out in prayer to heaven and then listen in response to the Voice that calls back and finds us waiting.

We are, nevertheless, full of inadequacies and are always reminded of our humanness, but life does not stop and wait. And no matter how dark the night, our eagerness awaits the morning with expectation for the day.

God has provided for us to live in the Spirit in spite of all the contradictions in life brought on by sin. In our humanity our natural reasoning determines our decisions. How little do we recognize the power of God's grace that enables us to carry on.

Our power of expression is so limited, we cannot say what we mean or tell what we want. He whose "mercy endureth for ever" (Psalm 136) and whose "grace is sufficient" (2 Cor. 12:9) still owns us as His creation and responds in love, for He understands the need.

He has made us to live, but He made us to live for himself, and the grace of God is equal to the miracle.

PRAYER: *O God, we sense our inadequacies, and how that we are human. While we know our weakness, we know the power of Your grace. Make our weariness less by making our strength in You more. Show us that there is much yet beyond to be possessed by Your grace. Amen.*

■ FEBRUARY 7

Be still, and know that I am God: I will be exalted among the heathen, I will be exalted in the earth.
(Ps. 46:10)

The listening ear, the attentive heart, the obedient will—the basis for all Christian living!

The secret lies in the listening and the hearing as well as in the obedience. There must be a listening time in the relationship to redemption when the soul will be revealed to itself by the voice of God. We live in a rush of tumult and excitement that tends to detract from hearing the still small Voice that speaks. How to sift out the sounds and keep only that which carries the "thus saith the Lord" is the great concern.

We begin with listening. We end with obedience. God will always speak to the listening heart. He is long-suffering to the slow in understanding. He blesses the consecration of the obedient will. He will bear with us until we close the doors; love never rests.

Salvation is an outward experience, something beyond ourselves speaking to us in words that we cannot mistake. And best of all it comes with a voice of authority on which we can base our claims to godliness. It is hidden in our hearts to be recalled in the dark nights of doubts and affirmed in every point of living. Probably in no other area of living can we have such a clear voice from heaven and assurance from God himself.

I listen. I hear. I obey. This could have been the testimony of Paul, for his final words were, "I have kept the faith" (2 Tim. 4:7).

It is still the pathway to victory!

PRAYER: *O God, we pray that You will tune our listening ear to catch the voice of eternity as we walk through the garden of Your revelation. In the Holy Book and in the holy sanctuary or in our walk through the day, give us hearing hearts and obedient wills to grasp the overtures of love ever springing from Your heart. Amen.*

FEBRUARY 8 ■

They that hate me without a cause are more than the hairs of mine head: they that would destroy me . . . are mighty.
(Ps. 69:4)

An old grudge; grudges; grudging—the most ugly word in the world. How the devil makes use of it!

One night at an altar of prayer a man looked up from his dealing with God and said to me, "Preacher, I have a grudge to settle with [and he called the man by name], and then I'll come back and pray." He never returned. A lady spoke out her anger to another member of the church concerning a deep hurt, "I can forgive her, but I'll never forget it." A nearby neighbor used to boast, "My motto is, 'You kill my dog, I'll kill your cat.'" Today in the arrangement of a funeral service the wife said, "Over my dead body will those people have part in the service." And on and on the troubled breast holds the bitterness and animosity built up over years of unforgiven grudges.

Not much room left to stand when the heart is full of hatred. Too often life is lived so far outside the reach of love that it is lost in an ugliness that mocks and destroys. The old grudge throws its color on simple relationships that will tarnish until time is no more.

Even good people are often hit by lack of self-discipline in this area and need to be watchful, for no liberty can be taken outside the love of Christ.

To look at this issue outside the Cross is nothing more than trying to lessen the sinfulness of sin. And to understand the dilemma, one must understand that meaning of the Cross.

At the Cross love claims all grudges, all hurts, all enmity and surrounds them with the forgiveness of eternity and says, "There are no boundaries here."

PRAYER: *O God, we bow at the Cross, for only here is found a forgiving spirit. Make it the beginning of a new life in many hearts today, and a gateway opening upon eternal blessedness. Reach out to people everywhere with the gospel of forgiveness, as Your judgment makes way for Your mercy. Amen.*

■ FEBRUARY 9

But Christ as a son over his own house; whose house are we, if we hold fast the confidence and the rejoicing of the hope firm unto the end.
(Heb. 3:6)

Today I typed a statement outlining rules regulating the activities of a certain group, and it concluded with "... is nonnegotiable."

"Don't call a board meeting, or set up any committees, or send a delegation to lobby—this is final!"

In our wishy-washy, do-anything world, how good to know that there are some things that are "nonnegotiable."

"If thou be the Son of God, command that these stones be made bread" (Matt. 4:3). An appeal to the immediate necessity. An address to the appetite of the moment. Who will ever know!

"If thou be the Son of God, cast thyself down: for it is written, He shall give his angels charge concerning thee" (v. 6). Develop your faith. Presume upon God. Test His strength. Try out the promises.

"All these things will I give thee, if thou wilt fall down and worship me" (v. 9). Temptation to turn the good into better. Shortcut to higher position. An easy road to riches over a good name and a good reputation.

The battle lines were drawn, and the only condition of mind that Jesus knew left no argument. No theological debating necessary! No hesitation. "Old devil, these things are nonnegotiable, for 'It is written . . .' [vv. 4, 7, 10]."

How well we know the temptation and the tender voice of the tempter! When he comes today with the same superficial speech and hollow temptation, I can stand in the affirmation of the Eternal One. The finger of God has written like lightning flashing across time to eternity, "It is written." Today my faith is founded on divine truths that are nonnegotiable.

PRAYER: *For those who have taken a stand for truth down through the ages, we are grateful, O God. They have fought with courage and dared to challenge a hostile world even when it meant death. May the joy we find in their faith clothe us with gladness and make us bold and daring for You. Amen.*

FEBRUARY 10 ■

I have been young, and now am old; yet have I not seen the righteous forsaken, nor his seed begging bread.
(Ps. 37:25)

The Psalmist recognized it many years ago: "The Lord is my shepherd; I shall not want" (23:1). Reporting again on the happy state of the godly person, he wrote, "Yet have I not seen the righteous forsaken, nor his seed begging bread."

Paul lived in this assurance and passed on the promise, "My God shall supply all your need according to his riches in glory by Christ Jesus" (Phil. 4:19).

A student walked by my door today whistling it: "For out of His infinite riches in Jesus, / He giveth, and giveth, and giveth again!" This morning we sang it at a funeral service: "All I have needed Thy hand hath provided." And through rich experiences in my life I have seen the barren desert blossom like a rose in the overflowing bounties of His blessing.

Sometimes we come into close quarters with God; and even though the battle may not always be on a grand scale, yet He reminds us that there are matters of concern greater than the last check in the book or the last bit of meal in the barrel.

In tenderness, in love, in understanding, in comfort, and in care His sufficiency is adequate, and His desire to supply is always measured by the urgency of the need. What a wonderful confirmation of this truth when He reminds us, "My grace is sufficient, too!" (See 2 Cor. 12:9.)

This is the law of eternity, and God has a way of doing things for us that bring contentment and refreshment to the soul in whatever condition it finds us.

It is God's glorious way—and it satisfies!

PRAYER: *O God, all of our necessities are known to You. Some are too deep for our words to express. Some we can only express to You, for no one else cares or understands. But You know all that we need, for You go beyond our speech, and You read the motives of our heart. We can talk to You. Thank You, God. Amen.*

■ **FEBRUARY 11**

And he said unto me, My grace is sufficient for thee: for my strength is made perfect in weakness.
(2 Cor. 12:9)

The whole world was stunned! One of the most disturbing bits of news to hit the airwaves came out of a ball of fire over Cape Canaveral—the space shuttle had blown up.

Through a series of unrelated circumstances, I found myself stranded in a New York City airport with many disgruntled travelers. Babies were crying, mothers were frustrated, and fathers were of little help. Everybody was on edge as they discussed the terrible news of the day.

A uniformed man mingled with the crowd. He joked with a rabbi who had missed a convention in Miami, answered questions about flight changes, took messages, and gave orders over his radio. He picked up a crying youngster, circled the room to the tune of his own singing rhythm, and said, "There, there, Sonny, it ain't all bad, it ain't all bad."

In a moment the frustration had dissolved, and the cloud of gloom and anxiety was gone, and the man disappeared as quickly as he had come. One old rabbi turned to his group, shook his head, and through tears of relief shouted, "Thank God, it ain't all bad."

Let's rest here for a little while. Call in your frustrations, disappointments, heartaches, anxieties, and recall your own dark nights. Call to mind those things that made yesterday so upsetting. Put them all in one big bundle and lay them on the balance scales of God's grace. As you pile your burdens on one side, His grace will offset them on the other. You cannot throw God's scales off balance. For His grace is sufficient.

Now, stand back and take a good look at them. "Thank God, it ain't all bad."

PRAYER: *Though we had the tongues of men and angels, and understood all mysteries and all knowledge, we could still not speak adequately of Your grace, O God. Through Your grace we find Your peace. Give us that peace today, we pray. Amen.*

FEBRUARY 12 ■

Because thou hast been my help, therefore in the shadow of thy wings will I rejoice.
(Ps. 63:7)

God was there all the time, and I did not know it." What a revelation! What a lesson! What a point of victory!

Jacob awoke one morning from a dream, took his pillow and drove it in the ground as a pillar of victory, and "called the . . . place Bethel," witnessing to the ages, "Surely the Lord is in this place; and I knew it not" (Gen. 28:19, 16).

· A pastor came into my office a few years ago and talked to me about the prayer meetings the students used to have here in the Canterbury. Pointing to a certain spot, he said, "Just about here God met me in sanctifying power." He closed his eyes, looked up, consecrated it anew with his tears, and thanked God for this place of victory. He turned to me and said, "Here is my Bethel pillar. I have pointed out this spot to the enemy many times in my life."

My Bethel pillar! God met me here! I have used it as a point of reference many times in my life.

When the enemy gets you at a disadvantage, throws his whole weight against you, and tries to draw you into the dark shadows of doubt, can you point back to your Bethel pillar?

God provides a place in your Christian experience that will find its basis in the past. Your Bethel times will return and enlarge and expand into greater victories. And no Bethel is small, for it holds within its power the potential for a thousand victories in your times of testing.

The enemy will dissociate you from this place of power and from any source of sustenance. But nothing can bring greater victory to you and greater defeat for him than your Bethel experience, "God met me here!"

PRAYER: *O God, we know that the things You have for Your people are more in number and greater in quality than all the powers that are arrayed against us. How grateful we are to know that to be with God is to be in the majority, and to be associated with You is to be assured of victory. We thank You. Amen.*

FEBRUARY 13

My hands also will I lift up unto thy commandments, which I have loved; and I will meditate in thy statutes.
(Ps. 119:48)

What would we do if we could not blame Murphy for everything? I heard it again today: "Oh, well, it's Murphy's Law at work!" When everything goes wrong, it's Murphy's fault.

In a way this is good, for it provides a scapegoat for our faults and absolves us from any blame. How ruthlessly we work to remove the blame from our own shoulders so that we can securely place it on the back of another. And the boundary lines between our faults and our failures are pretty fine.

Our religion rests on a foundation that says, "Bear ye one another's burdens, and so fulfil the law of Christ" (Gal. 6:2). This is not a license to load someone else down with our faults for the wilderness trip.

God knows our human frailties, and He knows that under the pressures of our own guilt we need help other than our own. He knows that our hand, our head, and our heart are under the effects of sin, and there must be a deliverance.

Paul recognized his utter helplessness in his own power and gave us the assurance that "all things work together for good to them that love God" (Rom. 8:28). This message delivered to our shortcomings does not change with the times.

As a Christian I can say that I am not under Murphy's Law but under a law of love that says, "I can do all things through Christ which strengtheneth me" (Phil. 4:13).

This becomes a matter of faith, not a human endeavor, and this faith is the gift of God—and it defies Murphy's Law.

PRAYER: *We thank You, O God, that You have shown us our shortcomings. Show us by Your Holy Spirit what we might be if we follow on in obedience to Your ways. Comfort us in our failures with Your gospel, and crown our efforts with the triumph and majesty of Your Son. Amen.*

FEBRUARY 14 ■

Let not your heart be troubled: ye believe in God, believe also in me.
(John 14:1)

The heart is a very vital part of the human body, but the use of the term in spiritual matters far outweighs its usage in any material sense.

It is used as a symbol of love, and many cards will appear in mail slots today with hearts depicting love in strange and various ways. Bumper stickers use the heart to display love, and recently I saw one that said in symbol, "I love Jesus."

The Lord says, "The heart is deceitful above all things, and desperately wicked: who can know it?" (Jer. 17:9). Christ tells us that "out of the heart proceed evil thoughts . . . blasphemies" (Matt. 15:19). It is the heart that holds the hurt of a wasted and ill-spent life, but it is also the heart that "crieth out for the living God" (Ps. 84:2). It is the heart that is softened by the work of the Holy Spirit or hardened by the power of evil.

The heart breaks under grief and bears burdens that reach beyond human endurance. In many a heart is buried a grief that cannot be shared, as it weeps inwardly, shedding no visible tear.

Out of the heart comes a stumbling prayer, misunderstood and mocked, but with an eloquence that moves heaven. It knows its own bitterness and delight, and it passes through agonies where no one can trace the sacred pain.

The blood of Jesus Christ can cleanse the heart so that it can be full of joy and peace and carry a cheerfulness that mocks the hurt that it holds. It will care as much for the little as for the great, for the poor as for the rich, and make no distinction of kind, for its vision will always be forward.

Keep it clean; it is God's universe, God's dwelling place, God's sweet retreat. He will always meet you there!

PRAYER: *The heart is deceitful and wicked and is self-mocking and self-ruining. Save us, O God, from ourselves, for out of the heart proceeds all things. Do the cleansing and renewing and make us clean in Jesus' name. Amen.*

FEBRUARY 15

Search me, O God, and know my heart: try me, and know my thoughts: and see if there be any wicked way in me, and lead me in the way everlasting.
(Ps. 139:23-24)

The neighborly custom that cemented friendships and made country living a unique experience was the ability to borrow a cup of sugar or a tablespoon of vanilla in times of need. The same held true when the need called for a handsaw or a special tool for some out-of-the-ordinary job.

An interesting bit of genius surfaced when I was sent to borrow a brace and bit to make a ladder. My neighbor told me that his had just been loaned and that he had only his good set left. It was then that I learned that he kept "lending tools" of inferior quality to accommodate the borrowers. He said, "Never would I lend my good tools to anyone." At that time it was amusing, but I have discovered that this kind of thinking does not confine itself to neighborhood relationships.

How well I remember the church folk who bought new furniture for their home and donated the old to the parsonage for the new pastor, thinking that God would be pleased with their generosity and consecration.

Is this any different from the struggling at the altar when the "lending tools" are placed before God as complete consecration? How God must be insulted by the hypocrisy of the act when He is looking for real devotion. He is trying to make a saint but is offered second-best material for the job.

In God's workshop the eternal is brought to bear on the temporal; the divine upon the human; the sacrificial Blood upon sinful nature; the end is forgiveness, adoption, sanctification, and heaven. And His plans call for the best in material and workmanship.

God will not settle for our "lending tools." It must be the good set!

PRAYER: *O God, we pledge the best of ourselves to You this day. It is our complete and solemn vow, and we make it in the spirit of love. All of this we must do in Christ and by Christ, without whom we can do nothing. Amen.*

FEBRUARY 16 ■

**Thy righteousness is like the great mountain;
thy judgments are a great deep: O Lord,
thou preservest man and beast.**
(Ps. 36:6)

What is my responsibility today—to God, to others, and to myself? How can I know the meaning of it in relation to my ability and my opportunities?

Our speeding days are built into God's eternity, and our responsibilities are part of the eternal plan. In this throbbing, pulsing process of moving on in the divine order, the eternal need is still forgiveness, and the everlasting want is rest for the soul. But the ones who need me most see only the work of my hands and never know the urgency of my heart.

Where is the minister who has not listened to the sad plight of the man who has just arrived in town with his wife and small baby, tired and hungry, but discovered his money has been stolen? Where does the burden rest when the truth of these and other pleas are not too well defined? Where is my standing ground, and who can tell the range or explain the mystery of responsibility here?

In a far deeper sense than I can know, I am my brother's keeper. I cannot know how near he may be to the uttermost fringe. Every opportunity I have of revealing to him something better draws me deeper into the realm of my responsibility. And my voice to him must be the voice of love, calling him to a better way.

My responsibility for today comes within the reach of the outstretched arms of the cross of Jesus Christ, without which there can be no help and no hope. It is at the Cross that I exchange my responsibility for obedience. God can use this obedience to bring hope and strength to a destitute and discouraged life.

I can be at peace if I have been able to share this part of myself with them today.

PRAYER: *O God, You have given us great responsibilities, and now we ask that You would enable us to know their meaning and our place in Your purpose. Let Your blessings be our portion in the great burdens we share so that that which begins in mystery will end in grace and glory. Amen.*

FEBRUARY 17

> **But let all those that put their trust in thee rejoice: . . . let them also that love thy name be joyful in thee.**
> (Ps. 5:11)

The morning was dull, drab, and dreary, and I was trying to be as cheerful as possible in greeting the people at the door. One elderly lady had walked to church through heavy rain, and I was commiserating with her over the weather. She held my hand for a moment and smiled and said, "Pastor, 'This is the day which the Lord hath made; we will rejoice and be glad in it.' He made it and gave it to me, and I am going to use it for Him."

Wow! I needed her message then, and I need it today: "He made it and gave it to me, and I am going to use it for Him"!

Today! Who can explain it? Who can account for it? The God who holds the sun, the moon, and the stars in His hands gives me one day and says, "I made it for you. It is clean and spotless, and it is yours. Use it!"

Sometimes we do not say in words exactly what we mean, and often our motives are misunderstood, and it is easy to complain when we don't intend to. And so much depends on where we place the emphasis, and often the true message is lost in the interpretation. Sometimes God gives us a greater message than we could have anticipated.

Each new day can be a growing period into maturity while the sting of the moment is lost in the true message from God. He brings us face-to-face with the issues that matter most.

There is no debate in this argument, for every day is a day that God has made. Today belongs to you and me. He gave it to us. Let us use it for Him!

PRAYER: *O God, all of our days are gifts from You. We believe that Your purpose is for us to use them well and return them as talents that have been used at work in the Kingdom. Give us yet another day, and help us to fill it with the strength of Your eternal greatness, and we shall be satisfied. Amen.*

FEBRUARY 18

Blessed is the people that know the joyful sound: they shall walk, O Lord, in the light of thy countenance.
(Ps. 89:15)

One of my early recollections was of an old man with flowing white hair and beard walking with two canes along the old country road, singing to his own tune, "And He walks with me, and He talks with me." I do not know if he had ever learned more of the hymn, but I sensed that he knew the One who was walking beside him.

How glad I am that God did not fill His universe with people and then go away and leave them alone to cope with the madness of an evil world. On the other hand, this same God never forces His attention on any one of us.

He comes to us in relation to the needs that He knows we have, and then He treats us as if we were an only child, and gives us attention as if we were the only traveler on the road. He is always watching our footsteps and understands our need by the trail we are leaving behind us.

The assurance that He gives to us for the journey is touched by the shadow of the Cross.

—"If any man . . . open the door, I will come in" (Rev. 3:20).
—"Ye shall seek me, and find me" (Jer. 29:13).
—"Come unto me . . . and I will give you rest" (Matt. 11:28).
—"He that believeth . . . shall be saved" (Mark 16:16).

This tells us that we may deepen our Christian experience, enlarge our communication with heaven, and find a sure defense for the battles of time. He is dealing with our weakness and is sending out an invitation of loving concern to our faith.

Only eternity will reveal the effect of the old man's message, but God is still walking with His people.

PRAYER: *O Christ of God, You come into our hearts only by consent and an invitation of love. May Your searching ministry draw us to the peace of Your eternity. We would think nothing or do nothing that is not under the inspiration of the Holy Spirit. Amen.*

■ FEBRUARY 19

If ye have faith as a grain of mustard seed, ye shall say unto this mountain, Remove hence to yonder place; and it shall remove; and nothing shall be impossible unto you.
(Matt. 17:20)

To say, "I care not today what the morrow may bring," would be an absurd statement were it not for its foundational truth that I'm "living by faith in Jesus above." Today people are chased by fear, and there is no rest but in God. The troubled heart can find no peace except in the grace that is all-sufficient. So if our fear is great, we need to begin to mend our faith so that we might have a deeper fellowship with heaven.

Many times we stand beside the father who cried out with tears, "Lord, I believe; help thou mine unbelief" (Mark 9:24). We gather up all our faith and look to God to complete the deficiency. If the night is spent in terror and the day with foreboding shadows, it is our faith that needs a renewal.

Can we take a lesson from Paul? He fought a good fight, he never drew back in the contest, he never asked for pity, and he died a victor. The one thing that explains all the rest is found in his own words, "I have kept the faith" (2 Tim. 4:7). It is impossible to do anything good in the kingdom of God except in proportion as we keep the faith. The explanation of life is not in the circumstance but in that mysterious connection with divine power.

God does not want us to be partly one thing and partly another. It is not His idea for us to be partly fear and partly faith; one works against the other. He wants us to be one thing only, and it is impossible to unite the two.

We do not have to live in little selves maintained by fear. We can live in great possibilities that yield their riches to a faith in the Omnipotent.

PRAYER: *We pray, O God, that our faith may be established and that it may be large and unshaken, strong in the Lord and in the power of His might. Increase our faith so that it might be better tomorrow with a confident and constant hope in our eternal God. In Jesus' name. Amen.*

FEBRUARY 20 ■

My voice shalt thou hear in the morning, O Lord; in the morning I will direct my prayer unto thee, and will look up.
(Ps. 5:3)

This morning is the beginning of a brand-new day. God is continuously giving us the morning. Each one is a welcome from the Maker and an open gate to opportunities. In the most significant moment of the next 24 hours He has placed tremendous significance for us. We will be living in the continuum of time as it merges into His eternity.

My grandmother used to pray, "O God, pour out a fresh 'tetch' from heaven on our souls this mornin', for the blessin's of yesterday will not surfice fer today." She expected great things for the day as she reached out to God in the morning.

Too often we look at the beginning of the day with a sense of profitless existence in our routine of living. Sameness marks the way—same faces, same places, same work tied down with that same short string.

Too often the morning is marked with chastening, sickness, sorrow, thunder, and unbearable circumstances. We begin by putting together today and tomorrow and the next day, trying to anticipate some purpose, but never being able to arrive at conclusions. The day continues in frustration.

When our morning does come along a path that is strewn with blighted hopes, unfinished plans, and disappointments, we fail to see God working out in our life a higher refinement, a greater purpose, keener insight, and a truer devotion.

This is God's morning. He made it and gave it to us. To time we must add eternity. To man we must add God. To our reaching out we must add faith.

We cannot live today on yesterday's experience. He has a new touch for us this morning!

PRAYER: *O God, we pray this morning that You will help us to be true, courageous, and determined for the day. At the close may we be able to say, "In Thy wonderful name we have done our work," and then leave the rest in Your hands. Amen.*

FEBRUARY 21

Hide not thy face from me in the day when I am in trouble; incline thine ear unto me: in the day when I call answer me speedily.
(Ps. 102:2)

Life is filled with meetings and meeting places. We seem to be always on our way to a meeting—committee meetings, board meetings, staff meetings, meetings with friends and sometimes with enemies, and meetings with God.

Some meetings are for a moment of time, while others are lengthy and are history-making events. Meetings have helped shape the destiny of our world.

God has allowed our little orb of life to be filled with these encounters. Often they have brought to us new hope, new beginnings, new opportunities, and new challenges. Often they have been occasions of review, when values come in for questioning, and often they have been a reaffirmation of hope in the love of God.

In every life there is an encounter when the first intimation of the divine movement meets the soul. The greatest questions of life are settled within the perimeters of this sphere: sometimes small because they are distant; sometimes large because they are close; sometimes blurred because they are unsettled. God sees them in true perspective and settles each one with us on its own merit. This transaction between the Divine and the human, the human and the Divine cannot be refused or denied.

A personal encounter with Jesus Christ is the greatest experience that can ever come before an individual. The final encounter for everyone is with the enemy called Death, and from this there can be no refusal.

Doctrine and fact merge here into an eternal mystery to be revealed in God's afterward of truth. Blessed is the servant who shall be found watching, waiting, when the Lord cometh.

The Great Meeting—His coming!

PRAYER: *Drive back the enemy, O God, and according to the fullness of Your grace may we have that meeting place where we will find complete recovery from the enemy and be set in the liberty of truth and love. May each encounter be full of God and full of heaven. Amen.*

FEBRUARY 22 ■

Make a joyful noise unto God, all ye lands: sing forth the honour of his name: make his praise glorious.
(Ps. 66:1-2)

There are many sounds in our world that perplex and make us afraid: sounds in the day, sounds in the night, sounds of disappointment, sounds of grief, sounds of death.

There is an inward sound that speaks to the soul. Sometimes it comes as a still small voice. Sometimes it is a word spoken in thunderous tones. Sometimes it is a light illuminating a dark corner of the heart.

We are brought face-to-face with the Christian consciousness that has to sort out this range of sounds as they relate to the speech of God. We want to be sensitive to His undertones and the persuasive whispers and entreaties He is ever breathing upon His people.

There are some circumstances in which we must take a firm stand, as these relate to heaven and earth. Every person has a degree of conviction by which his life is moved and without which he can neither hope nor rest. God allows each of us to make his own determination and tell his own tale.

Today I must live near the Cross, for amid all the other sounds its eternal truth still stands up under the examination of God. I must take my daily inspiration from here and daily return here for the renewal of my confidence.

How wondrously heaven moves in over our human weaknesses with revelations larger than our capacity. Sometimes in burning judgment. Sometimes in quiet understanding. Sometimes in loving care. God is always speaking and urging us in words that will make us noble in eternity. We must keep alert so that we can respond, "Speak, Lord, for thy servant heareth" (1 Sam. 3:9, see v. 10).

To hear and to sort out the voice of God and to understand His will is to apply our hearts unto wisdom.

PRAYER: *O God, Your voice is powerful, yet it can be a still small voice. It finds out with infinite tenderness the broken heart and the wounded spirit. The weary one knows its sound, and it speaks music to those who have no hope. Keep us ever within the range of Your tender call, we pray. Amen.*

■ FEBRUARY 23

> **Leave me not, neither forsake me, O God of my salvation. When my father and my mother forsake me, then the Lord will take me up.**
> **(Ps. 27:9-10)**

As we sang in prayer meeting tonight, I sensed there were others who shared my reaction: "It has not always been this way." We sang about belonging to the family of God

Family speaks of enjoyment, good times, good things, comfort, sharing, and home. It speaks of a place where the ugly and the deformed are loved as well as the brilliant and beautiful. It does not allow for selfishness or hatred in any sense of the terms. It does not downgrade but loves to encourage. The pattern was laid down by God before the family was ever formed. How the enemy has thrown discord into this pattern of living, debased the dignity of life, and mocked the great purpose of God!

God always looks for the fulfillment of the divine ideal, and in His family it is still love. When pressure is on and efforts fail, energy is gone and wrong takes the lead, and judgment is made against me, in His family I can still find acceptance in the great miracle of love.

Here is an enlarged life! We are miracles of His family. We live under the hospitality of God, where the strong are called upon to help the weak. We are little children looking up into the heavens as the star guides us to Bethlehem and on to Calvary where all families are held together.

It has not always been this way! The bitterness of sin, laying waste a life in tragic circumstances, was writing the story. The touch of love, the voice of trust with an invitation of concern, and adoption into God's family made the difference!

"I'm so glad I'm a part of the family of God."

PRAYER: *Almighty God, once we were strangers, outside Your family. Now we are of the household of faith in Christ Jesus the Son. How our hearts rejoice to know that Jesus wept and sighed and pitied and worked miracles because He loved the family. We would continue in Your family. Amen.*

FEBRUARY 24 ■

He that worketh deceit shall not dwell within my house: he that telleth lies shall not tarry in my sight.
(Ps. 101:7)

Every spring a man with a horse and buggy came to our little community with crude instruments and a suitcase full of eyeglasses. His sales pitch was that his wares would improve your looks and enhance your chances of getting a mate.

One young fellow listened in amazement, and the revelation hit a responsive chord, for his success in this field had been far from fulfilling. He was satisfied that glasses would improve his appearance, but he had one reservation. His proposal was, "If I can see as well with these things as I can without them, then I will buy a pair."

It's the old problem of trying to live outside the will of God and still reap all the benefits of Christianity. He had not fully accepted the necessity, but if there were benefits, he wanted to be a recipient. "Lord, if I can get along as well with Your plan for my life as I am doing without it, then I will be a Christian."

God's demand precludes this kind of commitment. It is impossible to break all the commandments of heaven, defy the spirit of the Cross, deny the God of the Bible, and still have the blessing of God on a wicked and wayward life-style.

He accepts the broken heart, the stammering tongue, and the repentant spirit only when the problems of sin and guilt are ready to be sacrificed at the Cross. How shameful is the sight of that one who stands on the edge of commitment and enjoys the comforts of the Church but still reaches out for the glamour and handshake of the world.

The one who is in kinship with eternity and in full consecration prays, "Not my will, but thine, be done" (Luke 22:42), is already beautiful in the sight of God.

PRAYER: *O God, You ask for our whole heart, and we want to give it to You without reservation. But often we take it back again to our own unsafe and unsteady hands. How gracious is Your compassion and long-suffering to us whom You love. Help us to throw ourselves wholly upon Your omnipotence and grace this day. In Jesus' holy name. Amen.*

■ **FEBRUARY 25**

For the word of God is quick, and powerful, and sharper than any twoedged sword ... and is a discerner of the thoughts and intents of the heart.
(Heb. 4:12)

"Well, why don't you write a Bible of your own if you don't agree with this one?" was the retort of a gentle old man, offended by criticism for his devotion to the old Book that had served him so well.

Good question! But what would you say if you had to retell the Bible?

The Creation bringing light and life, trees bearing fruit, and animals bringing forth after their kind would have to begin the Book. And you could not leave out the sunny days and moonlit nights fresh from the hand of the Creator. God's mighty design marred by the serpent and sin's temporary victory would be included with the flaming sword at the gate of Eden.

Humanity with family life (including Cain and Abel with the advent of jealousy and murder), love, fear, hatred, and all the inconsistencies of mankind would find a place in the retelling.

Temples warm with the fire of the Lord would find their places beside the houses of vain and corrupt idolatry. The conflict between the worship of the true God and all the variations of truth in other religions would be there.

The noise of battle, the piercing sword, and the pursuit of power could not be barred from the Book. But a large place would have to be made for the songs of victory, and the giant would have to buckle before the mighty hand of God.

The Book would not be complete without David and his songs, Jonah running away from God, Elijah's mantle, Job's patience, and Isaiah's vision of the coming of the Prince of Peace.

(Continued tomorrow)

PRAYER: *Let Your Word open itself to us, O God, and become an old word with a new message. May we reverence it as coming from eternity and apply it as addressed to our immediate needs. May we know it to be true because of the answering voice from within that responds to the message. In Jesus' name. Amen.*

FEBRUARY 26 ■

Thy word have I hid in mine heart, that I might not sin against thee.
(Ps. 119:11)

If the Bible had to be retold, there would have to be wild dreams, spectral hands on the wall, baffled magicians and truth-telling prophets, and a remnant of God coming through every crisis.

How could one rewrite the Psalms, for which no music is good enough, or the Proverbs, which glisten with wit and wisdom?

The Book would have to be filled with promises, but they could stand only on the grounds of Omnipotence. Then would come the tithes and firstfruits and the outpoured blessings dependent upon man's faithfulness.

The human mind could never recapture the songs from the night sky while shepherds watch in amazement and then make their way to the manger, or follow the holy life of the Son of God as He lived among the people.

The pen would go dry and the mind would go blank before the majesty of the Cross, the glorious Resurrection morning, and the imminent return of the Man of Calvary in judgment and hope.

The establishment of the Church, against which the gates of hell shall not prevail, and the spread of the gospel of Jesus Christ through a Gentile world with all the hatred and persecution could never be conceived by the mind of man.

Let us not suppose that we could rule out a personal God who answers the prayers of the saints and still walks with them in the cool of the day.

When I think of all this, I know that the Bible had to be written by the hand of God. It is His Book—an inspired, divine, and authoritative revelation of the will and love of Heaven. I love and support this old Book, because it does belong to Him!

PRAYER: *Almighty God, we pray that You will keep Your Word ever within our hearts. It is our Counsel and the Guide of our entire life. There is no other word that carries the truth of God. We know that it belongs to You because of the response of our love. In Jesus' name. Amen.*

FEBRUARY 27

Every man according as he purposeth in his heart, so let him give; not grudgingly, or of necessity: for God loveth a cheerful giver.
(2 Cor. 9:7)

When the question of stewardship is raised and we speak about possessions, the danger is that the words may come out of a spirit of pretense. When a right spirit prevails, the right questions will be asked; but in a context of selfishness, the questions come from a wrong spirit! It is only on the condition of a giving heart that we can receive the fullness of God for our lives.

It is easy to keep company with the prophets, apostles, and evangelists and absorb all the utterances they have received from heaven and still be ignorant of all the ways and counsels of God. The command is, "Freely ye have received, freely give" (Matt. 10:8). The intent of heaven is a fearlessness of soul that will dare to accept the whole will of God. And this relationship does not preclude the divine element in our stewardship.

Jesus singled out the poor widow to be remembered forever in His endeavor to teach us the complete consecration of our stewardship in the kingdom of God.

The truth of the doctrine that He taught so frequently was that to be rich was to be poor, and the test of the doctrine was found in the heart of the giver. Our righteousness rises to its rightful position when we can say to God, without reservation, "I have given all."

Our stewardship will be our victory and selfishness will have no resurrection when we are resigned to a deep and loving trust in God. For out of this resignation will come sweet joy and a peace as deep as the calm of heaven.

The commitment that covers it all is, "Take myself and I will be / Ever, only, all for Thee."

PRAYER: *Your purpose for us, O God, is that we should hold everything with a light hand. You have given to us and are at any moment free to take it back again. We are Your stewards and trustees. Help us to be able to give a faithful account of the things You have left in our care. In Jesus' name. Amen.*

FEBRUARY 28

**Thou shalt guide me with thy counsel . . .
My flesh and my heart faileth: but
God is the strength of my heart,
and my portion for ever.**
(Ps. 73:24, 26)

The night was dark, the day had been discouraging, and I walked on to make the last call in a home that was broken by discord and resentful of intrusion. As I walked down the sidewalk, music filled the air, and I followed in words the message from the hands and heart of the organist.

"Guide me, O Thou great Jehovah, / Pilgrim through this barren land. / I am weak, but Thou art mighty. / Hold me with Thy pow'rful hand."

God's hand is always working in our midst, shaping our lives and pointing out the way we should go. He sends us on errands that tend to terrify, but He goes before us and fixes the times and circumstances. The things that terrify us are attractions to Him, for He was always raising the dead, opening the eyes of the blind, quieting the stormy seas, and meeting the tempter on His own terms. He touches the extremes of our life with the strength of His omnipotence.

Within my experience I can find something answering to the attention of God, and my apprehension is swallowed up in a power that overcomes my fears. Purpose finds its utterance and expression in His calling, and my task becomes an errand of God.

When I speak to the one who has fallen down and pray with the one whose life is in despair, I do not have to speak in judgment but extend His offers of love and mercy. New stars hang in the background of the night's gloom when I know that the powerful hand of the great Jehovah is at work.

The expression of gratitude that fills the heart can only be, "Songs of praises I will ever give to Thee."

PRAYER: *Make Your light shine upon us, O God, give us the strength and guidance we need, and work in us the spirit of loving obedience. Help us say with great meaning, "Not my will, but thine, be done." In all sincerity of heart we ask that You will direct us in every footstep. In Jesus' name. Amen.*

■ FEBRUARY 29

> **Behold, the eye of the Lord is upon them that fear him, upon them that hope in his mercy; to deliver their soul from death, and to keep them alive in famine.**
> (Ps. 33:18-19)

"This has been the worst week I have ever spent!" Have you ever heard that statement? I heard it today, with complaints of problems caused by other people, concluding with, "How can you win?"

Job said that he had moaned and he had prayed. He had defied God and charged Him with injustice—he had nothing more to add.

Paul lists the things that happened to him without a cause, which included beatings, loss of friends, false accusation, and even imprisonment.

Jesus said, "Let this cup pass from me" (Matt. 26:39). He later asked His Father, "Why hast thou forsaken me?" (27:46).

Good people are brought to this "What's the use?" point very often. We see *things* when we should be taking in *horizons,* and we miss God's purpose for the circumstance. There are struggles and urgencies that challenge us to higher levels and to ardent prayer, and they can be avenues to a greater awareness of God.

God is working out a daily benefit in us, but our attitude to these plans could thwart the purpose of the Almighty. Who can inspire like the one who has known the weight of agony, the load of grief, or the loneliness of bereavement? We look at Job's suffering, but do we forget the victory and the lessons for the ages?

The sorrows, loss, desolation, and cruelty would be lost upon us if we fail to see that "it is God" working "both to will and to do of his good pleasure" (Phil. 2:13).

"This has been the worst week of my life" could turn out to be that God was using the week to prepare us for eternity.

PRAYER: *We thank You, O God, for life, notwithstanding its pain, shadows, and disappointments. You have made it a great joy and challenge to become enlarged in experience, ennobled in character, and glorified in eternity. Help us to receive life in this spirit. Amen.*

MARCH 1

No lion shall be there, nor any ravenous beast shall go up thereon, it shall not be found there; but the redeemed shall walk there.
(Isa. 35:9)

The language we use to express the most ferocious and the most gentle characteristic of our nature is borrowed from God's creation—the lion and the lamb. If March comes to us with fierce winds and winter's blast and leaves us with the gentle breeze of spring, it is said to have "come in like a lion and gone out like a lamb." And vice versa. And in the coming Kingdom, Isaiah has the wolf, the lamb, the cow, the bear, and the lion all eating together in peace and contentment (11:6-7).

Peter compares Satan with "a roaring lion," going about "seeking whom he may devour" (1 Pet. 5:8), while Isaiah sees the Messiah gathering His flock like lambs in His bosom and carrying them in His arms (40:11).

Who can mistake the simplicity of the language of the Book of God? In His care over us He reminds us that the very hairs of our heads are numbered, while His love is expressed in death. It is the gift of the sacrifice of His only begotten Son, to live, to die, to rise again, and to pray for us in intercession in heaven.

God knows that His message would be without value if we could not understand it, so He did not camouflage it with theories but made it so plain that "wayfaring men, though fools" would be able to find it (Isa. 35:8).

When God speaks to us out of the depths of His unfathomable truth, He adapts it to our own nature and need. Then we find that the mystery is in our sin and not in His truth, in our rebellion and not in His redemption.

Jesus takes the lion of our nature and makes it capable of being carried in His bosom as a lamb.

PRAYER: *O God, You are gentle and kind, always waiting for the best in us. To Your gentleness and mercy we would come. We have no hope in justice, for it can only bring the flash of the avenging sword. We come to the Cross. Here the terror that comes out of our inadequacies is lost in the joy that comes out of our salvation. We pray in Jesus' name. Amen.*

MARCH 2

God hath chosen the foolish things of the world to confound the wise; and God hath chosen the weak things of the world to confound the things which are mighty.
(1 Cor. 1:27)

God chooses His own way of answering prayer and His own way of revealing His secrets to His people. His enabling grace and the power of His omnipotence comes to minister in ways beyond human understanding. His voice is heard in the mighty thunder, and His power is held in the tiny atom. The agencies of God are humbling and terrifying, yet they are all messengers of heaven—how often we miss their meaning!

There is no meanness or misunderstanding in the work of God, and His love is in all the things that He does. All things are His—death, life, angels, principalities, powers, the past, the present, and the future. They all work together for good and are hidden in the secret chambers of eternity for His eternal purposes.

When life is sharpened into pain and sorrow, and loss swiftly succeeds loss, eyes are filled with mist, and the strong hands tremble in fear, do we dare to call it God? Providence?

Last week the life of a friend was suddenly snuffed out in an automobile accident, leaving a brokenhearted family and a devastated church. It is probably to our shame that we were quicker to acknowledge the sting of death than to own the victory of the Resurrection. Our cry was louder than our hymn, and our fear was more evident than our understanding. And it made life smaller in its meaning.

This experience must take in all that it can of the purposes of God. The weakness of our understanding must be hidden in His wisdom.

God is wise. God is love. God is good. God's will be done.

PRAYER: *O God, there are hurting hearts in Your world today who are bereaved or in circumstances of special distress. Out of Your compassionate heart send angels to speak to them of Your love, care, and wisdom. Show us all that even in the darkest hour there is meaning in all the chastening providences of life. In Jesus' name. Amen.*

MARCH 3 ■
But God forbid that I should glory, save in the cross of our Lord Jesus Christ, by whom the world is crucified unto me, and I unto the world.
(Gal. 6:14)

One of the great sidetracks in our Christian experience comes from a wrong understanding of God's challenges. We are taught to pray for great things and are not abashed by the greatness of our requests. The problem is that here is where we excel—praying for things.

The intent of the scriptural injunction is to pray for the greatest thing of all—that we may be transformed into the likeness of God's Son, Jesus Christ.

We have walked with Him through the Gospels, we have listened to Him as He taught along the way, we have been amazed at His simplicity, and we have stood in awe over His infinite mysteriousness. Here is One who has no guile in His heart, no vice in His hand, and no wavering in His behavior.

He revealed the Father to us and called upon us to be perfect as our Father in heaven is perfect. He was "the only begotten of the Father [and is] full of grace and truth" (John 1:14).

We look at Him in His purity, wisdom, and love. But when we try to pray to be like Him, our strength fails, our hope is buried in darkness, and our confidence is lost in fear. We learn that to be like Him, we must pray at the Cross.

Here heaven is open, peace comes in, and prayers find their greatest answers. In the spirit of His sacrifice there is new meaning when we pray, "Oh, to be like Thee, / Blessed Redeemer, pure as Thou art!"

No greater prayer can we make than to say in complete consecration, "Stamp Thine own image deep on my heart."

PRAYER: *O God, we thank You for Jesus Christ, the Gift of Your love, the Seal of Your grace, and the redeeming glory for a sin-sick world. We have seen that glory, the glory as of the only begotten of the Father. We would gladly suffer with Him so that His glory may be revealed in us. Make us fit to share this mystery. In Jesus' name. Amen.*

MARCH 4

My soul waiteth for the Lord more than they that watch for the morning: I say, more than they that watch for the morning.
(Ps. 130:6)

Today is a new day in your life! The thing that you will strive to do most anxiously will be the thing you want above all others. The beginning of the day will be bright with anticipation, and the night will be filled with apprehension. The pendulum will swing from enthusiasm to disappointment in striving for the noblest goals.

This week I had dinner with a friend who has spent a life in service for others. Sometimes he rode high on the train of success, sometimes he was condemned for failure. Sometimes the whole scheme of his life was caught up in that mystery called success—full of grandeur and meaning. Sometimes he was caught in the tunnel where darkness overpowers and friends are barren in sympathy. Now that he senses his time is running out, he summarized his outlook: "I have quit trying 'to do'; from here on in I just want 'to be.'"

Is there not a good deal of all our lives resident in this experience? How much of life is striving to become king, only to discover in the end that another hand reached for the crown? When you were ready to take the throne, it was lost to another pursuer. Here we suffer the supreme trial of our faith and the supreme agony of our sensitivity.

Resignation! "I just want 'to be.'" In the human heart there is born an irrepressible and holy desire for God. No pain, no fear, no dread of tomorrow. Let life bring what it will, it will be one loud, triumphant song.

Today is a new day in your life. Strive "to be" for God. His will be done! Here the crown is sure!

PRAYER: *Help us, O God, to live out the few more days that remain to us as little children in simplicity and love. Make us to know the measure of our days so that we might redeem the time, using every opportunity eagerly and as a sacred trust from heaven. In Jesus' name. Amen.*

MARCH 5

Then flew one of the seraphims unto me, having a live coal in his hand, ... and he laid it upon my mouth, and said, Lo, this hath touched thy lips; and thine iniquity is taken away, and thy sin purged.
(Isa. 6:6-7)

Our God is glorious in holiness. "Holy, holy, holy, Lord God Almighty, which was, and is, and is to come" (Rev. 4:8).

The call of the Master to His followers was to holy living, and He urged upon them, "Be ye therefore perfect, even as your Father which is in heaven is perfect" (Matt. 5:48). The Hebrews affirmation is that "without [holiness] no man shall see the Lord" (12:14).

Only He whose hands are filled with Omnipotence can work this miracle in the heart of a wicked and condemned generation. Only the Holy Spirit can baptize with fire. Only the Holy Spirit can perform what is needed for sanctification. Only the Holy Spirit of God can descend upon the human heart in Pentecostal power.

It was in the darkness that surrounded Isaiah that his inner eyes opened the vision of his heart and the sight of his soul. Isaiah became a seeing man! He saw the Lord in His holiness! Then as he saw himself in relation to God's holiness, he saw his need for that touch of purity.

God does not overlook the earnest prayer for holy living. When the burden of sin has been felt, He does not keep one waiting, groaning, and suffering under the intolerable pressure. His holiness is proof that He will help every one of Adam's race in pursuit of a holy character. He hears and answers when we ask for pardon. He hears and answers when we ask for purity.

Herein is real communion and vital fellowship with the Holy One. Here we can "grow in grace, and in the knowledge of our Lord . . . Jesus Christ" (2 Pet. 3:18).

PRAYER: *O God, You have forgiven our sins. Now we pray that You would cleanse our hearts by the purifying fire of the Holy Spirit. Establish Your throne in us so that Your will might be carried out in our lives every day. May the whole course of our actions be done in Your will. In Jesus' name. Amen.*

■ MARCH 6

He that believeth on the Son hath everlasting life: and he that believeth not the Son shall not see life.
(John 3:36)

How blind we are to the wonders with which we are surrounded every day. The miracles of God never cease, but our powers of seeing them seem to be very limited. They speak to us of the care, love, and tenderness of a loving Heavenly Father.

Jesus said, "He that loveth me . . . I will love him, and will manifest myself to him" (John 14:21). The focus of our spiritual insight is measured by the relationship of this love. He did not come to our cleverness or our genius, but He did come to our love, our simplicity, our need, and the contrite heart.

Here is the ground on which all can meet the Heavenly Father. Before us is the Holy Book, the place of prayer, and the point of communion with the Holy One. And here we find the miracles of God. In these we grow in wisdom, understanding, and love of the Holy One. Here is where character is built and humanity finds its completeness.

The wonders of redemption become real to us as we remember His going to death bearing the Cross. We watch as He is nailed to the tree, and we witness the Son of God in His last agony. We stand amazed at the wonder of the uplifted Cross, the pain and forsakenness, the darkness, and the thunder and death!

Then we hear it all again as for the first time, "For God so loved the world, that he gave his only begotten Son, that whosoever believeth in him should not perish, but have everlasting life" (John 3:16).

This tells it all! It satisfies. It comforts. Out of it comes the joy of heaven. "Oh, the wonder of it all!" Just to know that love was behind it all.

PRAYER: *O God, we are amazed by the wonder of Your power, Your wisdom, and Your love. You regenerate the heart that was dead in trespasses and sin. You give light to them that sit in darkness. For those who are afar off You bring them back by the way of the Cross. Oh, the wonder of Calvary! Help us to keep in the shadow of the Cross. In Jesus' name. Amen.*

MARCH 7 ■
Jesus said unto him, If thou wilt be perfect, go and sell that thou hast, and give to the poor, and thou shalt have treasure in heaven: and come and follow me.
(Matt. 19:21)

Jesus said it would not be an easy thing for rich people to get into the kingdom of God. But He did not say that the entrance requirements would be any easier for the poor. The kingdom of heaven is not gained by wealth, nor is poverty the criterion; wealth and poverty are both external circumstances. Jesus loved the young man whose inquiry elicited the requirements for eternal life, but He could not make the gate any wider than it had been made already.

Calvary can never become the sport of popularity. The Cross can never become a custom for serving the day. The spirit of Christianity can never be subservient to the demands of convenience. Only by the way of the Cross do we pass into the kingdom of God. It is the way of denial before it can be the way of acceptance.

Christianity has been called the greatest impossibility in the world. And Jesus often calls us to do the impossible so that we may be stirred by higher purposes and greater faith. The old foundations must be torn down before He can begin to build. The rubbish must be removed before the gold of His presence can inlay the walls. The old self must be removed before His Spirit can rule and the divine influence can become the master.

Jesus Christ loves the rich and the poor. He loves the lame and the well. Twenty-twenty vision does not reach out for special privileges, nor is blindness a ticket to eternity.

Jesus Christ is the Savior of the world, and the way of the Cross is the only way to heaven. "His blood can make the foulest clean; / His blood availed for me." And you!

PRAYER: *O God, we cannot be satisfied with time and sense alone. When we have thrown our arms around all our possessions, we find we have nothing but poverty. We can be satisfied only with the living God. Then our poverty is swallowed up in the unsearchable riches of Christ—precious, more precious than gold! Satisfy our souls with these things. In Jesus' name. Amen.*

MARCH 8

In God I will praise his word, in God I have put my trust; I will not fear what flesh can do unto me.
(Ps. 56:4)

Probably one of the greatest afflictions of humanity and yet one of the greatest safeguards is the problem of fear. The Bible lists many things that we should flee from in fear, but it challenges us to stand fast fearlessly before a host of other things. David said, "Though I walk through the valley of the shadow of death, I will fear no evil" (Ps. 23:4). He would have had no justification for the bold assertion had he not concluded with the reason, "For thou art with me."

The peculiarity of the Christian religion in whatever the situation is a trust and confidence in God that expresses itself in calmness and dignity before the fears and superstitions in every daily encounter. We can give God no greater pleasure than to cast all our cares upon Him and entrust Him with every concern and care in absolute consecration.

God's way always brings peace and courage, and in His presence there is security. This is our joy, our hymn in the valley of the shadow of death, our psalm in the night, and our victory throughout the day. We will fear no evil, for the rod and the staff of God are our strong defense.

We need have no fear if the Son of God walks the valleys with us, climbs the steep hills beside us, and shields us from the enemy in ambush along the journey. Up and down the mountains and the valleys of the soul there is no place for fear if God is there.

And the emphasis is not upon fear but upon God, and what is done under any circumstance of life is carried out on the battlefield of His choosing with His weapons of warfare.

"What time I am afraid, I will trust" (Ps. 56:3).

PRAYER: *Dry the burning tears, O God, and save us from the fears that cripple the soul and the despair that shields us from Your love. Bless us with the inspirations and the confidence of hope and the strength of those whose trust is in the living God. In Jesus' name we pray. Amen.*

MARCH 9

My brethren, count it all joy when ye fall into divers temptations; knowing this, that the trying of your faith worketh patience.
(James 1:2-3)

It is very difficult to "count it all joy" when we fall into temptation and when adverse situations come upon us. Temptations are usually swift and strong, and they come unheralded and urge themselves upon us without pity. To count it all joy in the midst of storm and in destruction, with plans and purposes thrown into confusion, calls for all-out preparation.

There must be a lesson to be learned in the purpose of God in this respect. God is ever teaching us that we should hold everything with a light hand, saying, "The Lord gave and at any moment may take it away." We are only trustees and stewards and need to give a faithful account of things in our care.

This can be done only in total surrender at the Cross, for there is no other school in which we can learn such wisdom or offer such commitments. Only in complete surrender can we say, "This is hard to bear; nevertheless, by the omnipotence of the grace of God..."

Every activity of the day is preparation for the next. Our foot is continually moving forward in our progress, for we seek a city not made with hands. While we are enjoying things, they fade away, and nothing is of itself worth gathering. Uncertainty, speculation, doubt, and fear mingled in a strange emotion mark our days. At best they are few and evil upon the earth.

But we walk by faith, and our affections and temptations are turned into a sacrament, and our pain becomes a disguised blessing. Our life is His miracle, and it lies in the palm of His hand.

At midnight we can sing songs in the prison and stand firm in front of the furnace, being assured that the presence of the Fourth will be there to sustain.

PRAYER: *Lead us not into temptation, but deliver us from evil, our Father; for Thine is the kingdom and the power, and the glory, forever. May we rest in the all-encompassing breadth of this prayer and hide ourselves in the sanctuary of Thy love. In Jesus' name. Amen.*

MARCH 10

As also ye have acknowledged us in part, that we are your rejoicing, even as ye also are ours in the day of the Lord Jesus.
(2 Cor. 1:14)

Paul tells the Corinthian people that they are his "boast" in the Lord. Beyond his own personal comfort and self-gratification his greatest satisfaction is found in their salvation. He was saying, "Part of me has become part of you, and you have become part of Jesus Christ, and in this I find great joy."

He was always looking for redeeming qualities in every person he met. Those who beat him, threw him into prison, and treated him with disdain were still possibilities for God. He believed that people are forsaken by people long before they are forsaken by God.

Paul was fully aware that sin is a debasing factor in life and that it blights whatever it touches. He knew that the heart is deceitful, and that it has strength only in the measure of its devotion to truth. He saw Jesus Christ as the Truth that makes the difference, and he believed that he was the son of God. Being one with Christ placed an urgency upon him to share this knowledge.

Is not this the crown of Christian experience? We stand in the grace and strength and hope of the gospel of Jesus Christ. We glory in nothing other than the Cross and its message to a dying world. We live in this spirit, enjoying all the meaning and purpose of the shed Blood. We find our security in the One who loved us and gave himself for us.

Paul said, "Woe is unto me," if I do not share this truth (1 Cor. 9:16). This is the whole plan and scheme of it all. This is God's glorious way! This is the rock on which the Church is built.

But God needs to hear it from us as well as from Paul. He needs to know where our "boast" rests today.

PRAYER: *Wherein we have done wrong in the past, O God, You have told us that Your mercy is greater than our sin. We rejoice with those who have found the answer to their iniquity and helplessness in the Cross. Here may we learn more of Your gospel of love. In Jesus' name. Amen.*

MARCH 11

Trust in the Lord, and do good; so shalt thou dwell in the land, and verily thou shalt be fed.
(Ps. 37:3)

A lady without much schoolhouse education but well established in natural wisdom and with a great heart had opened her home to several children from a broken marriage. One day the welfare people came to place them in a more permanent dwelling. In her plea to maintain guardianship, my friend reported, "I told 'em I'd learn 'em all I know'd and feed 'em all I could," but she concluded, "I guess it wasn't enough."

"I guess it wasn't enough!" How much is enough?

There is not sufficient in the finite to satisfy the soul. The inward demands more than all outward sources can supply or satisfy. There is something within every person that requires a greater sufficiency than any hand can gather.

One man decided to tear down his barns and build bigger ones to satisfy that ever-increasing demand of his greed. His wealth had become his poverty, and his riches crushed him into the dust. His unsatisfied soul was required of him before morning in his quest for enough.

Apply this demand to any area of living, and you come up with an increasing desire for more. The world offers its best with the invitation, "Come and drink!" But in the quest for satisfaction the eyes lose their glitter, the mind becomes devoid of thought, and the tongue babbles foolishness, while the soul cries out for contentment.

How much is enough? The Psalmist said, "Delight thyself also in the Lord; and he shall give thee the desires of thine heart" (37:4). God knows just what we need. He cuts slices from His loaf until we want no more. And He gives an inward joy that cannot be touched by the hand of the thief.

How much is enough? No amount until God has touched it, broken it, blessed it, and called it sufficient!

PRAYER: *O God, when our food was exhausted, You found bread for us in unexpected places. Water springs for us out of the rocky places. We have seen the overabundant supply of good things from the hand of a loving God, and we have said, "It is enough!" In Jesus' name. Amen.*

MARCH 12

Whether he be a sinner or no, I know not: one thing I know, that, whereas I was blind, now I see.
(John 9:25)

When the easy flow of life encounters obstacles, sharp bends, and barriers, we are baffled and vigorously question our lot. We chafe under the discipline of heaven and complain about our yoke of bondage. It is human to live in the spirit of apprehension and with the fear of famine next year. Our tears are met with mockery, and the world offers no healing balm.

God is always creating, calling, and amazing us with flashes of glory and unexpected disclosures of His grace. Even affliction is meant for our good, and our loss is intended to be the beginning of our gain. What is impossible under human conditions becomes possible when the soul meets God. The call from the heart always reaches the listening ear of God.

When shall we learn that the bondage of this world is the beginning of great unknown possibilities of grace? Our admonition: "Pray without ceasing. . . . Wait on the Lord. . . . Rest in the Lord, and wait patiently for him" (1 Thess. 5:17; Ps. 37:34, 7). Our reward: "A man that is called Jesus . . . anointed mine eyes . . . and I received sight" (John 9:11).

This changes all of our standards and methods of looking at things, so that now we see the brightness where we saw nothing but gloom. The wilderness rejoices, and the stony places are beautiful with flowers.

Then we come to know the power of the Spirit within ourselves. Fear is destroyed. Vision is enlarged. Love takes over from complaining. And forgiveness rules within the heart. We learn the meaning of waiting upon God.

When God's Spirit dwells within, the spirit of apprehension disappears. This is the miracle of redemption!

PRAYER: *O God, we would see with new eyes, hear with new hearing, and answer the appeals of Your providence with a new voice. Grant us this miracle from eternity! Open our eyes to the understanding of those mysteries hidden from the eyes of flesh. Do not hold yourself from our sight. In Jesus' name. Amen.*

MARCH 13 ■

Open thou mine eyes, that I may behold wondrous things out of thy law.
(Ps. 119:18)

The tapping of the white cane broke the silence as the blind student groped his way down the hallway, bumping into a wall and then a door. The cane counted out the steps as he struggled to find the piano bench. Then he dropped his cane and stretched his legs under the piano as his fingers reached for the keyboard. In an instant a symphony filled the room as the master took control of every movement, and the moment belonged to him.

In my limited vision I had seen only the blind boy; I had not seen the musician. How well we see the coming and the going of things every day as the usual marks out our routine. But the great events, the special circumstances, and the inner beauty escape our vision. A deeper knowledge of God and understanding of our fellowman is obscured by the noise in the hallway.

We recognize very little as it really is. While we are examining, estimating, and deciding, the real meaning is already escaping us. The mysteries that darken our midnight also gladden us with the morning sunrise. We are slaves on one side, while the liberty of the skies are at our disposal. We fail to touch things or see them or know them in their reality. We are mocked and laughed at and put down because we stumble, while God has placed something in each one of us that is beautiful.

We need to see great sights and hear great voices and think great thoughts that are not of this earth. We need prejudices destroyed, views enlarged, and love illuminated. We need to see the miracle of God in every human being.

I need to see you at the keyboard as well as in the hallway! I need to see in you what God sees in you!

PRAYER: *O God, who can tell the mysteries that work each day in Your people? Who can say where Your ministry of mercy ends or where the limitations are? We do not know how You will work out Your plans and understandings toward us. We do know it will be worthy of Your wisdom as measured on the scales of eternity. Open our eyes that we might see it. In Jesus' name. Amen.*

MARCH 14

> ... and yet hast thou not known me, Philip? he that hath seen me hath seen the Father; and how sayest thou then, Shew us the Father?
> (John 14:9)

The mystery of the Godhead is far beyond the grasp of the finite mind. Every move we make, every step we take, every breath we breathe, and every thought that enters our mind, in fact, every action within the limits of space, time, and sense is never out of the reach of God. Who can know the depth of meaning in Almightiness, Omnipotence, Holiness, or God? How can I know what God is, what God does, what God thinks, what God desires, or how He governs His world?

He has not left us without an answer, for while we are asking the questions, Jesus is saying, "He that hath seen me hath seen the Father." When we have looked upon Jesus, we have looked upon God. In Jesus, God was manifested in the flesh.

Here we can lay aside our intellectual imaginations and fix our whole mind, heart, and soul upon the life of Jesus Christ of Nazareth. That life is, within its own limits, the biography of God. The true grandeur of God we begin to see in the simplicity of Jesus Christ as a man living in our world.

In all the currents of human life our redemption and His providence are intertwined in the Godhead. We see Him feed the hungry, but we see Him planting the Cross at Calvary. He is no less God when He feeds the multitude than when He thunders for the grave to yield its prey. He is no less God when He talks to the child in His arms and blesses him than when He orders the storm to be quiet. He is no less God when He weeps over Jerusalem than when He throws over the tables in the Temple.

What it all is we cannot tell; but when we have seen the Christ, we have believed, and when we have seen the Christ, we have seen God.

PRAYER: *Almighty God, You have come to us in the person of Your Son. We cannot see You, but we see Jesus, the Son of Man and the Son of God. We can hear His voice, feel the power of His words, and answer the tenderness of His appeal. Through Jesus we have come to know You. We are satisfied. In Jesus' name. Amen.*

MARCH 15 ■

Therefore, brethren, stand fast, and hold the traditions which ye have been taught, whether by word, or our epistle.
(2 Thess. 2:15)

Determination has made the difference between the greater and the lesser in every generation. One person's determination leaves relics and monuments for other generations to admire and emulate. The deciding factor in the success of most major achievements has been the relentless decision "to do" when the impossible has mocked the intention. A spirit of determination supplies the energy, purpose, and unchangeable resolution in any endeavor.

Building a Christian character requires no less determination, and our concept of the task must be as great and worthy. A great Christian character bespeaks a great God; a great God calls for a great devotion; a great devotion comes from a great consecration; a great consecration is the result of a great determination; and a great determination is born of a great faith in a great God.

This is God's miracle in the life of an individual, and it is not in that person alone to be able to do this. This is the mighty working of the Holy Spirit of God, and it may be done in any one of us—the poorest and the lowliest. We can be touched by God so that every tear will be fraught with confidence, every laughter will be a renewal of strength, and every prayer will be an upward reach.

God never forgets the work of faith or the step of confidence. And He places His omnipotence at the disposal of the man or woman of courage. There is no green pasture in all the paradise of heaven that does not welcome the determined saint of God.

To be sure, our best efforts are often smothered in failure. We stumble and we fall and sometimes we fail, but God takes its meaning and mixes it with our spirit of determination and says to us, "I'm satisfied!"

PRAYER: *Keep us, O God, in the love of the truth and steadfast in Your holy cause. Save us from hesitation and uncertainty of mind, but give us that determination that rests upon the Rock. May our security be in the Cross and our hope in the blood of Jesus and His righteousness. In His name. Amen.*

MARCH 16

Search me, O God, and know my heart: try me, and know my thoughts: and see if there be any wicked way in me, and lead me in the way everlasting.
(Ps. 139:23-24)

Of all the well-laid plans that I have constructed and placed before God as "the only way that it can be done," very few have ever been accepted. God always seemed to have a different way. Many times I have rebelled against His way, and sometimes I have refused to accept it. Often I have taken it, and in every situation I discovered that it turned out best in the long run.

Naaman had leprosy, and he heard about a man who could cure it; but he also had a plan in his own mind how the cure must be effected—"I will use God to the point of my own convenience." He failed to take into account that God never meets us halfway to do His assigned part while we do the other half on our own.

God's way comes to us with a simplicity that actually baffles our understanding, and it comes with a directness that startles us. He has already taken note of the good things and the little things about us and reveals to us those secret things that we had tried to hide from Him. He stands us before himself as open as we would ever have stood before a bar of justice.

Sometimes the nonbeliever has a better crop than the man who has prayed from seedtime to the harvest. Sometimes Christ followers are put down, while the ridiculer is praised in the marketplace. Sometimes the honest man can hardly make it through, while the man without principle lives in affluence. The violence of the outcome often rebukes the man who has chosen God's way.

But we have not yet turned the next page of the book. It says that God is from everlasting to everlasting, and in the long run He will justify His providence to man. So today I will say, "Not my will, but thine, be done" (Luke 22:42), and tomorrow I can say, "He hath done all things well" (Mark 7:37).

PRAYER: *Speak to us in such clear tones, O God, that we will not mistake Your voice saying to us day by day, "This is the way, walk ye in it." May our immediate answer be, "In no other way will we walk, for this is the way of God." Then we will know in our hearts that "God's way is best!" In Jesus' name. Amen.*

MARCH 17 ■

For the kingdom is the Lord's: and he is the governor among the nations.
(Ps. 22:28)

How often I have wished that I had the power to perform miracles. I would have cured every sick child, healed the hurts of every broken home, dried the tears in every weeping eye, put bread on every table, and clothed every stripling on the street. I would have filled every church every Sunday morning, emptied every barroom, torn down every place of ill repute, and left every hospital room vacant. Often I have been critical of the One who had the power but did not seem to carry out my demands.

Most of my attempts ended in failure, and my prayers came back without having done their work. In my desperation for success I had to recognize that God just might be working out some mystery of wisdom and was rebuking my arrogance and my vain imaginations. How terrible if all were given the gift of miracles to dispose as our limited minds and hearts demanded!

Gehazi came back to Elisha and said, "Here is the staff, it has done no good—the child has not wakened." It is not everyone who can use the staff of Elisha. It is not everyone who can wear the armor of Saul. It is not given to any of us to know the mind of God or be entrusted with His wisdom and power.

There are failures in Christian experience, and He knows there are temptations in success. We need the empty purse to show us our limitations and that the excellency of the power is of God and not of ourselves.

How often I have had to go back to the wrestling match, till dawn, till midday, till midnight: "I will not let thee go, except thou bless me" (Gen. 32:26)—and teach me, and show me! Only then did His omnipotence conquer my feebleness, and my feebleness became my strength, and I said, "The battle, O God, belongs to You!"

PRAYER: *O God, the greatest miracle of all is the miracle of redemption, and it comes from You. We pray that You will complete this miracle in everyone. We put ourselves in Your hands for the miracle of mercy performed at the Cross, where the penitent find pardon and the pardoned find peace. In Jesus' name. Amen.*

MARCH 18

That they all may be one; as thou, Father, art in me, and I in thee, that they also may be one in us: that the world may believe that thou hast sent me.
(John 17:21)

One of the great lessons to be learned from the ministry of Jesus Christ is the way He showed us that in the midst of great diversity we can have spiritual unity. How wonderful to listen to a church board discussing in as many opinions as there are personalities, yet running through every judgment is a unity of love!

Look at Jesus in His board meetings! Here is a servant cured who was about ready to die. Here is a dead man raised to life while he was being carried out for burial. Here is a sick man being let down through the roof of the boardroom, and Jesus immediately forgives his sin—and heals him. Remember how Jesus handled each individual case? Remember the criticism! Remember the difference! But remember the touch of the Master! It brought a bit of eternity with it and put every other argument to shame.

Sometimes this unity eludes us. Jesus praised the prayer of the publican. He praised the donation of the widow. He praised a servant in the most endearing terms—"good and faithful." Jesus did not pay tribute to their genius but placed His benediction on their action of faith. While we are arguing for His miracle, Jesus is looking for our faith. And when it is brought together, it must be all of the same quality—unity in love.

He is easily touched with the feeling of our infirmities. And when we need Him most, and cannot see for our tears, He will move heaven and earth to help us. When John sent a message of doubt to Jesus, he answered with a gospel of hope.

Only we can supply the conditions of the miracle, and Jesus will never disappoint honest expectation in the spirit of love!

PRAYER: *O God, we pray that You will work the wonders of love until we see unity in all the diversities of mankind. May our agreements be greater than our differences, and may our union in Christ bring all our differences under the control of heaven. We throw ourselves in complete faith upon the infinite heart of Your love. In Jesus' name. Amen.*

MARCH 19

There is therefore now no condemnation to them which are in Christ Jesus, who walk not after the flesh, but after the Spirit.
(Rom. 8:1)

In a serious conversation between two very outstanding people this week I heard this startling statement: "There is a time in every person's life when an attempt is made to get God out of the way altogether." There was only one life that I could examine for the truth of the remark, and the evidence I found seemed to corroborate the comment.

Sometimes in life goodness prevails and all is well. At other times evil seems to have the upper hand and waits for the right moment to destroy. Life seen through this maze becomes a farce, and any attempt to control it ends in failure. This confusion is common to every person who faces life as it is in the raw. Paul was caught up in the middle of this dilemma: "O wretched man that I am! who shall deliver me . . . ?" (Rom. 7:24).

But we do not have to play this hide-and-seek game with eternity. Sometimes in, sometimes out. Sometimes up, sometimes down. Sometimes on top, sometimes on the bottom. We do not have to live in spiritual imprisonment that shuts out part of God.

In the moral confusion of our world, when it seems that evil has been mistaken for good, and we are tempted to think we can do better without God, we need to look at our moral failures. Life takes in yesterday, today, and tomorrow, not just the immediate glittering point of time. We are in our greatest danger when we cease to hold on to the hand of the Almighty with determination and hopefulness.

Our life does not have to be "O wretched person that I am," but it can be "I thank God through Jesus Christ" (Rom. 7:25). I do need Him every hour.

PRAYER: *O God, we need You. Our hearts cry out for You, for the living God. There were times we did not think that we needed You, nor did we seek You with earnest determination. But we have learned that without You we are nothing and we can do nothing. We do need You every hour. In Jesus' name. Amen.*

■ MARCH 20

> For, lo, the winter is past, the rain is over and gone; the flowers appear on the earth; the time of the singing of birds is come, and the voice of the turtle is heard in our land.
> (Song of Sol. 2:11-12)

We awoke today with all the hopefulness of spring breathing around us, with many signs of returning life as is experienced only in New England. It was so natural to announce with great exultation, "I saw a robin this morning," and to hear in response other evidences that the long winter was past.

God is beginning to rewrite His promise in every opening flower and every bursting bud. And in this revolution of the year we see the rewriting of some of His most tender words. If you lived within the confines of these happenings, you would sense the whole springtime in your heart and a heavenly breeze upon your soul, with a new light bathing the whole breadth of your being.

God's springtime serves to remind us of the way we should take in view our own responsibilities and opportunities. We need to see the measure of our lives and understand the brevity of our days so that we might be found, at the last, as they who wait for the Lord. At the same time we must not rule out of our concern other families, the afflicted, the downtrodden and the poor, our nation in all of its crises, and the minds of men, so vulnerable to the forces of evil in our day.

The greatest springtime in any land would be a blessing coming to every darkened heart, a consciousness of sins forgiven, a delight in the Holy Spirit, and a renewal of life through the One who brings the springtime in its season.

PRAYER: *The years belong to You, O God, for You mete them out one by one. You do not give out time in five years to one, and to another two. You give to each of us one year, one season, one day, one breath; thus You teach us the uncertainty of life and the coming and final judgment of all things. Help us to seek out Your best each season—each moment. In Jesus' name. Amen.*

MARCH 21 ■

**Mine enemies would daily swallow me up . . .
What time I am afraid, I will trust in thee.**
(Ps. 56:2-3)

Retirement is a term filled with dread, and too often it carries a load of grief to be dumped on the recipient. It should be a joyful anticipation with pleasure as the happy issue in the act of retiring. At the end of years of labor, stress, providing, caring, and holding the line, there comes the time of release when the torch is passed on to another.

But retirement is a frightening experience, and time can be an appalling monotony. Nothing is so dull as a day that has no business as usual, no special engagements for faculties that have been prepared for long hours of work, or to tee off on No. 1 hole alone. Memory supplies happy occasions and produces the scorecards for previous 18 holes, and anticipation glitters the future with diamonds, while the heart continues to beat in loneliness.

In retirement there must be the element of hopefulness; without hope we die. This hope must be multiplied within oneself so that in the year of release there will be found new chances, new opportunities, and fresh beginnings. The fear of retirement must be taken away so that life will be young again, for God has filled it with the possibility of good things.

Life is full of beginning again. Springtime sends the green tulip shoot up through the cold earth, reaching for the ray of the sun. Christ's own resurrection comes with the gospel of hope, the gospel of a new beginning, and the gospel of a large opportunity. The old year dies and buries itself, and a new year comes with the proclamation that "I will begin again."

God seems to have filled life with the law of larger compensation, and the reward is within the individual. "What time I am afraid [of retirement], I will trust in thee."

PRAYER: *Dry the burning tears, O God, and save us from the fear that cripples, dejection that stunts the soul, and despair that discourages and blinds us to Your love. Give us confidence and hope in our latter years with the strength of those whose trust is in the living God. In Jesus' name. Amen.*

MARCH 22

The Spirit itself beareth witness with our spirit, that we are the children of God: and if children, then heirs; heirs of God, and joint-heirs with Christ.
(Rom. 8:16-17)

Every generation has been noted for its men and women of wisdom, accomplishment, and place in history. Some have been in the field of science, some in government, some in religion, and others for challenging the normal and attempting the unusual. It seems that God is pleased to make revelations of His power, and He is always distributing human talent and influence among us.

The Bible gives us the records of Abraham, Moses, Elijah, Isaiah, Esther, and Paul, to mention only a few who have been set apart for great missions. It has been noted that "it is not the first 500 feet that gives a mountain its name, but the last 10 feet." There is a sameness in all individuals, but in some there is that larger liberty—the "last 10 feet" has made the difference.

But God has not forgotten the rest of us; for whether we are Moses or Esther or Paul, He tells us that "all things are yours; . . . and ye are Christ's; and Christ is God's" (1 Cor. 3:21, 23). We can lay claim to this, and it takes the limitation off for each of us. He made us all with the infinite cunning of omniscience, and He will take the hand of each of us to lead us through the darkness.

We are children of the dust, and there is a natural tendency to the normal and things that would drag us down. But we are also the children of the Holy One, and to each He has given a lifting up of the heart according to the measure of light in Christ Jesus.

The good part is that in His own good time we shall all be like the angels, loving God with undistracted hearts and serving Him with undivided strength throughout eternity.

Having this hope, we can stand with the greatest as heirs of God and joint heirs with Jesus Christ. What greater claim to fame can anyone claim?

PRAYER: *O God, we have often read to You our slates of greatness, but in Your wisdom You already know what we really are. Your mercy is extended beyond the reach of our own conceit. Bury our smallness in the heart of Your greatness until we shall know that the power of our lives is truly the power of God. In Jesus' name. Amen.*

MARCH 23

Thou hypocrite, first cast out the beam out of thine own eye; and then shalt thou see clearly to cast out the mote out of thy brother's eye.
(Matt. 7:5)

This morning I listened to a scathing indictment on the shortcomings of a good man. I came away with a heavy heart. You see, the condemnation of my friend was meant to be a recommendation for the one in the judgment seat. We have set up for ourselves laws of social penalties, and they all seem to be operating in one direction. How sad when we have to condemn others in order to complement ourselves.

The Pharisees sought to destroy the Master because He had broken their Sabbath-day laws. But in the laws they had made for themselves, to eat with unwashed hands came under greater condemnation than killing a man. In the definition of their own piety they could make the noblest acts unholy and even bring condemnation upon God himself.

Jesus kept on healing and loving and doing good, endured the Cross, and despised the shame because He was looking onward to the glory that was to come. And His life carries its message to us: "Let this mind be in you, which was also in Christ Jesus" (Phil. 2:5).

Jesus never used His miracles and marvelous works as a means of putting others down, nor was His primary aim to use them in support of His claim to Messiahship. But He made more of the obstinacy of His own countrymen than any other person would have made of it.

Jesus Christ came to seek and to save and was willing to prove it at the Cross. This is the whole meaning of the Incarnation; following this, everything else falls into its proper place.

When I am tempted to condemn for my own gratification, I must bring the condemnation by the way of the Cross.

PRAYER: *Deliver us, O God, from vain ideas and impulses that would extend our boundaries and promote our influences in our own name and strength and at the expense of another. Help us to know that only by Your good hand can we conquer. May our victories be made at the Cross. In Jesus' name. Amen.*

■ **MARCH 24**

And she shall bring forth a son, and thou shalt call his name JESUS: for he shall save his people from their sins.
(Matt. 1:21)

The Christmas season with all the festivities is fading farther and farther into the distance. The manger scenes and wreaths have been packed away for another year, and the tree has gone up the chimney in smoke. We do not sing the carols anymore, and the last of the broken toys have been discarded. Our programs have become memories, and Christmastime now has become more of an anticipation than a memory. With all the trimmings gone, there still remains the reason for which we celebrated the occasion.

We must have the Christ child, the hope of glory, born in our hearts again today. His birth time on earth must be a birth of the Child of love and redemption in our spirits. Our hearts were made for Him, and God's intention is that we receive Him day by day, to live in Him, and for Him to live in us.

But we look toward Easter with the triumphal march, the dark Friday, the Resurrection morning, and the Ascension into heaven. Our minds turn from the manger Babe to the One sitting at the right hand of God.

In between stands the mighty Cross by which we are bound together in fellowship in the infinity of love. While we stand at the place called Calvary, our vision encompasses his life from the cradle to the crown. Not only do we see the Crucified One, but also we see the angel of God who shall liberate from the tomb all those who die in Christ.

Today we do not ask for great visions that fill the skies with splendor, but we do ask that we might touch the swaddling clothes of the Child, take up our own cross, be raised in the resurrection, and at the last be worthy of His proffered crown of glory.

PRAYER: *O God, we have been to the manger, and now we come to the throne by the way of the Cross. We do not bring any virtue of our own, but we come bringing a great hope, and we know that we shall not be disappointed. It is the open way into heaven's eternal peace, and we come this way. In Jesus' name. Amen.*

MARCH 25

And God is able to make all grace abound toward you; that ye, always having all sufficiency in all things, may abound to every good work.
(2 Cor. 9:8)

Every person is familiar with the question from the puzzled mind of the child, "Why can't I . . . ?" Often the parents are not far enough removed from the dilemma themselves to have found a definite reason to satisfy the inquiry. All they know is that life is marked all over with boundary lines, and the child looks on them as limitations and unfair restrictions. The parents try to identify the varied circumstances of life and work within these boundaries according to their understanding.

The lines can be very subtle, and sometimes they do make life a prison, but they can also be marker points for the claim of independence. The problem is that most of them are invisible, and their definition is hidden in controversy. Who can show the lines of love or measure the boundaries of goodness? Where does evil stop, and who can tell the point where it has invaded the bounds of truth?

Boundaries mean discipline, and often the lines pose a threat between what we possess and what we think we want. To keep within our own lines, whether we have little or much, is life's highest discipline, but the possibilities are extended to everyone.

The Christian commitment recognizes that all who live within the boundaries that God has set for them are wise. For His is not only a hand that rules but also a heart that loves, and right and wrong are terms that apply to His concern. God will make up to us any loss we sustain, for His love is the guarantee of our well-being.

The encouraging Voice from heaven is that God's grace is available within the bounds that He has set for His people.

PRAYER: *O God, we cannot tell how You work out Your plans toward us. But we do know that it will be worthy of yourself and will be measured on the scale of eternity. Your way is glorious in majesty and tender in compassion. May Your signature be placed on the bounds of our living, and the length of Your love extend to our eternity. In Jesus' name. Amen.*

MARCH 26

> Know ye not, that to whom ye
> yield yourselves servants to
> obey, his servants ye are
> to whom ye obey ... ?
> (Rom. 6:16)

One of the frightening things of my childhood was the constant reminder that an all-seeing God was keeping a record of everything that I did. This did not make me very happy, because I performed some childhood pranks that I did not think needed to be recorded in heaven. I believed that the angels would find it difficult reading, and some of the language would probably be unfamiliar to them.

Mine was a recorded life, and it made me nervous. I knew there was a determined and inevitable power leveled against my freedom and childhood independence. I was never told that this God looked down on me in love or with any degree of concern and protection.

Too often childhood is ruled by fear, and the imagination is left to magnify the penalties of evildoing. Even a threat meant for good is seen in its ugliest consequences and not as an escape from penalty. Obedience as a daily discipline against one's will may force one into submission, but it is an obedience that brings no good and often leaves a mask of rebellion. It can become an acquiescence to please and not a discipline for good.

The whole problem can be resolved best in the question that most individuals often ask, "Why do I have to ... ?" whether it involves obedience, behavior, or morals. The answer can be discovered in observing how Jesus conducted himself under the demands made upon Him. His was the ultimate demand: "who for the joy that was set before him endured the cross" (Heb. 12:2).

I discovered that the God who keeps the records and asks for obedience is also the God who forgives in the spirit of caring and love.

PRAYER: *Help us to know, O God, that we have no law in ourselves. If we would live wisely, we must live obediently. And whatever the challenge, its reward will be large in eternity. Let the joy of true obedience enter into every heart like the singing of angels sent down from heaven. In Jesus' name. Amen.*

MARCH 27 ■

And, behold, I send the promise of my Father
upon you: but tarry ye in the city of
Jerusalem, until ye be endued
with power from on high.
(Luke 24:49)

Heaven on earth"—words used to express good things that happen to us, or to express enjoyment in circumstances that make us happy. We think of heaven in terms of hard labor ending, battles won, tears dried up forever, and days without weariness. This is the purpose for which Jesus came into our world—to bring happiness and to make us good. He did not delight in seeing life lived in pain, or ending in drab death, or endured in daily darkness.

When He came, He was not understood by His contemporaries, His friends, His disciples, or the leaders of His day. He gave assurance to them that He had not come to destroy but to bring salvation, but they were threatened by His presence. Yet when He called His disciples and ordained them to go out into the world, He painted a dark picture for them. He told them they would be persecuted, treated with contempt, and brought before the authorities for death. Many of them could not understand it all.

Then came His cross! He became obedient even unto death —"not my will, but thine, be done" (Luke 22:42). There had been the slaying of animals and the outpouring of blood and the offering of the gifts, but now He became the Priest and the Victim.

His words seemed to be very discouraging and in the immediate light of the Cross devastated their brightest hopes. But they were followed by acts of greatest magnitude and words of greatest encouragement. For after the Cross He spoke to them about tremendous possibilities, "after that the Holy Ghost is come upon you" (Acts 1:8), and He opened a new day for the world.

Heaven came to earth in the form of love withholding no good thing, but we did not know it until we saw the empty grave and Pentecost! Heaven on earth!

PRAYER: *O God, we pray that You would show us something of Your majesty and glory. May we have access to Your power, grace, wisdom, and love. Give us the supply we need for our daily necessities. Satisfy the hunger of the soul. In Jesus' name. Amen.*

■ **MARCH 28**

The Lord is my strength and my shield; my heart trusted in him, and I am helped: therefore my heart greatly rejoiceth; and with my song will I praise him.
(Ps. 28:7)

Today the backward look gives cause for much praise, for no power but that of the Holy Spirit could take one through the yesterdays as God has done. In the forward look praise must fill the heart, for the grace of God has provided larger revelations and infinite possibilities in the march onward. Open windows of heaven, in abundance beyond measure, have been promised as the answer to obedience and prayer. All that the heart needs in courage and cleansing is made available through the Easter Sacrifice.

Words fall flat and too few and feeble to express the emotions of love and gratitude of the soul as we bring our praise to God. He has gone before us through the wilderness, has rolled back the billowing seas, made the giants as grasshoppers in our sight, and has given us the fruit of the land as a witness to His benevolent care. This is the Lord's doings, and we rejoice in psalms of loudest praise.

In looking back and in looking forward, we know that we do not live in ourselves, but we live in God, and in Him we move and have our being. But this is His promise and the encouragement of the heart, and here we take our stand. His Word is our inspiration and foundation and the hope of every victory yet to be taken.

We meet at the Cross, for this is where the victory of the Christian is written. Here the joy of forgiveness enters into the heart like a singing angel from heaven. Here fellowship begins and prayers find their answers and love leads the way through temptation and sorrow to our final triumph.

Today my heart sings, "Songs of praises I will ever give to Thee."

PRAYER: *Help us, O God, to praise You every day, and make us to know that all of our times with You are moments of peace. We seek that rest that comes from You; yea, our whole existence here is an anticipation of everlasting tranquility. We give You praise for that peace today. In Jesus' name. Amen.*

MARCH 29

And after that they had mocked him, they took the robe off from him, and put his own raiment on him, and led him away to crucify him.
(Matt. 27:31)

The darkest day the world has ever known was that day when darkness spread over the whole earth at the sixth hour and lasted until the ninth. Our minds fail in their quest to follow all the mighty works of God in this event.

We see the Son of God staggering under a heavy Cross, and we hear the hammers, steel hitting steel, and we cringe at the piercing spear and weep with the loved ones as they watch in vain. We see Pilate wash his hands to try to rid the guilt, and we witness the soldiers gamble for his robe while the thief curses on his cross. We hear Him cry out from His cross and ask, "Why . . . ?" (Matt. 27:46), and then darkness hides the face of the earth as He dies in shame. But in that darkest hour "the veil of the temple was rent in the midst" (Luke 23:45).

Oh, day of darkness! Oh, day of light! The way to God has been opened through the Crucified One—the only way by which we can find access to the throne. The long-awaited answer of God to the wickedness of the world has come within the grasp of every child of Adam's race. The soul buried in the depths of darkness can now know that the night of earth is the beginning of the day of heaven.

As we stand by the Cross and look upon the dying Savior, our sins find out the meaning of His great work. "He was wounded for our transgressions, he was bruised for our iniquities: the chastisement of our peace was upon him; and with his stripes we are healed" (Isa. 53:5).

Today the Cross stands through all the darkness and through all the light, and sin has been swallowed up in the victory.

The Day of the Cross! The secret of our hope, and the security of our peace. Our Good Friday!

PRAYER: *O God, we pray that You will enable us to feel the great mystery of the Cross that we cannot understand. Show us that we no longer need be in the bondage of darkness but can walk in His light, enjoy His peace, enter into His gladness, and live in the inspiration of immortality. May every day be touched by the Cross. In Jesus' name we pray. Amen.*

■ MARCH 30

My God, my God, why hast thou forsaken me? why art thou so far from helping me, and from the words of my roaring?
(Ps. 22:1)

The Sayings on the Cross by Jesus give us a complete revelation of the humanity of our Lord. But so much more is hidden from us than we are able to see.

"Father, forgive them, for they know not what they do" (Luke 23:34).

"To day shalt thou be with me in paradise" (Luke 23:43).

"Woman, behold thy son!" (John 19:26).

"My God, my God, why hast thou forsaken me?" (Matt. 27:46; Mark 15:34).

"I thirst" (John 19:28).

"It is finished" (John 19:30).

"Father, into thy hands I commend my spirit" (Luke 23:46).

We take these expressions and play them on the screen of our own humanity while eternal purposes standing before us are swallowed up in our vision of the moment. The cycle of time merges into God's immeasurable cycle of eternity as we live within our limitations and watch Him die. What decrees were fulfilled! What prophecies came to pass! What truths passed by in review on Calvary's hillside that day! And we knew it not, for we heard only the human cry. We gave Him vinegar to drink when He cried out for water!

The Atonement was completed that day! The answer to the law was perfected. The way to the Father was opened. The love of God shone through in our world without a cloud to cover its light. And a covenant was fulfilled. But we only heard the thunder and felt the quake, then we walked away in despair.

What we saw that day was but a dim hint of the glory that shall be revealed. We were lost in that love!

PRAYER: *O God, we saw Your Son going to His death, carrying His own cross. We watched as they nailed His hands and feet to that accursed tree, and we heard the cry of victory reverberate around the world. And we asked, "Why?" Then You told us that "God so loved the world, that he gave . . ." And we believed, and our hearts cry out, "Hallelujah!" In Jesus' name. Amen.*

MARCH 31

Fear not ye: for I know that ye seek Jesus, which was crucified. He is not here: for he is risen, as he said, Come, see the place where the Lord lay.
(Matt. 28:5-6)

As the first rays of the morning sun hit our part of the world, voices out of the semidarkness and shadows sent the thrilling sound across the chilly morning air, "Hallelujah, Christ arose!" Choirs in every part of the Christian world repeated the praise. Congregations took up the strain as these triumphant words expressed the joys of Easter morning. Triumphant because of the week of sorrow and the dark Friday when the enemy of the Cross would have claimed victory. Today we express joy because death could not hold her prey, and the rolled-away stone gives testimony to the enemy's defeat.

The teaching of the New Testament is that the Church is the Body of Christ. And the identification of Christ with the Church makes the very soul of Easter morning a personal thing. It brings a closer relationship, a oneness, and a unity to the Church. The message that comes out of the heart of the tomb to us is, "If ye then be risen with Christ, seek those things which are above" (Col. 3:1). This is the challenge of the Cross, and it is the demand of love. And it belongs to us.

Oh, the mystery of the Resurrection! Oh, the mystery of love! Sometimes we think we know it, and then we feel we know nothing whatsoever regarding it. Sometimes we think we see its meaning, and then it fades beyond our grasp.

But for every radiant hope, for everything that makes our soul cleaner and better and stronger, for every new relationship and responsibility and quiet resignation and song of praise, we are grateful.

This is our resurrection and our hope of eternity!

PRAYER: *O God, You have set among the days of time one glad day—Resurrection Day! It is the very climax and glory of time. Help us to enter into the experience of this zenith day and be glad. Help us, in the spirit of the Master, to endure the sufferings of the Cross and despise the shame so that we may be partakers of the glory of the Resurrection. In Jesus' name. Amen.*

■ **APRIL 1**

And, behold, there was a great earthquake: for the angel of the Lord descended from heaven, and came and rolled back the stone from the door, and sat upon it.
(Matt. 28:2)

Last fall my driveway was paved with a new layer of asphalt. A spot near the house where a small garden plot had been was filled in to make easier access to the car during the snowy winter.

Then came springtime! A tulip bulb that lay buried in the cold ground and under four inches of black, tar-laden asphalt refused to die! With an obstinacy that confounds the prejudice of the human mind, this tulip is showing about two inches of green blade up through its black surroundings.

In a very precious moment in my garden this morning, I called out in surprise, "Who rolled the stone away?" as I experienced a Resurrection morning.

The grave was empty; the angels were filling it with light. The stone that represented the power of the Roman Empire, that black asphalt of sin, moved aside—was hurled back by the mighty hand of Omnipotence! Out of the depths of death the voice of the Resurrection was heard around the world. "He is not here: for he is risen, as he said. Come, see the place where the Lord lay. And go . . . and tell" (Matt. 28:6-7). Resurrection knows no impossibilities!

This message cannot be buried in the tomb, for it belongs to eternity. Humanity, shattered and torn, lying in ruin without shape or meaning, with prayers falling back from heaven unanswered, and covered by layer upon layer of black filth of sin, can have a Resurrection morning.

God is still breaking through the asphalt, rolling away the stone, liberating the captives, giving a new dawn, and witnessing to the enemy, "Come and see."

PRAYER: *Almighty God, we come to the throne by the way of the Cross and the empty tomb. We come crying out of our necessities and conscious of the great void without You. We also bring great hope, for the Resurrection morning is not a disappointment as we tarry by the tomb. This is the place of our redemption. In Jesus' name. Amen.*

APRIL 2 ■

Make me to understand the way of thy precepts: so shall I talk of thy wondrous works.
(Ps. 119:27)

The day of miracles is not past, nor is the day of receiving special revelations from God over and gone. Every time the Bible is studied with open minds and hearts to receive, the Holy Spirit uses the occasion as an entrance to give light to the soul. However, there is no real light apart from the Word, nor is there any truth.

In our day we need to be inspired by the Spirit of truth. We need to see the goodness of God as His gentle acts, long-suffering patience, and enduring love pass before our vision. In seeing His goodness, we are prepared for that greater privilege of heaven— the revelation of the glory of God.

It is to the tender care of God that we go when courage fails. It is God who has dried our tears with a soft hand and a touch of love. It was God who spoke to our hearts in a voice that did not deafen with thunder. It was God who stooped with omnipotence to lift us up in our weakness and brought it to bear on our feebleness. He spread our table in the wilderness and opened the rock for our thirsty souls. He put laughter in our heart when life was far spent, and while the grave was yawning at our feet, He showed us that its sting was swallowed up in victory.

He is still able to send Easter blessings upon His people and give us a resurrectional glance at the infinite glory that will awaken our best hope and rekindle our desires for more of His love.

Today He calls out of darkness and gives us a new resurrection through the Cross and the sacrifice of His Son, our Savior Jesus Christ. These are miracles of His grace, and they are still happening today!

PRAYER: *We look upon our salvation, O God, and we say herein is the miracle of the Cross and the triumph of the Holy Spirit. We stand before You redeemed through a name we cannot portray in human tongue. This is the miracle of grace. This is the marvel of the Holy Spirit, when the penitent find pardon and the pardoned find peace. We thank You for this miracle. In Jesus' name. Amen.*

APRIL 3

The thief cometh not, but for to steal, and to kill, and to destroy: I am come that they might have life, and that they might have it more abundantly.
(John 10:10)

One day Jesus Christ passed through our world. Bethlehem put Him in a stable to sleep. The leaders treated Him with suspicion and ruled Him out of their plans. His own people rejected Him with disdain. Out of a spirit of jealousy and hatred He was condemned as a criminal and put to death on a wooden cross. He came as had been prophesied as an apostle to the captive. The brokenhearted and the mourning reached out to Him as a lamp of hope.

Jesus Christ came into our world today. His name is still above every name, and it is still associated with the Cross. He hears the petition of every heart offered in His name, and He responds in kind. He says, "I did not come to destroy lives, but to save them. I will not reject your poor, your lame, your children, or your aged. I will not turn My back on the sinner, nor will I hide myself from the coward and the weak. I will care for you according to the need in your heart."

He knows that every heart has its own cry, every life its own bitterness, and every individual his own sorrow. When we invite Him in, He makes our house a pleasant place and reveals himself to our need, our expectant love, our brokenness, and our contrite heart. Though we have no words to explain His presence, we will know Him by the tenderness of His touch.

He is the only answer to our sin, the only consolation of our sorrow, and the only meaning on which our life can rest. In Him is our today and yesterday and tomorrow, for He is eternal. These are the creations of love and the outcome of the Cross.

PRAYER: *You come to us, O God, in the person of Your Son. We cannot see You, but we see Jesus, the Son of Man and the Son of God. We can hear His voice, feel the power of His words, and answer the tenderness of His appeal. The world can offer no such treasure. Come to our hearts, we pray. In His name. Amen.*

APRIL 4 ■

I will bless the Lord at all times; his praise shall continually be in my mouth.
(Ps. 34:1)

Sometimes when we try to pray, we find no response on the other end; it is as if we were surrounded by covers of blackness. We can discover no reason within for this lack of communication, but it's there nonetheless. A veteran missionary reported having gone through such an extended period, when the walls and ceiling were like cement barriers, and his prayers returned in mockery at his feet.

He said, "One day I quit praying and began praising God, and the walls crumbled around me, and I found myself in His presence." His conclusion was, "When you can't pray your way through, you can always praise your way through."

God's mercy and love are always around us, for we live under their influence every day. But we are also surrounded by cement walls, and we travel on a road where there are giants waiting to slay, lions to devour, and miry places to swallow us up.

We must never forget that we come to God by the way of the conquering Cross and are actually walking the footsteps of the Man of Galilee. We stand beside Him as our Priest, and through Him we have the assurance of forgiveness and a "joint heir" relationship with heaven. We have been brought out of the place of darkness and live in the joyfulness of a new light from the throne.

We do not need to live in our own littleness and always walk on the brink of defeat and live on the edge of despair. We can enjoy the favor of God and move with the courage of the conqueror. Our God is the God of Elijah, Isaiah, Jeremiah, and the great company of apostles, and the record of His failure will never be written.

May God take us from the alphabet of prayer to the deeper reading of praise.

PRAYER: *O God, Your words to us have ever been marvelous in love, and we praise You for it. You have magnified mercy in the midst of our need, so that we see eternity in Your work. Make our praise to be eternal to meet the demand of Your love. Help us to live the upward life with our eyes fixed on heaven. In Jesus' name we pray. Amen.*

■ **APRIL 5**

And they said one to another, Did not our heart burn within us, while he talked with us by the way, and while he opened to us the scriptures?
(Luke 24:32)

In every great experience there is an "after" condition to face. Sometimes it is a letdown and pulling loose ends together. Sometimes it is putting broken pieces back together and re-grouping and beginning again. Jesus had been with His disciples for three years, but then came the Cross, followed by disappointment and discouragement. To be sure, there was the Resurrection, but the truth had not yet sunk in, and it was back to the fishing nets.

There is a principle here of very wide adaptation, and it includes that point in which leaning and dependence have to cease. It is that point where the eaglet must fly all by itself. It is the point where faith, courage, and spiritual consciousness say, "I can do it now!"

After Easter, what then? There was the Emmaus road experience when Jesus met them; later "he led them out as far as . . ." (Luke 24:50); then He left them. Cruel? No! It is here that faith takes over, and they are no longer dependent on the visible, but they must depend on a higher level of life for their victory.

Jesus is always leading His people "as far as . . ." and then saying, "Now, you do all you can in your own strength; 'and, lo, I am with you alway, even unto the end of the world'" (Matt. 28:20). But He is always leading on to something larger, even when it seems that we are left with no answers, and the solutions have completely eluded us.

Today Jesus is still going with us "as far as . . ." and saying to us, "You must go on from here." But at the point of parting He is showing us the larger truth that the enabling power of the Holy Spirit is ever available at the point of our need.

PRAYER: *Often we fail, O God, but in our failures is our success. Our weakness becomes our strength, for what we would do if we could is taken as if we had already done it. Your mercy and omnipotence glorify their own tenderness, and in them we find that our strength is made perfect in weakness. In Jesus' name. Amen.*

APRIL 6 ■

Let thine hand help me; for I have chosen thy precepts. I have longed for thy salvation, O Lord; and thy law is my delight.
(Ps. 119:173-74)

You can read any old book or trashy magazine in any public place, and no one pays any attention. But the person who opens the Bible to read in public is branded and comes under severe scrutiny and ridicule. Too many people treat the Bible with suspicion. It is not a divine revelation to them but something about which they have to be apprehensive.

How should we read the Bible anyway? Is it just a jumble of words, difficult to understand, without any central meaning? Is there an underlying point the writer wants to say to us? Is there a theme, a story, a purpose, or an experience that we should try to find?

The Bible wants me to believe that "God created the heaven and the earth" (Gen. 1:1). It wants me to believe that the serpent betrayed Eve, and sin entered our world through disobedience. It wants me to believe that God gave Moses the Ten Commandments on Mount Sinai. It wants me to believe in the meaning of the Cross, which says that the world is "not redeemed with corruptible things, as silver and gold, . . . but with the precious blood of [Jesus] Christ, as of a lamb" slain "before the foundation of the world" (1 Pet. 1:18-20). It tells me there is a power mightier than death, and its sting is swallowed up in the victory of the Resurrection. And it tells me more.

After people have belittled it, ridiculed and disputed it, and mocked it, they have not really touched the Bible. When we understand this, our reading will take on new meaning, and we will find truth in the midst of all the turmoil. And in it we will find God, who "is our refuge and strength" (Ps. 46:1).

The Bible speaks to the soul. It is God's Book. The world is afraid of it!

PRAYER: *Thank You, God, for the Book! Help us to read it with clear eyes, to receive it with honest hearts, and to embody it in obedient lives. It contains all truth, all wisdom, and all light. It is like a golden gate opening into heaven. It is Your Book. Help us to receive it as such. In Jesus' name. Amen.*

■ **APRIL 7**

Eye hath not seen, nor ear heard, neither have entered into the heart of man, the things which God hath prepared for them that love him.
(1 Cor. 2:9)

People today are looking for answers, proofs, things that can be looked at and handled. We like to see everything in black and white so that we don't have to make decisions. We want it to be there when we come back looking for it. If we cannot see it, we cannot believe it. From this point of view we have tried to construct everything with which we have to do, including our religion. Maybe this is the reason Jesus told us that "the kingdom of heaven is like unto . . ." and began to fill in with types and symbols and things that were familiar to us (Matt. 13:33, 44, 45, 47; see 24, 31).

We think about God as a man and give Him a human form as its only possible expression. Even when we try to think about Him as merciful, righteous, and holy, we have a tendency to put these in terms of an infinite, almighty Man. We speak of His eyes, His mouth, His hands, and His feet; He rises, He sits; He walks, and He rides; He comes down, He calls, He grieves, He rejoices—all of these are human expressions, and we limit them by human uses.

Our Lord said that "God is a Spirit: and they that worship him must worship him in spirit and in truth" (John 4:24). This baffles us because we have no image that represents this idea. But when God says that He is a Father, a King, or a Shepherd, we can relate to these human characteristics.

Jesus told us, "He that hath seen me hath seen the Father" (John 14:9). And our hearts tell us that the movement of life is from the less to the greater, and that the half has not been told us! (See 1 Kings 10:7.) What has been seen is as nothing compared to what has yet to be revealed.

What a day that will be when we see Him as He is! "Eye hath not seen, nor ear heard . . . the things which God hath prepared for them that love him."

PRAYER: *O God, we are still upon this old earth and think in terms of its earthiness. But You did breathe into us the breath of divine life, so that we are not all earthy. Look upon us in love and renew again the love we once had, so that we may grow more and more like You. Show us more of yourself as we learn more about the Christ of Calvary. In Jesus' name. Amen.*

APRIL 8 ■

And hope maketh not ashamed; because the love of God is shed abroad in our hearts by the Holy Ghost which is given unto us.
(Rom. 5:5)

Life is pretty much geared to the clock and the calendar. Our working day, with all of its activities, has a time set for a beginning and for an ending. To witness the lineup of workers, standing by the time clock with cards in hand, waiting for the clock to tick out the last minute of the shift, is an interesting sight. How drab the day would be if there were no "five o'clock" to anticipate.

Life must have an element of hopefulness; without it we die. We live by it, and we call its partner faith. God has placed a portion of himself in the heart of every Christian, and He has called it hope. It sings to us when right is being tested, when shadows fall on our way, and when the scheme of our planning is spelling out defeat. We look upon the everlasting for the long haul, but hope sees victory in our now.

The Resurrection came with the gospel of hope, the gospel of a new beginning, and the gospel of larger opportunities. The old year dies, but life comes forth in a new one and says, "You can begin again." In all of the ups and downs, the inconsistencies, the uncertainties, and the disappointments, it writes with a careful hand. Step by step through all our opportunities God places the ladder of hope, and He never asks for obedience without offering His promise of larger compensations.

Within this circle lies the victory or the defeat of every person in God's universe. We are made in His own image, and His gospel has filled His children's lives with the power of hopefulness. When we are surrounded by darkness, pitfalls, and temptations, it says to us, "There is a light ahead."

PRAYER: *We thank You, O God, for all Christian hope and confidence. We need this in the dark times, on cloudy days, and when the sun is shut out. It tells us how great is Your love, how tender Your pity, and how precious the dew of Your tears. Help us to ever live in this hope. In Jesus' name. Amen.*

APRIL 9

**Stand ye in the ways, and see, and ask for the
old paths, where is the good way, and
walk therein, and ye shall find rest
for your souls.**
(Jer. 6:16)

Often we hear critical remarks when people recall the good old days and recount in great detail occasions that are still dear to them in memory. On the other hand it would be sad if these precious moments that had been such a vital part of life had been forgotten. And sadder still is the possibility of forgetting God and His providences in the lives of many individuals.

In every life there are experiences worth remembering and reliving. How many kind words have been spoken to us in encouragement? How many great and ennobling prayers have we heard on our behalf? How many lives have mingled with ours from whose love has been gathered strength and comfort? How many voices have urged us to keep going when it would have been easier to give up? To empty the memory is to silence the tongue of praise, and not to cherish the recollections in life is to hamper the progress of the soul.

Moses suggested a way to accomplish this same purpose: "Lest thou forget the things which thine eyes have seen . . . teach them thy sons" (Deut. 4:9). In other words, talk about the good old days, dwell on them, be grateful for them, and never forget the day of your deliverance, and recall the special revelations that God has granted to you. Keep your recollections up-to-date and repeat them often.

How much we lose when we never recall the good things God has done for us, for the personal experience enhances the power of Christianity. When we have been to the Cross, we are in a better position to preach Christ, and a witness of salvation becomes more real in the recollection of our commitment.

Let the spirit of recollection be bound up in the spirit of anticipation, lest some good thing be forgotten!

PRAYER: *Every moment, O God, that we spend in Your presence makes us feel more keenly that we have been taught in the mysteries of Your life and purpose. May we recall these times of refreshing, lest we forget Your goodness. Make Calvary real to every generation, renewing again and again with Your fullness, and we shall be satisfied. In Jesus' name. Amen.*

APRIL 10 ■

And they rest not day and night, saying, Holy, holy, holy, Lord God Almighty, which was, and is, and is to come.
(Rev. 4:8)

Holy, holy, holy, Lord God Almighty." The Bible clearly expresses this attribute of God. Peter used the same truth of God's holiness in his admonition, "Be ye holy" as your Father in heaven is holy (1 Pet. 1:15-16). The Hebrews writer warns that "without [holiness] no man shall see the Lord" (12:14).

The imagination is staggered before this demand laid on a fallen and sinful world. This is either a promise within the reach of possibility for the human race, or it is a mockery of God and a false temptation to holiness. Who can work within a depraved humanity the miracle of purity resulting in the likeness of our Father in heaven? This divine demand baffles the heart that is held under the bondage of sin.

The answer is God. God reigns and holds everything within the grasp of His almighty hand. And He can make us pure in His sight. What we need for our sanctification is available to everyone. The Holy Spirit can baptize with power and descend upon His people today as in the Pentecostal hour. The day of God is still open to people everywhere. There is still salvation at the Cross. It stands above the ages, and the superscription written by the finger of God is still, "Whosoever will!"

God's promises have not changed with the time. His requirement for salvation is for us to forsake our wicked ways and thoughts and return unto the Lord with penitent spirit, and He will abundantly pardon. And His promise of the Holy Spirit to all who seek holds true in every generation all over the world.

In this hope we live; in this hope we can never die. "Holy, holy, is what the angels sing," and we can join in the song!

PRAYER: *Holy Father, continue to grant us the comforting ministry of Your Holy Spirit so that we may be able to live in harmony with Your gospel every day. Without Your help we can do nothing. May we know that we have passed from death unto life because of this new love we have received through Your Holy Spirit. Amen.*

APRIL 11

And he shall judge the world in righteousness, he shall minister judgment to the people in uprightness.
(Ps. 9:8)

An interesting cover-up in common usage in recent years was the explosive retort, "The devil made me do it!" This was supposed to justify the act, dissolve any indiscretion, and put the guilty one in a not-my-fault and without-blame condition in society, leaving the devil with the full load of responsibility.

There are other alternatives to wrongdoings, even though it is part of human nature to take the avenging route in circumstances. There is something better than vengeance, and for every spirit of hatred there is a spirit of forgiveness and love. The Christian way is to live in God, trust in God, and commit all things to God. He said that He would handle vengeance and blame in His own way and time.

God's purposes concerning His people are always good, and His mercy is extended forever to all who would be good. In the face of all that the devil may try to inveigle us into, the grace of God is available in greater abundance than the sin that tries to conquer.

God is right; righteousness is at the heart of all His purposes. Maybe He does move slowly from our perspective, and the devil does try to bury hope in despair; but God still moves with infinite certainty. And His movement is toward justice, right, and truth. In the controversies with Satan we do not have to succumb to his demands, for we are called upon to love God, to fear God, and to trust God.

"The Son of man is come to seek and to save that which was lost" (Luke 19:10). There are difficult battles that we cannot fight, but there is a refuge always open to us. When we are lost in wonder, love, and praise at the cross of Jesus Christ, the power of the devil carries little consequence.

PRAYER: *O God, if You will look upon us in love, we will take heart again; we will be strong and fearless, and our whole nature will reverberate with praise to You. In ourselves we are without hope, for the enemy is too great, and our defenses are too small. Our hope is built on nothing less than Jesus' blood and righteousness. Here is our claim. In Jesus' name. Amen.*

APRIL 12 ■

Yea, the darkness hideth not from thee; but the night shineth as the day: the darkness and the light are both alike to thee.
(Ps. 139:12)

On Sunday I am happy, on Monday full of joy, / On Tuesday I have peace within that nothing can destroy; ..." And on the chorus went, taking in one whole, every-day-happy week, and that was good. So often religion becomes a thing that is useful here but useless there—good for Sunday but unnecessary for Monday and Tuesday. A Lord who is good in the crisis but not needed on the hilltop. A religion that is good for the dark and dangerous places but unnecessary when the way is clear and the dangers are past.

How grieved must be the heart of God when we call Him in for the rough occasions only. He wants to be included in all the purposes of life conditions—body, soul, and spirit. He wants us to live and move and have our being in Him—every day!

Today, be it Sunday, or Monday, or Tuesday, when "I ... lift up mine eyes unto the hills" it is gratifying to know that "my help cometh from the Lord, which made heaven and earth" (Ps. 121:1-2). He can be brought into my daily experiences. He can take part in the minute-by-minute details of my life. He wants to fill the earth with His morning and bless the journey with His presence, and He weeps over the city that rejects Him.

Today He is my God in the valley of troubles, but I need Him on the hill of my strength and joy. When life dips into steep places or faces disaster at the bend of the road, and when the beasts roar in the field and the vultures scream in the air, He says to me, "I want to be with you in every situation, even to the end."

"If I take the wings of the morning, and dwell in the uttermost parts of the sea; even there shall thy hand lead me" (Ps. 139:9-10), so that every day, in every situation I can have peace "that nothing can destroy."

PRAYER: *Help us, O God, to meet You every morning of every day so that we might find strength for each task that we have to do. Take us to the top of the mountain and be with us there, and then go with us in the valley and through the wilderness. Keep us in the morning of every day as we seek Your presence throughout our whole life. In Jesus' name. Amen.*

■ APRIL 13

Great deliverance giveth he to his king; and sheweth mercy to his anointed, to David, and to his seed for evermore.
(Ps. 18:50)

It has always been gratifying to read about people in the Bible who "did that which was right in the sight of the Lord." The failures recorded are numerous, and great is the number from whose "countenance the image of God has faded." Behind both are traditions and environment of the most corrupt kind. In every situation there comes a point of yielding to the evil of the environment or resisting it. No one can trifle or compromise with it. One must either take a firm stand for God or be prepared to fall!

There is no easy life in the Christian faith, even in a Christian community. In proportion as one bases his life on righteousness, honesty, decency, and faith in God will he be struck down with antagonism and opposition. This holds true in every department of life where any assault is made against wrong and evil-doing. But good men and women have gone out at great personal cost, and by the power of the almightiness of God, and "did that which was right in the sight of the Lord," and have set up a better world for us.

Even as people go on for good, the fist of evil will ever be waved in defiance, temptation, and mischief in their face. The enemy will take you to the "high mountain" and display his kingdom of possessions and challenge you with the false promise of security. But while he is teasing, testing, and tempting, the frail threads of truth can be broken by the proven "thus saith the Lord" of the Bible.

In the final analysis it is not necessary for you to find the answer, for God will defend His own cause. Never forget that the finest answer in favor of Christianity is in a life that "did that which was right in the sight of the Lord."

PRAYER: *O God, You are always revealing new things to the human mind when we are able to accept it. We take our stand on Your truth as You constantly fill us with new surprises beyond our natural inclinations. We would do that which is right and honorable in Your sight so that we might know more of Your ways for us. In Jesus' name. Amen.*

APRIL 14

Therefore speak I to them in parables: because they seeing see not; and hearing they hear not, neither do they understand.
(Matt. 13:13)

One of the complaints that Jesus made when He was here on earth was that people would not look, would not hear, would not consider, and would not sit down and think for themselves.

You have ears; but instead of hearing sounds in tune with the music of goodness, you listen for gossip, noise, and sordid tales.

You have eyes; but you see only surface appearances and a confusion of the immediate and the vulgar. You are blind to the finer things and neglect that which would uplift and edify.

Jesus is pleased when we ask honest questions, and He listens when we wonder why and state our doubts, and He is in tune with the aching heart. He is saying, "Empty your heart. You can be yourself with Me. Speak out like a child when he makes his inquiry." We do not understand the Master, and we do Him an injustice if we think He is not interested when we are perplexed and ask questions.

He came here as one of us and was in all points tempted as we are. He was God, but He also was man. He does not want us to throw away our experience. He knows every intricacy of our lives and shows understanding to guide us through the complexities of life, and He wants us to talk with Him about them. The whole ministry of the grace of God is available to the searching one.

His benediction was, "Blessed is that servant who shall be found waiting and watching and inquiring when the Lord comes" (see Matt. 24:46).

Jesus Christ is still in the business of receiving sinners and leading them gently through every question of life until they reach heaven.

PRAYER: *O God, we pray that we might see, hear, and understand Your truth and goodness. Then give us the unfailing desire to follow after them. May our pursuit be with an ever-burning zeal and with a completeness of devotion that leads to heaven. In Jesus' name. Amen.*

■ APRIL 15

And herein do I exercise myself, to have always a conscience void of offence toward God, and toward men.
(Acts 24:16)

The man from the IRS was reporting to the TV audience the number of people expected to go wrong on their income tax this year. He outlined reasons, which ranged from the insignificant to the complicated and on to the ones that would require a computer to define. His final words of warning were, "It is better to do it right now than to try to find reasons later for having done it wrong."

This probably relates to the darker side of our society, but many do get caught in the dilemma. But there is a brighter side, and this always drives us back upon the yesterdays. For repentance knows no halfway measures, and there is no statute of limitations for the honest person. The Christian man and woman write the evidence of their Christianity even on their Form 1040.

It is difficult to try to live in the gloom or in the resurrection of buried deeds of the past. Zacchaeus felt the power of this in his encounter with Jesus and immediately responded, "If I have taken any thing from any man by false accusation, I restore him fourfold" (Luke 19:8). Christianity makes this kind of a person. Whenever you see one making amends for the past, drying the tears he caused to start, or renewing right relationships, you have found a person who has met Christ.

How early in life we should learn that truth can be found only in Christ, the Living One. Those who are feeble within themselves find strength in the power and comfort of divine truth.

Through Christ we can be partakers of the riches of His grace and truth, "with a conscience void of offence toward God, and toward men"—and the IRS.

PRAYER: *O God, help us to manifest Your truth in all our words and deeds. Make it dwell in us, touching every point of our lives, giving us an outreach over all lesser things in the time of testing and dismay. We would know more fully its riches. In Jesus' name. Amen.*

APRIL 16 ■
He was wounded for our transgressions, he was bruised for our iniquities: the chastisement of our peace was upon him; and with his stripes we are healed.
(Isa. 53:5)

The anticipation of the world was that One would come down like rain upon the mown grass and as showers that water the earth. It had been prophesied that One would come who could save the poor and needy and be a helper to those who had no friend. He in whom all nations would be blessed was promised to earth.

He has come! We have seen Him! We have followed Him from His birth even to His death. We have seen the nail prints in His hands and have thrust our hands into His wounded side. We heard from His lips the Beatitudes; no more tender words in all heaven were ever uttered upon earth. He was wounded for our sins and carried our transgressions to the Cross. And through His Spirit He lives with us today.

The way of salvation is made known to us through the God-man mystery in the life of Jesus Christ. He was a Man who hungered, thirsted, got tired, slept, and walked like we do. Yet there was a line of limitation in the kinship, a point of approach and a point of separation. He loved, but He rebuked. He obeyed the laws of time, but He commanded with the authority of eternity. Heaven was in His smile, but there was fire in His judgment. He cried out to the Father in His pain, but He defied death in His resurrection. He claimed earth for His own, but He called heaven His home.

We take our stand beside Him in relation to this prophecy and the fulfillment, for no person can remain on neutral ground. The highest thought of our soul encompasses Christ and moves us to the Cross. Here His gospel of love invites us to be partakers of His glory.

God's love is never greater than when He sees us coming with a broken and a contrite heart.

PRAYER: *O God, how beautifully You have revealed yourself to those who would seek after You. In the prophecies we find the gospel, and in ancient times we find the Lamb slain before the foundation of the world. Your entire revelation is resident within the spirit of the Cross. We have found Him. In Jesus' name. Amen.*

■ APRIL 17

Verily I say unto you, Inasmuch as ye have done it unto one of the least of these ... ye have done it unto me.
(Matt. 25:40)

One of the absolutes in our world is that we will always have the poor and needy with us, while the cry for help is louder than the desire to respond. Innocent children are caught in the dilemma, the culprit goes free, and the victim is left with the scars. The age-old question is still with us, "Does anyone care?"

This is the same world that Jesus passed through. He was always surrounded by the deaf, the dumb, the blind, the poor, the brokenhearted, the weary, the hungry, and those who had been left to suffer without help. The hope in His world was that a Messiah would come to the brokenhearted and to the hurting.

It's the same world. But we reach out for a comfortable place where we cannot hear the cry. We shut ourselves up in our dens while we enjoy our TV and snacks. We warm ourselves by our marbled fireplaces and shut out the cries of distress and the screaming for help. We tell ourselves that life is tolerable and comfortable, while we sing, "What a wonderful world!"

Oh, we hear the complaints, but we call them exaggerations. We read about the human distresses and poverty, and we call them fillers. We blame the poor for their poverty, the sorrowing for their sorrow, and the lonely for their loneliness.

Jesus stopped for a time in this world. Its distresses fluttered in expectancy. The blind heard His footstep. The deaf knew of His presence. Sadness prayed with new hope. The sick reached for the hem of His garment. And when He left, the dead had been raised to life, and love had left its mark.

Today I saw Jesus place His crown on an individual who had heard that cry in the night and had responded to redeem a life from destruction.

And I prayed, "Lord, open my eyes so that I might see—and be and do!"

PRAYER: *Lord Jesus, as You wept at the grave of Lazarus, so Your tears flow today when the heart is broken. Help everyone to be able, by Your grace, to bear life's burdens when the poor little bundle of strength has given way to weakness. We know that when our cry is the greatest, we will find that Your help will be the most tender. Amen.*

APRIL 18 ■

Thou art Peter, and upon this rock I will build my church; and the gates of hell shall not prevail against it.
(Matt. 16:18)

When God comes into the life of an individual, the Church says, "He is a new creature," and continues that "old things are passed away; behold, all things are become new" (2 Cor. 5:17). It is spoken as if everything pertaining to personality, abilities, relationships, and minds were obliterated, and God had formed a new and holy creation. All of this sounds good, but that is not exactly the way it is!

The stones of the old building are not crushed to powder and thrown to the winds, nor is the timber burned to ashes to be forgotten in hidden places. The old stuff of which our life was made is simply taken out of the hands of the enemy and placed into the hands of the Master Builder. He takes every stone, every old board, and all the old material and finishes it to build a palace.

Dangerous? Yes, but for one thing. God oversees the finishing.

There was danger in entrusting the revelations of Christianity to a few fishermen and others, ignorant and feeble in every aspect of social importance. But Jesus did!

There was danger in selecting as the leader of His Church a man who had cursed and sworn and denied his Lord. But Jesus did!

There was danger in leaving His missionary world with a man who had set out to persecute the Church and put to death all her followers. But Jesus did!

He did not disguise or change the identity, but out of the intensity of the persecutor He made an evangelist. Out of an impulsive personality and on the rock of ruggedness He built His Church.

He can work on what we give Him, so that someday when people ask, "What meaneth these stones?" Jesus will answer with a sense of accomplishment, "Out of the pieces given to Me I have built a sanctuary."

PRAYER: *O God, we are aware that no person lives without some mark of Your handiwork upon him. All things that have ever been built have been backed by the wisdom of the Master Builder. We invite You to lay the foundation, place every stone, and build according to Your design, so that it may be Your dwelling place. In Jesus' name. Amen.*

■ APRIL 19

But when he saw the multitudes, he was moved with compassion on them, because they fainted, and were scattered abroad, as sheep having no shepherd.
(Matt. 9:36)

Whatever a person might think of Jesus Christ, there is one thing that cannot be overlooked: He was a Man of great compassion. We have seen the tears, listened to the urgency in His voice, witnessed the caring in His actions, and been touched by the passions of His deeds. It does not come across as a display of power for a selfish purpose, but it is written full of love and an exemplification of the mercy of God.

When we read the life of Christ, we read the story of One who took upon himself all the pain, all the feebleness, all the poverty, and all the anguish of those who suffer most. He took upon himself our sins. He carried our iniquities. He took our infirmities. He is "not an high priest which cannot be touched with the feeling of our infirmities" (Heb. 4:15). He knows every one of us through and through. He is All in All, the fairest of 10,000. He is the Son of Man.

He was moved to compassion by the multitudes; the little children blinded Him to any need of His own; the sick guided His hand of mercy; and He made a way from Calvary to paradise. He saw people as sheep having no shepherd, and He became the Good Shepherd. He came from heaven's glory and made himself of no reputation that He might reveal His purpose, sympathy, and love. He knows the language of the heart and all the emotions of the human spirit, and He became one with humanity so that He might bring new hope to the soul.

The key word of His ministry was *compassion*—a relationship that makes all others fall into their right perspective and proper place. Here we begin and here we end. This is the consciousness of every human heart.

PRAYER: *O God, You have given us comfort by Your grace and healed us from the leprosy of sin. Because Your compassions do not fail, You have spared us to this hour. We are monuments of mercy, witnesses of grace, and miracles of Your love. This shows Your love for Your people. In Jesus' name. Amen.*

APRIL 20

Then came Peter to him, and said, Lord, how oft shall my brother sin against me, and I forgive him? ... Jesus saith unto him ... Until seventy times seven.
(Matt. 18:21-22)

Today I talked to a man who had been taken through some very irritating extremes of life. He was wavering between two possibilities as the result of his experience. There was the normal drive to let the past embitter his spirit and become embroiled in controversy. Or he could look on the past with a broken heart and become richer in his spirit for not having succumbed to resentment and hatred. As he talked, I knew he would survive the storm, for a new tone charged with the music of sympathy came into his voice, and his feet were anchored in a spirit of forgiveness.

Here we ought to learn a lesson. How easy to come out of those dark nights of the soul embittered and resentful with a spirit of getting even. How easy to sit on the throne of judgment and mete out hateful injustices. How easy to let an injury of the soul fester into an angry sore of contempt!

I saw the real spirit of Christ shine through my friend today, and I saw the miracle of the water of hatred turn into the wine of forgiveness and love. I took knowledge of him that he had been with the Master. He remembered all that happened to him, and the hurt will be a long time in healing; but God had applied the balm of tenderness to an aching heart. It was not difficult to grasp the spirit of Job: "He knoweth the way that I take: when he hath tried me, I shall come forth as gold" (23:10).

Today I talked to a Man who had come up against gross injustice, prejudice, slander, betrayal, and death. On His cross, with arms outstretched to the world, He said, "Father, forgive" (Luke 23:34). Today His holy gospel lifts its sweet voice amid all the tumult of conflict and hatred and says, "Seventy times seven!"

PRAYER: *Our hearts rejoice today, O God, that Your love reaches out to us with the gospel of forgiveness as Your judgment makes way for Your mercy. We bow at the Cross and wait, for only here is there to be found forgiveness. We pray that forgiveness will be given to every one of us in the measure of our need. In Jesus' name. Amen.*

■ **APRIL 21**

**Let not then your good be evil spoken of: for
the kingdom of God is not meat and drink;
but righteousness, and peace, and joy
in the Holy Ghost.**
(Rom. 14:16-17)

"Leave well enough alone." "Don't upset the applecart." "Don't kick over the traces." And so on.

Admonition: If life is going smoothly, don't do anything to spoil it. You have built your house in a good neighborhood. You have a good job. Your family is a credit to you and society. Settle in for the long haul and be content to remain there in comfort the rest of your life.

All of this seems to have a religious look about it, and it produces the image of a pious contentment. And is not the human need to be rid of pain, disappointment, and care, and to live in peaceful surroundings and invest yet another dollar in a solid market? No better paradise could be found on earth.

The problem is that there is another side of the street where the applecart has been upset! While we sit in our comfortable gardens where the flowers bloom and the birds sing and the babbling brook lulls us into a contented slumber, the cry of need and the hand for help from the other side spoil the paradise. And the burning question, "Am I my brother's keeper?" (Gen. 4:9), must be resolved in the comfort of every person's garden.

The Bible recognizes the existence of affliction, sorrow, pain, and death in the midst of comfort and unconcern. The Book of Psalms would have to step aside but for the fact that at the root of human life there is the curse of human sorrow. And these things will not go away, even if I do hide myself from them. So God's kingdom of peace and joy becomes a kingdom of duty and responsibility; it was never meant to be a refuge of comfort and unconcern.

Life, then, must speak to me in the language of sympathy and caring, from which I cannot escape, for I am part of the kingdom of God.

PRAYER: *Our Father, we pray for those who are living one day at a time. Prepare their chamber so that peace and happiness may move in with the Unseen Guest to dwell forever. May Your grace and strength be used to encourage a deeper faith for others as we live in Your love that never fails. In Jesus' name. Amen.*

APRIL 22

... knowing in yourselves that ye have in heaven a better and an enduring substance. Cast not away therefore your confidence, which hath great recompence of reward.
(Heb. 10:34-35)

The ups and downs of life under which we live are either in the enjoyment of good and happy days or in the anticipation of them. The Bible tells of bright days for the people of God. His ultimate promise is that time when clouds and storm will be gone and peace with all things beautiful will be the crowning point of everything. Sorrow will be forgotten in God's eternity. This we have come to know as the meaning of love.

We live in this hope. We encourage one another with this expectation. We endure and grow and become strong in the faith through the promise of this bright and glowing revelation.

In God's promised day righteousness shall be the rock on which we stand, and the strength of it shall rest in the almightiness of the eternal God. In that day violence will be under control, all iniquity will be put down, and God's eternal Sabbath shall dawn upon earth.

This is the hope of the Christian and the prophecy that has given strength to the weak, encouragement to the downcast, and purpose to those who hold on in blind faith. The times are in God's hands and the ages in His keeping, and all things are under His direction. The years are given to us one by one as we are shown the uncertainty and brevity of life.

God knows the need of every heart, the pain of every life, the shadow that darkens every path, and the hope that beats in every breast. The outpouring of His grace is dependent upon our faith in Him. From Him comes courage to move forward. In Him is our hope for immortality.

Heaven is the promise and the glorious climax of it all!

PRAYER: *How we thank You, O God, for the hope of heaven—the place of purity and love that You are preparing for Your people. Our lives are lived here in preparation and in anticipation of that city not made with hands, eternal in the heavens. This is the meaning of love. Make us to know that we belong there. In Jesus' name. Amen.*

■ APRIL 23

O Lord; in the morning will I direct my prayer unto thee, and will look up. For thou art not a God that hath pleasure in wickedness: neither shall evil dwell with thee.
(Ps. 5:3-4)

There was a sense of awe and sacredness in the house of God. You got ready and went to church, knowing that God would be there when you arrived. You did not go to talk, but you went to listen, and you left all the noise outside except when you prayed. When you prayed, you prayed loud, and then you opened your ears toward heaven and waited for God to answer you.

The church was not a place for entertainment. There was an altar there, and God was there, and you went penitently with a purpose and a heart full of expectation and a desire for good things. The only voice to be heard in that sacred place was the voice of God speaking truth through the minister.

The congregation was small, but they sat with bowed heads, silently praying and lovingly expecting. God liked that because He knew their hearts were open and waiting for His faintest whisper. They knew that God was righteous and had set himself against the wicked, and that His purpose was to get rid of the evil in the world. They knew that if they allowed any evil to linger in their hearts that it would be difficult for God to talk to them.

The lesson they took home was that religion is a good thing. They believed that the prayer of Jesus beginning with "Our Father which art in heaven" (Matt. 6:9; Luke 11:2) was suitable for all occasions. They believed that they could be right in matters of business only as they were right in their relationship to God. They believed that God would never forsake them if they trusted Him. They knew He would not turn His back on the weak and brokenhearted. They believed that God's whole thought was in terms of love and well-being.

The days of the week went better because they went to church on Sunday where God was.

PRAYER: *O God, we believe that You love the Church because You have established it through Your Son, Jesus Christ. He told us that the gates of hell should not prevail against it. You have arrayed it with the armor of righteousness in the battle against sin. We come to it to worship, we stay to praise, and we leave to serve You in a sinful world. Help us, in Jesus' name. Amen.*

APRIL 24

Happy is he that hath the God of Jacob for his help, whose help is in the Lord his God ... which speaketh truth for ever.
(Ps. 146:5-6)

My college French professor could always seem to find some spiritual application in the old classics when everyone else saw only the darkness and evil. How often I have heard her expressions, "*C'est dommage, mais attendez ...*," when she would pick from the most ugly circumstance a thread of goodness developing. She carried us along through events and issues to something that was not yet expressed—but she saw it. She led us through darkened paths and evil strongholds and found indications of that which was intensely spiritual.

Today we look away back to lost Eden with the angry flaming sword through animal sacrifice and people wearied with impotent ritual. But in every generation the prophets saw the promise of a deliverance and the expectation of hope. Through the shadows we saw God's hand write a New Testament and build His grandest altar, and we saw the Son of God face His darkest hour. Then Light broke into our world!

Out of the darkness of human existence Jesus introduced the highest word ever spoken and the greatest thought ever to come, "Thou shalt love ..." Love means sacrifice. Love means daily worship. Love means hope. Love does not destroy any of the old elements that entered into the mystery of true worship. It is not a mere sentiment, but in our walking and serving it constitutes the divine sonship of the soul. It was there all the time, but we could not see it.

God often hides His purpose from us, and He leads us one step at a time according to our capacity to understand. But He places His glimmer of hope even in our darkest circumstance.

PRAYER: *We thank You, O God, for our Christian hope. Our hope in the living God chases away the deepest shadows, fills our being with a tender light, and floods the soul with ineffable glory. This all comes from heaven and is the crown of the gospel. May we never lose this hope. In Jesus' name. Amen.*

■ APRIL 25

There is a sore evil which I have seen under the sun, namely, riches kept for the owners thereof to their hurt.
(Eccles. 5:13)

A great fallacy built up in our minds that influences every phase of our living has to do with possessions. We say, "This is mine, and this is yours." We think we are the gods of our own security and the makers of our own money, but we forget the Source of our blessings. We see God in the creation of the world and in the operation of His universe but fail to see Him in the everyday affairs of living. Too often He is left behind when we lock the doors of the church on Sunday night, or He is crushed between the moroccan covers of the Bible after morning devotions. He wants to be in the office, in the kitchen, in the car, in the factory, and in the boardroom.

God and business. God and finances. God and decisions. God and good times. God and home. These all go together; God wants to be part of every day. When the tools for our achievements have been laid on the table, we must never forget who provided them and where we got the ability to use them. The builder who takes pride in the work of his hands must never forget who made the tree.

God makes it clear that the outpouring of His blessing is dependent upon two principles—our recognition of His ownership and our observance of His laws of giving. To fail in these areas is to miss His principle of possessions. In understanding this, we begin to understand something of His greatness and His concern for His people. We cannot work for God without reward, and we can never owe our failures to His oversight.

When the day comes to face the account of our work, we will find that God will have already recorded the whole course of action. And we must never forget that the Lord our God who commands the universe also whispers to us, "Ye are not your own . . . ye are bought with a price" (1 Cor. 6:19-20).

PRAYER: *O God, You have made us rich with promise, and now we pray that You will make us rich with the possessions that make us free. May we use our possessions to advance Your kingdom, as we are delivered from the prison of selfishness and greed. May we be able to say, "Thine is . . . the power, and the glory." In Jesus' name. Amen.*

APRIL 26

Jesus answered and said unto him, Verily, verily, I say unto thee, Except a man be born again, he cannot see the kingdom of God.
(John 3:3)

Much attention is being given by the news media recently to the concern of being "born again." A great part of the reporting is in ridicule, and very little of the press comes across in a serious manner. How harsh their column appears today, when Jesus attached primary importance to the doctrine of the second birth and identified it with the special function of the Holy Spirit.

The questioning by Nicodemus is still heard in our time: "How can these things be?" (John 3:9). But didn't the common words of Jesus always create confusion between himself and His hearers? For when He spoke about giving them living water, it was taken to mean water from the well. He always chose those things that pointed toward the most solemn necessities of life. So with the word "born": It was to describe the great transition by which we turn from the despair of a sinful life to the hope of glory through an inward regeneration.

Jesus did not attempt to explain the mystery of regeneration. He has always allowed it to be its own witness. It does not destroy the primary individualities of human nature. After their encounter with Christ, Peter is still ardent Peter, and Paul is still courageous Paul. But each, through Christ, had to add a dimension that lay far beyond his own power.

In laying down the doctrine of the new birth, Jesus showed how fundamental was the change that human nature must undergo as condition for entrance into the kingdom of God. Being "born again" as He taught it turns one to a new life in God and away from the old one in trespasses and sin!

"How can these things be?" asks our modern Nicodemus. And we reply, "With God all things are still possible" (see Matt. 19:26).

PRAYER: *O God, whatever power of love and grace You displayed for Your great creation, You have outdone it all in the redemption of lost humanity. The Cross rises higher than our mountains of iniquity and reaches deeper than the roots of our sinful nature. For that born-again experience we give You thanks. In Jesus' name. Amen.*

APRIL 27

Come now, and let us reason together, saith the Lord: though your sins be as scarlet, they shall be as white as snow; though they be red like crimson, they shall be as wool.
(Isa. 1:18)

I looked in awe as I stood before a terrible painting of the Garden of Eden. Terrible, because a man and a woman were being driven from it and a flaming sword guarded the gate. It looked as if God himself had turned against His creation, and the ones He had loved were being banished forever from His care. I could sense bitterness and pain in the rebellion, as the voice of thundering and judgment was being heard on earth for the first time.

God could have retired into the depth of infinite space, shut himself away in His own eternity, and refused to have anything more to do with those who had disobeyed Him. Yes, He could have, but He didn't! He could have except for the spirit of mercy, the spirit of hope, the spirit of love, the spirit of the gospel.

The gospel made the difference! You see, it is as old as God, as ancient as eternity; and as for the cross of Jesus Christ, it was built before a tree ever grew in the Garden. Out of the disappointment of God and the flaming sword, a new order was set in motion. God did return, and He said, "I will give you another chance."

He said, "Come . . . let us reason together." The proposition came from God. It was initiated by Him, on the part of the Almighty himself. The possibility of salvation for Adam's race comes from God's own redeeming grace.

He who was offended by sin bears no malice and seeks no retribution but says, "Come now, and let us reason together . . . though your sins be as scarlet, they shall be as white as snow."

PRAYER: *O God, we thank You for the blessed gospel that tells us that Jesus Christ came to seek and to save the lost. We thank You for an impartial salvation. It touches our sin and throws the light of hope upon our despair. It is, indeed, a great and wonderful work of love. We need this salvation. In Jesus' name. Amen.*

APRIL 28

I am crucified with Christ: nevertheless I live; yet not I, but Christ liveth in me: and the life which I now live in the flesh I live by the faith of the Son of God, who loved me, and gave himself for me.
(Gal. 2:20)

One of the great lessons I have learned over the years is that a vital Christian experience must be a *personal* relationship with Jesus Christ. No religion has much worth if it cannot be identified with an actual personal experience with God himself.

John Wesley made this point very clear in his testimony to his own experience: "And an assurance was given me, that he had taken away *my* sins, even *mine*, and saved *me* from the law of sin and death."

Charles Wesley sang it: "I felt my Lord's atoning blood, / Close to my soul applied. / Me, me, He loves, the Son of God, / For me, for me He died."

Paul puts his experience in similar words: "I live by the faith of the Son of God, who loved me, and gave himself for me."

In these testimonies we have the universal element in the thought and language of every partaker of salvation. Man does not invent his own faith or bring about his own quest for repentance. This comes from God to the individual. So also is worship a matter between man and his God—one person and one God.

It is interesting that the Bible deals with universals, ages, nations, master races and minds, and addresses worlds in all the ages of progress. But every individual sees his own place in the Word of God, and it speaks to him in his own area of concern.

I must see God's purpose for myself and be faithful to that which comes within the limits of my own vision. I cannot account for the revelation given to someone else—it must be mine!

And in this personal encounter, "I press toward the mark for [my] prize of the high calling of God in Christ Jesus" (Phil. 3:14).

PRAYER: *O God, we thank You for that personal relationship we have with You. Help us to be humble, true, sincere, and obedient so that we may live the Christ life and be true representatives of the Cross. In Jesus' name. Amen.*

■ APRIL 29

Thou art Peter, and upon this rock I will build my church; and the gates of hell shall not prevail against it.
(Matt. 16:18)

The distraught mother sighed, "Well, that's over. I have been in a panic all day long." The health of a little one had been in jeopardy, and the guardianship of love was on the line. There are necessities that arise in every life and experience that require a strong and fearless love for control. Every day there are threatenings directed against us, and many succumb to the crushing blow, so that panic reigns in place of peace.

Attacks do not always spell defeat. Jesus said that even the gates of hell would not prevail against His Church. Attacks? Plenty! Defeat? Never! Assaults will ever be made upon Christian strongholds, and Christian doctrine will ever be assailed. But the end of the report is in God's favor, so that the bottom line reads, ". . . shall not prevail against it."

It is human to panic and to report the works of the enemy in a trembling voice from a heart of fear. But all things are in God's hands, the great and the small, the stars in the heavens and every blade of green grass that covers this earth. He holds the nations in His own power and places them as He pleases. He binds up the broken heart and knows every sparrow that falls. His throne is on the circle of eternity, and His purpose is love. He has no pleasure in the death of the wicked, and for those who oppose Him, His heart cries out for their salvation.

The Christian cannot expect to defeat the opposition in the strength of his own genius, nor should he attempt such a bold act. He hands the whole thing over to God, for he is living upon a divine assurance and standing upon a divine promise.

God works through human frailties, and His impossible answers to our faith. "What time I am afraid, I will trust in thee" (Ps. 56:3).

PRAYER: *Dry the burning tears, O God, and save us from fear that cripples and despair that blinds us to Your love. Bless us with the inspiration and confidence of hope and with the strength of those whose trust is in the living God. In Jesus' name. Amen.*

APRIL 30

Lord, who shall abide in thy tabernacle? ... he that backbiteth not with his tongue, nor doeth evil to his neighbour, nor taketh up a reproach against his neighbour.
(Ps. 15:1, 3)

My stepfather used to have great confidence in the destructive powers of his children. Often, in jest, he would threaten, "I'm going to get the devil for you kids to play with, for you will destroy him in no time at all." This simply pointed out one great lesson in life. How easy it is to destroy! One touch may damage what a lifetime could never repair. Bring an accusation against a person, and the charge will be remembered long after the defense is forgotten.

The Christian person must ever be on guard so as not to get trapped in these matters. To whisper that a person is not what he ought to be is to stab that person in the back. Suspicion, judgment, and contempt will follow the whisper even beyond the grave of innocence.

Actually, every one of us lives within one step of destruction at every moment of our lives. One move of the pen, one misstep on the highway, one wrong judgment, one decision in haste can mar a lifetime. People who would never commit murder do this very thing when they attack a character. "Fear not them which kill the body ... but rather fear him which is able to destroy both soul and body in hell" (Matt. 10:28).

Through the gospel of Jesus Christ we are called to a larger life and a deeper commitment, and the journey is always upward. The rule is to believe every good thing that is said about a person. Never let a good action perish for want of publicity.

The one thing that holds our world together is the grace of God. How corrupt is the evil heart, but, "If any man be in Christ, he is a new creature" (2 Cor. 5:17). Herein lies the hope of our daily dilemma!

PRAYER: *Deliver us, O God, from those things that tear down and destroy. Build us up in works of love, pity, and helpfulness. Make us to know each other, and may the true meaning of Calvary shine through our lives every day. Help us to lift up the fallen one and to show them that Your way is best, for it is the pathway of peace. In Jesus' name. Amen.*

MAY 1

The face of the Lord is against them that do evil ... The Lord is nigh unto them that are of a broken heart; and saveth such as be of a contrite spirit.
(Ps. 34:16, 18)

Many years ago I worked in a lumber camp with a man who was very wicked. I listened to him curse and swear all day and watched as he sat before the wood fire at night, keeping his pipe burning with live coals from the stove. Every word he spoke and every step he took seemed to beat in rhythm with evil, while wickedness ruled his thoughts. Early in his life he had shut the doors of his heart against God, and for 70 years Love was defied by an evil will.

One day he came face-to-face with Jesus Christ, and he saw the whole scheme of redemption played out before him for the first time. A new paragraph was written in church history that day that belonged to him and God alone. And I heard him testify to his personal encounter with his Savior, and I saw God's hand work in the life of a very wicked person.

When I think about this encounter, there are three words that stand forth as the greatest need of human life—"To see Jesus." A person is infinitely better or he is infinitely worse by coming in contact with Jesus, for one either accepts Him or rejects Him. The signature of sin had been inscribed on my friend's entire life, and despair had written his story—until he saw Jesus.

It is an easy thing for a person, wicked and hopeless, to run counter to the current of concern of the Church. But when the human heart that has been shut up in the cold, dark night of sin is exposed to the Sun of Righteousness, it opens as the flowers to the morning sunshine. This experience proves again that the pathway of God's love runs across the pathway of the impossible.

Jesus Christ still receives sinners. He is mighty to save and unwilling to destroy.

PRAYER: *O God, You always know what we want and what we need and what is best for us. And best of all, You did not turn Your back on us when we were in sin searching for peace. Help us stand in the love of the Cross, where we will find our victory in the Son of God. We would see Jesus. In His name. Amen.*

MAY 2

As for Saul, he made havoc of the church, entering into every house, and haling men and women committed them to prison.
(Acts 8:3)

Saul attacked the Christians as they had never been attacked before and made havoc of this society of followers of Jesus Christ. In his determination to annihilate, he left a trail of blood from the prayer cell to the prison house. What began as Saul, the foe of the Church, turned out to be Paul, the glorious friend. As Saul assailed the Church, it responded in a louder and clearer voice of heavenly authority until the foe became the conquered.

The power of the Church has always been seen to excite the worst passions of mankind. Christianity either kills or it saves; there is no neutral ground. It is either the brightness of the day or the darkness of the night in a person's life. It came with the angels' song in the air, "Glory to God in the highest, and on earth peace, good will toward men" (Luke 2:14). It continued with the voice of God in the heavens, "This is my beloved Son: hear him" (Mark 9:7; Luke 9:35; see Matt. 17:5). It attacked the most formidable thought, prejudice, and error and brought upon itself the fist of retaliation.

Joy was the word associated with the language of the Church. "I bring you good tidings of great joy" was the word from the angel (Luke 2:10). The church ought to be the very fountain of joy, delight, and triumph. There should be no tears of tyranny in the church. There should be no fear of death in the church. There should be no sighing, fainting, or doubting in the church. God's house should be a place of music, rejoicing, and great festivals of joy.

Persecuting Saul tested its security, and through the fires of persecution he found a Force greater than the persecutor. He was to learn that he was mightier when he prayed than when he persecuted.

PRAYER: *Thank You, God, for the Church! Give it power in proclaiming the gospel. As You have clothed the morning with brightness and the evening with the glitter of stars, we pray that You will array Your Church with the armor of righteousness in the battle against sin. In Jesus' name. Amen.*

MAY 3

I know whom I have believed, and am persuaded that he is able to keep that which I have committed unto him against that day.
(2 Tim. 1:12)

Every morning I used to hear my mother pray, "We do not know what today holds for us, dear God, but if we have the assurance of Your presence, everything will be all right." Her God was the God of the living, and for every part of the day. There were days of darkness and tears, but she lived in the quietness and peace of God through it all. Her God was without limitations or qualifications, and her life backed up what she believed.

The most important thing that any person can say is, "I believe in God." But after that has been said, it should be followed with the reasons why. Does my God have limitations? Does He direct all my ways every day? Does He go with me in all of my daily activities? Does God have all of my life to do with as He pleases? Do I worship my own personal God, or am I worshiping someone else's God?

The all-important factor in my life should be, "What does God mean to me today—*now?*" The God of Abraham, Isaac, and Jacob can give me inspiration, and I can sing the songs of the God of David and rejoice with Isaiah in his vision of the Wonderful Counselor. But the only God I can worship is the living, present, and personal God who met with me this morning.

I believe in a God I can know today. I do need to know Him by my feeling, by my experience, and by the divine certainty He has placed in my heart. I need to know Him by His presence in all the painful, disappointing times in my life. I need to know His sincerity when He said, "I am with you alway, even unto the end" (Matt. 28:20). And to know that He has never failed yet.

With this assurance I know that everything will be all right.

PRAYER: *Almighty God, continue Your goodness to us, we pray, and give us that sense of Your presence near to us every day. Make our souls grow in quietness so that when the end of our experience here on earth comes, there shall be that more abundant life in glory. We wait for You, for we cannot go one step without You. In Jesus' name. Amen.*

MAY 4 ■

Let us run with patience the race that is set before us, looking unto Jesus the author and finisher of our faith.
(Heb. 12:1-2)

An ironic expression that has been used in ridicule of a certain athletic exercise has to do with the "happy jogger." The pained expression betrays the effort through which the jogger paces himself in an effort to achieve his goal. No one seems to run simply because he finds pleasure in the activity; the object lies beyond the exercise itself.

Life is full of "happy joggers" who accept today's suffering in preparation for greater accomplishments tomorrow. Often the things of the moment are grievous, but when the next trial comes, one will be better prepared to bear it.

Every life has its own jogging trails. Youth looks to maturity as the end of the hard run. Middle age looks to the senior years, when responsibilities and cares will fall on younger shoulders. Old age sings about the "Sweet By-and-by" as the solution to earthly woes. The strongest, with the merriest laughter, have bitter hours, experience pain, and endure tragedy though mingled with an inner peace.

Many joggers promise well when the trail is all on level ground, only to discover that in the hill country knees begin to buckle. One really does not know what life is until affections have been torn away, hopes have been turned into disappointments, and the truth from an honest heart has been turned into bitterness in the mouth.

In the Gethsemane darkness Jesus set the pattern for the bitter trails of life when He prayed, "Thy will be done" (Matt. 26:42). So when the battle is set, and life tumbles in, and the hills are long, we can have a smile even when we run.

PRAYER: *O God, in all of the perplexities of life You have given us grace, day by day, and have enabled us to bear the strain and find in it the mystery of joy. You have brought us through varied disciplines, and we have found in them holy meaning. You have given us strength and light in the darkness of our own confusion. For Your way with us, we give You praise. In Jesus' name. Amen.*

MAY 5

The Lord is my light and my salvation; whom shall I fear? the Lord is the strength of my life; of whom shall I be afraid?
(Ps. 27:1)

A friend of mine bought a new car this week but was unable to add the special package of extras that would classify the purchase as being "loaded." But the convincing salesman proved the necessity of the antitheft device to fortify it against possible loss. My friend could not afford this item either but realized the wisdom in adding this bit of assurance.

Our lives are run under similar circumstances as we fortify our dwelling places against intruders. Our tendency is to dwell on the strong points and not upon those that are doubtful in connection with our Christian experience. This is the genius of Christianity. A person can believe God, love God, obey God, and wait patiently for God without having to construct a whole package of arguments to load an experience. God loves us when we work within our capacity and power.

Every person must fix his own strong points and take a stand upon actual experience as tested out in the living. The man in the Gospel of John who was cured of blindness asserted the one thing he did know, and he became strong in his affirmation. "Whether he be a sinner or no, I know not: one thing I know, that, whereas I was blind, now I see" (John 9:25). It is not necessary in order to be a happy Christian to be able to answer every question that the world may throw at you. The strength of the Christian is to enjoy profound and often silent communion with God. He has set in value above all rubies and precious stones the broken and contrite heart that accepts Him on simple faith.

From eternity God bends down to hear the prayer of that one who is working within the lines of his own strength, whatever the level may be. And He will "keep that which [we] have committed unto him against that day" (2 Tim. 1:12)! Amen.

PRAYER: *O God, how thankful we are that You give power to the faint, and to them that have no might You increase their strength. We find our confidence in Your omnipotence, and we can do all things through Christ who strengthens us. May we accept our responsibility, knowing that You are working in all things and that Your whole purpose is love. In Jesus' name. Amen.*

MAY 6

Go to the ant, thou sluggard; consider her ways, and be wise: which having no guide ... provideth her meat in the summer, and gathereth her food in the harvest.
(Prov. 6:6-8)

God has placed many different kinds of things in His world. Different in appearance. Different in character. Different in ways of living. We are constantly comparing everything with the human and are amazed at what we discover. Every encounter is a lesson, and maybe God has meant it to be so.

Creation is full of teachers, and it is a mistake to think that we can learn only from the highest and biggest. God has written a lesson for us in the smallest works of His hands. The infinite variety of His creation is but the expression of the infinite aspects of His mind, but all come to us as sermons written by His hand.

"Consider the ant," says the wise man, "and see the wisdom of making the best of our opportunities." Then he leads us into that great lesson on foresight and away from the false idea that everything will turn out all right if we go away and leave it alone.

Foresight keeps us from wasting God's most precious gift to us: time. The greatest people have always been the most severe economists of time. The person in the church who can always be counted on "to get the job done" is usually the one who has already filled the day with plans and activities. Never leave the job with the one who has time only to sit beside the fire and criticize others for their indolence.

Beware of the one who is always on time for work but has no time for worship. Fear the one who never missed an appointment with man yet has never kept one with God. Pray for the one who was never late for a trip but has never planned for heaven.

Through His creation God is teaching us to prepare, to watch, and to be ready. He is never wanting in His training!

PRAYER: *How often, O God, in our lack of foresight we have fallen into the trap of ungratefulness and selfishness. Show us that every good thing comes to us as a gift of love from a God who loves and cares. You know the things that we need, and You have given us an abundant supply. Out of the depths of sincere gratitude we say, "Thank You, God." In Jesus' name. Amen.*

■ MAY 7

If I take the wings of the morning, and dwell in the uttermost parts of the sea; even there shall thy hand lead me, and thy right hand shall hold me.
(Ps. 139:9-10)

How far away the Garden of Eden appears when we read the Book of Genesis! The stories of Joseph and his coat of many colors, Moses and the Red Sea, and Daniel's night with the lions are events that occurred thousands of years ago. What interest can they have for people today? If we were merely studying the events, their significance would soon be lost in the retelling. But we study the events only as we study the God who lived in the circumstances.

The God who brought about the beautiful reunion of Joseph and his family in Egypt and visited with Moses on the mountain is the God who lights the lamp of every morning and draws the curtain of darkness on every twilight in our time. The events may long ago have died, but God still lives. When we stand with Moses at the burning bush or walk with David beside the still waters, we are in company with the God who unites all history and gives priority to the well-being of His people today.

No age is to be the perpetual custodian of God's truth, for it cannot be locked up in the years. Nor is it merely a set of words or an elaboration of sentences. It is God in the soul, and He breaks in and out of circumstances as we move on in the mystery of His action.

"Great is the Lord . . . and his greatness is unsearchable" (Ps. 145:3). He cannot be measured by reason, nor can the mystery of the Godhead be understood by human understanding. But He can be worshiped in spirit and in truth away from language, event, or representation.

Without the God of the Garden and the wilderness we can do nothing in our time, but we can still meet Him on the mountain or in the lions' den.

PRAYER: *One thing we know for certain in this present world, O God, and it is that You live with us today. Our lives are witnesses, for they are wrapped up in the biblical account of redemption. Ever remind us that now is Your accepted time, and now is the day of salvation. Today we need the Blood, which cleanseth from all sin. In Jesus' name. Amen.*

MAY 8

For your Father knoweth what things ye have need of, before ye ask him. After this manner therefore pray ye: Our Father.
(Matt. 6:8-9)

It has happened on one or two occasions in my life when I sensed in a very real way that I was given an "asking time" with God. It was that moment when a special freedom was given to me to say anything to God and ask anything from Him. It did not come from any set of words or great praying on my part. It was a God-given and self-answering prayer. I did not try to interpret it then, and I do not pass judgment on it now.

We must accept the fact that God has always been giving. We turn His giving into prayer-asking as we remind Him of the past: "O God, You fed Elijah. You supplied oil and meal for the widow. You rescued Jonah. You delivered Daniel," and so on. But we see no miracles, and no soul is healed, and no problems are solved. And often we sense that we did not pray at all.

Prayer cannot be judged by one occasion or another, for we would either be swallowed up in despair, or we would be overcome in our ecstasy. The great Teacher on prayer gives us the secret that unlocks the mystery chambers of eternity: "Seek ye first the kingdom of God, and his righteousness; and all these things shall be added unto you" (Matt. 6:33).

Great answers do not come from great prayer speeches. God supplements our weakest prayer by the sincerity and honesty He finds in the heart when we pray. Great answers come and great miracles are accomplished within the opportunities that our faith gives to God for His purpose. The one condition that opens the way says, "Thy will be done in earth, as it is in heaven" (Matt. 6:10).

When we send this prayer to heaven by way of the Cross, there shall come back to us answers like the cool rains on a hot summer's day.

PRAYER: *O God, if our prayers were our only hope, we would be in dire straits. But we mingle our petitions with the intercession of the one Priest and commit them to the mystery of the mediation of Jesus Christ himself. With the Cross as our altar and our Savior as our Advocate we are assured of God's reply—His great Amen. In Jesus' name we make all of our petitions. Amen.*

■ MAY 9

There is a river, the streams whereof shall make glad the city of God, the holy place of the tabernacles of the most High. God is in the midst of her.
(Ps. 46:4-5)

Have you ever known the joy of relaxing in a tent pitched beside the shore of a lake far away from all man-made disturbances? The sound of the lapping waves along the shore mingled with the screaming of loons and the distant call of the night owl provides music that enlarges the soul. A slight breeze rustles through the trees as a squirrel rushes, busily gathering another spruce bud for the winter, and the mother bird brings one more morsel to her brood. As you close your eyes, your heart sings in response to the touch of God on your soul.

Isaiah's little song in chapter 12 could well have been written under these conditions. Here the sky seems to be clothed with the summer, the day is quiet with the very spirit of peace, the music is sweet, and the soothing sound of the waves is very near. Moving out of the dark prophecies of the work of God's hand on the Egyptians, as his people return from exile, he sings the song that only a person who has been there can sing.

Who has not known the violence of thunder or felt the hard hand of oppression or seen hope dashed into destruction before their eyes? Then out of the long process of sorrow and hardship comes a song that makes the heart sing and the dumb speak again. How much more this is so in life when the power of sin has been broken. The desire to sing becomes natural.

You do not have to search the ancient hills for God. Search your own life for God's shoreline, pitch your own tent beside His still waters, and sing your own song of praise to His glory. You will discover that every wave becomes a gospel of peace singing the wonders of His love.

PRAYER: *O God, we know that where You are, there is peace. Lead us beside those still waters and give us the assurance of Your presence in the midst of the enemy. May Your peace flow like a river and righteousness like the waves of the sea. We would be among those who live in the presence of Your peace. In Jesus' name. Amen.*

MAY 10

Wherefore take unto you the whole armour of God, that ye may be able to withstand in the evil day, and having done all, to stand.
(Eph. 6:13)

This week I took a friend to the doctor for his regular checkup. A casual remark to his examiner was, "One of these days I'm going to retire and get out of this rat race and do absolutely nothing for the rest of my life." The doctor's quick response was, "Don't do it, for we will be burying you in six months; keep active!" The words hit home and carried great significance for my friend.

The Christian life is this way. Jesus is always calling us away to some higher altitude, to some greener pasture, or even beside some more peaceful stream. And it is always in preparation for His greater purpose and finer achievements. The Church is always under inspiration for something greater. God is always telling His people that this is the time for marching, advancing, learning, and obeying. The call of God is to go forward!

There is no place in a Christian experience when God says, "You have made all the progress you can make. Now sit down and relax until I get ready to take you to heaven!" The call is "Arise, come away! You have not seen it all yet. You have hardly begun the journey." He whispers to the weakest saint, "As you gain strength to bear it, there are many things that I have yet to tell you."

When we sit down and tell ourselves that this is the end, we become as broken clay in the hands of the potter. Our Christianity is proven by our progress. And our tomorrows are captured in the spirit of the strength God gives us for today.

Every new day will bring with it some message from God calling us to higher things. And it always comes with the promise, "Lo, I am with you alway, even unto the end" (Matt. 28:20). Amen.

PRAYER: *O God, we pray that You will keep us patient in our progress toward the Kingdom. May we understand the meaning of working as well as waiting for God. Bring to our hearts the assurance that we are in Your will as You make known to us the further mystery of the Cross. Lead us in Your own good time and in Your own way. In Jesus' name. Amen.*

■ **MAY 11**

Remember now thy Creator in the days of thy youth, while the evil days come not, nor the years draw nigh, when thou shalt say, I have no pleasure in them.
(Eccles. 12:1)

Many times we have heard the lament, "I can remember things that took place 40 or 50 years ago better than I can remember what happened last week." How we envy the youth time, made to grasp details and able to hold them forever. What becomes impossible with age is routine activity with youth. So we enjoy or regret in old age the things we gather in the gleaning years.

God sends us reminders of these conditions of life and says, "Remember now thy Creator in the days of thy youth." In the seedtime of living the wise person puts the Creator first in anticipation of harvest. Set God at the front of all your thinking. Include Him in all the plans, hopes, and visions of the future. Remember in your youth that God deserves all, demands all, and only in giving all can one realize the full potential of life.

Reverence for God will lead to obedience, and it is well to learn early in life that we are not to make the commandments but to obey those that have been laid down for us. Youth will see them as hardships and recognize that often they do not fit the mold of his generation and are often not in the supposed best interests of his peers.

Learn also that after one has been inspired by the Holy Spirit and trained in the school of God's wisdom, there is true liberty in obedience, there is true harmony in living. We will never know how vain mere things really are until we come to know God and keep His commandments.

The greatest message that youth of any generation can hear is, "Live in God, obey God, love and serve God. Leave all the outcome with God." Then the memories of old age will reflect a happy and wholesome life.

PRAYER: *O Father, help those who have the youngest, tenderest, and freshest memories to take to heart early in their lives the sacred pages of the Word of God. When they once read it, they will never forget it; if they once see it, it will become an eternal presence. This will outlast instruction and will manifest itself in the end to Your glory. Make it so in Jesus' name. Amen.*

MAY 12 ■

We are more than conquerors through him that loved us. For I am persuaded . . . nor any other creature, shall be able to separate us from the love of God.
(Rom. 8:37-39)

Life seems to be a great big battle of overcoming obstacles, fighting giants, and adjusting to growing problems. This observation is quite commonplace, and it is associated with all that is devastating and tragic in life. Often God is blamed for the condition, while the problem of evil, the main instigator, goes without reproach. What cunning there is in the power of evil, and it is not within human ability to deal with the foe!

One danger for the Christian is to imagine that wickedness has gone in advance of the divine, and that God has more work to do than His omnipotence can undertake. Such is false thinking, for God has everything under His control, and in His own time and in His own way and with His abundant supply will He vindicate all evil actions and cleanse the earth of opposition. There is no problem that God does not share.

Another danger is in underestimating the power that opposes the Church. These powers are not to be sneered at or left in an unguarded moment. The world is full of pitfalls and traps, and the devil never allows any person to go through life without confronting them. Life is a battle, a daily conflict, and with many it is a tremendous struggle. There is no moment when the Christian can take liberties as if heaven had been easily won.

The one lesson for the Church is that the power to overcome is not in the individual but in God. God is our inspiration, our strength, and our confidence. God's grace is sufficient, and we do not have to try to add anything to it.

In our world we can be more than conquerors, for God has placed the Cross between us and the enemy.

PRAYER: *O God, it is the battlefield and the enemy that give us the right to pray. Help to begin where Christ began, walk where He walked, and follow Him in all things, taking up our cross every day. We know it will be the way of the battleground, but it is Your way and the gateway to heaven. Be with us on this Your way. In Jesus' name. Amen.*

■ MAY 13

Search me, O God, and know my heart: try me, and know my thoughts: and see if there be any wicked way in me, and lead me in the way everlasting.
(Ps. 139:23-24)

We have come through changing times and have seen the temper turn to ridiculous proportions. We watched the old give way to the new, while our ways were replaced with things that could not take their place. Life was controlled by the master motive of ushering in a new day with a new life-style. Under the influence of a new liberty, laws were set aside and gods were set up to cover a false act of worship, while the tabernacle was left empty on the inside.

It is not necessary to pour contempt on this life-style, for it was soon learned that no one can remove the need for God in the heart. The Church learned a long time ago that no form of worship can be looked upon as typifying the entire kingdom of God. But all ministries must bow before Him, while every individual form must be examined before the Cross.

When will we learn that the two opposing forces we face every day can never be reconciled? Earth can never understand heaven, and heaven will never bow to the demands of the earth. There is danger, however, that those who are wicked should influence for ill those who are heavenly-minded. For it seems easier to do harm than to do good, to cool enthusiasm than to create it. To keep up the faith life in all of its eagerness has always met with opposition.

The call to the Church in every changing generation is to the sufficiency of the grace of God and His conquering power through the Christ of Calvary. Prayer creates its own life-style, and love creates its own language. Out of it will come an endurance to stand the test of our times.

No way can be right except it be right with God, and no way can be right with God except by the way of the Cross.

PRAYER: *Almighty God, we pray that You would show us the wonders of Your way. Keep us in expectant silence before Your majesty, and keep us from interfering with the course of Your providence. Help us say from a heart of sincerity, "God's way is best." In Jesus' name. Amen.*

MAY 14 ■

God is a Spirit: and they that worship him must worship him in spirit and in truth.
(John 4:24)

The missionary showed her slides of the feast day that involved the worshipers carrying idols down the streets with offerings of sacrifice and worship. She remarked that their gods could not respond in affection and concern as the worshipers poured out their adoration with great pain and beating of the body. How grateful one becomes in comparison to worshiping the Son of God, where praise is given and recognition received. There is no idolatry in Christian worship when the worship is directed to the Son of God.

Every day we should praise God that we live in a Christian land, where we have the freedom of Christian worship. Our God does respond, which proves the truth of His being. An idol does nothing in return. A wooden deity makes no reply. A stone god shows no interest in an adoring worshiper. To pour out the heart to such an unanswering god is simple and fruitless idolatry.

Our redemption does not come through corruptible things such as silver and gold; we are redeemed through the precious blood of God's Son, who was dead but is alive forevermore. To every overture of worship He responds in love and care. We cannot give even a cup of cold water in His name without receiving His recognition. We cannot pray with Him one hour without the promise of sharing in the triumph of His resurrection. Every note of praise sent to heaven comes back as a new song in the heart.

In no other form of worship can there be found the reciprocal action as between Christ in heaven and His Church on earth. This is the marvel of grace and the mark of true worship.

"My soul ... hope thou in God" (Ps. 42:5, 11).

PRAYER: *May our worship, O God, be in spirit and in truth. Turn our eyes to Calvary and bind in Your heart all the affections we offer. Show us a love deeper than the human can go and more tender than we can know. Renew our strength as we wait patiently and worshipfully upon the living God. In Jesus' name. Amen.*

MAY 15

Then Abraham fell upon his face, and laughed, and said in his heart, Shall a child be born unto him that is an hundred years old? . . . O that Ishmael might live before thee!
(Gen. 17:17-18)

One day I walked into the study of a very frustrated pastor who was deep in discussion with several members of the Building Committee. The city inspectors had just returned the blueprints for the proposed building, and many changes had to be made in order to pass code regulations. Their expectation was that the blueprint they submitted would receive immediate approval.

"Behold, I thought, He will surely come out to me, and stand, and call on the name of the Lord his God . . . and recover the leper" (2 Kings 5:11). Naaman had made a plan, complete in every detail, for the healing; but when it did not receive official sanction, his mind could not grasp the dilemma.

The mistake of the ages, from Naaman until now, is that we think we can blueprint our own religion and simply submit the plans to God for approval. Religions are continually invented that are not confirmed by the revelation contained in the Book. But the religion of the Bible has never accepted a compromising position. The first thing the Bible does is to rebuke these liberties and dash the homemade imaginations to the ground. And we do not like it at all.

Who are we that we should invent ways for divine action and methods for divine activity? The Christian is urged to take a stand and say, "Lord, 'not my will, but thine, be done.' I will not conjure up any plans that will set themselves between me and God."

God's surprise is that He has made the way for us so simple that no one should miss it, yet we complicate it with our impossibles. What are God's ways? Believe. Wait. See.

We bring our blueprints for approval. God has already placed the stamp on His revelation!

PRAYER: *Help us to know, O God, that You have made marvelous plans for Your people. If You stop us in our way, it is that You may lead us aright. If You lay us aside, it is that we may be healed with an immortal healing. Make us to know that Your way is the way of heaven, and help us walk by Your law, looking forward to Your eternity. In Jesus' name. Amen.*

MAY 16 ■

Fear not: for I have redeemed thee, I have called thee by thy name; thou art mine. ... For I am the Lord thy God.
(Isa. 43:1, 3)

Standing beside a dear friend in a hospital room at the bedside of her husband, who had undergone extensive surgery, I tried to console against that ugly question, "Why?" She looked at me and said, "But Reverend ..." and proceeded to list the extremes in distress, heartache, and hatred that had made up her life. A cloud of gloom dispelled all light, as I tried to tell her that God finds no satisfaction in the darkness.

God is too big to turn aside in judgment on any life just to prove His omnipotence. But He does return again and again for any sign of submission that will allow Him to come in where there is hurt. He does not delight in judgment, and He has no pleasure in death. Every thought of God in relation to humanity causes Him to stand with open arms of compassion, love, and understanding and an invitation to come to Him.

How often the horizon is loaded with gloom as the sunset has made way for a long night of darkness! The ills of the moment have become as prison walls, and the gatekeeper has retired with the keys! The bedside in the intensive care unit has played havoc with homes and life-style and has mocked any semblance of happiness!

Is there One who can come out of our flowery terms in which He has been clothed and satisfy these hurts? Isaiah says there is, and he called Him "The mighty God" (9:6; 10:21). Matthew said there is and recorded, "Thou shalt call his name JESUS" (1:21). When earth has taken its love away, and foundations crumble, and tears magnify the hurts, then there comes a clear voice from God that only the heart can hear, saying, "When thou passest through the waters ... rivers ... fire ... I will be with thee" (Isa. 43:2).

Throw away the long ladder of adjectives and worldly concepts, for God's love cannot be limited in language. He is there when we need Him. He has never left the bedside!

PRAYER: *Be with us, O God, for the few days and nights we have yet to remain here in time. They go and we cannot recall them. Help us, through the presence of Your Holy Spirit, to be better today than we were yesterday. Make our tomorrows an anticipation of Your grace and glory. In Jesus' name. Amen.*

■ MAY 17

For God so loved the world, that he gave his only begotten Son, that whosoever believeth in him should not perish, but have everlasting life.
(John 3:16)

The startling report from a seminary recently was that 28 percent of its students preparing for Christian ministry were there against the wishes of their parents. Further revelation portrayed the ugly life-style in which some of the aspiring ministers had lived. The picture was unlovely, but the message was that if you want to be a follower of Jesus Christ, you can do so.

Of course, we know that the opposite is true also. If you do not want to come to Christ, you can easily find an excuse for escape. If you do not want to go to church, you can easily find reasons for not going. Excuses do play a very subtle part in the tragedy or comedy of life. The coward never wins many battles, and the lazy man never reaps the rich harvests, but the person who wants to find Jesus Christ can do so.

Nicodemus found a way. He determined not to rest until he had spoken to the Man. He waited for the night, and it closed him in with the Master until the truth could be conveyed. Out of the night the infinite secret found response in the heart of this inquiring master of Israel.

Zacchaeus found a way. He was a small man, and his vision was cut off by the bigger people. He found a sycamore tree, and he was not afraid to climb. When Jesus passed by, heart and heart met in a life-changing experience.

A certain woman found a way. She knew that if she could touch the hem of His garment, all would be well. The touch that elicits healing from God and virtue from the Cross made contact with Divinity, and Jesus knew it. Faith called the act complete.

Contact with Jesus Christ is not without its battles, nor is it without determination. The road is over a place called Calvary. And you "shall know Him / By the print of the nails in His hand."

PRAYER: *O God, we pray that You will give us a determination for those things pertaining to the kingdom of God and the Church. May this grow as we experience more and more of that love that is from heaven. We cannot forget that we are children of time, but we have been redeemed with a great price through Calvary. May we be lifted up in Your likeness. In Jesus' name. Amen.*

MAY 18

Take ... no thought for the morrow: for the morrow shall take thought for the things of itself. Sufficient unto the day is the evil thereof.
(Matt. 6:34)

Can anything be more baffling to the human mind than the idea of a tomorrow? What is tomorrow? Who has been able to define it? Who can be sure there is one? What will it be like? How long will it last? Will there be another one after that?

The wise man warned, "Boast not thyself of to morrow; for thou knowest not what a day may bring forth" (Prov. 27:1). It is not to be treated as belonging to us, for we can claim no right to it! God gives it to us as a gift to be used in the spirit of faithful stewardship.

Jesus is emphatic in His warning not to be anxious about tomorrow. He showed the folly of building greater barns to take care of needs for the tomorrow that may never come. He showed us that we can build barns, but we cannot build the future. He is urging us to understand by what limitations we are bound and then to work within these limitations with all thankfulness.

The great paradox is the part that "tomorrow" plays in the human drama. Time is not ours, yet we cannot do without it. We have never seen it, yet we grasp it with a firm grip. The industry of the ant is held before us as wise action, since tomorrow's food comes from today's labor. And it all comes with God's approbation, "Well done, good and faithful servant" (Matt. 25:21, 23).

We cannot shut out the mystery of tomorrow, for we live continually in its shadow. Our faith tells us, "Commit thy way unto the Lord; trust also in him; and he shall bring it to pass" (Ps. 37:5). The Christian has no tomorrow as a fear. He does have an everlasting tomorrow as a hope in the things of God. This hope is enveloped in time to open as a rare bloom in God's eternity.

PRAYER: *A thousand years, O God, are in Your sight as yesterday. How we are filled with wonder when we think of time. But it is in Your divine plan, and we are caught up in it. In the confusion of our todays and tomorrows help us know that we are also creatures of Your eternity. In Jesus' name. Amen.*

MAY 19

Why art thou cast down, O my soul? and why art thou disquieted in me? hope thou in God: for I shall yet praise him for the help of his countenance.
(Ps. 42:5)

A sadness in reading the Bible in my early years still remains with me today. God offered so many good things to His people, but they were always living contrary to His purpose. One king would do "that which was right in the sight of the Lord," but the heir to the throne would run a corrupt kingdom. They made alliances with heathen nations and married strangers whose religion was calculated to deprave the heart. Isaiah said, "They please themselves in the children of strangers" (2:6).

How difficult it has been for God's people to carry out discipline in every department of life! How hard to keep the well-defined lines and to keep from running after the glitter of gold and accepting the proffered fruit of Eden. Every age has had its own apostasy and withdrawal from God. The ancient witchcraft and magic have cleared out, only to return to work under new names. People are still seeking other avenues to heaven and revelations other than what God has given them.

God has always rebuked disobedience, for nothing good has ever come out of it. This is the thing that has always troubled the church, divided families, and left lives open to enemy attack.

The same Bible has recorded the happy story of those who have returned to the old Book and the altars of God. They have found in the eternal fountains of God's promises all that was needed for the satisfaction of the soul. Life under stress and sorrow must always return to the one eternal God for lasting peace.

Over the years I have learned that God is not a companion of heathenism, but He never forsakes a life whose trust continues in Him.

PRAYER: *O God, our hope this day is in all of the good things You have promised to Your people everywhere. We do not need to go to other gods, for You have promised Your peace and Your blessing to Your people. When we live in this hope, it brings us near to Your altar, where we find our peace. Keep us ever in this place, we pray. In Jesus' name. Amen.*

MAY 20 ■

Thy kingdom is an everlasting kingdom, and thy dominion endureth throughout all generations.
(Ps. 145:13)

Every Sunday morning the Apostles' Creed is repeated, with little thought given to the battles through which it became a dogma of the Church. The enemy has never stood aside to let the people of God pass through with fresh supplies for any battle against sin. The message of Jesus Christ has always met with hostility. We must not think that we are wrong simply because we come up against opposition.

Great names have been associated with battlefields in the Church: Luther, Calvin, Knox, and Wesley. Great questions have been surrounded by great controversies in the Church: inspiration, authority, miracles, Atonement, and immortality. The historical ground of the Church is a record of battles, but the same record has become her most precious possession. The ministry of the work of the Holy Spirit has been evident as well as the testings of the devil. How often the enemy has become the servant of God in fulfilling his purpose for the Church!

Who can fight against the Almighty and prevail? Place a marker near the scene of every battle and write the epitaph for the Church, "The gates of hell shall not prevail" (Matt. 16:18). There is only one way of victory in life, and that is the way of obedience, trust, and love. There is nothing along the road of sin but failure, disappointment, shame, and death. Here the great gospel of Jesus Christ takes its stand to breathe its benediction upon the Church.

When I stand with the congregation and repeat, "I believe in God the Father Almighty and in his Son Jesus Christ . . ." it is more than a creed. It is a testimony to the sovereignty of my conquering God in the daily conflicts of life.

PRAYER: *Your Word, O God, speaks to us of battles as well as victories. Every forward movement of Your Church has had its battlefield, just as every life is wrapped in strife. But You did establish Your Church a long time ago not to be betrayed by the enemies from hell. To all who overcome, You have promised a place in Your presence. This we seek. In Jesus' name. Amen.*

MAY 21

They got not the land in possession by their own sword, neither did their own arm save them: but thy right hand.
(Ps. 44:3)

Sin has enveloped our generation into the spirit of megabucks and the lure of the lottery. "To have more is to be happy" is the motto, and to regulate happiness by possession is the urgency that drives it along. To build bigger barns to hold great possessions is the program of greed, as it unfolds itself looking for a heaven it cannot find.

The message that sin hides is the message of the aching void. The heart cannot be satisfied with ashes, nor can the mind be satisfied with its own conquests. There is still the cry for a better answer. Hear the words of the wise man, "I made me great works; I builded me houses . . . [I chartered ships to sail the seas, and] I looked on all the works that my hands had wrought . . . all was vanity and vexation of spirit" (Eccles. 2:4, 11).

Jesus told us that "a man's life consisteth not in the abundance of the things which he possesseth" (Luke 12:15). And John added, "If any man love the world, the love of the Father is not in him" (1 John 2:15). The supreme lesson in Christian experience is that there is something better than what we see or receive from the world. For when the gardens and the houses and the ships return to dust, the soul is still searching.

God is in charge after the world has failed to satisfy. When sin has ruled out the gates of pearl, silenced the harps of gold, dried up the fountains of living water, and drawn its black curtain over God's sunshine, there still remains the unsatisfied heart.

In the midst of all the greed, hatred, and despair, God's message is, "Blessed is every one that feareth the Lord; that walketh in his ways. . . . it shall be well with thee" (Ps. 128:1-2).

This is his answer to sin in any degree or measure!

PRAYER: *There is so much, O God, that we deeply desire that we do not possess, yet we know that our not possessing can be an advantage. May we use the possessions that satisfy to advance the kingdom of God. Deliver us from the prison of this present life, and may our joy be found in things eternal. In Jesus' name. Amen.*

MAY 22

Blessed be the Lord, that . . . hath not failed one word of all his good promise, which he promised by the hand of Moses his servant.
(1 Kings 8:56)

The bills were piled high on my desk, the phone kept ringing from the calls of the creditors, and there just were not enough receivables to go around. In despair, I went for a walk and stopped to stretch my credit still further with needed supplies. On the wall my eyes spotted the words, "God hath not promised . . ." This reminder I did not need; I already knew. I read on. "But God hath promised . . ." I could go no further. As I recalled the things He had promised, the tears started, my heart began to sing, and the burden rolled away, even though I knew that my desk was still piled high with unpaid bills. I said, "Thank You, God, I needed that!"

Who says there are no mysteries in Providence? Things we pass by and never notice today may meet us tomorrow as a messenger from God. Who knows what mottoes God has placed on the walls of sorrow to soothe some aching heart tomorrow. Often the things that we pass by and never notice come before us later in a greater capacity of spiritual understanding.

In every providence of God there is a Calvary, and in every deed of love there is the beginning and pledge of an Atonement. Whatever God does in relation to our world He does with a view to recovery, redemption, and encouragement. God's voice is always for good, His omnipotence is on the side of the helpless, and He never turns aside from the defeated one.

He is the mighty God! He is the strong Deliverer! No living person ever filled the finest meaning of all these names but One. His name is Jesus. And I need His encouragement every day!

PRAYER: *O God, You know when we pass through waters and through the fire. You know the best of one and the violence of the other. But they are all under the control of a mighty, loving Heavenly Father. Into Your hands we fall and find our rest. In Jesus' name. Amen.*

■ MAY 23

The earth is the Lord's, and the fulness thereof; the world, and they that dwell therein. For he hath founded it upon the seas, and established it upon the floods.
(Ps. 24:1-2)

One of the startling questions to come out of a Christian experience is the one that asks, "Where was God when I needed Him?" The question comes when we think that God is not dealing in harmony with all the necessities that may arise in our lives through disappointment and discouragement. And judgments are often directed against God before His meaning is ever understood.

How many assaults have been made against Christian doctrine, the Christian Church, and the idea of God when His wisdom has overruled demands! The greatest words of the Master were unfairly attacked. When He was dying on the Cross in the place of His offenders, their cry, "Crucify Him!" was still ringing in the judgment hall. In great power of expression accusers have mocked the movement of the Church, while the faithful followers have written the martyrs' story in blood.

God's message to the Church is that the gates of hell would not prevail against His work. He is the Keeper of Jerusalem, and His people are ever reminded that the battle belongs to God. How sad when the standard-bearer faints under the burden, the saint on his knees loses the perspective, and even the fainthearted question God.

The song of Zion is still "God is our refuge and strength, a very present help in trouble. Therefore will not we fear, though the earth be removed, and though the mountains be carried into the midst of the sea" (Ps. 46:1-2).

Faith comes through in the long run, and God's people have an inner peace even when hell is thundering at the gates of the city. And God is there when we need Him most.

PRAYER: *O God, You do not forget us, but You send reminders continually of Your concerns for us. We are graven upon the palms of Your hands. Help us not to forget You but to acknowledge Your goodness and mercies. Make us fit for Your kingdom and obedient to Your commandments; and hide our shortcomings in Your mercy, which endures forever. In Jesus' name. Amen.*

MAY 24

And such trust have we through Christ to God-ward: not that we are sufficient of ourselves to think any thing as of ourselves; but our sufficiency is of God.
(2 Cor. 3:4-5)

The speaker told the graduating class that God does not choose a person for a task without intending to qualify him for it. The challenge was followed quickly by the remark that God has never been able to work with that person who feels that his qualifications are already adequate for the job. God never turns down the trembling one, who comes to Him with eyes full of tears and a stammering tongue. Whomever he calls, God will qualify and crown.

We must learn that it is not the word of man but the Word of God that matters most in our universe. The command given to Moses still holds, "Ye shall not add unto the word which I command you" (Deut. 4:2). Man has tried to invent a Bible, but he has left out the breath of God and done away with a personal devil and put out the fires of hell. He has invaded it with a pale light that can find no sin and leaves no place for the fellowship of the Holy Spirit.

It has never been in the power of human adequacy to accomplish anything for God. But the nation and the people who prayed and who lived by the strength of the Book of God have been the ones who have crossed the Red Seas and torn down the strongholds of sin.

God's call to every person is to begin at the point of his own understanding and take his stand there. This requires faith but is the standing point at which God's meeting takes place. This way takes the larger view, and the battleground is at the foot of the Cross where victory has already been won.

God's way produces a harvest as certain as the seedtime when it has been touched by His hand.

PRAYER: *Help us, O God, to find our sufficiency in You and not to look for it in ourselves. May we hear Your Word coming to our waiting need. Make it mighty as thunder but gentle as a breeze. Make it full of music and full of strength, saying to us, "My grace is sufficient for thee." In Jesus' name. Amen.*

MAY 25

I will lift up mine eyes unto the hills, from whence cometh my help. My help cometh from the Lord, which made heaven and earth.
(Ps. 121:1-2)

We use the words so often that the meaning is in danger of being lost in expressing the encouraging remark, "Keep looking up!" In the deep moments of the soul where despair has been encountered along with bereavement, sickness, and loss that takes away security, it is natural to encourage, "Keep looking up." It is as if a benediction and an Amen had covered the occasion, and there is no more to be added.

The benediction is not new. It has been God's encouragement for wounded hearts and bruised lives. He said to ancient Israel, "Lift up your eyes on high and behold," and then called their attention to the mighty hosts of heaven before their view (Isa. 40:26). When Jesus was taken up into heaven, the disciples stood steadfastly looking upward. The gaze is still to the hills, "whence cometh [our] help," and heavenward for His promised return.

In the same manner were the women reluctant to move away from the empty tomb, for they caught a vision of eternity. There is a time when sorrow becomes sweetness and loss turns into a source of gain. The great paradox of the gospel is "When I am weak, then am I strong" (2 Cor. 12:10). Every heart tells its own tale, and the soul turns to heaven as naturally as the opening bud to the morning sun.

The question was asked, "Ye men of Galilee, why stand ye gazing up . . . ?" (Acts 1:11). And the question came from God. Our positive response testifies to the deity of Jesus and fills the waiting heart with sacred delight and the expectation of His imminent return.

The greatest challenge of God to His Church in any generation is still, "Keep looking up," for "of that day and hour knoweth no man" (Matt. 24:36; see Mark 13:32).

PRAYER: *Encourage us, O God, in all our searching after You. Make us to know that You have made us for yourself and that only in You can we find Your purpose for us. Keep our gaze heavenward, and let a bit of heaven descend upon our souls. May our courage never fail and our hope be as a burning light as we look for the return of our Lord. In Jesus' name. Amen.*

MAY 26 ■

The Lord is my shepherd; I shall not want. . . .
Surely goodness and mercy shall follow me
all the days of my life: and I will dwell
in the house of the Lord for ever.
(Ps. 23:1, 6)

One of the most frequent questions I have heard over the years of my ministry has been, "How can I know that there is a personal God who really cares that I exist?" One man said to me, "To find identity with the God of the universe blows my mind; I just cannot fathom it!"

It is important that every person have a window through which he sees God and understands Him, and we go so far as to personalize Him so that we can understand Him better.

Probably David said it best for all of us: He "is my shepherd; I shall not want." It brings God in from the heavens and places Him down here where His people live. Follow David through this beautiful psalm and see the enrichment of his soul through a personal God who really does care!

The waters of comfort brought him near to God as the stars led to Bethlehem's manger. And the peace of God's resting-place provides a stillness and restores every soul that is in conflict.

He saw the valley of the shadows as the valley of night and death, where the darkest part of it must be passed alone. But David knew that his God would be there and that fear belongs only to this earth.

His God spread the banquet table where the enemy looks on in rage and helplessness. The rod, the staff, the table, and the cup all belong to God. He uses these to make each of us His own special child.

He gives us a place in His house where dwells truth, wisdom, holiness, sacrifice, and worship—it is also nearness to God.

He has bread enough and to spare, and they that put their trust in Him will want no good thing. He does care!

His people can say, "I shall dwell with Him forever."

PRAYER: *We thank You, O God, for Your care! We cannot tell where it begins, and we do not know where it ends. May our lives be witness of Your care as we daily testify to the presence of Your Holy Spirit. Your love goes beyond our asking, and Your giving far exceeds our greatest expectation. And we thank You. In Jesus' name. Amen.*

■ MAY 27

There is therefore now no condemnation to them which are in Christ Jesus, who walk not after the flesh, but after the Spirit.
(Rom. 8:1)

The evil in God's beautiful world has set loose a power difficult to understand, a power difficult to confront, and a power difficult to overcome. Those who are in the business of doing evil constantly appear to enjoy doing evil. "Out of the heart proceed ... murders, adulteries, ... thefts, ... blasphemies" (Matt. 15:19).

Paul talks about a work of evil in the heart that controls a person against his own desires. He said that because of it, he did evil even when he did not want to do it. He wanted to do good, but because of evil he found himself unable to accomplish his own good purpose. He hated evil, but then he went out and did it (Rom. 7:15-19). This is different from the state of the heart that loves to wallow in evil continually.

From whatever basis sin operates, evil brings its own penalties. Oh, the mystery of human nature that allows itself to be willfully taken down the pathway of death where the eternal loss of the soul is the reward. Whether the loss is little by little or sudden and without warning is the option the devil reserves for his own judgment. Nevertheless the trickery of sin is played out by the master hand.

But thank God, the rule operates on the other side as well. There is a delight in doing the will of God. God also delights in making His people happy, in setting the sinning person free, and opening the prison door to them that are bound by evil. We can commune with God in such a way that the evil is torn aside, and we are given a vision of the Father through the Son.

In this evil world the Holy Spirit can still take the things of Christ and reveal them to us. Let us pray for this gift of the Holy Spirit of God, who works for good in our world of sin.

PRAYER: *Our sins have kept good things from us, O God, and our iniquity is gathered like a cloud between us and You. But by penitence and brokenheartedness and hope in God we were able to take the burden to the Cross. Help us always to be ashamed of sin, lest the enemy turn upon us and gain the victory over our lives. In Jesus' name we pray. Amen.*

MAY 28 ■

Delight thyself also in the Lord; and he shall give thee the desires of thine heart. Commit thy way unto the Lord; trust also in him; and he shall bring it to pass.
(Ps. 37:4-5)

Today I attended the promotion exercises of a grade five class on their way to the next grade in public school. Awards of achievement were passed out, and winning essays on the theme, "Moving On," were read by the winners. The little girl who had placed second asked the searching question, "I wonder what the future will be like?"

What is the future? What is tomorrow? Who can define it? Who can be certain as to what it will be like or even how much of time "the future" contains? It does not belong to us, we have no right to it, but we must receive it as a gift and use it in the spirit of faithful stewardship.

The little grade five girl was not allowed to mention God in her essay, for in her school system they have to leave Him outside the classroom. I wanted to tell her that we are simply living according to the will of God, and we take our moments one by one as precious gifts to be used to the glory of the Giver. I wanted to tell her that Jesus warns us not to be anxious about it, for He will take care of it. I wanted to tell her that we should make the most of today and leave the tomorrows in God's hands.

A lesson comes out of the query greater than the question itself in regard to the whole mystery of the future. Ours should be a spirit of dependence, and we should build our life on the principle, "If the Lord will, we shall live, and do this, or that" (James 4:15). We are to hope continually in God and be assured that He who made yesterday will not leave tomorrow outside His love and care.

We may not be able to shut the mystery of tomorrow completely from our concern. But we can have a living faith that says, "Commit thy way unto the Lord; trust also in him; and he shall bring it to pass."

PRAYER: *O God, You have shown us how great is eternity, how immeasurable is heaven, and how precious is love! How we thank You for this vision while our eyes are bound by time. We do not live wholly in the future, for You give us joy in abundance here and now. We accept Your will for today, and there is no murmur or complaint. In Jesus' name. Amen.*

MAY 29

Be sober, be vigilant; because your adversary the devil, as a roaring lion, walketh about, seeking whom he may devour.
(1 Pet. 5:8)

The memory remains clear even today of the dear old saint walking the aisles of the church, warning the young people, "Beware! Beware! Beware! Satan is on the trail like a roaring lion, seeking whom he may devour." The admonition became commonplace through repetition, but the spirit in which it was given still lingers in the hearts of the hearers. Evil ingenuity plays supreme in tearing down where the strongholds are not well fortified by the Spirit of God.

The list of weaknesses of Christianity are on the front page of the devil's workbook, and he knows that no one can hurt the cause of Jesus Christ as much as the one who professes to follow Him. No infidel power can hurt the Son of Man as much as that one who has been touched by the Cross and has followed the Christ in communion and prayer. The work that Satan began in the Garden he continued into the very ministry of the Lord: "Then entered Satan into Judas surnamed Iscariot, being of the number of the twelve" (Luke 22:3).

It has been said that no man is as strong as when he is on his knees in prayer. But it is also on bended knee that the Christian faces the fiercest battle where the black seeds of doubt are planted to bear harvest tomorrow and the next day.

Today, I must hold on to the commandments and promises of God, and there must not be a shadow of doubt in my heart as to His holiness and divinity. God has promised to do all things well; here I must put my trust. To take doubt and prayer together to the throne is an insult to God Almighty.

I cannot live in terms of philosophy and speculation without argument, but the devil has no right to take from me my faith in a God who loves me.

PRAYER: *O God, in a world rocked and wrecked by satanic power, it is difficult to keep a Christian experience. As we fight these battles on our knees, help us to keep our treasured love safe in the shadow of the Cross. Here our victory over the enemy is assured by Him who died for us and rose again. Our faith is in Your great love. In Jesus' name. Amen.*

MAY 30

Praising God and having favour with all the people. ... Now Peter and John went up together into the temple at the hour of prayer.
(Acts 2:47; 3:1)

The Day of Pentecost ushered in a new day for our world, and the Holy Ghost from heaven was poured out upon the waiting family of God. There had never been such a day before, and the Church could never be the same again.

Men saw visions and heard voices, ambitions were born, and an inward stirring set plans for great undertakings for God. The people of God were filled with a new delight, and all the impossibilities fell out of sight. And all who believed were together, and all things became common possession. People were praising God from morning until night; and "they, continuing daily with one accord in the temple ... did eat their meat with gladness and singleness of heart" (Acts 2:46). It was a high day for the Church!

Then a very significant thing happened. "Peter and John went up together into the temple at the hour of prayer." A person is not made to live on the mountaintop of ecstasy all the time. There has to be a quiet time for the nourishment of the soul. God grants times of refreshing, hours of enthusiasm when all of life seems to open doors into the upper room of heaven. But we cannot always live in these luxuries of life, for we grow in the ordinary routine of worship and prayer.

The Day of Pentecost also took the hour of prayer out of the commonplace. To be able to have communion with God through the Holy Spirit was a new experience. When we realize the scope of this kind of praying, when the heart beats in communion with God's Holy Spirit, there can be nothing commonplace about it. This was given to the Church at Pentecost.

Every Christian life must have its own personal Pentecost and prove it through the sacred place of prayer.

PRAYER: *Give us power in our praying, O God, through the Holy Spirit. May we be more than conquerors when we come before the throne to make known our supplications and wrestle with You for victory. Warm our hearts as we pour forth our psalms of praise to You whom we love. In Jesus' name. Amen.*

MAY 31

Take heed unto thyself, and unto the doctrine; continue in them: for in doing this thou shalt both save thyself, and them that hear thee.
(1 Tim. 4:16)

Life for a Christian is basically not a very simple route, and it has not changed in character over the years. God's demands have never changed. There must be works of violence performed in every Christian life: "to uproot and to destroy and overthrow" (Jer. 1:10, NIV). There has to be *"Break down every idol, cast out every foe"* before there can be a *"wash me* and I shall me whiter than snow."

This is the message of every teacher, minister, and missionary who would shoulder the gospel yoke and set out to Christianize any class, congregation, or nation. The language of victory has not changed much over the years. The enemy is killed, false altars are burned, graven images are hewn down, and flirtation with foreign idolaters comes to an abrupt ending.

God's intention is to establish the throne of His righteousness and to clear out anything that could obscure the brightness and beauty of His presence. But His purpose is still the salvation of all persons of every age. Paul was always warning the young converts, "Take heed unto thyself," and the Church, "Let [every] man examine himself" (1 Cor. 11:28).

God never makes the burden heavier than we can bear, and He has made heaven to condescend to the limitations of earth. Calvary has run through the ages, and the condescending, saving Cross has been for all time, and Love has never been out of the reach of the one who would repent. Touch life wherever you will, and you will find the Cross pointing the way to God.

In whatever age God has met the honest seeker the testimony has been, "He must increase, but I must decrease" (John 3:30).

PRAYER: *O God, You know those who are carrying heavy burdens, whose eyes are full of tears, and whose feeble hands can no longer do their work. Don't put them to shame but deliver them by the magnitude of Your grace. Cleanse from all sin. Destroy all evil. Make us pure. Prepare us for heaven. In Jesus' name. Amen.*

JUNE 1 ■

And he said unto me, My grace is sufficient for thee: for my strength is made perfect in weakness.
(2 Cor. 12:9)

The question, "Do you find the rules of 'fare' play too difficult to live by?" was posed in jest on the golf course today, but the message introduces a startling truth that needs to be examined every day.

It brings us down to the fareway of life where every person must watch himself at the weakest point. Examination must be made in those areas of living where others might least suspect a problem. Every person should try himself as by fire and undergo a personal scrutiny of the value system of life. The Book of Deuteronomy warns to "take heed to thyself" (12:19), and Paul speaking to the Church said, "Let [every] man examine himself" (1 Cor. 11:28), bringing it all down to an individual matter.

We have the demands of heaven on the one hand and the limitations of earth on the other. Our weakness is the basis of negotiation, and when the weight is too heavy to carry, God meets us with His strength. But the rules of fair play, honesty, integrity, and truth never change.

This is the greatness of God that we often miss, and because of our failure to recognize this truth, we go down in defeat. God's grace and mercy go hand in hand. His statutes are written with tears and surrounded with love and understanding. He is concerned about our lives today, and when we find the rules too difficult, His strength is supplied for our weakness.

God knows the burdens that weigh heavily, the lives that are full of tears, the bodies that are full of pain, and the pressures that keep the spirit under bondage. There is an answer in heaven to all the necessities of earth, and His rules are not made to put us to shame.

PRAYER: *O God, how thankful we are to know that You give power to the faint, and to them that have no might You increase their strength. Help us to carry our burdens in the strength of Christ and in the power of the Holy Spirit. May we find our confidence in Your omnipotence. In Jesus' name. Amen.*

■ JUNE 2

Then came the officers to the chief priests and Pharisees; and they said unto them, Why have ye not brought him? The officers answered, Never man spake like this man.
(John 7:45-46)

Great multitudes of people heard the words of Jesus, and they followed Him in His journeys from Nazareth to Jerusalem and back again. Great multitudes begged for His death, and the multitudes watched Him die. He spoke many things to them in parables and did many miracles that they did not understand. When He went to the Cross, the multitudes challenged Him to come down, for they did not know what was happening.

The words of the Messenger said many different things to the many listeners, but His message never changed. The subject was the kingdom of heaven, and He illustrated it from every quarter of life and nature. The multitude failed to get the point, and the meaning of His truth went beyond their understanding.

They gave Jesus credit for having spoken like no other man. But the message—the nugget of gold, the treasure more precious than rubies, the mystery of heaven, the heart of His heart—was lost to them as water running through a basket.

The multitude that followed Jesus is present in every age in human history. They are sitting in the pews of every church and running with every messenger whose voice is made audible by whatever means. Some hear the Word and understand it, while some see it for the moment but go out and forget it and are led away by the crowd that cries, "Crucify Him!"

Jesus still stands today crowned above all other messengers, mightier in power and more tender in gentleness. His words have made Him a Shepherd, a King, a Father, a Brother, a Root out of the dry ground, the Flower of Jesse, the Lily of the Valley, and the Rose of Sharon. These are words that speak to the heart.

They lead us to His cross while we watch Him die, and we try to understand.

PRAYER: *O God, once we did not understand the message of Your kingdom, for it was the message of suffering and the Cross. Now You have shown us that it is Your very heart, and who can know the great depths of its meaning? But You have shown us that it is the message of love, and we are part of it. May we be worthy, in Jesus' name. Amen.*

JUNE 3

And when they had prayed, they laid their hands on them. And the word of God increased; and the number of the disciples multiplied in Jerusalem greatly.
(Acts 6:6-7)

One of the purposes in prayer is so that God can get our attention to tell us about things He wants us to do. And when He gets our attention, He names the purposes that He has in mind for us. Isn't this like the love of God? He does not suddenly hit us like a bolt of thunder, but He gently, gradually, and with much care prepares us for the particular assignment that He has for us to do.

Jesus told His disciples to pray for laborers for the harvest. When they had prayed, He said to them, "You are the laborers; *go!*" How often when we get desperate in our praying for God to send hands, feet, and finances, He says to us, "Thou art the person!" And when we pray, "O God, send a revival in the church," God answers, "Begin it in your own heart." God's plan seems to work around the principle that the one who prays most is the one best prepared for the task!

God is always calling, always creating, always shaping us to new and challenging things within the abilities that He has given us. But the greater invitation is to get nearer to Him through the avenue of prayer. The nearer we get, the softer His voice and the more gentle the call.

When God awakens within an individual the call to service, He also empowers that one for the task to which He calls. Jesus gave His disciples power to relieve burdens and distresses, to heal diseases, and to soothe aching hearts. And the power was given as it was used and needed, and it came after the prayer was made.

God expects us to begin where He calls us. Through the pathway of prayer must be the way of everyone who would do and be for God in any capacity.

PRAYER: *Hear us, O God, when we pray. May the end of our communion be greater wisdom and better preparation for the things You are calling us to do. When our prayers fail, may Your answers be multiplied, so that we might be conquerors in following Your will. In Jesus' name. Amen.*

■ JUNE 4

For he that is called in the Lord, being a servant, is the Lord's freeman: likewise also he that is called, being free, is Christ's servant.
(1 Cor. 7:22)

One of the greatest expressions in the Bible is Paul's description of himself as "a servant of Jesus Christ" (Rom. 1:1), also translated as "a slave of Jesus Christ" (Williams). He never did seek to be crowned the prince of servants but was willing to be the least of slaves that he might magnify the name he sought to honor. God took what Paul gave and clothed the gift with His Spirit for a special ministry.

We all have to state our position before Jesus Christ for ourselves. It must be written down in the inner being. Not what we wish the world would suppose us to be, but what we actually know we are in the inmost soul. And it must be written upward toward God. It does the soul good to put in words what it is, what it thinks, what it wants, and what it hopes. The final definition is impossible outside the touch of God, but it is a commitment and a testimony to where we stand.

Faith is greater than any definition of faith, as God is greater than any definition of God. The marvelous terms may mean 100 things. Sometimes it is as an invisible angel leading the soul to the Cross. Sometimes it talks in whispers in the darkness and speaks of the morning when not a star is in view. Sometimes it moves one to give, to work, to suffer, and to sacrifice, so that someone else might have. In the same sense love is greater than any definition of love. And being a servant of Jesus Christ is far greater than our mere testimony to the fact.

Our reasoning often blurs the way to the Cross when we place it in forms of our own making. We live in love, in faith, and in experience, but we need the touch of God for the fulfillment of the relationship with Jesus Christ.

PRAYER: *O God, this day we would offer ourselves as servants of the living God. Once we were dead in trespasses and sins and worshipers of self and did not know You. We would receive Your will and begin our eternity by spending our few earthly days as Your servants. Then ours will be a living service that knows no ending. Make it so. In Jesus' name. Amen.*

JUNE 5 ■

**Many are my persecutors and mine enemies;
yet do I not decline from thy testimonies.**
(Ps. 119:157)

How simple a thing it is to throw difficult questions at the believing Christian! How difficult it is to find a satisfying answer to every query! Yet the Bible exhorts us to "be ready always to give an answer to every man that asketh you a reason of the hope that is in you" (1 Pet. 3:15). Therefore, we ought to be prepared to answer each question with some degree of certainty. It is good to be instructed in the doctrine so that we can have a clear understanding of the religious arguments that would confront us.

Moses told the Israelites that questions would be asked of them. The son would ask the father the meaning of certain monuments and institutions, and the father would be obliged to reply.

How disheartening to the cause of Christianity if in the presence of inquiry as to our commitment, we were dumb to the question! Moses said, "Tell them what God has brought you out of, and where He has placed you today, and what He has promised you for tomorrow." We cannot adapt a better reply. No argument is required here! Here is the only reply that will stand the test of reason and the wear and tear of time.

Moses is saying to the ages, "Don't be afraid to make it personal—speak about your involvement and your own vital relationship to the Almighty God. Connect yourself with the thing that is happening." The man in John 9 said, "I was blind . . . I met a Man . . . and now I can see." What greater answer can be given to the one with the question?

Question: "What meaneth this stand you have taken among us?" Answer: "I met a Man called Jesus . . ." Argument: There is none!

PRAYER: *Keep us, O God, in the right way by the continual revelations of Your truth. Make the testimonies of our lives stand off the mighty enemy of Your Holy Spirit. Enable us to know that through all the mysteries of life You are bringing us to Your place of rest and perfection. In Jesus' name. Amen.*

■ JUNE 6

And we compassed mount Seir many days. And the Lord spake unto me, saying, Ye have compassed this mountain long enough: turn you northward.
(Deut. 2:1-3)

A good deal of banter sometimes follows the testimony of one who is still living on past experiences and tries to envelop everyone else in the "good old days." Some people seem to be content to linger there while present opportunities pass them by. In the Christian life there is a standard of progress, and we are putting the knife of destruction in our own souls when we remain at the altar after the fire has ceased to burn.

God knows how long we have been there, and He knows when we have been in one place long enough. When we have "waited patiently for the Lord" (Ps. 40:1), He tells us when to stay, when to rest, and when to move on. God will always provide answers to our prayers—not always a heavy commandment to perform but often a simple commingling of spirit with Spirit in doing His will. Infinite is His wisdom with the honest seeker.

It is human to get attached to the mountain. We need change. We cannot live by building tabernacles of remembrance, and God knows that our impulse is often spoken in ignorance. Often our testimony is an utterance of the emotion of the moment, which soon dries up. God says to us, "Ye have dwelt long enough in this mount" (Deut. 1:6).

While we are saying, "It is good to be here," God is saying to us, "Go down off the mountain!" He does not want us to build any heaven for Him on earth, for the foundations on which we would build are shaky. God always places His people where the action is—in the valleys, on the seashore, in the battlefield, and where the hand is reaching out for help.

It may be difficult to leave the mountain, but when God takes us to the plains, the taking itself can be a vision of heaven.

PRAYER: *O God, we pray for such a vision of Your greatness that we shall remain calm when our cherished mountains are carried into the midst of the sea. We will tell You to take the mountain with its sham security and place us where Your action calls for our help. Then we shall be satisfied. In Jesus' name. Amen.*

JUNE 7

But he knoweth the way that I take: when he hath tried me, I shall come forth as gold.
(Job 23:10)

The Psalmist states that "the fool hath said in his heart, There is no God" (14:1). How difficult to try to live without God! How difficult to define right and wrong or discover the best way to heaven. The biblical doctrine is one of human dependence upon God. He has made the way so plain that "the wayfaring men, though fools, shall not err therein" (Isa. 35:8).

The deep desire of every seeking person is to find the will of the eternal God. The Bible speaks to the heart that asks with reverent earnestness. This is the beginning of faith, and the Christian is led on by trust, the result of which is a conviction that no argument can disturb. The testimony to this divine mystery is that God has provided a way, and "he that doeth the will of God abideth for ever" (1 John 2:17).

God is always training, leading, rewarding, and encouraging. His delight is in the glory of human obedience. In our earthiness we have only understood such words as still waters, fountains, fig trees, vines, and shepherds, but God has used them as spiritual props to lead His people onward.

God also allows chastening for those whom He loves. "Whom the Lord loveth he chasteneth" (Heb. 12:6). This does not always mean punishment; often it is a trial of patience so that we might be taught the habit of waiting, and it may become the beginning of prayer. We learn in hunger what we could never understand in fullness, for in the end God means to do us good.

God's way is the way of hope, of a new beginning, and of larger opportunities; and step by step He leads us onward and upward. This is the God to whom we sing, "I need Thee every hour."

PRAYER: *We put ourselves in Your hands, O God, and pray that Your great knowledge of the way shall be our determination. Lead us that we may not stumble. Help us to find the city of God where human effort shall end and our direction shall come from the throne. In Jesus' name. Amen.*

■ JUNE 8

> O God, when thou wentest forth before thy people ... the earth shook, the heavens also dropped at the presence of God: even Sinai itself was moved.
> (Ps. 68:7-8)

The Old Testament words "The battle is not yours, but God's" (2 Chron. 20:15) could easily stand beside most of the problems encountered in any Christian endeavor. In the extremities of life and in the crises of peril the call is for childlike trust in the merciful and almighty God of heaven. And the key word is trust. The converse was given in the New Testament where Jesus "did not many mighty works there because of their unbelief" (Matt. 13:58).

It is human to take our problems upon our own shoulders, to work as if God had died, and only when the battle is lost to begin to pray. How poor a thing it is to depend entirely upon our own wisdom and power!

God has ways at His disposal that have never entered into the mind of man. We look at things that are seen. We make calculations. We may lay aside the supernatural. We substitute faith for reason. We forget that God is there all the time.

God can turn armies one upon another. God can cloud the reasoning powers of man. God can turn comrades into enemies. God can make the sun and the moon to stand still for the battle to be won. When God stands at the head of the battle, all heaven becomes the reply to our need.

Often our strength is found in standing still—waiting patiently for God. The true test of our Christianity is the depth and reality of our repose. When problems move in and the enemy is at the door, the depth of our piety will be in our calmness before God. Calmness is not weakness, nor does waiting prove lack of ability.

Our anxiety is often our shame, and our fear is an accusation against God, because "the battle is not yours, but God's."

PRAYER: *Almighty God, in the day of battle, when great fear would descend upon us, and distress of soul would become our portion, be our delivering Hand, we pray. Prepare us for the great encounters of life, and may we know the restfulness of Your rest. Keep us on the victory side. In Jesus' name. Amen.*

JUNE 9 ■

Blessed is that servant, whom his lord when he cometh shall find so doing.
(Matt. 24:46)

Life is a curious thing and how utterly unmanageable when we try to control it ourselves! On the other hand, life is a beautiful thing and well-proportioned in every aspect when God is in charge.

God has set out plans for His creation. The part of wisdom is to do our day's work with patience where God has placed us. By following this commitment, we shall get rid of a great deal of fretting, worrying, and concern in becoming entangled in our own impossibilities. The confirmation of the gospel is that the servant following God's directions shall be blessed at the coming of the Lord.

We lay plans as if we were going to live forever, yet we know that at any moment we may die. Our plans for business, our plans for home, our plans for living—not one of them are limited to the day. We will not allow ourselves to be bound by the sunrising or the sunsetting. We set our life in plans that shall endure for the years and the ages. Too often God has not even been consulted in the things we are trying to accomplish.

In our ways there must be a point of commitment and trust. There must come a place where we act on confidence in God, who knows the way and is in control. Every morning we need to take a good look at His blueprint for our day. The Great Architect has mapped out, put down, and set to scale every little minute of it. We need to go often to the place where the plans are kept!

The next task to be done, the next turn in the road, the next foundation to be laid is on God's map. His designs lie far beyond the reach of our imagination. Life can be beautiful when it is shaped by God.

PRAYER: *Make us Your servants, O living God, we pray. We give You our heart, our mind, our affection, and our loyalty—withholding nothing. We would receive Your will even in our limited understanding and spend our earthly days as servants of the Most High God. Make us servants of men only because we are first servants of You. In Jesus' name. Amen.*

■ JUNE 10

For the word of God is quick, and powerful, and sharper than any twoedged sword.
(Heb. 4:12)

One of my earliest recollections of Sunday School was memorizing the books of the Bible to repeat without error or hesitation before a critical congregation. This was followed by an analysis of the chapters and verses in each book. One member of the church encouraged us by the many times she had read the Bible through, being very careful to note the date for each accomplishment.

Interesting and useful as this might have been, in reality it was nothing, for in it all we never saw God in the Book that carried His name. It is so easy to get caught up in the secular that we miss the message and spirit of the Word. We measure the miles from Dan to Beersheba while we miss the way of the Cross of Calvary.

It is possible to build a church and never utter a hint of prayer from the heart. It is possible for men to lay bricks for the sanctuary while they mix the cement with their blasphemy. It is possible to endow a church with riches while living in the poverty of our own piety. It is possible to attend church and support it financially and never have a heart-to-heart encounter with God. It is possible to live in the chapter and verse and never enter into the sanctuary, where God is the eternal Flame.

Beware, lest when we have quoted all the dimensions of the Bible, we have never found the Spirit of God in the Book. Beware, lest when we have paid our tithes and kept the commandments, we have failed to pray the publican's prayer and brought the cleansing of heaven down in our heart!

The Bible is more than a book with chapters, verses, and readings to be noted on the flyleaf. It is a revelation, blooming and expanding, grand and rich with the joy of God.

PRAYER: *We give You thanks, O God, that You have written a Book for us. Make every chapter a spiritual event and every sentence a meeting with heaven. Our desire is to live in Your Revelation, the Word, with wisdom to understand and wills to obey. In Jesus' name. Amen.*

JUNE 11 ■

I have fought a good fight, I have finished my course, I have kept the faith: henceforth there is laid up for me a crown of righteousness.
(2 Tim. 4:7-8)

The Vietnam War brought many changes in the thinking and activities of the nation. The outlook on patriotism and the viewpoint on warfare were analyzed. The Church was criticized as a warfaring unit, and the hymn "Onward, Christian Soldiers" came under severe scrutiny. The idea that the Christian life had anything to do with the battleground was frowned upon.

The argument supported the belief that as soon as one joined the church, he settled into a state of selfish enjoyment. The idea of soldierliness was removed from Christianity, and the follower of Jesus Christ was placed on the sunny side of the garden.

The real biblical teaching is that Christianity is a contest, a race, a struggle, fighting forces of darkness. And to "endure hardness, as a good soldier" (2 Tim. 2:3) is a biblical emphasis.

Jesus Christ was the Prince of Peace, but He was against everything bad and opposed all that was not founded on eternal truth. He never met evil without engaging in conflict. The victory of the Resurrection came after the battle of Gethsemane and Calvary.

The battle of the Church is not geared to the blare of the trumpet, the clash of carnal metal, or the bloodshed of the pointed sword. Jesus Christ won by tears, tenderness, sympathy, patience, love, and the power of peace. And His gentleness became the very strength of His sword.

The Church goes forward into battle every day! And she is mighty by the power of the Holy Spirit to pull down the strongholds of selfishness and ingratitude and rebellion of heart. But "Victory in Jesus" comes only after the battle is over.

PRAYER: *O God, how good to know Your presence in the midst of the battle against sin. The fight has been won, and Calvary stands as our symbol of victory. Cover us by the omnipotence of Your power and give us the tenderness of Your presence. Hasten the day when all fighting shall cease, and Your peace shall abide forever. In Jesus' name. Amen.*

JUNE 12

> For bodily exercise profiteth little: but godliness is profitable unto all things, having promise of the life that now is, and of that which is to come.
> (1 Tim. 4:8)

A young athlete, heavily involved in the Summer Olympic Games, was being interviewed before a television audience. The questioner probed concerning his physical training that enabled him to outclass his competitors. His answer was, "In every practice I ask myself, 'How much more can I do?'"

There is a "how much more" thread running throughout the Scriptures. Whatever there is good in a person, whenever the end of the attainment is reached, there is still the question, "How much more?" It has pleased God to make us seekers after His perfection.

Human love is but a drop of God's love and a mere symbol of His affection. It is a mere speck to begin with; but when we know its agony, its passion, its mystery of suffering, and multiply this by infinity, we can say, "This is the beginning of God's love." And we learn that the "how much more" of love is as boundless as God's eternity.

Jesus teaches us about the possibilities of faith and finds a theology in the grass, the lilies, and the flying birds. When we see what God is doing in nature, "how much more" we can expect from Him who loved us even to His own death.

God does not want us to live superficially when we might have "life ... more abundantly" (John 10:10). The welcome of His hospitality is to the feast and not to continue in our famine. The call of the Kingdom is not to do little things, but the call is upward and onward to greater things. The call is to enlarge our capacity for more of His grace.

"Bodily exercise profiteth little," but how much more does godliness profit. Eternal values are much more precious than gold medals.

PRAYER: *O God, we pray that You will help us know what is important and what is not important. We have learned that the soul is more valuable than the body, and the future far outshines the present. Make us obedient to Your will, wherein true value is eternally resident. In Jesus' name. Amen.*

JUNE 13 ■

But he knoweth the way that I take: when he hath tried me, I shall come forth as gold.
(Job 23:10)

The thought had never been so real to me before as when I awoke this morning: This day belongs to God. As the sunbeams played across the room and the birds sang their morning song, the neighborhood began to vibrate with the sounds of the day, and everything seemed to belong to Him. Everything with which we have to do is an expression of God. He comes out of His eternity to share my narrow space of time.

If this be true, then I can have no secrets from Him today. He knows everything that will come to my mind: all of the unspoken murmuring of the heart; the deepest and most bitter expressions of the soul; thoughts that are soundless to the human ear; and anticipations that may never become actions. God says, I know them all. I know what you are thinking. I know your imaginations.

Greater still, God knows the way of the soul. Here is an evil thought against a friend. Here is a little plan for mischief. Here is a little coveted thing, free to be taken. Job says, "No thought can be withholden from thee" (42:2).

But the very thing that is a terror to the bad man is a comfort to the good man. The Christian can rejoice in His omniscience and find the answer to sin in the atonement of His Son. Because He knows me, He will deal with me according to His understanding.

There are prayers that we dare not tell our friends, and prayers that are prayed only when the door is shut, bolted, and sealed. But God knows them and hears the heartbeat behind them. His very omniscience is my crown of glory if my purpose is right.

PRAYER: *O God, You know our deepest thoughts. There is not a word on our tongue or a thought in our heart that Your eyes have not penetrated. May the words of our mouth and the meditation of our heart be acceptable in Your sight, our Lord and our Redeemer! In Jesus' name. Amen.*

JUNE 14

Verily, verily, I say unto you, He that believeth on me hath everlasting life. I am that bread of life.
(John 6:47-48)

To understand the purpose of Jesus Christ, the Son of God, one must study His Gospels. His use of the word "Amen," by paraphrase or translation, shows us the positive message of His ministry to an eager people.
—In the Gospel of Matthew He uses it 31 times.
—In the Gospel of Mark we have 14 instances of it.
—In the Gospel of Luke He uses 7 Amens.
—In the Gospel of John we find it 25 times.
This is the Christ with the everlasting "Yes" to a people awaiting some great positive answer. Now it has come. The Amen of God.

We cannot live on suppositions, and the message that Jesus brought from God confirms heaven's intent in the salvation of the world. The message is the living truth.

—"The Son of man is come to seek and to save that which was lost" (Luke 19:10).

—"God so loved the world ... but have everlasting life" (John 3:16).

—"The Son of man is not come to destroy men's lives, but to save them" (Luke 9:56).

The everlasting "yes," the "verily" of everlasting love, was written in heaven, brought to earth by the Son of God, confirmed by the Cross, and sealed by the Resurrection.

Today Jesus Christ must be believed and preached in this spirit. He wants His gospel given, not defended. We must call men to the positive Christ who gives a positive pardon and a positive peace and prepares them for a positive heaven.

This is Christ's representation of himself to the world, and this is His representation of God. Heaven has nothing to say to the critical unbeliever but has a positive gospel to speak to the heart of the honest seeker after righteousness.

PRAYER: *Help us, O God, to know the truth of Your ministry among the children of men. May it dwell in us as a positive force touching every point of our lives, giving us victory over all our daily happenings in our temporary stay here. Fill us with Your Holy Spirit and lead us homeward. In Jesus' name. Amen.*

JUNE 15 ■

**It is good for me that I have been afflicted;
that I might learn thy statutes.**
(Ps. 119:71)

Suffering and sorrow are mountain peaks that seem to dominate every life-style. There is not a person living who does not know what is meant by grief and pain and suffering and sorrow. All history has a black line of affliction weaving through the events of the ages. The image throws its shadow over the whole area of the Bible. The thesis of the Book of Psalms shows that at the root of human life gnaws the worm of human sorrow.

In a book so full of joy, happiness, peace, tenderness, and love, what does God mean when He afflicts the children of men? What is the meaning of loss, grief, disappointment, and affliction in all of their devastating ramifications? The brief, grim, horrible answer is—SIN!

We will never be able to fathom the mystery, but how often we have been drawn closer to God through our tears than through our laughter. There can be no holy life until we have seen and heard and obeyed. From the beginning God's purpose for His people has been obedience. This is a discipline that tests the highest human qualities and places our will within the will of God.

Another mystery of affliction is that it will do what no amount of argument or eloquence could ever accomplish. God allowed His servant Paul to have "a thorn in the flesh" so that he should not "be exalted above measure" (2 Cor. 12:7). Job's testimony to affliction was: "When he hath tried me, I shall come forth as gold" (23:10). How often affliction turns to prayer and penitence and trust in God.

Remember this: He will not allow us to be tried beyond what we can bear, and with every trial He makes a way of escape. Even our affliction is under His control!

PRAYER: *O God, we cannot understand the mystery, but we know that affliction brings peace and that death comes to the saint with a blessing in its hand. Help us to bury our burdens at Calvary, and through the Cross give us a vision of the throne. Keep us under Your care and guidance. In Jesus' name. Amen.*

JUNE 16

> If ye then, being evil, know how to give good gifts unto your children, how much more shall your Father which is in heaven give good things to them that ask him?
> (Matt. 7:11)

How is it possible for someone living here on earth to be able to talk to someone in heaven?" The question sounded its own disbelief this week as two elderly gents were discussing their theological differences on a park bench in the Plaza. The question does become very startling as you think about it and surround it with the impossibilities that our humanness imposes.

It seems that Matthew believed in the possibility, for he recorded the words of Jesus, "How much more shall your Father which is in heaven give good things to them that ask him?" He believed that an interchange between heaven and earth was perfectly honest, straightforward, and possible.

How beautiful the simplicity of faith—ask, seek, knock, and find. Jesus believed it, and He laid it before His followers as a possibility. And He was speaking about an earthly appeal finding its answer in heaven. There is no theological underbrush here to wade through. There are no questions here to suggest uncertainty. We bring our own mystery to it.

We stand before Heaven's Giver as a child stands before a wise father, for sometimes God says, "No." We must learn to put our prayers before heaven and, having delivered them with an anxious heart, learn to say, "Nevertheless not my will, but thine, be done" (Luke 22:42).

God is greater than our asking and knocking. The greatest gifts of heaven in redemption, in life, in responsibility are determined by the will of God and not by our prayers.

If our spirit is bathed in the love of God, our link between earth and heaven is already complete.

PRAYER: *Our Father in heaven, Your patience is so great when You know that our life here on earth is resolved into one big daily need. Yet You have told us to ask and we would find. We are always asking, and You are always giving. Your supply is never exhausted. How amazing! We will never understand. We thank You in Jesus' name. Amen.*

JUNE 17 ■

He that cometh to God must believe that he is, and that he is a rewarder of them that diligently seek him.
(Heb. 11:6)

There are many things about God that we shall never find out or understand. His ways are above our ways, and His thoughts are greater than our imaginations. We reckon time in minutes and hours, days and weeks, months and years, and we dare to go so far as to speak about a millennium; but our minds give way as time runs into eternity.

We use the word *love*, and we place upon it such descriptive terms as our minds can grasp. But there comes a point where contemplation can go no further. And Love passes into Sacrifice and goes beyond our reach by the way of the Cross.

God created man and placed him in His Garden. We can understand this, but even here we find something that is beyond our knowing. We hear God say that He made man in His own image, and we get lost in the meaning.

Our relationship with God is set in ways beyond our finding out. Jesus brought heaven to earth when He told us to pray, "Our Father which art in heaven . . ." (Matt. 6:9; Luke 11:2). Whoever He is, the word "Father" suits our circumstances and brings heaven much closer.

What we do know of God, we know through experience, which is like a tiny gate opening upon infinite possibilities. And the best description we can give is great, wise, good, just, and eternal. Experience tells us that God is, and that "he is a rewarder of them that diligently seek him."

Beyond words and deeper than words is an abiding confidence through the eternal Son of God that allows us to believe, worship, and trust. And this satisfies the heart.

PRAYER: *We pray, O God, that You will come down to us as a light and as a cooling dew upon the parched grass. Bring to our memories every recollection of our sins and then show us the Cross of Redemption. May we know no rest until we worship You in spirit and in truth. In Jesus' name. Amen.*

■ JUNE 18

Thy word is a lamp unto my feet, and a light unto my path.
(Ps. 119:105)

Since we depend so much on the Bible, we wonder how the people got along without it before it was written. It is difficult to know its beginning or to know its ending, for as we grow in intimacy with its spirit and meaning, dimensions of time and place have little significance. When we go to its pages for help, we determine its value by our own experience with it.

There is a sense in which every writer had all the Bible with him. We look at the Psalmist, who seemed to have the whole gospel in his heart and expressed it in so many ways. We are startled by the new beauties and the righteous ways he reveals to us. Yet he sensed there remained something he had not grasped, for he prayed, "Open thou mine eyes, that I may behold" (Ps. 119:18).

His concern was our concern! Can we read the Word of God so as to have all the "wondrous things" (v. 18) of God revealed to us? Have we caught the meaning of God as "our refuge and strength," or accepted the challenge to "Come, behold the works of the Lord," or been struck by the openness of His invitation, "Be still, and know that I am God" (Ps. 46:1, 8, 10)? Can we know it as the Psalmist knew it? "Thy word is a lamp unto my feet, and a light unto my path."

There is more in the Bible than even the writers knew. They tested it in the palace, in the lions' den, in the prison, and in the deep midnight. We have tested it in our day-by-day experience with God. The Bible and Christian faith have stood the test of experience, and we have never exhausted all the wonderful resources available to us.

The Bible is not a man-written book, for it is full of God—awful, solemn, and sublime. It stands forever, because the world forever needs it.

PRAYER: *O God, we tell ourselves that we have read the Bible when we have merely skipped through a few verses in haste. Teach us the meaning, by which we will be able to understand the wonderful works of God. Keep us close to the Book so that we might know the Giver in all His omnipotence, lest we lose our way. In Jesus' name. Amen.*

JUNE 19

Wait on the Lord: be of good courage, and he shall strengthen thine heart: wait, I say, on the Lord.
(Ps. 27:14)

God's waiting time is part of every Christian experience. Waiting is not in the normal makeup of most of us. If we could fully understand the meaning of that word and would fearlessly apply it, there would be less reason for impatience in the crises encountered. Few of us have mastered it so as to be able to use it fearlessly and with perfect ease.

The strength of the Church is in waiting on the Lord. The weapons of her warfare are kept within the sacred custody of that most simple yet inexhaustible word—wait! It contains all that is necessary for the most complete revelation of God. It throws us back on ourselves, our impatience, our fears, and our failures and says, "If you want to know—wait."

To find out what God is asking, go into your closet of prayer, shut the door on all of your world, fall before God, and wait! And listen! You will find deeper depths, inner secrets of mystery, and possibilities beyond comprehension, for God is always in advance of His people. When He said, "Be still, and know that I am God" (Ps. 46:10), the invitation was to "wait" and to "know."

No person can ever be the same at the end of a waiting time with God as he was at the beginning. Those who were reared in a Christian home and sung to sleep at night with snatches of Christian hymns and nurtured in the fear and love of God can never stand before God as someone who had never heard the name of Christ spoken in love.

So our waiting times are God's times, for here is the secret of our fellowship, our hope, and our victory.

PRAYER: *O God, we pray that You will keep us quiet, patient, and at ease before You. May we understand the meaning of waiting for You as well as waiting upon You. Give us the assurance that Your messenger will come with great answers to the heart. Then make us more than conquerors and accommodate Your omnipotence to our weakness. In Jesus' name. Amen.*

■ JUNE 20

Make a joyful noise unto the Lord, all the earth: make a loud noise, and rejoice, and sing praise.
(Ps. 98:4)

An accumulation of sickness and sorrow had spread a blanket of gloom over the home. Happiness was smothered in the darkened pathway of death. Strength had yielded in silence, while the weak remained to carry the flame. But an interesting thing happened in the midst of the gloom. A little boy had a birthday! The day bloomed into a ray of light with every hour a burning candle. And a mother carried a lamp into the gloom lighted by a divine and comforting Presence.

This could have been happening in any family, for it carries a principle for every home where darkness has moved in. Every month has its own memory, every day tells its own story, and every night holds its own darkness. The events of life call for a reach upward, even though many are set in despair and lived out in sorrow.

God's purpose for every life and every home is that it be filled with joy and happiness. But a turn of events took place in the planning, and sin moved in with fear, hatred, hopelessness, and death to mar His wonderful design.

God's keyword is still "Rejoice." Rejoice and be glad. Rejoice and give thanks. Rejoice and sing, and love and worship. And this is meant to include the fatherless and the widow, and it includes the little boy's birthday party. God's joy does not shut doors and close windows and pull the shades and silence the children's laughter. His joy turns the night into gladness and makes every day a day of heaven.

God's delight is to make us children of heaven and eternity and not of earth and time, and to bring the Light of heaven into the gloom of every home.

PRAYER: *Sometimes, O God, we sing and cry at the same time. We know what it is to be joyful even when our tears flow in sorrow. Your joy is that everyone, great and small, be found at last within the arms of Your love and in Your heaven. Make it so, we pray. In Jesus' name. Amen.*

JUNE 21 ■
The days of our years are threescore years and ten; and if by reason of strength they be fourscore years, yet is their strength labour and sorrow.
(Ps. 90:10)

"The days of our years are threescore years and ten," said the Psalmist. Today I attended the funeral of one who had gone beyond that allotment of time by one score and four years.

In childhood we look with awe on this vast mountain of time. In youth we turn away from the giant with unconcern. In the aging years we treat it with reluctant respect. As the years advance, the span of time shortens, and we measure the days very carefully.

At best this time is hardly a breath when measured by God's eternity. We mourn about our little day and lock ourselves up in our prison houses of uncertainty and worry. God means to challenge us with immortality and not dishearten us by our frailty. He wants us to live with endlessness in mind and not to die in the narrowness of our sphere of threescore and 10 years.

Jesus Christ knows our days, for "He brought life and immortality to light through the gospel" (2 Tim. 1:10). He knows our weariness and has promised rest to our weary days. He knows our sin, and He came to reply to its agony and to destroy its power. He knows that we are dust, but He also knows we are immortal creatures in God's plan.

When we sense the immensity of eternity and how short is the measure of our time, He comes to us with a higher revelation. He speaks to us of the possibilities that do not lie within the compass of our "threescore years and ten."

We discover that life can be a building up toward heaven as part of the divine fellowship and God's eternal purpose. Then the terror of time is lost in the miracle of His grace.

PRAYER: *O God, how great is the assurance that though we are always dying, yet we cannot really die. You have given us immortality, and our spirits shall rise to praise You in eternity, the duration of which is beyond our grasp. We thank You for this hope through Jesus Christ, our Lord. In His name. Amen.*

JUNE 22

Be ye therefore perfect, even as your Father which is in heaven is perfect.
(Matt. 5:48)

God's ideal: "Be ye therefore perfect, even as your Father which is in heaven is perfect." But how can I be perfect as God is perfect unless I am God? Or is this ideal what we ought to be and ought to do, but cannot be and cannot do? Is it something to look up to and something to strive after? Or did God mean it to be a quality to be prayed for and worked for, with nothing marring the endeavor? It is God's eternal plan that we should strive to be perfect!

The march is ever onward and upward, and there is no looking back. It is an abhorrence of that which is evil and holding on for dear life to all that is good (Rom. 12:9). To be bathed in the fellowship of divine communion and then descend to play the game of Satan is not in the plan of God for His people. The closer one gets to God's perfection, the more he shows forth a spirit of God's holiness.

The ideal of God keeps one busy with the Lord's business. God is in the center of everything. His direction, management, wisdom, and concern are placed in every burden to be carried and every decision to be made. God is not left out of any transaction.

The Christian knows what it means to be "rejoicing in hope; patient in tribulation; continuing instant in prayer; distributing to the necessity of saints; given to hospitality" (Rom. 12:12-13). The greatest days of the Christian are enfolded between the sunrise and the sunset of these miracles of Calvary.

God's ideal does not allow His people to claim infallibility, but He does urge them to "press toward the mark for the prize of the high calling of God" (Phil. 3:14).

PRAYER: *Release us, O God, from the demands of the world, and help us to strive for that perfection that is found in You. Draw every faculty and desire of our soul toward You, that in all the times of our lives we may find the strength to be like Christ. We would be holy as You are holy. In Jesus' name. Amen.*

JUNE 23

For yet a little while, and the wicked shall not be ... But the meek shall inherit the earth.
(Ps. 37:10-11)

Longfellow felt the problem very keenly when he wrote, "For hate is strong, and mocks the song / Of peace on earth, goodwill to men." Here is one of the great mysteries of life that only God can understand: that good causes and good people should meet with constant opposition.

Where is there a good cause today that does not have some ugly head rise against it in opposition? Where is honesty? It has an enemy! Where is wholesomeness? It has an enemy! Name any good purpose, and there will arise an enemy of equal stature to cut it down. The great Head of the Church was "despised and rejected of men" (Isa. 53:3) and put to death with the spike and the sword.

The person who would be good must fight a battle. The person who would pray and intercede before God on bended knee must fight the evil forces of hell. The person who would lead a crusade for righteousness has the power of darkness unleashed against the endeavor.

Longfellow concluded, "The wrong shall fail, the right prevail." And history has recorded that opposition to God always means loss in the long run. Evil has never been at the table for the final victory, and good will never sign the bad man's check.

No one can break God's commandments, defy the spirit of Calvary, denounce the God of the Bible, and live a bad man's life, and be able to testify to a lasting peace in his heart. While we wait for the testimony, we can call an army that will testify that "the way of transgressors is hard" (Prov. 13:15).

God is always leading His people so that He might make them know the joy of victory in a far greater measure than they have ever known the pain of defeat.

PRAYER: *O God, we believe that Your goodness will live because You are good. We would live by Your example and rest our weary spirits in the care of One who loves and understands. Give us the assurance that the steps of a good person are ordered by You. In Jesus' name. Amen.*

■ **JUNE 24**

For verily I say unto you, Till heaven and earth pass, one jot or one tittle shall in no wise pass from the law, till all be fulfilled.
(Matt. 5:18)

When Jesus talked to the multitude and to the individual about the problems of their day, He was also speaking to my day and to yours. He was familiar with the circumstances of His time, but what about those days that lay out in the distant future?

One of the earliest sermons in my childhood memory was based on the text "Thou God seest me" (Gen. 16:13). It was very disturbing to me at the time. What made me uncomfortable then has become an anchor with time as the God of yesterday has been present in every crisis of life.

Jesus talked to His people as if His words carried the answers for any age and any era. He did not step in at some intermediate point. He brought originality in His concepts and left a "thus saith the Lord" in every conclusion.

He did not ask questions about any particular person or circumstance. He went beyond and said that everything must be judged by a divine purpose. Our "glass darkly" views and narrow controversies are set aside, and He goes to the basics where the real problem has taken cover.

Sin is not a modern discovery, nor is the human heart a development in today's expanse of knowledge. If we want to know what sin is, we must let Jesus take us back to the Garden. Time has confounded us with details, but sin must be placed in its proper perspective.

The Lamb slain before the foundation of the world was not an afterthought, not an accident in history, not something immeasurable in time, but a heavenly purpose without which no problem in any age can find an answer.

PRAYER: *O God, You know all things, for You know the end from the beginning. We cannot tell what a day will bring forth, and we have no way to reckon time—it belongs to You. Help us to know that we are working in a small corner of the universe of which You are the center. May this make a difference in our lives. In Jesus' name. Amen.*

JUNE 25

And they said unto them, Why have ye not brought him? The officers answered, Never man spake like this man.
(John 7:45-46)

Today I saw a Man!
His face glowed with intense radiance, and His eyes changed from pity to judgment and from judgment to pity. His voice was like thunder, yet it soothed like hidden music. Men and women followed Him, and little children tugged at His flowing garments. The lame, the blind, and the leper called Him "Healer." He was worshiped with all the grace of heaven yet hated with all the fury of hell.

He was a lonely Man and went away secretly to the mountains to pray through long, cold nights. On His knees, with face turned toward the starry canopy, His lips moved in speechless communication. He knelt alone as a Priest between God and His people.

He was very young, yet the aged looked to Him for wisdom. He spoke the language of the soul with an accent that none could imitate. He was called Jesus by the angels, but to others He was nameless, for no lips dared to call His name.

He was held in a tight grip. A silent Man in the presence of imperial power. A Man on a grim Cross built with savage delight and plunged into the stony ground with the joy of cruel triumph. An unresisting Victim with crown of thorns crushed on His temple and a spear thrust into His side.

Darkness. Winds. Thunder. A cry, "It is finished" (John 19:30). Praying fails. Fears prevail.

The Light comes back. Yonder on a mountain stands the risen Man. Descending clouds receive Him as a chariot into the heavens, where the angels sang His birth story.

And I cried, "Glory! Glory to the Son of God!"

PRAYER: *Almighty God, we have seen Him of whom Moses and the prophets wrote, even Jesus of Nazareth, Your divine Son. To Him we give, without reservation, our heart, our mind, our soul, our strength, and our hands—yea, our whole being. Accept us, now and for eternity. In Jesus' name. Amen.*

■ **JUNE 26**

Behold, I shew you a mystery . . . thanks be to God, which giveth us the victory through our Lord Jesus Christ.
(1 Cor. 15:51, 57)

Last summer a dear friend of mine was drowned while vacationing at the beach with his family. This week I met his young widow and held her in my arms while trying to console the grief. Amid the sobs she said to me, "A million times I have asked God, 'Why?' but it remains a mystery!"

I think I knew it all along, but I heard it again! There are insoluble problems in connection with our understanding of God. We try to have all mysteries dwarfed to the measure of our own wisdom. When we fail in the endeavor, doubt begins to argue against God to deny His loving providence.

Sometimes our condolence is lost in the cry of the broken heart, and the mystery veils God's purpose. But first of all and last of all we must know that God does right, or He is not God. We must not look at the incomplete pieces as a basis for judging the wisdom and righteousness of the Almighty.

When I think of God, who is "glorious in power . . . doing wonders" (Exod. 15:6, 11), prayer is clothed in a broader meaning, and sin takes on a deadlier blackness. But out of the wilderness of sorrow He makes a path to the city where every tear shall be wiped away.

When language fails and sentences are broken by choking sobs and life loses its meaning in mystery, it just might be that God is drawing us closer to an altar where He intends to meet us for greater meaning.

Still a far greater mystery! Love says, "Come unto me . . . I will give you rest" (Matt. 11:28); and in accepting this invitation, we can find God's greatest answer.

PRAYER: *Somehow, O God, You allow us to see glimpses of the mystery of life. You have promised to make known to us someday the meaning of darkness and pain, awful tears and sudden heartaches, with all the tragedies of life. Until then, hold us steady in our misunderstanding of it all. In Jesus' name. Amen.*

JUNE 27

For in the time of trouble he shall hide me in his pavilion: in the secret of his tabernacle shall he hide me; he shall set me up upon a rock.
(Ps. 27:5)

There are some experiences in life that can never be forgotten. How often we hear the expression, "I shall never forget . . ." then stand by and listen to a supporting tale of woe. Often the terror has gone, but the shadow is still there. The victory has been won, but the sounds of battle boom on forever. No one can go through life without encountering some of these rough experiences at some time or in some way.

Have you ever stopped to think that the most jovial person in the crowd just might be trying to find a way through this same wilderness? I think Paul knew it and urged the Galatians to "bear . . . one another's burdens, and so fulfil the law of Christ" (6:2). I think he is saying to us, "Never offer a prayer selfishly, but always think of the one who is carrying the heavier burden."

Was it not in these places that we received the most precious touch from God? Can you remember how He looked at you in your dark moments, with no blaze of condemnation in His eye, but in the reach of love rescued you from the terror of the way? We owe much to the wilderness that made us afraid, for we found God there.

Wherever the crowd and however jovial the sound, get beneath the charade and you will find broken hearts, burdened lives, and sorrow-laden souls looking for a way out of the dark shadows.

The Christian life is a tribute to the power and the grace of God. We stagger under great burdens. We lose our way. We take wrong roads. But in the darkness we find a hand—bruised and nail-scarred. It will lead us through.

I shall never forget the wilderness! I met God there.

PRAYER: *We do not need to tell You, O God, that sometimes we pass through rough places and can't seem to find our way. Make us to know that our way is under the control of Your loving leadership. Give us the strength of those whose hearts have been touched by Your hand, and save us from despair. In Jesus' name. Amen.*

JUNE 28

> O let me not wander from thy commandments.
> Thy word have I hid in mine heart, that I
> might not sin against thee.
> (Ps. 119:10-11)

God's Book has a message for every condition of life, and it speaks to the need of every day. The message comes from eternity, clothed with "thus saith the Lord," and stands without apology, asking that it be heard.

Never has there been a worthwhile person so great in his own wisdom or so sufficient in his own power that he has not recognized the need for a message direct from a higher wisdom. A marvelous faculty is set within the heart of us all that knows right from wrong, the noble from the mean, and the noise from music. And the reach of the soul is for the higher rather than the lower, the greater over the lesser; it is unsatisfied until it finds God. It is this that gives the Bible its place in the ages, for it speaks to this need.

God knows every hour of the day. He knows the pulsebeat of every moment. We have no sorrow to tell Him, or joy to express, that He has not known from the beginning. He has spoken deeper words to the human heart than ever were spoken to it by any other voice.

The Psalmist felt the assurance of God around him, and he expressed his delight in many ways. He said he could "run against a troop" or "leap over a wall," for his God was "a shield to all who trust in Him" (Ps. 18:29-30, NKJV). And again, "In the name of our God we will set up our banners" (20:5). All of this and more can we do, but it is in God's name and by the power of His Word.

We can stand tall in this faith, for it sets the soul free. "The Lord is King for ever and ever" (Ps. 10:16), and His Word is the final reply to every need in His world.

PRAYER: *Heavenly Father, we thank You in this evil day for Your Word, the Book of God. Help us to search it, study it, and make it familiar for our need and a wise counselor in our daily living. May it become part of us as an answer to every temptation and a place of confidence in the trials of life. In Jesus' name. Amen.*

JUNE 29

But seek ye first the kingdom of God, and his righteousness; and all these things shall be added unto you.
(Matt. 6:33)

A little boy in elementary school had just finished looking over a medical school dissertation by his older brother. The language and content was a bit deeper than his training had prepared him to absorb. Looking for some common ground on which to base his assessment in a positive response, he made the honest comment, "Well, I know what 'is' means!"

How much like the elementary student we are in our relationship to the wisdom of heaven! It was the big bunch of little questions that some people poured out on Jesus when He was here. The religious leaders were more concerned over His eating with publicans and sinners than in the Bread of Heaven that He talked to them about. They were more confounded by His healing on the Sabbath than His being the Lord of the Sabbath.

Jesus was judged critically by small inquiries, and great occasions were belittled by lack of vision. To their little questions Jesus answered to the ages, and they could not absorb the meaning. Their questions expressed momentary concerns. His answers spread beyond the immediate occasion to His cause and kingdom for all time.

There are those that are least in the kingdom of heaven, and there are those that are the greatest—but all are in the Kingdom. He that is least in God's kingdom is greater than he that is greatest outside. Whatever the level, God looks for the honest intent and will always supply an answer that will satisfy.

God does not ask whether we are giants in the Kingdom, or whether we are children with limited vision. He will never refuse the honest inquiry.

PRAYER: *O God, there is so little of this life of ours that we understand! We cannot see enough of it to make an honest judgment. Our trust is in You, the living God, who is working out His immeasurable purposes in every area of our lives. Give us the power of a life that is turned over to You. In Jesus' name. Amen.*

■ JUNE 30

Go ye therefore . . . teaching them to observe all things whatsoever I have commanded you: and lo, I am with you alway, even unto the end of the world.
(Matt. 28:19-20)

As I walked across Boston Commons one afternoon, I met people asking for money and saw others lying on the grass, too far gone to beg. An ambulance picked up a man lying unconscious under the elms. An elderly lady lay on the park bench beside paper bags holding her earthly belongings, while a blind man stood at the subway door with his tin cup. I watched hundreds of people in fine clothes pass by unconscious of the need.

In the world that Jesus passed through, He encountered the deaf, the dumb, the blind, the poor, the brokenhearted, the weary, the hungry, and the helpless. There were those in His world, comfortable in their nice homes, who shut out every cry of distress.

When Jesus came into a city, the blind knew He was there, the deaf recognized His presence, and the lamp of hope burned in every window of despair. He condemned the priest and the Levite for their selfish response to the needy but praised the Samaritan who lingered to redeem a life from destruction.

The work of Jesus Christ for the needy does not take a large book to make itself clear to us. We need to follow His footsteps through the highways of need to find the blind, the deaf, and the poor. We must not be afraid of the obedience of love that opens our hearts to the needs of our world. For Jesus the healing of the heart was of greater importance and a greater work of love than walking or hearing or seeing.

Every good thing we see in Christ is an obligation laid upon us if we are His followers. The urgency upon us is still, "Go . . . and tell" (Matt. 28:7).

PRAYER: *O God, You are always healing the bodies of Your people. We do not have any disease that is outside the touch of Your hand. We thank You for the quietness of soul in the midst of earth's great tumult. Here is the greater healing, and here we come for the final salvation of our being. In Jesus' name. Amen.*

JULY 1

To day if ye will hear his voice, harden not your heart, as in the provocation, and as in the day of temptation in the wilderness.
(Ps. 95:7-8)

Today I heard a mother praying for her children who had grown up and gone away from home. Her prayer was, "O God, keep them in Your will just for today!" But the interesting thing is that this was her prayer for them yesterday, and I suspect she will make the same prayer for them tomorrow morning. This is really the command of the Bible, "Thou shalt keep . . . his commandments . . . this day, that it may go well with thee" (Deut. 4:40).

This is not far from the prayer that Jesus taught His disciples to pray, "Give us this day our daily bread" (Matt. 6:11). And is not this the strength of Christianity, for its appeal has always been a here-and-now experience. Christianity has always been judged by its declared intention regarding the present state of an individual's experience with God.

Christianity has never made homes unhappy. It is judged by the Christ who founded it and by the good people who have made it work. No other religion can excel Christianity, for it holds homes together and makes its people strong, courageous, disciplined, and not afraid of tomorrow.

The greatest heritage any person can possibly have is to be born in a Christian atmosphere; be trained by Christian parents; be brought up under the influence of Christian ministries; live under the light of the Cross; be educated by Christian teachers; and enjoy the liberties of a Christian civilization.

How sad to see some boy or girl who has been prayed over by Christian parents and loved with all Christian love turn against the morality of Christ and say, "I have found a better way!"

No person has ever found a way that surpasses the way of the Christ of Calvary. On this we shall all be judged!

PRAYER: *O God, whether our days be many or few, may they all be given to You, and may they be lived in the strength of Your divinity. Help us spend our days here so that there will be created within us a burning desire to know the things You have in store for us tomorrow. May this day be Yours, lived out with Your richest blessings. In Jesus' name. Amen.*

■ JULY 2

Lead me in thy truth, and teach me: for thou art the God of my salvation; on thee do I wait all the day.
(Ps. 25:5)

For those things that are behind we are enabled to remember. And we can view with great accuracy those things that have already taken place. We have not been given the ability to know the future; we are simply told to "Watch." We cannot tell the time, nor the way, nor the specifics of events yet to come or the way of the enemy in tomorrow's battles.

God gives us one day at a time, and each day is set in its own circumstances. We must not trifle with the moments or allow the ideals of God for the day to be smothered in our own vain ambitions. Paul set the stage for us: "But God forbid that I should glory, save in the cross of our Lord Jesus Christ, by whom the world is crucified unto me, and I unto the world" (Gal. 6:14).

A friend of mine used to pray in the morning, "O God, today is a new page in life, white as snow, and without blot or blur—help us keep it clean all day. Amen." Isn't it good that God does give us new days as places to begin again. We begin at the top and write, line by line, down to the bottom of the page. How carefully we must try to write without a blot or blur.

What treasures God entrusts us with for each new day! We have seen the Son of God. We have watched Him die on the Cross. We have heard His welcome to pardon and peace. We have not despised the Blood of the everlasting covenant. We look forward to His coming to receive His Church for eternity. This is God's today—and it belongs to us.

Today every move can be pure, every impulse can be for good, and all our love can be under the direction of heaven.

PRAYER: *Sometimes we wonder, O God, at the time it takes to make up a day, a year, or a life. Sometimes it is long. Sometimes it is very short. Yet we cannot tell what it is. In our journey in time help us to listen to Your voice and keep Your commandments. Do not let us forget that we are also creatures of Your eternity. In Jesus' name. Amen.*

JULY 3 ■

For what is a man profited, if he shall gain the whole world, and lose his own soul? or what shall a man give in exchange for his soul?
(Matt. 16:26)

Recently I came across a paper outlining changes that had taken place within the last number of years. The writer was born before television, penicillin, polio shots, plastics, and contact lenses. Numerous other things were given in detail that make up our present-day civilization. The amazing conclusion was that without all the deprivation people had been able to survive very well.

The truth was missing that our civilization has turned human life into a daily warfare. We live in the midst of contention, burglary, murderings, and fierce conflicts of every kind. All of this while God has placed His law in our midst, calling us to see life in its sacredness, and telling us that we are temples of the Holy Ghost.

God's boundaries are still set around human life today in spite of our advanced style of living. His written and unwritten laws still have their rewards and penalties. And when choices have to be made and integrity is on the line, there should be no hesitation as to which way the judgment is made.

A long time ago the one truly good Man asked the question, "What is a man profited, if he shall gain the whole world, and lose his own soul?" Our civilization is forcing us to answer, and the price of victory is often high. Too often it is forcing a sacrifice of something too sacred to lose and impossible to replace. The greater question in life does not involve things but, "What is God's highest purpose for me in my life?"

Even today God allows people the desires of their hearts, but at the same time He sends leanness into their souls.

PRAYER: *O God, we pray that our whole life may be set to the music of Your will and to the purpose and victory of Your divine planning. The powers that rule the air and direct the world would destroy us forever. Our victory is in the Cross, where battles have never been lost or victories forfeited. Lead us through our brief days here, and hold us steady. In Jesus' name. Amen.*

JULY 4

And Joshua said unto all the people, Behold, this stone shall be a witness unto us; for it hath heard all the words of the Lord which he spake unto us.
(Josh. 24:27)

Names without faces! Some long and difficult to pronounce, others simple and without meaning to us. Yet they serve to remind us how great human history has been and the place that every name had to occupy. They show us how vividly separated everything is in that which goes to make up our day. But they remind us that this great family of souls are all the children and heritage of God—and we are part of that family.

Names, only names! And we sense the impossibility of association with them in any common thought of worship.

We could learn from the early followers of God. They delighted to begin with Abram and lead on toward Canaan land. They never forgot their affliction in Egypt or their triumph over Pharaoh. They remembered the pillars of cloud and of fire in the days and nights of their need. The grandeur of the Sinai and the thundering voice of God was ever in their hearts and minds. The Sabbath with its sacred rest was not forgotten. God gave them kingdoms and nations and lands and blessings as their history rolled on, and they remembered!

We lose standing ground when our association with our history becomes blurred and dim. We need a sense of belonging to the people of God. We need to walk with Abraham to the mountain, and around Jericho with Joshua. We need to stand with Daniel in his purpose to be true, and to hear the lament of Jeremiah for his people. We need to walk the hill of Calvary and go with hearts aglow to the Resurrection tomb.

All of this and more we need to do, for we are part of God's great family, whatever the name happens to be!

PRAYER: *O God, we pray that You will establish us in the great truths of eternity. Help us to learn from the men who knew You best and to see the Cross of suffering as well as the crown of victory. Make us worthy of our standing with You as we look for the eternal meaning in the richness of Your revelation. In Jesus' name. Amen.*

JULY 5 ■

Depart from evil, and do good; seek peace, and pursue it. The eyes of the Lord are upon the righteous, and his ears are open unto their cry.
(Ps. 34:14-15)

Did you ever realize how difficult it was for Jesus to say no? That cold, harsh word did not fall freely from His lips in response to the human heart that asked a question of Him. With all the sympathy of love Jesus wants to say yes to every human desire and to every yearning, loving spirit. But when He said no, it was a final and firm assertion, and He meant to stand on His pronouncement.

Jesus never said no to the sick, the weary, the brokenhearted, the bruised, the helpless, or the wounded spirit. He never said no to the one who came before Him in the innocence of a little child. But standing in front of an evil and adulterous generation seeking signs for His condemnation, He could say, "No, there shall no sign be given." He who would much rather say yes to every human prayer finds it necessary to say no.

Jesus never came to satisfy the mere intellect of any individual. The scribes and the Pharisees, in asking for a sign, were seeking intellectual gratification as another link in the chain of arguments against Him. The gospel of Jesus Christ still has nothing to say to the stiff and blind intellect in its godless pursuit to destroy.

"The secret of the Lord is with them that fear him" (Ps. 25:14). The meek, the tired, the worn, the humble, the honest heart, along with the mourning and tearful, have an open avenue to the compassionate heart of God. Jesus Christ has always kept His answers for the meek, the childlike, and those who know Him as Lord and Master.

He has a positive answer today for the "Whosoever shall do the will of my Father which is in heaven" (Matt. 12:50).

PRAYER: *O God, we have tried in our own intellect to find peace, but we have failed in our vain pursuits. We long for true happiness that can be found only in You, the living God. Our hunger has brought us to Your table, where none are turned away, and to the heavenly fountain, where all honest longing is filled. In You our souls are completely satisfied. In Jesus' name. Amen.*

■ JULY 6

> There is no fear in love; but perfect love casteth out fear: because fear hath torment. He that feareth is not made perfect in love. We love him, because he first loved us.
> (1 John 4:18-19)

Love is the greatest word in the literature of any language, creed, or country. In all ages and in all places it has created new heavens and a new earth and has written a literature that no eye but its own can read and fully understand. Love works with the things we know and gives new meaning to the mundane and new purpose to the ordinary.

The object of love for the Son of God was the kingdom of heaven, and He compared it with everyday things. It is like a sower, a goodly pearl, treasure hidden in the field, a grain of mustard seed, and virgins going forth to meet the bridegroom. Through these simple things He tried to explain to us the Kingdom on which He was to build His empire of love.

Jesus did not live merely in parable and poetry, but He brought His love out in the open where the common people lived. He laid an obligation on all whom He met, and the challenge was, in the words of James, "To him that knoweth to do good, and doeth it not, to him it is sin" (4:17). We are to be transformed by love, for it is impossible to see Christ without this work of love.

He also showed us how this love works. "Not every one that saith unto me, Lord, Lord, shall enter into the kingdom of heaven; but he that doeth the will of my Father which is in heaven" (Matt. 7:21). We may go with Him to the Mount of Transfiguration; but when we choose to stay there and build tabernacles, He shows us a cold and heartless world waiting for a display of love to their needy souls.

Life is real, it is tragic, and it is sad; and it does long for love in action from God and from His people.

PRAYER: *O God, we come to Your throne by the only way possible—by the way of love. Because of a love You have created in our hearts, we cannot be content with the darkness. Our longing is toward the morning, where we stand and partake of hymns of praise that extol Your love and grace. We cling to that love that will not let us go. In Jesus' name. Amen.*

JULY 7 ■

After that he poureth water into a basin, and began to wash the disciples' feet, and to wipe them with the towel wherewith he was girded.
(John 13:5)

He stood before his people on Sunday morning with white shirt, tie, and suit in immaculate condition and with shoes shined to match. In the middle of that week he was seen on his hands and knees digging out a blocked sewer for a widowed lady of his congregation. What a vast difference in appearance, yet in purpose the first and the last are related.

Maybe Paul had something like this in mind when he talked about being all things to all men that he might be able to save some (1 Cor. 9:22). Probably he would say that the man who was willing to dig in the gutter on Thursday would be a better man in the pulpit on Sunday.

The principle works anyway. The one who cannot weep and feel deeply for a need can never do any great and permanent work in a congregation. The one who is not willing to fast can never claim an effective ministry for God. The one who will not pray and ally himself with the omnipotence of God can never stand with courage in the heat of the battle against sin. The one who cannot hear the cry of the hungry can never hear the "Well done!" of the One who fed the 5,000.

Circumstances develop people, and there is no final exercise in God's economy. The Bible principle is that he who would save his life must know that he will lose it. He who would have all things added to him must seek first the kingdom of God and his righteousness.

This is the spirit of the Man who girded himself with the towel and stooped to wash the feet of His disciples. He said that whoever "will be the chiefest, shall be servant of all" (Mark 10:44).

PRAYER: *Undertake for us, O God, in all things, for we would be servants in Your congregation. You have made us wonders to ourselves and mysteries that have no answer in time. We would serve You with all faithfulness, love, and sincerity. Our prayer is that You will accept our offering. In Jesus' name. Amen.*

JULY 8

For in him we live, and move, and have our being; as certain also of your own poets have said, For we are also his offspring.
(Acts 17:28)

There is a sense in which each one of us lived in the days and times of every Bible event recorded in the Book. We measure everything by our own experience and consciousness. We live in every command, every blessing, every defeat, and every victory as we see them develop throughout the Bible.

There is a powerful gospel here. People cried out to God, "'Is there no balm in Gilead; is there no physician there?' [Jer. 8:22]. Is there no love in heaven? Where is the Almighty power and infinite wisdom to rule the world?" To this cry God showed us the Cross, the Savior and a way out of it all. A faith from the hunger of a helpless heart saw a God who is able to do the "exceeding abundantly above all that we ask or think" (Eph. 3:20).

It has not been by power of the mind or the strength of the hand that the greatest battles in life have been fought and won. We fight with the heart. We live with the heart. We return to battle because of the inspiration of the heart. No person can lay a fisted hand upon heaven's pillars and challenge the power of the Almighty.

The ashes of Nebuchadnezzar's furnace would bear the remains of three brave men, Jericho's wall would still be standing, and the roar of Goliath would still be heard in the land if there was not "the heart" that "believeth unto righteousness" (Rom. 10:10).

Who can roll back the purposes of God for His people? He has vowed that His word would not return to Him void. "And the Lord said, . . . As I live, all the earth shall be filled with the glory of the Lord" (Num. 14:20-21). Our hearts are content to leave it there!

PRAYER: *O God, we thank You for the sacred things that fill the aching void of the heart and make the little great and turn the insignificant into the sublime. This is the work of the gospel. This is the miracle of faith. And it is Your way. Through this gospel we accept and we believe. In Jesus' name. Amen.*

JULY 9 ■
But God hath chosen the foolish things of the world to confound the wise; and God hath chosen the weak things of the world to confound the things which are mighty.
(1 Cor. 1:27)

We used to sing a chorus in Sunday School: "Shamgar had an oxgoad. David had a sling. Dorcas had a needle. Rahab had a string." Then we filled in with Samson and Moses and anyone else that would rhyme. The conclusion was that each simple item was used for some outstanding work for God.

I always got nervous when we sang it because the teacher would turn the lesson against our delinquent behavior and lack of progress in memory work and Bible study. She insisted that the results determined everything and chided us that with a simple oxgoad used for God, Shamgar stood rejoicing over 600 defeated foes. For a long time I held a grudge against this woman for showing us up when we had so many advantages.

Is not this the best answer for the church to a criticizing world, when souls are converted, homes are held together, lives are pulled out of the mire, fear is driven away, and new families are finding God? The church may well point to such results and be stirred to keep on going, rather than to succumb to the sting of criticism of those who pay more attention to the instruments than to the results. Has not God chosen the weak things of the world to throw down the things that are mighty?

What meaner instrument can there be than the wooden Cross on which Christ died? Has it not pleased God by the foolishness of preaching of the Cross to save them that believe? Are not the highest things hidden from the wise and the prudent and revealed unto babes? God's way is that no flesh should glory in His presence.

And the cross of Christ will stand when all else fails—it is for eternity!

PRAYER: *Almighty God, how grateful we are that You give power to the faint, and to them that have no might You increase strength. You gather the lambs in Your arms and gently lead those that are with young. We would find our confidence in Your omnipotence. In Jesus' name. Amen.*

■ JULY 10

And the Lord God called unto Adam, and said unto him, Where art thou?
(Gen. 3:9)

One of the great attributes of human nature is the quality of the inquiring mind. When the child begins to ask questions, the parents may be hard put for an answer; but there is joy in observing an alert young mind. "Why, Daddy, . . . ?" can go on endlessly as one question suggests another. But it is a sign of intellectual progress, and Daddy's ego swells with pride as he reports the questions that Junior has posed.

How soon in life the child comes to a question that Daddy cannot answer! There is a question-asking that is in vain, for it touches on the impossible. There are questions that reach the eternal boundary where it is written, "Hitherto shalt thou come, but no further" (Job 38:11).

The devil comes to the heart and the mind with subtle and vicious suggestions. He asked the first question in the Bible, "Yea, hath God said, Ye shall not eat of every tree of the garden?" (Gen. 3:1). So simple his question, but so full of mischief; and it fostered discontent and led to further inquiry and the Fall. He will ask questions about every sincere prayer you ever pray, every decision you will ever make, and with a black finger of interrogation he will mark every word you ever speak.

God has given His people the power to counter with questions to His almightiness. Moses asked, "When I go who will I say sent me? Give me a name!" And what an answer! "Tell them, 'I Am That I Am!'" (See Exod. 3:13-14.) The inquiry was sincerity from an honest heart, and God provided an answer.

Probably our greatest question will be, "Lord, what wilt thou have me to do?" (Acts 9:6). God will always give an answer!

PRAYER: *O God, we cannot see enough of this life of ours to make an honest judgment. We live by faith and not by sight, and our trust is in the living God, who is working out His immeasurable purposes in this world. The only power that can reach out and give an answer to the impossibilities of life is the gospel of Jesus Christ. Here is our hope. In Jesus' name. Amen.*

JULY 11

And let us not be weary in well doing: for in due season we shall reap, if we faint not.
(Gal. 6:9)

This week I sat with a young man who had tried six new jobs in the last six months and at the present time is unemployed. He did not inquire within himself for an answer to his problem, but he placed abundant blame on each place of employment. He was always hopeful at the beginning of each new job but was equally critical when he dropped out of each responsibility.

The problem he faced was that he did not have the stamina to go manfully through when the initial enthusiasm broke down in the process.

We must accept the solemn fact that life is a process. It is more than an enthusiastic beginning with a dull ending; it is more than a cradle and a grave. The "in-betweenness" determines whether life takes the throne of victory or ends in the gutter of defeat. There are streams that must be bridged, and mountains to climb or to tunnel through. There are gates to guard, roads to block, and new trails to make. This is life!

The process takes on a different aspect when viewed from the end of the road. There have been many narrow escapes. There have been difficulties to surmount. Many nights have been long, and many days did not have much sunshine. Sorrow often waited at the gate, and discouragement vied for companionship. But the process included the all-covering and ever-shining mercy of God. And there were pools in unexpected places. There were divine triumphs to gladden life and to give inspiration and courage in the dark and cloudy days.

My greatest advice: Live in the process of your life so that you can point back to your yesterdays and find God there!

PRAYER: *O God, we owe our whole life to Your faithfulness to us. When we were discouraged and life was full of terror and meaninglessness, You showed us a better way. We were lost and You found us. The moment of pain was consumed by the awareness of Your presence. Today we look back in wonder and say, "You led us all the way!" We thank You in Jesus' name. Amen.*

JULY 12

And he hath put a new song in my mouth, even praise unto our God: many shall see it, and fear, and shall trust in the Lord.
(Ps. 40:3)

The night was dark and the road was long, but in the darkness I could hear a song. My friend said, "When I sing, I am not afraid!" And his song was so beautiful that the enemy would have to stop and listen and then move off into the shadows.

One commentator, writing about the Psalmist, said that he often sang himself out of trouble. Every person does not have the gift of song, and to sing along the road of trouble is not a universal possibility. Musical notes lend themselves to expressions of joy and victory as well as to trouble and fear. And the dark places along the road accept the discords and create a music that heaven can understand.

The message of God would seem to be, "Sing or speak out all that is in your heart; keep nothing back. If trouble has come, or if joy has spread flowers along your way, pour it out in the most expressive terms possible to the soul."

God always encourages frankness. If the way is dark and you are afraid, spare nothing in your description to God. God will listen to an honest expression, whatever it happens to be, from the fearful or the happy heart. The Psalmist complained of neglect and forgetfulness as often as he extolled the wonders of God from a heart full of happiness.

My friend's song kept his mind off the darkness that made him afraid. When a person can look at God and sing of His wonders, the enemy fades into insignificance and is no longer a threat. A song of triumph always comes from the heart that is filled with the Spirit of God.

A song in the heart is the light of the morning, the crown of the noonday, and the star of the night. And the music from the heart is always sweet to the ear of God.

PRAYER: *O God, You give Your people songs in the nighttime. You go with us in the morning and give us shade for the noonday. Our song is large and full of meaning, for we remember the mercies of heaven. Accept our song of praise, as it comes from our heart to Your throne. In Jesus' name. Amen.*

JULY 13

I thank thee, O Father, Lord of heaven and earth, because thou hast hid these things from the wise and prudent, and hast revealed them unto babes.
(Matt. 11:25)

We reach for big words and big ideas as one tries to impress another by greatness of thought and depth of understanding. This probably has its place, for some minds have delved into areas of thought and action beyond the reach of the ordinary mind.

There must be something that we have missed in our grasp for greatness. When Jesus called a few men to be His disciples, He did not call those of intellectual greatness, and He did not surround himself with the philosophy and culture of His time. He called 12 who had been fishermen and men of ordinary stature, who probably could not have answered any of the great questions of their day.

Then He placed a little child in the midst of His generation and said, "He that is most like this little child is the greatest in the family of God." He disappoints our calculations and He blinds our wisdom, but our childlikeness can ask, and there is nothing that His hand will hold back.

The salvation Jesus came to bring does not come through our intellectual capacity. He saw in the child a mind that is open to receive without question from God, and a love that is answered by God's love.

God's best things are hidden from our cleverness, and His revelation is not the result of our ingenuity. His best things are hidden "from the wise and prudent, and . . . revealed . . . unto babes."

How can we understand that when we are weak, then are we the strongest; and when we are most like little children, then we are most like the angels of God. This is the message that Jesus brought to us from heaven.

PRAYER: *Make every one of us like little children, O God. This is the greatest prayer that we can make. We would live by Your power, and because of Your love and tenderness and daily grace, we would become dependent upon You. May we learn from the little child that Jesus would not turn away. In Jesus' name. Amen.*

■ JULY 14

> Can a woman forget her sucking child, that she should not have compassion on the son of her womb? yea, they may forget, yet will I not forget thee.
> (Isa. 49:15)

The word "forget" can be one of the most beautiful words in any language, yet it can put terror in the soul of the bravest. God has made the hearts of millions to rejoice by the assurance of sins being forgiven and forgotten. Others have gone into eternity in despair, because they were sure they had been forgotten by God.

The Psalmist faced this possibility in his thinking. He is afraid that his prayers are not getting into heaven but are lost somewhere in the darkness. His soul is full of trouble, and his strength has given way, and he is sure that his grave will mark the place of a forgotten man. He bows his head and in grief cries out to God about His forgetfulness!

There is a silence that is terrible! There is a fear that our names may be blotted out of the book of life (Rev. 3:5). There are days when prayers fall back to earth, and heaven closes the door on our weak faith. There are times when life is a burning pain, and the grave would speak to us of an end of our existence.

The Christian message is that Omnipotence finds no place in all its infinity for sin. And all sin that is forgiven is forgotten. Let us never suppose for any reason that God has forgotten the person He has forgiven, nor does God forget that person's most humble service to Him. So great is our God that He will never forget even a cup of cold water given to a disciple in Christ's name.

Through a process known to us by the beautiful name "forgiveness," there comes a state in the divine mind that is known by the human word "forgotten." This is the sweetest message that heaven ever sent to earth.

PRAYER: *O God, our life is shortened day by day, and every pulsing throb robs us of our brief heritage of time. Help us to think of the purpose of it all, then the way to Calvary will be buried in forgetfulness in the joy of heaven. This will make it all worthwhile. In Jesus' name. Amen.*

JULY 15 ■

Neither pray I for these alone, but for them also which shall believe on me through their word; that they all may be one; as thou, Father, art in me, and I in thee.
(John 17:20-21)

The man came one day to tune our piano. He took it all apart and exposed the inner workings to the family, who watched with eager interest. He pointed out all the wires, long and short, stout and thin, and called them the church. He demonstrated the disharmony when everything was out of tune, and even gave position names to some of the discordant pieces.

The moment came when all was reassembled, and he sat down and played the piano, tuned by the professional ear. He looked up with a smile of satisfaction and said, "Preacher, this is how it should be—harmony!" and continued his discourse on a proper church. I listened. I hope I learned!

Harmony. This is how it should be! A togetherness. Unity! Didn't Jesus pray that His people should be one as He and His Father were One?

The deepest meaning of this spirit is unity with Christ. Oneness with the Son of God. Identification with Jesus Christ in spirit, purpose, and mission. A love and trust that sees the best in every person. A love that recognizes Christ in the Christian. It is the Church on its knees. It is not formal; it is spiritual. When the spiritual concept is lost, we become as discordant strings on a piano.

Spiritual unity is the only thing that can permit honest diversity in the church. One key differs from another on the board, but the whole is in harmony. How wonderfully Jesus Christ can develop human nature in its possibilities of working in harmony with the plans of God.

Unity means many people and many ways of doing things, but only one motive—to serve God and to answer to His ministry.

PRAYER: *O God, our aim is that there might be a unity of spirit in our relationship with You and with others. As life reveals itself to each of us in different ways, may Your light shine in our minds and hearts, making us all channels for Your will and for Your purpose. In Jesus' name. Amen.*

■ JULY 16

The kingdom of heaven is like to a grain of mustard seed, which a man took, and sowed in his field: which indeed is the least of all seeds.
(Matt. 13:31-32)

Jesus Christ spoke to the people of His day in a gospel that was meant to be understood. Volumes of explanations have been written since to try to explain what He meant when He said what He did. The teaching on the kingdom of heaven was to be grasped by the human mind and reproduced by human speech and in human life. For what other reason would Jesus have left these great words to a group of unlearned fishermen?

To be sure, it is not given to every person to understand equally His revealed truth. But is not this the rule of all of life? He never meant for the little sparrow to fly as high as the eagle, nor for the tiny mouse to run with the lion. God wants us to keep within the limits of our own understanding and capabilities.

Jesus must have meant for His words to be understood, for His command was, "Go ye into all the world, and preach the gospel to every creature" (Mark 16:15). In the proportion that understanding and wisdom and power is given, we are to go and tell and teach. And beneath every bit of human effort there will be found a rock of divine wisdom, because He also said, "I am with you alway, even unto the end" (Matt. 28:20).

Our understanding of His Word may be lost in the greater calling of being a witness. People will take knowledge of His followers, "that they had been with Jesus" and learned of Him (Acts 4:13). The one who has been with Him will bear the heart of His message and a testimony of His presence.

We are to speak by that which we know, for by this does God's kingdom come, and His will is done on earth as it is done in heaven.

PRAYER: *When we go out into this old world, O God, may we go as men and women who have seen You and have been sent by You. May our lives be a living witness to the message we have heard from You. And may Your message be to every soul a whisper not made by human breath. In Jesus' name. Amen.*

JULY 17

And he said unto them, The sabbath was made for man, and not man for the sabbath: therefore the Son of man is Lord also of the sabbath.
(Mark 2:27-28)

The question came up in Sunday School, "Why do we make so much of the Sabbath when Jesus never kept it at all?" This always makes for a lively discussion, and the question is usually asked by those whose preference would be for a less binding schedule.

It is true that Jesus did not treat the Jewish Sabbath according to the wishes of the Pharisees. And the controversy over the day occupied a large portion of their differences. Jesus Christ was getting ready to establish a Sabbath that would override the ceremonial custom of His day. He saw that the Pharisees were also breaking the Sabbath in their very act of keeping it.

God has laid His hand on one day and called it His. We are asked to set aside that day to worship Him. We are asked to rest in Him. We must not steal His Sabbath away from Him or deface it for our own gain or greed. Works of necessity must be done, but if more time is required for personal reasons, it should not be stolen from God's time.

Jesus said His Sabbath was made for man. But He did not say that man could do what he pleased with it, and He did not intend for man to destroy it. It was set apart for man. It is God's gift to the human race. It is a hint of heaven initiated on earth when God and man meet—alone!

The Sabbath is also the Lord's Day. "This is the day which the Lord hath made," and we should "rejoice and be glad in it" (Ps. 118:24). In a sense it is a resurrection day when the morning opens with angels and empty tomb and risen lives and offerings of peace.

Jesus Christ gave it to us, and we should keep it holy as He intended it to be!

PRAYER: *O God, we thank You for the Sabbath Day. It is a day of triumph. The grave was robbed of its victory by the rising of Christ from the dead. Now He has gone on to make us free forever. This is our Sabbath! Keep us in that day until the end of time and the beginning of heaven. In Jesus' name. Amen.*

JULY 18

And as Jesus passed forth from thence, he saw a man, named Matthew, sitting at the receipt of custom: and he saith unto him, Follow me. And he arose, and followed him.
(Matt. 9:9)

One day a lady came to the church with a hand open for a touch of friendship and a heart open for a touch of love. She had survived in a world of people whose back was turned toward her, and she had made her way by the strength of her character and the will to keep going. Sorrow and sadness had plagued a big part of her life, and tears were often in her eyes. The people opened their hearts to her needs until she became one with them and testified to the love of a Christ she had come to know.

Does this scene not harmonize with those things that Jesus said and did while He was with us in the flesh? Matthew's statement was, "And as Jesus passed forth from thence, he saw a man." He saw a possibility, an undeveloped seed, a hand reaching out, an aching heart—He saw Matthew.

Jesus saw a man in his working clothes—a publican, a tax collector, a man facing Him from the opposite court, for Matthew was not a likely candidate for His message. He also saw Zacchaeus, a little man who was to stand tall like a king. He saw a woman who was amazed at His knowledge of her past. And to the very least and meanest He gave the invitation, "Follow me!"

Jesus never hurled His omniscience against anyone, nor did He lay His mighty hand on anyone to take them against their will. His invitation is always inspired by love, and the act of obedience to follow Him is done with all the spontaneity of love.

It is in the power of the Church, under the blessing and special call of God, to reach out a hand of love to those who would follow Him today!

PRAYER: *We bless Your name, O God, for every church that opens its door to those who are seeking a touch of love and friendship. They cannot find satisfaction elsewhere, and they come to Your house so that they might find a haven and a home. This is the work of Your Church; help us to do our share to make it so. In Jesus' name. Amen.*

JULY 19 ■

That he might present it to himself a glorious church, not having spot, or wrinkle, or any such thing; but that it should be holy and without blemish.
(Eph. 5:27)

Jesus loved the Church! He was absolutely positive of its survival. He defied the powers of hell in the battle against that which He had come to establish. The Cross was the mark of its redemption through which He proposed to present His Church to the Father without spot or wrinkle. A glorious Church!

Through the years it has faced the unleashed cruelty of a defiant hell in opposition to the mission of Jesus Christ. It has been persecuted and hated, has suffered all manner of distress and evil, has been pursued by an enemy thirsty for the blood of its martyrs, and has been in a battle without pause day or night. It has suffered every variety of pain, indignity, humiliation, and loss.

In our peaceful times we are thankful for our solitude and are happy that our churches meet at undisturbed and specified hours. How easy to forget that the sanctuary whose security we enjoy is founded in blood, and the walls that contain our hymns of praise are built on the bones of heroes, valiant soldiers and standard-bearers of the Cross.

While we value peace and are thankful for our security and praise ourselves for our possessions and contributions, we should thank God for those who counted not their lives dear to themselves so that they might stand tall for God and for His Church!

The great day of the Church is established in heaven, when right shall reign, we will see justice take her stand, and peace will be the victor on the battlefield.

At that day He who is immortal and the Prince of Peace shall bring home His Church to reign with Him forever. Amen!

PRAYER: *O God, You have called Your Church, charged it, and sanctified it; and all the processes of holiness are promises of the final and everlasting crown. May we be found in the Church of Jesus Christ, which He has redeemed with His own blood, and be part of that great number that shall be presented to the Father without spot or wrinkle. In Jesus' name. Amen.*

JULY 20

When thou passest through the waters, I will be with thee; . . . For I am the Lord thy God.
(Isa. 43:2-3)

From what I had been able to gather about being a Christian, it seemed that it was a road to glory with all the avenues of evil blocked off and every enemy entrance under strict surveillance. Any thought of encounter with evil forces to hinder had never been considered.

One day the preacher spoke about the checks in the progress of the Christian, and I wished he had not spoken about them because he was in territory that was unfamiliar to me. The enthusiasm of being a new Christian was real, and I was still in the honeymoon stages of a love relationship with God.

He spoke about one's prayer life being up-to-date and everything by way of commitment being in proper order. Then, with all conditions being as they ought to be, there would yet appear an invisible wall through which one could not pass and over which one could not climb, and the Christian life would come to a standstill. In my happiness I could not accept this barrier on my road of Christian living.

Then suddenly there was a dead stop in the machinery for which I could not account. The sun refused to shine. The days were long, the nights were cold, and no friends seemed to understand or care. I began to question God and the experience that I had been led into.

Out of this experience I learned a very important lesson on the sovereignty of God. I learned that dry places will come, but God will stand by sincere, honest, and bold consecration. Having this confidence, we can have a peace deep inside even when the day is the darkest.

PRAYER: *O God, keep us where our cry of victory will be, "We will not despair!" Bring comfort to those who are bowed down, and lift up that soul that is at the point of surrendering to evil. Give us grace for our daily needs and help us to look through the darkness to the light of Your promises. In Jesus' name. Amen.*

JULY 21

Justice and judgment are the habitation of thy throne: mercy and truth shall go before thy face. Blessed is the people that know the joyful sound.
(Ps. 89:14-15)

"Did you feel that earthquake?" was a frequent question among the neighbors this week as each reported their relationship to it. It was not too high on the Richter scale but enough to let us know that we had been witness to an unmanageable phenomenon. A most interesting expression came out of this dangerous three-minute calamity: "We began to pray!"

The next day everything was following its normal course of activity, and the memory was lost in the varied experiences that surrounded its coming. How soon an earthquake becomes a familiarity and a calamity becomes the topic of common gossip!

Why is it important to recall such an incident? Simply because it illustrates the part of life that baffles but does not change. People know the ill effects of wrong living, but they will repeat the wrong tomorrow and the next day and the next. They see what comes of evil activity, but they no sooner look at the punishment than they go away and repeat the same thing. It is good to know that mercy holds back the hand of judgment, while God continues His salvation of love as the best way.

The events of life are related to one another, and so subtle is the intertwining that in the day of fear our confidence must be in God.

The church does not stand in its great songs. The preacher does not stand in the eloquence of his preaching. The priest does not stand in the greatness of his prayers. Nor does the evil work fall in its disobedience. We all stand or fall in our relationship to Jesus Christ.

In the day of the earthquake we do not need to fall on our faces and pray; we can stand on our feet and praise! "Jesus Christ [is] the same yesterday, and to day, and for ever" (Heb. 13:8)!

PRAYER: *O God, we have read it many times in Your Word that the secret of the Lord is with them that fear Him. Take away all other fear so that we might learn more of the secrets of Your great heart. Bless us with the inspiration and confidence of hope and with the strength of those whose trust is in You, the living God. In Jesus' name. Amen.*

■ **JULY 22**

I know thy works, that thou art neither cold nor hot: I would thou wert cold or hot.
(Rev. 3:15)

Halfheartedness has been the blight of every program and the big block hampering the progress of God's Church since the beginning. To go into any endeavor without being completely sold on it is to spell defeat and disaster. To be neither good nor bad, to straddle the fence, and to say, "Well . . . yes—maybe!" does not make a good foundation for any kind of permanence.

The call of God is for absolutes! We are called to grow, to advance, to march forward, to become wiser, and to continue day by day in that mysterious daily addition that leads to completion.

But God does see things from a true perspective, and He who makes the judgment has already appraised the intent of the heart. Only God knows how much temptation has been resisted, and how much suffering has been carried on in silence, and He knows the barriers that have blocked the way to heaven. Only God knows what some have to endure to be a Christian, and He keeps the judgment in His own hands.

God in His mercy is always talking to us at the level He finds us. He sees the one who has been mighty in prayer but has come under ruthless criticism and has fallen under the crushing power of Satan. He finds the one who has been brilliant with the Bible but has stumbled over a misinterpretation by voices that have whispered untruths. He meets that one who obeyed yesterday, disobeyed today, but is determined to try again tomorrow.

God knows the sincerity of every heart, and He keeps the way open to the Cross, where the cry for mercy is never lost in judgment.

PRAYER: *Heavenly Father, we come to You as the God of mercy and pray that You will know the intent of our hearts and withhold Your judgment from us. Help us to bury any semblance of halfheartedness in our sincerity. You are kind to all, and Your tender mercies are over all. Hold us steady. In Jesus' name. Amen.*

JULY 23 ■

He came unto his own, and his own received him not. But as many as received him, to them gave he the power to become the sons of God.
(John 1:11-12)

The words are often used in jest after the new couple have come through days and weeks or months of getting used to their new status of living and have run headlong into some differences, and the first response is, "Looks like the honeymoon is over!" The give-and-take and realities of life are faced, and the tones of reproach are heard for the first time.

I discovered something like this in my devotional reading this morning. All of the dealings of Jesus with His people had been filled with utterances of love and hope, and offerings of healing and peace and joy. Then a new tone is heard in His voice. Rebuke! Reproach! "Woe unto thee . . . !" And it spoke of disappointment, for He saw a terrible judgment ahead for those who had "repented not" (Matt. 11:21, 20).

The disappointment had tones of rejection: He had come "unto his own, and his own received him not," and the great heartache of God is laid bare. No person can hear the welcome invitation of the Master and be the same after its rejection. Any offer of divine mercy or display of divine love is a crisis in the personal history of anyone, and its rejection is the beginning of a breakdown in the most intimate relationship.

Jesus never did hide His disappointments, and He never tried to conceal the failures of His own to respond to His invitations. He could weep over Jerusalem, Bethsaida, or Tyre and Sidon, and He was willing to say, "I came unto My own, and they turned Me down."

Herein lies the strength of the gospel. He sees us as we are, and He tells it like it is. This is not the end of the honeymoon; it is just the beginning of heaven!

PRAYER: *We thank You, O God, for the ability to repent. You do not turn Your back and walk away, for we heard the loving call, a tender voice, and a quiet whisper, and we recognized our redemption in You. We know the terror of Your judgment; now we will be led to the Cross and to repentance and companionship and heaven. In Jesus' name. Amen.*

■ JULY 24

> I was also upright before him, and I kept myself from mine iniquity. Therefore hath the Lord recompensed me according to my righteousness, according to the cleanness of my hands in his eyesight.
> (Ps. 18:23-24)

It was a strange statement, and it came out of circumstances that seemed unrelated to the immediate problem. The counselor saw it differently as he remarked in frustration, "The past is always catching up to the present!"

We live as if everything were lying on the surface with no reference to the past and no bearing on any unwritten and eternal law. Experience tells us that there is nothing as simple as it often seems to be. And every day brings its own judgment, and every moment has its echo in the past.

Who can estimate the indirect influence that one generation has upon another, or how one small act can reverberate down through the years? Who can tell the influence of a verse of Scripture, or a gospel well preached, or a life well lived? Who can tell the influence of a small untruth, an act of deceit, or a selfish concern at the expense of an innocent party? The final judgment will no doubt lay condemnation on the outworking of many deeds done in the dark of yesterday.

Maybe there is an admonition here! Whatever we do should be done in the name and fear and sight and love of God. This kind of living keeps the soul clean and pure and healthy. Jesus Christ will not abide in the heart with deceit, hidden iniquity, compromise, or any enemy of righteousness. How often little iniquities have kept back God's blessing, the hurt of which will be multiplied in the generations to follow. Our today gathers up into itself the influence of all the years that have gone by.

The greater blessing is that God is faithful, and He does not forget the works of faith and the labors of love. He is always harmonizing our present with the deeds of the past.

PRAYER: *How often, O God, we have worried and fretted about those actions, thoughts, and performances of the past. We know that our present is imperfect if our past is still impure, and the only thing that can help is the miracle of grace wrought through the Holy Spirit. Assure us this day of a new heart, a new spirit, and a forgiven past. In Jesus' name. Amen.*

JULY 25

Nevertheless I tell you the truth; It is expedient for you that I go away: for if I go not away, the Comforter will not come unto you; but if I depart, I will send him unto you.
(John 16:7)

It must have been a very difficult decision to accept. Death would be conquered, Rome would no longer be a threat, and truth would be victorious. All of the promises of the prophets were being fulfilled, and the Messiah had made His home among His people. Hell would now hold no terror, and it was all straight ahead from here on in. Then comes the sudden and unexpected change in divine movement, and Jesus tells His disciples, "I am going to have to leave you."

Who can know the mind of God or make a way for His providences? When God moves, it is not to disappoint or to tear down. There is that in divine government about which we cannot predict. Sudden revelations. Great answers to our long-standing prayers. Special disclosures for which we are entirely unprepared. Unexpected victories. Losses from which God multiplies our capacity for greater gain.

The disciples saw only the loss of their Leader. Jesus looked ahead to the greater blessing of heaven and said, "I am sending the Comforter!" We make preparations for our expectations, and quite unexpectedly God sends His angels with blessings we had never dreamed possible. He opens the windows of heaven and gives us blessings beyond our calculations.

God will not have our todays as our yesterdays, nor will He allow our tomorrows to be as our todays. He will come, not as we had planned but in His own way and time with blessings that are higher than the depths of our disappointments.

When we see confusion, God sees a plan. And when our Savior is taken, it is to prepare us for the advent of something the answer of which only heaven holds.

PRAYER: *O God, You have never disappointed the honest heart seeking after You. In the moment of our greatest loss You have turned our sorrow into bliss and our mourning into joy. Our past will become greater and our future brighter as our present rests in the security of the Cross. In Jesus' name. Amen.*

JULY 26

And the King shall answer and say unto them, Verily I say unto you, Inasmuch as ye have done it unto one of the least of these my brethren, ye have done it unto me.
(Matt. 25:40)

We have all seen it, but few of us are prepared to cope with it! A human being reduced to a state of helplessness and alone. In our society there is a good deal of this kind of thing—loneliness, helplessness, blighted hope, and defeat. Hand in hand with this plight is the selfishness that plagues our society with the scant care for the one in need.

Many are sitting beside the Bethesda pools, waiting for a helping hand. The long waiting has ended in disappointment when another has stepped in for the healing. Eyes see them but have no pity, while the struggle adds to the pain. None of those who have been cured at the pool stand by to give another the benefit of the strength received. Selfishness makes a world that is very small, cold, and gloomy. When deeds are used for selfish gratification and do not cover human needs, they soon fade and are forgotten. The teaching of the Master is that inasmuch as we have touched others, we have touched the heart of God and ministered to Him. The method of the Master was to do a kindness as if He were receiving it himself.

But Jesus went about doing good, and He did not simply wait for the need to come to Him. He did not wait for the lost; He went out to search for them. Whether His help was sought or offered, it was there at the point of need. And He always addressed himself to the loneliest and the most helpless.

The Christian method of service compels us to go and seek opportunities of doing good. Love is always at the poolside, offering a helping hand toward the healing waters.

PRAYER: *Look upon those today, O God, who are in peculiar circumstances of loneliness, pain, fear, or weakness. Spread the table of Your blessing before them until one loaf will be as many because it has been touched by Your hand. Give us the helping kind of hand that ministers to the one in need and touches Your heart. In Jesus' name. Amen.*

JULY 27

For this God is our God for ever and ever: he will be our guide even unto death.
(Ps. 48:14)

It is not an uncommon thing to hear critical remarks on the negative aspects of one's religious beliefs. "You can't do this or this or this—what can you do?" Then the emphasis is placed on those prohibitions that are questionable and where moral values are involved. The message comes across that these "things" are necessary for happiness, or at least to be "accepted," one must be a partaker.

One does not have to read far into the Bible to run into a number of things that a Christian person is not to do. The divine Voice is clear, direct, and final in stating principles for building life, and definite things to avoid in the process. This is the strength of the Book of God, that He knows His people, He knows the power of evil, and He is saying to us, "Let Me give you some guidance."

Here is the true relationship of God to His people everywhere. He blesses. He forbids. He leads. He puts out His hand and says, "No further!" He never comes with an apology or misdirection but always with the majesty of right. And He comes with the words we cannot do without: "I am with you!"

How do we explain God and His desire to protect His people? We cannot explain it. Yet we can know that it fills the deepest space in our being that no other means can fill. Know this, that God's commandments are not expressions of a sovereign will to control, but they are expressions of mercy, grace, pity, and love.

God has never assumed that we could find our own way through life, which has been darkened by sin. He has promised to guide us all the way, even to the end.

PRAYER: *Guide us, O God, all the days of our lives, and help us when the road is narrow and the signs for direction are dim. We cannot find our way alone, for the dangers are many, and the enemy is great. In all of our journey help us to be aware of the tenderness and strength of Your presence. In Jesus' name. Amen.*

JULY 28

> **I have trusted in thy mercy; my heart shall rejoice in thy salvation. I will sing unto the Lord, because he hath dealt bountifully with me.**
> (Ps. 13:5-6)

How cruel to condemn; how precious to praise! I recently met a man who had been under terrible condemnation for acts and attitudes for which he was accused of being at fault. He was down! His personality, his method of doing things, his deportment seemed to be standing in the way of his being accepted by the opposition.

We observed that many times a judgment is a backhanded compliment to the one who is condemning. We found qualities that excelled and abilities that went beyond the common and ordinary practice. We discovered that when the props of pride have been knocked away, a person still can maintain some dignity as a foundation for beginning again. We put in new lights, gave the accusations new angles, and ran it all through the gamut of a new outlook. Result? My friend walked away with tears in his eyes and a new spring in his step.

It takes true courage to face the subtle powers of antagonism. Witness how the Pharisees set out to destroy Jesus through an exaggeration of their own piety. But when His lips were closed by their hateful accusations, His hands kept on healing and working.

Jesus did not succumb to the difficulties of the moment, for there was an end in view greater than the persecution. He went on to endure the Cross, despising the shame, looking onward to the glory that was to come.

We can fall before our accusers and never pray another prayer and look forever at the dust that gathers at our feet and bring joy to the angels of hell for another victory.

Thank God, there can be a beginning again! After the Cross and the shame there was "the joy that was set before him" (Heb. 12:2)—and us! Hold steady; God still cares!

PRAYER: *Our sincere prayer today, O God, is that You will keep us near to You. The enemy is at work, and his condemnation is harsh and fierce. Hear our faint cry and give us strength for the need. We do not understand the mystery of Your love, but we would rest in Your care. In Jesus' name. Amen.*

JULY 29

Humble yourselves therefore under the mighty hand of God, that he may exalt you in due time: casting all your care upon him; for he careth for you.
(1 Pet. 5:6-7)

The message of God to His people has always been very clear. He has promised not to withhold any good thing that we are capable of receiving. The secret closets of heaven are unbarred to those who are ready for them. "Then shall we know, if we follow on to know the Lord" has been God's challenge (Hos. 6:3). We should find more if we looked for more; he that doeth the will of God shall know the doctrine (John 7:17). It tells us that they who begin in the twilight of God's grace can grow into the midday blaze of His glory.

All of these promises are based on a simple gospel of trust, and every page of the Bible is rich with the promises of this doctrine. We believe that God is over all, that we are in the hollow of His hand, and that nothing happens without His notice. He who watches over the tiny sparrow and flashes the morning light upon our windowsill says to us, "All things are possible to him that believeth" (Mark 9:23).

This is the very heart of the teaching of Jesus, who saw God's care over small things and reassures us that He also cares for the greater. "Wherefore, if God so clothe the grass of the field, which to day is, and to morrow is cast into the oven, shall he not much more clothe you, O ye of little faith?" (Matt. 6:30).

To know that we can attach our individual lives to the great chariot of God's providence is one of His great revelations. We can draw on Him for our strength for today. Our smallest affairs can be laid before Him with the assurance that He cares. He will keep our door against the enemy; and when we pass through the valley of the shadow of death, He will be our comfort.

All of this and more if we believe!

PRAYER: *O God, we thank You for all of Your tender care. When other love has run out, Your love has just begun. When other patience has been exhausted, Your long-suffering has been multiplied toward us a thousand times. Show us again that we can live in Your providence and in Your mercy, and that Your love never fails. In Jesus' name. Amen.*

■ JULY 30

My grace is sufficient for thee: for my strength is made perfect in weakness. Most gladly therefore will I rather glory in my infirmities, that the power of Christ may rest upon me.
(2 Cor. 12:9)

The effects of sin on society in our day has left the greatest mark on living since the Dark Ages." So said a news commentator this week—and it was not a religious broadcast. The remark had to do with the drug traffic, which has insulted manhood and taken away privileges, rights, and honor. However loud one might boast in its favor, the length of the chain of freedom is getting shorter.

Sin in any form is slavery, and it is a continual opposition to all that is good and pure and holy. It leaves nothing but big gaps that the world cannot fill, and all hope turns into the bitterness of disappointment. The hand of sin is heavy, and it is cruel, and no human power has the capability to break it.

The one observation that the newsman failed to make was that there is an omnipotent and gracious Redeemer, whose nail-pierced hands are extended in mercy and love to every generation of society. Not until heaven's door closes upon the redeemed person will the devil give up in his pursuit, but the greater assurance is that God "giveth power to the faint; and to them that have no might he increaseth strength" (Isa. 40:29). Sin promises trouble, persecution, heartache, disappointment, and torment, but it has never been able to rule out the triumphs of the grace of God.

Old influences, old habits, old companions, old associates, and old conditions with the ugly, black mark of sin in every degree that plagues society and the individual can fall before the promise of the Eternal, "My grace is sufficient."

The prisoner of sin can become a prisoner of God's love and be shut up in the great sanctuary of His heart even in our day.

PRAYER: *We have learned, O God, that Your purposes toward us are always good. Your mercy, which endureth forever, is far greater than our sin. Through Your grace may the world have some sense of the sinfulness of sin and a hatred for its abominations. Give us that grace that can pardon and cleanse within. In Jesus' name. Amen.*

JULY 31 ■

For now we see through a glass, darkly; but then face to face: now I know in part; but then shall I know even as also I am known.
(1 Cor. 13:12)

It is interesting to visit people you haven't seen for a long time but with whom you had been closely associated in earlier days! Memories fade and imagination fills the gap, while stories are related as new as if being heard for the first time. Some events need to be forgotten, while others gather embellishment in each retelling.

Life has a memory; but every day sings its own song, every night has its own story, and time is dull only when we make it so. Every event of life can have a bright side, and our moments of rejoicing can be many and varied. Every hour can be labeled with some deed of love, and the whole week can be marked by the joy of living. Every month of the year can be highlighted by some part of God opened to us. The eagerness of each new morning can find its fulfillment in a day lived in the presence of the Almighty.

Life does not have to be an expression of fear, hopelessness, and utter dejection. The Bible tells us to "rejoice before the Lord your God," "rejoice and be glad," "rejoice and sing," to rejoice and give thanks. This is the very essence of love. And it opens the door of the heart to forgiveness and service.

When we set God upon the throne of our life, all that is worthwhile comes back again. Hope becomes alive, and a new meaning is born for the day. And time becomes too short to know the full mystery of God.

God calls every one of us to hope while the events of the past are seen through a glass darkly. But in this hope we can prepare for God's greater revelation that is promised to faith, obedience, and love.

PRAYER: *We thank You today, O God, for Christian hope, which is in You. This hope chases away the deep shadows and fills the soul with joy and peace. This all comes to us from heaven and is the crown of the gospel. We would be led by this hope to Your altar, where our sacrifice has been made. In Jesus' name. Amen.*

■ AUGUST 1

> Behold, as the eyes of servants look unto the hand of their masters, and as the eyes of a maiden unto the hand of her mistress; so our eyes wait upon the Lord our God.
> (Ps. 123:2)

Did you know that the Bible is full of God? He comes down to earth, walks upon it, talks to His people, tells them what His will is for them, leaves them with His promises, and points out their destiny in graphic detail. He is always speaking to His creation while retaining the awesomeness of His deity. God is never very far away, and simple events are all filled with the mystery of eternity.

Man stands next in majesty to his God. He was made in the image of his Creator. But he was soon led on in his vanity to believe that he could become God. He was told that he could have "more"—more pleasure, more progress, more knowledge, and more freedom. This led on to what human nature is today. Now it required a redeeming God rather than a creating God to stop the course of sin that had entered into our world.

A simple theology begins early in the Bible. Here is a human nature that has been marred by sin, a divine government that is stung by disappointment, and the promise of One who should come to redeem. Here two of the greatest names in history combine, and Jesus is not ashamed to be associated with Moses. For when the great songs roll across heaven, it is the song of Moses and the song of the Lamb that touch and gather all the elements of salvation (Rev. 15:3).

In spite of whatever ridicule has been heaped upon the Bible, it has to be said that no person who has ever really read the Book with body, soul, and spirit has ever disbelieved it. And wherever it has been fairly treated, it has been received and adopted as a Book full of God.

There can be but one God, and His Word shall fill the whole earth!

PRAYER: *O God, we thank You in this evil day for Your Book. It is a light, a lamp, a tender comfort, and a standard by which our shortcomings are measured. There we learn about the Cross, which unites redeemed mankind and glorifies the Redeemer in the revelation of Your plan for a sinful world. May we ever live in the Scriptures. In Jesus' name. Amen.*

AUGUST 2

Jesus said unto them, They need not depart; give ye them to eat. And they say unto him, We have here but five loaves, and two fishes. He said, Bring them hither to me.
(Matt. 14:16-18)

The work of the Church of Jesus Christ has been hampered through every generation by well-meaning persons taking the stand, "It can't be done!" How often ideas for the advancement of the kingdom of God had come as angel voices from heaven but were dismissed as impossible endeavors. It is a fearful thing to argue against the purposes of God.

The disciples said, "We can't feed this multitude, because we have only five loaves and two fishes." Were they speaking for the multitude, or did their argument betray their own lack of faith? "Send them away, and we will not be under the condemnation of conscience or the judgment of the Master" was their argument.

How much better to go to Jesus with the problem and leave it in His hands. It is a great mistake to dictate and make suggestions for Divine Providence. Jesus said, "Bring them hither to me." We do not have to be left with fear and apprehension when the Master gives the commands.

We must not narrow the Church and dwarf it into a helpless institution while we send the multitude away to look for satisfaction in other areas. We must not send our young people, the weak, the doubtful, the troubled, and the fainthearted "into the villages" to "buy themselves bread" (Mark 6:36). The Church must be ready to supply all the necessities for the hungry, weary, and wanting souls.

We never know how much we have until we begin to give. And the amazing thing that the Church needs to learn is that whatever is given in the right spirit grows in the giving.

"It can't be done," said the disciples. But Jesus did it!

PRAYER: *O God, we have nothing that we have not received from You, and we are nothing except by Your grace. When we face the impossibilities that life presents, may we know that we are serving One whose specialty is the impossible. Then give us that confident hope in Your eternal person and make us to know again that You do all things well. In Jesus' name. Amen.*

■ AUGUST 3

If God so clothe the grass of the field, which to day is, and to morrow is cast into the oven, shall he not much more clothe you, O ye of little faith?
(Matt. 6:30)

This morning I was awakened very early by the fluttering of wings and the chirping of a small bird. I discovered, hidden away in some tall grass under the edge of a bush beside my tent, a tiny nest with three baby birds in it. For a long time I sat on the edge of the tent platform and watched the little mother flit back and forth to feed her precious babies.

It was morning devotion time, and I was in the big chapel of God's universe. Here was a vivid illustration of God's care and overpowering love. If God is so careful of a little birds' nest, how much more careful He must be of things of higher quality. The message of Jesus becomes very real at a time like this: "If then God so clothe the grass, . . . how much more will he clothe you . . . ?" (Luke 12:28). If God is so careful of the little birds' nest, how much more must He care for my heart, my home, and my family?

I learned again this morning that God is kind in little things as well as in things big and great. I learned that the quality of His love is one, whether it be shown in the redemption of the human race, in ordering my footsteps for this day, or in guiding a little mother bird in providing food for her babies. I learned that the power of our omnipotent God must be controlled by lots of kindness and mercy and love. I learned that God is not only a hand that can rule but also a heart that can love.

The message of Jesus, "Are ye not much better than they?" (Matt. 6:26), is meant for us today. The question answers itself when we know that He places within us a clean heart, sanctified by the Holy Spirit and made fit for the dwelling of God himself.

The little birds' nest showed me this morning the value God places on me—and you.

PRAYER: *We thank You, O God, for all of Your tender care. When other love has run out, Your love has just begun. We cannot tell where it begins, and we do not know where it ends. You work things out for us in ways beyond our dreams, and You give us solutions far beyond our own wisdom. Teach us that we live in Your mercy, because Your love never fails. In Jesus' name. Amen.*

AUGUST 4 ■

But Jesus said, Suffer little children, and forbid them not, to come unto me: for of such is the kingdom of heaven. And he laid his hands on them.
(Matt. 19:14-15)

One of my earliest impressions of the character of Jesus Christ was from a song by a missionary who had spent many years in Africa. It said that "Jesus loves all the little children of the world." That sounded good because it had to include me and my friends, all of whose behavior was in question at the time.

Over the years I have been able to learn more about the love and compassion of Jesus. I have seen His tears, have heard His plea to the people of Jerusalem, and have been touched by His passion in the deeds He has performed.

He could have come on as a genius, with a display of literary power, and overthrown kingdoms and turned away from the little children. Instead, His was a life of love, a story of compassion, and an exemplification of the most tender aspects of the mercy of God.

He is "not an high priest which cannot be touched with the feeling of our infirmities" (Heb. 4:15). He knows each one of us through and through; and because He is the Son of God, He loves us and accepts us where He finds us. He said, "Suffer the little children to come unto me, and forbid them not" (Mark 10:14; see Luke 18:16). If He could have taken any other course, He never would have been the Savior of the world.

Jesus saw that the people around Him were as sheep having no shepherd. He is called the Good Shepherd, because it is said that He knows His sheep and that He would lay down His life for them. And when one is lost, He leaves everything and goes on the search until He returns with it in His bosom.

That song has never lost its meaning. Jesus still loves all the children (and all the big people, too) of this great big old world. And that includes you. (And me.)

PRAYER: *O God, we look up from our dark world, and we see our suffering Savior. He is our Priest, our Hope, and our Redeemer. We have heard His words of love, and we saw Him take up the little children in His arms and bless them. We saw Him go to the Cross, and we know the power of His resurrection. He is God, and we claim Him as our Savior. In His name. Amen.*

AUGUST 5

> **Let the words of my mouth, and the meditation of my heart, be acceptable in thy sight, O Lord, my strength, and my redeemer.**
> (Ps. 19:14)

It seemed ironic tonight to hear a young man who had just made a commitment for the Lord say, "Now I don't dare go home; my parents will kill me!" Today when homes are broken, families separated, loved ones beaten, and lives torn to bits, opposition toward one who is trying to do good seems a bit out of character.

It is disheartening when a person's opposition to being good comes from his own home. A person who can stand up against a whole army of opponents on the outside may easily stumble over a mere straw placed in the way by a friend. The opposition of the enemy we can take, whereas one cross word from a loved one tears at the heart.

Nehemiah could stand up against the Sanballats and the Tobiahs and the camp of heathenism and encourage his people to keep on. Outward assault he could manage. But when he faced opposition on the inside from those within his household, he faced discouragement that nearly floored him.

Here is a challenge for the church! It must provide strength, maintain unity in the redeemed fellowship, and be unselfish and caring to all within its reach. The enemy is building his smoking altars at every corner, and many homes are under the influence of his tolerance of sin, grief, and hatred. The church must be united in love to rescue that one who would live right.

Probably the greater appeal is to the individual Christian to be firm in the stand for good, ready to encourage, and slow to criticize. In so doing, a new Christian within the fellowship will dare to go on.

PRAYER: *Give us courage, O God, to pray bolder prayers and to step out on brave acts of faith. Out of it may there come more of Your wisdom, grace, patience, and strength. May we dare to allow the Holy Spirit to be our Life and Light and Joy, and be able to grasp the truth of God as never before. Then our courage will beget liberty that makes people free. In Jesus' name. Amen.*

AUGUST 6 ■

But grow in grace, and in the knowledge of our Lord and Saviour Jesus Christ. To him be glory both now and for ever. Amen.
(2 Pet. 3:18)

Tomorrow is not yet here. No one has ever seen it, nor has its message been heard. Yesterday with all of its joy and sorrows has gone, never to be brought back again. But today is here! It is now! This is God's day—and ours!

God told Joshua, "This day will I begin to magnify thee" (Josh. 3:7). "This day"—today—was to be a growing day for him. New responsibilities were given to him as he was thrown into a new situation. And he stood up with new strength, and he began to tackle the greatest task of his life with courage and hopefulness. Joshua was a chosen man and a prepared man for God's today.

God has a magnifying experience for all of His people. No person can make himself great. All greatness comes from God, and He does not grant it all at once.

We can all be prepared for a larger area of influence. We can all be found watching, waiting, looking, and praying. We can use our one little talent as if it were a thousand. We can work our little corner of space in time as if we owned God's eternity. God always magnifies the humble, the contrite, the faithful, and the honest follower.

The strength of His people has been that they dared to stand in the name of God—today! They did not simply hope that God would be with them someday. They put God in the foreground and put His signature on every promise and every prediction. He wants His people to live in a "thus saith the Lord" atmosphere.

Today we can still have a faith and express it, and grow in grace through a mystery we cannot explain.

PRAYER: *Your purposes toward Your people, O God, are always good, and Your grace is far greater than all our sin. Magnify our experience in You that we might speak adequately of that grace. The depth of Your love can never be fathomed, but we answer its call and accept Your truth with confidence. In Jesus' name. Amen.*

■ AUGUST 7

Blessed is the man that endureth temptation: for when he is tried, he shall receive the crown of life, which the Lord hath promised to them that love him.
(James 1:12)

From some early classroom lectures on the Book of James the impression settled in that it might be wise to shy away from it. James was supposed to be a stern individual giving strict orders from a high pedestal. He was not to be trifled with, and his voice carried harsh words from the Eternal.

One day I heard an evangelist say, "Let us look at James as a slave—a slave of God and of the Lord Jesus Christ." A love slave! As he opened up the book, he said, "Love is never so happy as when stooping to serve, indicating the completeness of its devotion. And James sits down and writes his letter to the 12 tribes that are scattered abroad. And to us!" I learned something new about the book.

"Count it all joy," he says, "when you fall into various trials" (NKJV). Surely it is not in the human heart to want to find its happiness in the hard places! But read on: "Knowing this, that the trying of your faith worketh patience." We are not to be glad for the trials, but the pain works out a mystery bearing the gentle, quiet name of patience.

In this little gem of God we find not only patience but also wisdom, humility, and healing. All of these God wants to give to His people, for He never holds back any good thing from those who love Him. James is passing along good exhortations: Take care how you ask. In whose name you ask. For what reason you ask. Your prayer must be cleared of selfishness and filled with a desire for the fullness of God. Be sincere. Be honest. Be earnest. Let your yes be yes and your no be no.

James is saying that we must be a slave if we would touch the high points of consecration. Today I can handle that!

PRAYER: *Give us more of the good things You have in store for Your people, O God. Give us that patience that waits as those who would do Your will, and make us stand still for Your time and for Your answer. Bring to our hearts that sweet and tender peace of assured acceptance. In Jesus' name. Amen.*

AUGUST 8 ■

Then Simon Peter answered him, Lord, to whom shall we go? thou hast the words of eternal life.
(John 6:68)

One day I sat with a young man in a counseling session. He poured out his problems, accusing, condemning, criticizing and weeping—and then he was quiet. We sat for 20 minutes, and no one spoke a word. My mind played and replayed his sad tale, and I turned pages for a well-defined answer that I could not find. He walked over and placed his hand on my shoulder and asked, "Will you pray with me?" We prayed. He said, "Thank you, you have helped me. I can begin again." And he left the room.

"You have helped me. I can begin again." It all sounded so ridiculous, for I had not spoken a word of wisdom. The sense to feel the need was there, but the power to provide an answer was missing.

How often I have walked out of a sickroom leaving the patient in a worse state than when I had found him. I had tried to console. I had read passages from the Bible. I had prayed. I had tried to cheer. When I left the room, it was as if I had pulled a black shroud around the bed of sickness.

One day I learned that the speaker we must listen to is Jesus Christ, the Son of God, the Representative of the Father. He it is whose heart is broken with every earthly sorrow, whose love reaches out to every need, and whose lips spoke the words, "Come unto me, all ye that labour and are heavy laden, and I will give you rest" (Matt. 11:28).

One day I learned that it is not enough to try to speak the right word at the right moment, for in much of our chattering we say nothing. I learned that my task is to point them to the One whose voice melts in pity, whose words speak comfort, and to let them know that there is no pain Jesus Christ cannot heal.

Outside of this there is no adequate counseling chamber!

PRAYER: *O God, our world is sick and needs the listening ear of the only One who fully cares and can heal. Your love is a continual astonishment, and Your grace awakens within us unspeakable surprise! In You we find courage and strength to carry on. This is the divine miracle! This is the revelation of love! Keep us near to Your heart. In Jesus' name. Amen.*

■ AUGUST 9

I will sing a new song unto thee, O God: upon a psaltery and an instrument of ten strings will I sing praises unto thee.
(Ps. 144:9)

The words of the veteran missionary often come to mind as he reported some of the difficult experiences in his work in dark Africa. He discovered that during times when he was not able to pray a hole through the skies, he could always praise the way through to God. He continued in his testimony the many times he was able to sing and shout his way through problems and difficulties.

It is well for every person, even in the loneliest part of the journey, to try to sing. We have a natural tendency to express our momentary experiences of doom as if they were permanent factors of life. Granted, God always encourages frankness and honesty in sorrow as well as in joy. How often the Psalmist complained of neglect and forgetfulness, yet God did not turn away from him.

Jesus spoke to His disciples, not out of condemnation but out of concern, when He told them, "Without me ye can do nothing" (John 15:5). God wants to occupy the whole soul and be part of every living thought. He has a right to our praise, and we need to rejoice in Him, our Master and our Lord. The weakness of God is stronger than the might of man. We know this truth, and it makes us glad. And we need to sing about it. Our praise to God is the light of the morning, the crown of the noonday, and the star of the night.

The Psalmist found a way to the song. He said, "I have trusted," "my heart shall rejoice," and "I will sing." He does not begin with a song but with trust. And when trust has been established, joy begins to glow in the heart. What can come after joy but a song?

Our song must never be surrendered, whatever our calling in life!

PRAYER: *Almighty God, we bring our tribute of praise to You, small and unworthy though it may be. You do not cast aside our insignificant offering. We praise You for eyes to see and hearts to understand and tongues to proclaim Your truth. Our gratefulness rises for all these good things. In Jesus' name. Amen.*

AUGUST 10 ■

O the depth of the riches both of wisdom and knowledge of God! how unsearchable are his judgments, and his ways past finding out!
(Rom. 11:33)

Words become hollow and lose their meaning when we try to fit God into our human thought and language. All the great words that are in our thinking and speaking run far behind in expressing what God is, has been, or will be!

We reckon time in minutes and hours, in days and weeks, in months and years, and in centuries; and we even dare to speak about a millennium. But here we stop, for time passes into eternity, and we become lost.

We speak about love and call it by many intriguing names that charm and speak of trust and companionship and caring. But there comes a point where we can go no further, for love passes into sacrifice, and we are baffled as it leads us to the Cross!

Our great big world has taken us into its spell, and we reach out in our wide-open space and measure our distances in miles and light-years. But there comes a point where we can measure no more, and we throw down our instruments before the Milky Way. Space runs into infinity, and infinity we cannot comprehend.

How proud we have become of our power of reasoning, which places us next in line to God himself. Philosophers, scientists, and mathematicians have placed great ideas before us that we cannot fathom. But the wisdom of this world is transfigured into faith that merges into an image of eternity and the Creator.

So all of our great words that have their roots upon earth find their real meaning in Him whom no words can explain. Jesus made it so plain! He simply said, "When ye pray, say, Our Father which art in heaven . . ." (Luke 11:2). To this no man can add.

PRAYER: *Our Father, we have heard the words of Jesus, Your Son, as He tried to explain You to a weak humanity. Help us live in these words so that the royalty of His strength and grace will rule in every heart. May we know that the Word belongs to heaven because of the response of our love. In Jesus' name. Amen.*

■ AUGUST 11

For this is the message that ye heard from the beginning, that we should love one another.
(1 John 3:11)

When Jesus Christ spoke, His message was universal. It was not a message for one or two or a selected few. His message was complete, it was final, and nothing was to be added to it; nor was it to be modified by the ages. The message was God's, for it came from God.

Every generation has put the words, as well as the followers, of Jesus Christ to the test. Paul had to face the test of his belief in Jesus Christ. He was despised. The coat was torn from his back. He had no real place to call home. He came under every indignity of his day. He sang in the dark prison house and wept there for his accusers. But his ministry was founded upon the message of love and the cross of Jesus Christ—and it stood the test.

The message that Jesus left with His people also carried with it an "until the Lord come" aspect. It was temporary; it was for time. It was to carry His people onward to a greater day. It was an "until I come back again" message. Whether the message was given as an admonition for time, or for preparation for eternity, it carried a greater demand—that a person be found faithful "until." And this implies testing and trials so that through every crisis faithfulness will be the mark of character.

His message brings people from all over the world into one fellowship. We are one at the Cross. We are one in prayer. We are one in trusting the living Christ for redemption, forgiveness, and holiness.

His greatest message: "Seek ye first the kingdom of God, and his righteousness; and all these things shall be added unto you" (Matt. 6:33).

PRAYER: *We are ever reminded, O God, from Your message sent to us by Your Son, that our salvation comes by faith in the Eternal Son. Every day You come to our world with a new revelation and a new hope, bearing a new message for Your people. Help us recognize Your presence by the glowing love that burns in our hearts as we walk and talk together. In Jesus' name. Amen.*

AUGUST 12

And he arose, and rebuked the wind, and said unto the sea, Peace, be still. And the wind ceased, and there was a great calm. And he said unto them, Why are ye so fearful? how is it that ye have no faith?
(Mark 4:39)

In your devotions this morning what kind of prayers are you bringing to God? Are you facing some serious problems in your business world, and are you asking God to be your Co-partner? Do you feel too weak for the day, and are you asking God to make up what is lacking in your strength? Maybe things are going well with you, and you want to place your expression of praise at the throne and say, "Thank You!"

An old saint in the church used to pray, "Too many times our prayers are like a bird with wings too weak to get above the roof of the sanctuary!" Then he would add with great vigor, "Help our prayers to be strong and sturdy!" Jesus criticized those fearful disciples, "O ye of little faith" (Matt. 8:26). Prayers with no strength!

Are you coming to God this morning in your emptiness, but with a faith that opens the door of heaven? There is no mightier force in all creation than a faith that cannot be shaken. The cry of every child of God should be, "Lord, increase my faith!" (See Luke 17:5.) Faith is power. Faith is peace. Faith is prayers answered!

Difficulties and problems are going to come, even in the discharge of our most devout duties. The child of God is not exempt from sorrow, setbacks in business, suffering, and false attacks. In the hours of your deepest devotion storms will sweep in to put your calm sea in dreadful turmoil.

Let your faith reach out this morning to the One who is mighty to save, whose power is infinite, whose touch is emancipation, and whose look is a benediction. His answer to your prayer of faith is, "Peace, be still"!

PRAYER: *O God, You know our impatience, the wilderness of our impulses, and the difficulties we have in seeing our shortcomings. Help us to listen to Your commandments and walk in the ways of Your law, then peace will flow like a river and righteousness like the waves of the sea. Give us great answers of peace. In Jesus' name. Amen.*

■ AUGUST 13

For God so loved the world, that he gave his only begotten Son, that whosoever believeth in him should not perish, but have everlasting life.
(John 3:16)

John said that if all the things Jesus did were recorded, he guessed the world would not be able to contain the books (21:25). Yet if pen and ink could have captured the inner Jesus and written His deepest thoughts, little room would have been left for recording His acts. The real life of Jesus was not one of circumstances but one of thought, purpose, feelings, desires, aspirations—the inward, spiritual Christ.

To know Jesus Christ, we must know something of His thoughts, for out of them we have recorded His acts. To be sure, we will continually come upon things we cannot understand, nor will we be able to explain them, for they defy the intelligence of humanity.

An ailing woman came trembling through the crowd with hand outstretched for a mere touch of His garment. Faith had made its way through the crowd and found Him first. Jesus responded, "Virtue is gone out of me" (Luke 8:46). A woman's reach, a touch of faith, and a holy virtue mingled that day for a healing.

"If thou hadst been here, my brother had not died" was the twofold accusation (John 11:21, 32). Weeping. A groan. A prayer. A command, "Lazarus, come forth"! "Father, . . . I said it, that . . . the people . . . may believe that thou hast sent me" (vv. 43, 41-42). He was moved with compassion, and while He walked toward the grave, He cried.

The redemption of the world was upon Him. In His last agony He prayed when He had no hand to stretch upward to His God, "Father, forgive them; for they know not what they do" (Luke 23:34).

Who can know the real Jesus behind these great acts? Only love can explain it. How do we explain love?

PRAYER: *Herein is love, not that we loved You, our Father, but that You loved us; and while we were yet enemies of heaven, Your Son died for us. We cannot understand this, for we cannot understand His love. It is enough to know that our sins, which were many, are all washed away. Amazing love! How can it be? In Jesus' name. Amen.*

AUGUST 14

I have fought a good fight, I have finished my course, I have kept the faith: henceforth there is laid up for me a crown of righteousness, which the Lord, the righteous judge, shall give me at that day.
(2 Tim. 4:7-8)

This week I visited a church where many of the older folk had been my boyhood friends. During the prayer time, in which one was asked to participate, he prayed with great fervency for me who "is now going down the sunset side of the hill." I appreciated the concern, though at the time it did create some amusement.

There comes a time in every life when the road does become a downward slope toward the sunset, and the foot of the hill is the last earthly resting-place. This is the way of God, for every person must die. From the point of view of actual experience it is a sublime and appalling announcement to know that the bottom of the hill is in sight. But even the sturdy oak must yield to the ravages of time as the strongest gives way to weakness and affliction.

God educates His people to look beyond the sunset and the foothills to the land where flowers never fade and the summer promises to last eternally. His people seek a city on high whose Builder and Maker is God. The earth, but a handful of dust, loses its meaning, and there is a yearning for God and a restlessness that only the eternal can satisfy.

Christianity is a religion of faith. It is a faith that finds its way through the wilderness and sees a Canaan land ahead and marches to the drumbeat of eternity. It is a sight that sees the invisible and a hand that grasps the very omnipotence of God.

The sunset side of the hill for the people of God carries no fear, for if any man believe in Christ Jesus with the whole soul, he cannot die. "Whosoever liveth and believeth in me," said Jesus, "though he were dead yet shall he live" and "shall never die" (John 11:25-26). This solemn decree was addressed to the never-dying soul!

PRAYER: *O God, You have not neglected our life here on earth or in the anticipation of heaven. When the last scene comes, and it is time for the final farewell, You will be on hand with assurance, reestablishing our faith in eternal values. How vain and insignificant life would be were it not rooted and grounded in the love of Jesus Christ. Keep us in this love. In Jesus' name. Amen.*

■ AUGUST 15

And he said unto me, My grace is sufficient for thee: for my strength is made perfect in weakness.
(2 Cor. 12:9)

The speaker suggested that the little boy "gladly gave up his lunch" to Jesus so that He could feed over 5,000 hungry people. I did not say, "Amen," because I did not agree with him. I grew up as a little boy with brothers, playmates, and then with sons and grandsons, and I know that this is not the way that little boys think. Furthermore, I seriously doubt if the lunch was intact, because there is a nibbling quality about little boys that would support my theory. But the beautiful thing is that he did give it to Jesus, and Jesus blessed it and used it.

Look with me at the greater observation as we move from the lad to the loaves. The boy gave, Jesus blessed, the people ate, and the disciples gathered. The loaves grew under His breaking touch: He breaks until He is surrounded by piles of bread—and He still breaks and blesses. When the feast is over, He says, "Pick up the broken portion and don't leave a crumb of what I have broken." The overabundance of the grace of God!

We begin with a need, and we end with faith. We begin by asking questions, and we end by trying to understand the answer. We begin with inadequacy, and we end with God's sufficiency. We begin with the impossible, and we continue (for there is no ending) with the One with whom there is nothing impossible.

Jesus did more than "just enough" to save the sinner! He saves with an eternal salvation, an everlasting redemption, and His Cross is able to lift the world to heaven forever. God always goes beyond our asking!

Today I shall want no good thing, for God breaks and blesses what I give to Him. My soul shall be satisfied throughout the endless ages of eternity.

PRAYER: *O God, You have fed us day by day with Your overabundant supply. You have filled us with hope until we can say that the end is far better than the beginning. You have done for us the exceeding abundantly beyond what we could have asked. We give to You our loaves and fish and ask that You will accept and break and bless and feed. In Jesus' name. Amen.*

AUGUST 16

Looking unto Jesus the author and finisher of our faith; who for the joy that was set before him endured the cross, despising the shame, and is set down at the right hand of the throne of God.
(Heb. 12:2)

Just a simple word of encouragement has made the difference in many lives between going down in defeat or moving on to success. Who has not faced that overpowering sense of doom when the air filled with darkness and the sword was about to drop? Then when all the lights died out and the rock became mire and walls closed off the pathway, God worked His greatest miracle. A friend clasped your hand and said, "It's OK. Keep going!"

How wonderfully God's miracles fulfill human circumstances! He takes out the darkness and fills the place with light. He drives away the silence and fills the void with music. He makes the dry places become fountains of cool water and provides a shady place for the heat of the day. A friend places his hand on your shoulder and says, "I understand!" This is God's way.

God's miracle is not something that just covers the necessity, but it is always overflowing, losing the need in His overabundance. When the multitude was hungry, Jesus broke and blessed the bread. The miracle went 12 basketfuls beyond the necessity. When you want to understand the miracle, first understand the circumstance—God goes beyond that!

Never let us shut our eyes to the dark side of human life. Even good people need a word of encouragement; they are not always strong and successful. Stress and fear and sickness and famine visit the just as well as the unjust. The miracle! "Wait—joy cometh in the morning. God keeps the times and the seasons to himself. He will come!"

When there seems to be no road over which to travel on to heaven, God's miracle opens a way through the impossible. "Keep going!"

PRAYER: *O God, we pray that You will give encouragement to all those who are trying to be good. May their courage never fail, may their hope be as a burning lamp, and may their inspiration be renewed day by day. Place Your arms around this little world and say to each one in tones of comfort and encouragement, "I love you," and point us to the Cross. In Jesus' name. Amen.*

AUGUST 17

Ask of me, and I shall give thee the heathen for thine inheritance, and the uttermost parts of the earth for thy possession.
(Ps. 2:8)

There was always something special about missionary meetings. It was a grand time when a real, live missionary came with curios, another language, and positive reports on the work in another world. We expected to hear about miracles with heathenism and homes made into a living heaven. We expected to hear about a cry for the living God and a reaching out for something that was there but could not be found.

Is not this the hallmark of Christianity? It can do what no other religion can do, and its Central Figure has no equal! He is the Only Begotten of the Father. He is the Ruler of people everywhere. He is the One whose cry from the Cross encompassed the world that He had made. And Christianity did not come to approve the practices of heathenism, but it came to cure the problems of sin in the heart of heathenism.

Christianity has come into our world to tell the broken, self-condemning hearts everywhere that God is love. And when people condescend to a lower level of religion, they move away from the central purpose of the Cross.

Christianity still has the answer for trouble, sorrow, and broken dreams and can put into perspective those dreams that were lost yesterday. Jesus always answers everyone who comes to Him with an earnest and honest heart. His was a touch that took five loaves and two fishes and fed a multitude, opened the eyes of a blind man, and healed a woman who had been ill for years.

Christianity offers to heathenism at home or abroad a touch that multiplies, a smile rich as the summer dawn, and a voice of the most tender benediction. His name is Jesus!

PRAYER: *We pray today, O God, for the missionary church where men and women will hear about the Man of God for the first time. Be with that missionary who asks for the widest sea and the most distant shore so that he might blow the silver trumpet of salvation to those who have never heard. This is love! May we give it our full support. In Jesus' name. Amen.*

AUGUST 18

When I consider thy heavens, the work of thy fingers, the moon and the stars, which thou hast ordained; what is man, that thou art mindful of him? and the son of man, that thou visitest him?
(Ps. 8:3-4)

It is difficult to work into our thinking such words as *multimillionaire, billionaire, unknown quantity,* and *the unknowable.* When we read that something is 50 million miles in circumference, and the sun is nearly 100 million miles farther away from the earth than the moon is, and that something else is 5 million times larger than the earth, our minds go to rest.

We ascribe such terms to God as the Unknowable, the Undefinable, the Invisible, the Boundless, and the Almighty, and it is well that we should. But how easy it becomes to destroy Him by placing Him in a category beyond our comprehension! We boggle our minds with space and eternality and place God in this realm and make Him unreachable.

GOD! A Fire that may not be touched! A Life too great for shape or image! A Love for which there is no equal name! An Idea too deep for logic to capture! An Enigma for which there is no answer! All of this and the question continues to be asked, "Who is He?" And we are tempted to turn away in discouragement.

Out of this vastness there is a part that the God of the Bible plays in the life of the one who accepts Him and obeys Him with all the inspiration and diligence of love. This God comes down to where we are living and says, "I am with you alway, even unto the end" (Matt. 28:20), and inspires life and gives hope and makes heaven possible for His creatures.

Then He says, "You are part of My omnipotence; and 'When ye pray, say, Our Father which art in heaven, Hallowed be thy name.' . . . [Luke 11:2] Amen."

PRAYER: *O God, we have found Your greatness resident in Your goodness. Even though You are great, we have found You to be good and kind. Your omnipotence is promised to those whose trust is in Jesus Christ as Lord and Savior. Bury our smallness in the heart of Your greatness as our souls respond in praise, "How great Thou art!" In Jesus' name. Amen.*

AUGUST 19

> **Thus saith the Lord ... Call unto me, and I will answer thee, and shew thee great and mighty things, which thou knowest not.**
> (Jer. 33:2-3)

One day, in the early stages of my Christian experience, I was searching for promises and passages in the Bible that I had heard repeated in the testimonies of the saints. I came upon the following words, "Call unto me, and I will answer thee, and shew thee great and mighty things."

It was as if the curtains had fallen from the windows of a darkened room, or a great Niagara had hit the turbines of a mighty dynamo, sending light to the dark city streets. I thought that if I never found another thing in the Bible, this would hold me until the Lord called me home. And it tied in with something that I had found the day before, that He "is able to do exceeding abundantly above all that we ask or think" (Eph. 3:20).

The possibilities that God showed me that day have not been exhausted. Recognize My existence, He was saying to me. Rely on Me in every detail of your life. Come to Me as often as you want with all the problems that you will ever have. Never quit praying and believing, and always keep the way open. Do not depend on your own strength, for Mine is made perfect in your weakness. Remember that it is in answer to your call that I will enlarge your place and reveal greater things from heaven to you.

Over the years there has been much calling upon God, and it has come from the heart of need to the Source of supply. Sometimes it was a cry of pain and an agony of desire, and sometimes the cry came from the dark valley of death. Sometimes it was a cry of thankfulness and praise and commitment. All in all it was an enclosure with God in a loving communion when the world was shut out and one soul and one God were alone, together.

He had promised great and mighty things, and He has kept His promise.

PRAYER: *O God, You have given great and noble promises to Your people. In times of darkness You have held a light for our way. Work within us a new kinship with Your own nature. Give us joy in our peace, the assurance of liberty, and the richness of Your promises, and we will be satisfied. In Jesus' name. Amen.*

AUGUST 20 ■

Keep yourselves in the love of God, looking for the mercy of our Lord Jesus Christ unto eternal life.
(Jude 21)

My grandmother went to school only a few days in her life, but she taught herself to read the Bible by comparing passages with some she had already memorized. These she passed on as admonition or encouragement at every opportunity. But she kept a special one in reserve for that person in the initial stages of being a Christian: "Keep yourselves in the love of God."

It always seemed to me that the way she said it was more convincing than the exhortation. She knew that people cannot be lectured into love, and her message was that the love of God is an unchanging love. The urgency in her plea was saying, "Hide yourself, guard yourself, take refuge in the security of a love that will never change." I seemed to hear her say, "Build a fortification of love around yourself for the battles that will surely come."

What better admonition for any Christian at any stage of Christian living? "Entrench yourself behind the fortress of infinite love!" The enemy will line up his forces to bewilder the mind and distract the attention and unsettle the soul. And if we doubt that, the whole life will end up in failure. The heart of the matter is God's redemptive love through His only begotten Son, without which there is no answer even in God.

The fortress of infinite love! God loves me. He died for me in the person of His Son. He has given to me the pledge of that love. I can live in it, grow stronger, pray more boldly, and answer His eternal love with trust, simplicity, and obedience.

What greater admonition for this day? "Keep yourselves in the love of God."

PRAYER: *O God, we come before Your throne by the only way possible—by the right of love. May it be a great love, beginning at the Cross, sustained by daily grace, and made greater by the constant inspiration of the Holy Ghost. This is Your miracle. This is the wonder of life. In this revelation of yourself we would live. In Jesus' name. Amen.*

AUGUST 21

Thou wilt shew me the path of life: in thy presence is fulness of joy; at thy right hand there are pleasures for evermore.
(Ps. 16:11)

God had rescued His people from the tyranny of Pharaoh, brought them across miles of barren land, parted the waters, saved them from the hoards of pursuers, and landed them safely on the victory side of the Red Sea. He gathered them in the wilderness, ready to reveal His next move.

Partakers of one of the greatest miracles of history—how soon they forgot! The song had scarcely died on their lips when murmuring filled their mouths, and they were ready to turn on the One who had delivered them.

Witness the miracles of Jesus! They went for nothing to many of the people who had witnessed them. But soon the mob who had seen the hand of heaven move were crying for the death of the One who had worked wonders in their midst.

There seems to be a necessary logic here, for when one denies the miraculous power of God, he also goes down on the human side in like proportion. When faith in miracles goes, faith in all that is good and noble also goes. It is impossible to dismiss faith in God, in His miracles, and in the Bible and still retain the deepest meaning in life, on which good is built.

Note that it was God who led them into the wilderness, and His intention was to lead them out. Did they forget that God never leads one into a place that He cannot deliver from? God knows how far He is accountable for our circumstances, and to that degree He is faithful for the deliverance and for our well-being while we are there. He will find a solution for all the difficulties, however difficult they may be!

Lest we forget! God is repeating His miracles every day, and with each one He is trying to teach some higher truth!

PRAYER: *You would teach us, O God, how to be strong and possessed with a desire to do good. You lead us out of difficult places. Often there is no human way out of our entanglements, but the divine hand comes and brings us to the open spaces of liberty. You are able to do exceeding abundantly above all that we ask or think. We are satisfied. In Jesus' name. Amen.*

AUGUST 22 ∎

And she called the name of the Lord that spake unto her, Thou God seest me: for she said, Have I also here looked after him that seeth me?
(Gen. 16:13)

In the old farmhouse the parlor was a closed room except for special occasions such as funerals, visits from distant relatives, and my sister's Saturday evening date with her boyfriend. I was glad that it was this way, for there was a very frightening motto hanging on the wall. It said, "Do nothing that you would not want to be doing when Jesus comes," and this would curb my activities for several days after I read it. I was much more comfortable when the doors were closed.

One day I discovered that God is acquainted with everything that happens in my life anyway. And I discovered that He cares. Nothing has ever happened in my life that God does not know all about. Every word that I have ever spoken in anger or ridicule as well as commendation is well known to the Father.

One day I learned that a speaking conscience is God telling me what I ought to do. He portrays us to ourselves and shows us what we are in His sight. Then He brings us to the Cross—the bar of judgment—and shows us that after all the wickedness, denial, and blasphemy, He has provided for us a better way. Through tears of confession and heart overflowing with joy I discovered that I can look up and say, "Lord, Thou who knowest all things," and open the doors.

Our days fly past, and our moments are lost in the wind. It is scarcely morning before the night is upon us, and while we are walking in our youth, we are anticipating old age. Our doing, our going, and our being can have His continual blessing.

We must learn in the rush of time that only those things that are done for Christ and the Kingdom will have value in eternity.

PRAYER: *O God, You always see us as we are, and nothing is hidden from Your eyes. You know how near or far apart our intentions are from our actions. We cannot hide anything from You, for the darkness and the light are both alike to You. Guide us in the right way and make us to be more watchful in our daily walk. We pray this in Jesus' name. Amen.*

■ **AUGUST 23**

I am the resurrection, and the life: he that believeth in me, though he were dead, yet shall he live: and whosoever liveth and believeth in me shall never die.
(John 11:25-26)

Opening the windows and doors of the cottage to let the fresh summer breeze flow through, getting the first bucket of cold water from the spring well, putting the planks out for the wharf, and arranging the diving board—exciting? Yes! But it all carries a cloud of sadness, for time moves too swiftly toward the day of reverse process, when the camp with all its activities will be closed for another year.

The word *finished* has always carried a tantalizing connotation. Sometimes we are baffled by it as we try to give it meaning, for it seems to exhaust the imagination. We are scarcely born until we are facing death. And the new year celebration is still fresh in our memory when the aged man with sickle comes to pronounce its ending.

In a very real sense things are never finished. Students look forward to that day when "I finish my education." In education you only finish that you may begin again. You close your books as a pledge of your qualification to open another.

Heaven dawns in the Bible, and who can ever finish reading the Word of God? When we have read it, we have not finished it, for it can never be exhausted this side of eternity.

You can never finish love. Love just keeps on growing. It cannot die; it enlarges as the heart tends toward God, and it mellows with the swiftly adding years. Love touches the very fullness of the power of God.

In a sense camping is never finished, for memories remain; and no matter how poor it may be, there is love in every shingle, and every bucket of water is magical.

So it is with life. If it is owned and filled with the life of God, it keeps on living—throughout eternity.

PRAYER: *Our prayer is, O God, that our life, which seems so short to us here, may know a higher purpose than earth can provide. We look forward to the beginning that Your grace has provided for the ransomed and redeemed men and women. You have given it to us for eternity, and we cannot handle it without You. In Jesus' name. Amen.*

AUGUST 24

Whither shall I go from thy spirit? or whither shall I flee from thy presence? If I ascend up into heaven, thou art there: if I make my bed in hell, behold, thou art there.
(Ps. 139:7-8)

One of the earliest lessons I learned about God was that it is impossible to hide from Him. The voice of the early radio preacher spoke it: "If I ascend up into heaven, [or] dwell in the uttermost parts of the sea . . . thou art there" (vv. 8-9). It left no alternative. There is no escaping from God—all things are open and naked before Him.

God will not allow anything that He has created to be lost from His care, nor will He run away from His creation. As long as He can find one speck of value, one desire that is reaching out for something better, one hope reaching out to the Cross for redemption, or one leper sitting by the way waiting, God will be there.

God begins with the least little bit of goodness that He finds in the heart. He looks for the tear of penitence—that silent, glistening tear backed by a hunger that no words can express. It cannot speak its want, but it moves the whole soul. And it is never hidden from God.

God has not made a prisoner of himself in His own universe. Whatever He has done, all things are under His feet. He can turn the winter into summer, bring out of the heavens a beautiful calm after the storm, and make the snow but the background of the most glowing flower. No bird falls to the ground without His notice, nor can one drop of dew be siphoned from the rose petal without His knowledge. Then how can I, mortal man, hide from His love and care?

What a strange and comforting peace comes after accepting God as Friend, Companion, and Redeemer. Herein is the outcome of the Cross: "As I live, saith the Lord God, I have no pleasure in the death of the wicked" (Ezek. 33:11).

God made the universe for fellowship with His creatures—not a hiding place for them or from them.

PRAYER: *O God, our sincere prayer is that You will keep us near to You this day. We do not want to stray beyond the reach of Your hearing. Many times our praying is loud, and still we cannot seem to reach You. Sometimes we can only whisper, but we know You have heard our weakest cry. Give us strength for our need, for we put our complete trust in the Lord. In Jesus' name. Amen.*

AUGUST 25

There is therefore now no condemnation to them which are in Christ Jesus, who walk not after the flesh, but after the Spirit.
(Rom. 8:1)

No one likes to hear words that accuse or condemn; it is not part of human nature. The Bible speaks of false witnesses, people who have been paid good sums of money to tell big lies and cover the truth, or to say good things about bad people.

When Jesus came with the voice of judgment and the tone of rebuke, they turned their backs on Him. He dealt with iniquity and selfishness and falsehood, and they devised ways to remove Him from their company. But Jesus never accused anyone without looking into the heart and disclosing the reason for the accusation.

God does not condemn because He wants to show His omnipotence or exercise divine authority over the human race. He always reveals the basis on which He judges and points out His better way before He lays down His judgment.

He is always holding the door open. He says, "Ask, and it shall be given you; seek, and ye shall find; knock, and it shall be opened unto you" (Matt. 7:7; Luke 11:9). It is impossible to know the depths of mercy or the extent of love in the heart of God for the worker of iniquity.

The greatness of heaven came in the form of God's Son with something to say to every person in the tongue in which He was born. He walked beside the one who was seeking to do evil, and by the way of the Cross He was able to take the accusation himself that had been placed upon every bad person.

Wondrous beyond all other sights is Jesus sitting among the people, speaking words concerning themselves. His voice of thunder was an eternal challenge to evil. But His voice of love was an invitation to partake of His righteousness.

PRAYER: *O God, it is better to fall under Your judgment than to fall under the condemnation of our fellowman. You could have cut us off and thrown us aside, but You spared us and tried us and renewed our opportunities. We pray that by Your grace we might stand approved and be accepted into the family of heaven. In Jesus' name. Amen.*

AUGUST 26

He ... took a towel, and girded himself. After that he poureth water into a basin, and began to wash the disciples' feet, and to wipe them with the towel wherewith he was girded.
(John 13:4-5)

Did you know that Jesus never gets so busy that He cannot answer all the prayers, all the requests, and all the questions that we bring to Him? To what can we compare Him? We can say, "Jesus is like . . ."; but then we have to pause, for there is nothing that we can place beside Him!

Up to a given point He is just a good man, extremely kind, gracious and eager to please, answering every emotion in life that is around Him. Then we are lost, for in a moment He leaves all parallels and stands before us as God. And as God He defies all the standards by which we attempt to measure Him.

If we consider His message, we have to see Him as a Servant as well as the Master. He has no other plans when the heart really needs Him than to be where that need exists. He who would gird himself with the towel and wash the feet of the tired followers would also stand beside the tomb of sorrow and weep with the heartbroken family.

When Jesus stood before Pilate and was questioned in bitterness concerning His kingdom, He had nothing to say. When He was asked about greatness and position in His kingdom, He went beyond the question and picked up a little child in His arms and set Him in their midst. When He entered the chambers of sickness and sorrow and death, He used His healing touch, spoke to them about faith, and whispered about His resurrection.

People still come to Jesus in their helplessness, sorrow, pain, and emptiness. They know that nothing can touch the deepest need of the soul but the divine hand of Jesus Christ.

PRAYER: *We do not have to tell You, O Christ, that sometimes we pass through the waters and through the fire. You know all about the violence of the one and the heat of the other. You have been through every test and temptation common to mankind. Show us Your victory, stand beside us, and give us the strength of those who have been touched by Your power. Amen.*

■ AUGUST 27

For the word of God is quick, and powerful, and sharper than any twoedged sword.
(Heb. 4:12)

The man prayed today, "O Lord, give us some new meanings for those old words we have repeated so often." It bothered me! I had always thought that we should keep the meaning to those old words, for to change their old meaning would take away the real meaning.

When Jesus said, "no man can serve two masters" (Matt. 6:24), He meant that no man can serve two masters! It is impossible to belong absolutely to God and have some left over for the devil. This is what God demands. And the devil will settle for no less. The meaning of these words has not changed with the times.

When Jesus was tempted in the wilderness, His great defense came in those words, "It is written" (Matt. 4:4, 7, 10; Luke 4:4, 8, see 12), and the devil was defeated. This was an endorsement of Jesus Christ of all that was written in the Scriptures. We are not called upon to be geniuses in our conflict with the enemy, but we are challenged to use the Word.

The Sermon on the Mount, whose Preacher was none other than the Son of God, left us some of the most beautiful words ever spoken. What human wisdom can improve on them?

It says nothing of the blood of Christ, the Cross of Calvary, or salvation through believing on the Lord Jesus Christ. There is nothing in it on the doctrine of grace, justification by faith, or the assurance of adoption into the family of God. But the sermon would have no meaning had not man fallen from his first estate. When He said, "Love your enemies" (Matt. 5:44), it did not require any new interpretation to understand the meaning.

Let us read His words over and over again and again, but let us not do anything to them that will not stand the test of divine fire!

PRAYER: *O God, Your Word is sharp and clear to all those who come within its influence, and it has not changed with the ages. It is a lamp, a light, a trumpet, music, a song, and a friend. It is everything that can cheer and delight the soul. Apply it as a flame to our souls today, we pray in Jesus' name. Amen.*

AUGUST 28 ■

For I am the Lord, I change not ... Return unto me, and I will return unto you, saith the Lord of hosts.
(Mal. 3:6-7)

It seems that you can do anything you want to these days and get away with it" is an expression used frequently in our time. Part of the mind-set behind the words is an acquiescence to the nature of things as they presently exist. Part is still holding on to things as we would have them be. Beneath all the irregularities and uproar in life there is a steady line, a stable force, an unchangeableness, and a certainty that we dare not forfeit.

It can be the clashing of worlds, or ideas, or the fight between good and evil. It can be the superficial look that sees nothing wrong against the spiritual look to which one might trust for the true, the real, and the genuine. Through it all I must believe that there is an order of God that cannot be upset, and it is this order that rules all things in the long run.

How brief the work of our hands! Whatever they do, time will wear it out, for nature is the great spoiler of all human grandeur. But in the midst of it all God has placed His stamp of eternity. My hope, my security, and my eternity is in this spark of God!

If Christianity does anything, it teaches us how to behave ourselves in the changing times and varying of ideals. The Corinthian love chapter has not changed, and if we lose that love out of our living, we are nothing. And the words upon which our eternity is based are *humility, denial, crucifixion,* and *consecration.* And on these words God prepares us for His greater blessing, and it must not leave out the greater word: *obedience.*

"Strait is the gate, and narrow is the way, which leadeth unto life" (Matt. 7:14). This is God's way, and it does not change with the times.

PRAYER: *O God, everything in this old world is changing every day. But You do not change, and Your years do not fail. The earth grows old, and everything in it changes every moment. In You we can find our stability, our confidence, and our security. We are filled with delight in the midst of it all, for we know we are moving toward eternity. In Jesus' name. Amen.*

■ AUGUST 29

Come unto me, all ye that labour and are heavy laden, and I will give you rest. . . . For my yoke is easy, and my burden is light.
(Matt. 11:28, 30)

When I answered the phone, I sensed that my caller was facing serious problems; and as we talked, I knew he was holding back the thing that troubled him most. He had become involved in matters of legal consequence that could ruin his career, and there was serious danger of a rift in his home relationships.

In spelling out the details that had brought him to his present predicament, he finally blurted out, "But God will not leave me alone," and proceeded to spell out his problems. He wanted the gold of Barak, but he wanted the blessing of God, and he was having trouble with the latter. I responded, "These are the most beautiful words that I have ever heard in my entire ministry."

This is the way of a life that has been reared in a Christian atmosphere. God will not let people alone to go unhampered on the downward road to hell. He is not open to a compromise and will not adjust His concern to meet the whims of Satan.

God insists on having all and makes no room for a partner. He wants the whole heart, the entire will, and a mind that is fixed on Him. He comes upon us with His mighty hammer of love, which He wields with an arm of omnipotence, smashing every action we may conceive to replace Him. And He will not leave until our will has shut the door on His final plea.

Our God is a demanding God; His is a gospel of righteousness as well as a gospel of compassion, and righteousness can never confront unrighteousness without a battle. His gospel says, "Come out from among them, and be ye separate" (2 Cor. 6:17).

To every one whom God has created in His own image He is saying, "This world is not worthy of you, precious one, and I will not give you away!"

PRAYER: *Show us, O God, how terrible it is to allow opportunities to pass without accepting the responsibilities that are attached to them. Watch over us in love, and lead us in Your way. Teach us through the little to measure the value of the great. Do not leave us to our own imaginations, but follow us all the days of our lives. In Jesus' name. Amen.*

AUGUST 30

For I delivered unto you first of all that which I also received, how that Christ died for our sins according to the scriptures.
(1 Cor. 15:3)

No human mind could ever capture the full meaning of these words by Paul, "Christ died for our sins according to the scriptures." They reach beyond reason where faith takes hold and leads the way to the Cross. Paul had no New Testament, but he so read the Old Testament as to find Jesus Christ in it everywhere.

Jesus himself began with Moses, and from all the Scriptures He expounded to those tear-blinded disciples the things concerning himself. So loving was His appeal that the hearts of these despairing men felt a new glow and burning within them under the new reading of the old writings (Luke 24:27, 32). And when Paul read the Old Testament, he saw Christ dying for our sins.

Does not every reader of the Scripture, in a sense, see the Christ for himself as with his own eyes? After all the parade of witnesses have passed by, and all the glowing reports have been left behind, we can say, "I saw Him too!" Our Christianity is based not only upon historical evidence but also upon personal experience.

The theme of the entire Bible is captured in the Psalmist's song on Him who "shall have dominion . . . from sea to sea," "shall come down . . . as showers that water the earth," and "shall save the children of the needy" (72:8, 6, 4).

No matter how great in majesty and glory or how dazzling the diadem, we are assured by the Scriptures that He comes to save the poor and the needy. We who could never reach Him in His loftiness can meet Him in His condescension even at the Cross.

Here is the very crown of the Christian faith: "I have seen Him in the Scriptures, and I believe."

PRAYER: *O God, we thank You that You have written a Book on human life. Every chapter is an event, and every sentence is an occurrence marking each day. Beginning with Moses, we want to hear Jesus expound again to us the things concerning himself. Speak from Your own lips to our hearts. In Jesus' name. Amen.*

■ **AUGUST 31**

Ask, and it shall be given you; seek, and ye shall find; knock, and it shall be opened unto you: for every one that asketh receiveth.
(Matt. 7:7-8)

Heaven must be full of great and wonderful secrets. Our God has a way of revealing some of them to us as He sees we are able to receive them. When we think we have learned all that He has for us, He opens His Word and allows us another insight we had never known before. Life is full of mysterious and secret things, and God has kept many of His doors closed to us. In fact, in all of nature there is a point of unknowableness beyond which our minds cannot reach.

At the door of His knowledge God has placed a key: "Ask, and it shall be given you." It is through prayer, the highest asking and the most persistent application of human power, that God has chosen to reveal more of himself. The unseen hand holds the light, turns the pages, and reads the secret to the one who asks in earnest.

Who can know the work of God from the beginning? We look into the vastness of the heavens. We are baffled by the perfect sphere of the dewdrop. We speak often of the wisdom of the ant. Then we look within ourselves and realize that there is not a word on our tongues or a thought in our heart that is not known to God. And we cry out, "Great is the mystery of godliness" (1 Tim. 3:16)!

All the mysteries of heaven and earth are as a kindergarten compared to the mystery of the Cross. But in this mystery God has opened a door and shown us, in His love and mercy, His endeavor to rescue us from wickedness and restore us to His image and favor.

Today we know in part, but by faith we have a hope for His greater revelation tomorrow.

PRAYER: *O God, You have opened the door of heaven and shown us the power of Calvary in the Blood that takes away the stain of sin and removes the memory of our guilt from Your mind. You have revealed to us great and mighty things, and You have led us in strange ways. In Christ we have peace and joy. He leaves nothing to be desired, and we are thankful. In Jesus' name. Amen.*

SEPTEMBER 1 ■

The same came to Jesus by night, and said unto him, Rabbi, we know that thou art a teacher come from God: for no man can do these miracles that thou doest, except God be with him.
(John 3:2)

It has always made for an interesting prayer meeting when each person is called upon to relate the reason for being a follower of Jesus Christ. Whether it was used as a filler for lack of preparation on the part of the pastor, or whether it had been genuinely planned, the reasons given for being a Christian always varied greatly and showed the appeal of the Master to every individual. Every person comes to Christ for his own reason and sees in Him something that meets an individual need.

Nicodemus said that no man can do these miracles except God be with him. He saw in the power of Christ the possibility of a redeemed life. Others saw the miracle of the loaves and the fishes and declared, "This is of a truth that prophet that should come into the world" (John 6:14). As they saw this truth, they also saw a new beginning for themselves and their households.

Many of the Samaritans believed because of the testimony of the woman who declared that He "told me all things that ever I did" (John 4:29). Through her need they saw their own and found the water that satisfied their thirst.

People still see the conversion of friends, the work of Christianity in this world. They have seen the lion turn into a lamb, an alcoholic changed into a servant of God, and a broken home become a haven of love. The faculties of the mind have been opened, and the heart has responded to the One who gives the vision.

You can testify to the world out of your own experience and out of your own knowledge, and it will be eloquent and effective through the power of the Holy Spirit.

PRAYER: *We look upon our salvation, O God, and we say that herein is the miracle of the Cross and the triumph of the Holy Spirit. Wherein our old nature has been destroyed, we see the supreme miracle of grace through that name which is above every name. In Jesus' name. Amen.*

SEPTEMBER 2

Confess your faults one to another, and pray one for another, that ye may be healed. The effectual fervent prayer of a righteous man availeth much.
(James 5:16)

It has been observed that every great historical event has been marked by great prayers by good people. It is true that a great prayer marks a significant point in the life of a person or nation. The publican knew that he had prayed when he said, "God be merciful to me a sinner" (Luke 18:13). He had the answer in his heart before the last word ever escaped his lips. The woman knew when she had touched the hem of Christ's garment by the instant healing that had taken place.

We stand or fall by a spiritual relationship to the Divine. Our immortality stands in our relationship to Jesus Christ. We have no goodness or no charter giving us title to privilege in heaven. We are measured by eternal standards and judged in the courts of mercy and love. Everything we have we hold upon the merits of Calvary. Our prayers from lips of clay are placed before God by nail-pierced hands. Who can understand the miracle and mystery?

We know how to speak human wants in human words. We know the measure of our sorrow and the burdens that press most heavily. Often we pour out our petitions in many words, but sometimes there are no words to express the intent of the heart. Sometimes we pray as if we can break our own bonds and set ourselves free. We try and we fail.

There is only one Son of God. There is only one Cross. There is only one Atonement. There is only one hope. There is only one Source of prayer. Herein is the strength of the Christian way!

The great answer to prayer is an answer to the soul that only the soul can hear and understand.

PRAYER: *If our prayers were our only hope, O God, we would be in dire straits. But we mingle our petitions with the intercession of the one Priest and commit them to the mystery of the mediation of Jesus Christ himself. With the Cross as our altar we are assured of Your reply—the great Amen. In Jesus' name. Amen.*

SEPTEMBER 3

My help cometh from the Lord, which made heaven and earth. He will not suffer thy foot to be moved: he that keepeth thee will not slumber.
(Ps. 121:2-3)

Often through the years I have heard good people call upon God with the reminder that "one ... should ... chase a thousand, and two put ten thousand to flight" (Deut. 32:30). It sounded good, but the question remained of the incredibility of 1 man chasing 1,000 strong men armed for battle. All the probabilities of the case are against the statement, however good it may have appeared.

In my devotional reading this morning I came upon the statement again, but this time a little word stood out that made the difference! "Except." "Except their Rock had sold them, and the Lord had shut them up." In other words, "Except God had entered the scene with His power," victory would be out of the question.

Failure is certain, and the hosts of Satan surely would overpower every Christian person—"except." Except for faith in an omnipotent God, daily communion with Him, and spiritual renewal from those quiet times in prayer before the Almighty. Has it not been proven in the great battles of life, "If God be for us, who can be against us?" (Rom. 8:31).

Faith alone is not the big lesson here, but faith in a God greater than all the armies of evil in our world. The final answer always comes from heaven, and God will not turn His back on the threat from 10,000 enemies. There is no end to divine blessing. The challenge of God has always been, "Prove me now herewith, saith the Lord" (Mal. 3:10). God has always promised more as the battle with sin progresses.

Except for one thing our battles surely would end in failure. We could well say, "Blessed are they whose trust is in the living God, for they shall see the results of their labor."

PRAYER: *Your voice, O God, is powerful! It divides the flames of fire, yet it is a still, small voice. It discovers with infinite tenderness the broken heart, the wounded spirit, and the weary pilgrim, and it speaks peace to those who have no hope. We do not measure our strength by our own standards but by the omnipotence of God. In Jesus' name. Amen.*

■ SEPTEMBER 4

God that made the world ... hath determined the times before appointed, and the bounds of their habitation; that they should seek the Lord.
(Ps. 17:24, 26-27)

"Why can't I ... ?" These are about the first words a child learns to put together. Born into a world full of interesting things that little hands reach out after, the child is restrained by a higher authority. This is rather baffling, but it introduces a lesson that has to be learned, for life is marked all over with boundary lines. The option is ours whether we make them a prison or whether we use them as the road that leads to greater things.

We cannot get rid of boundaries, and life is full of limitations in ability, talent, gifts, intellect, and possibilities. And the acceptance of these distributions is one of the difficulties in life. Using to its uttermost what God has given to each individual is the great challenge of life.

There is nothing too little in the eyes of God. The poor widow with her mite may do more excellently than all of the rich men in the city. Jesus took the "little child" and set him in the midst of the disciples and said, "If you would be great, become as this little one" (see Matt. 18:1-4). Jesus placed His standard of greatness within the bounds of this young one.

Life's boundary lines spell discipline for all of God's people, and sometimes the line gets very fine between our love for and our bitterness against much of the discipline. The highest discipline—and it is possible to every one of us, whether we have much or little—is that we can be a child of God, God's servant, and a follower of Jesus Christ.

The command of the Master still is "Seek ye first the kingdom of God, and his righteousness; and all these things shall be added unto you" (Matt. 6:33). Try it today; it still works!

PRAYER: *You have placed us in some strange circumstances, O God, and You have caused us to pass under some very unusual disciplines. You have put in our spirit an eternal song and a determination in our soul that says God's will be done and His name be glorified. May Jesus Christ, the hope of glory, be formed in our hearts. In His name. Amen.*

SEPTEMBER 5 ■

But whoso keepeth his word, in him verily is the love of God perfected: hereby know we that we are in him.
(1 John 2:5)

There is scarcely a churchgoing person alive today who has not heard a sermon preached on the use of the word "know" in the First Epistle of John. He insists on a personal and definite knowledge of things pertaining to the ways of salvation. There is no think so, hope so, or guess so in his reasoning, but there is a definite "I know." And that is good, for John lived in the presence of Jesus and learned firsthand those things that were close to the heart of the Master.

The genius of Christianity is that it calls on its people to know. It gives them a faith that sweeps away the uncertainties and tells us that God loves, that He redeems, and that He also keeps. This kind of knowledge is not confined to the intellectual faculties, and it is not found solely on the library shelves or told only in logical propositions.

There is a knowledge of feeling. There is a divine certainty planted in the soul. There is a knowledge of the heart. There is a knowledge that comes from above. There is a faculty reaching beyond the grasp of the mind or the touch of the hand that gets hold of heaven and places an "I know" in its very depths. It lays hold upon God with a knowledge that earth cannot provide.

John backs up his statement and secures it with "And hereby we do know that we know him, *if* we keep his commandments" (1 John 2:3, italics added). It is a keeping-on process that never allows a vacancy in which one has time to doubt. It is praying without ceasing, watching with expectation, waiting on the Lord, listening, obeying.

When your soul is at its highest and best, then it can say with certainty, "I know."

PRAYER: *Help us know, O God, that Your Spirit dwells within us because Your words abide in us. Make us to follow on to know You better every day of our lives. Help us know that when human hope has gone from our world, Jesus will come through the gloom and make it glow with the brightness of the morning. In His name. Amen.*

SEPTEMBER 6

Salvation belongeth unto the Lord: thy blessing is upon thy people.
(Ps. 3:8)

We have heard it! We have accepted it. We expect to hear it often. Is it just routine, or is it real?

The man of God stretches forth his hand and asks divine blessing upon his congregation. It is a call for a melting tenderness and a sacred uplifting that will carry the people to a new level of service by a consciousness of the presence of the Holy Spirit of God.

We have seen the Emmaus Stranger mingle with His people. We have heard His message delivered straight to the soul of the seeker. We have seen the fire burn and hardened hearts recognize the Master. We have seen the soft, tender touch of God hover over the church with a deep sense of awe and mystery. We have seen love rise above circumstances and knew it was inspired by the Holy Spirit. And we said, "These are great days in the Church of Jesus Christ."

God never leads a congregation to a place of expectancy in order that they might be overcome by the power of the impossible. God never places an urgency of prayer upon a heart so that He might deny the petition. Petitions that are made in faith are their own answers.

God does want His people to know that He has a blessing of His own for every one who prays and believes. Jesus Christ has a tender word that none but the Son of God can speak. The Holy Spirit has encouragement and comfort more fitting than the human mind can imagine.

It is good to talk to heaven, to say what our requests are and name them one by one. On the mystery of prayer and faith God still places His benediction.

PRAYER: *O God, in our deepest need, when our eyes are turned toward heaven, You send down a blessing to rest upon the weary soul. Then You tell us that You will never leave us nor forsake us. We are overwhelmed by this blessed assurance. Give us a song and a touch of tenderness for the last mile of the journey. In Jesus' name. Amen.*

SEPTEMBER 7

What man of you, having an hundred sheep, if he lose one of them, doth not leave the ninety and nine in the wilderness, and go after that which is lost, until he find it?
(Luke 15:4)

Trees had grown up around the old church, hiding it from view. The roof had caved in, and the plaster from the ceiling and walls covered the floor. The windows had been smashed in, and the doors creaked on rusty hinges. An old man stood by, recounting the glory days, while my friend and I salvaged some pews for our home mission church a few miles away. Tears of joy streamed down the old man's face as he saw that some good was able to come out of these shambles of time.

A church standing in ruin! A human being reduced to a state of helplessness! Loneliness! We amuse ourselves with the song about "This Old House" that we are not going to need much longer, and we detail the pieces that are wearing out. But the mirth is lost in the reality of sadness for the one who is experiencing the loss of the days when life was full and exuberant. Then the great house is given up and the proud head stoops beneath the roof. The hand that was a symbol of authority droops by the side in pitiful weakness, and the voice becomes faint and without meaning.

Our society is full of loneliness, helplessness, blighted hope, and undetermined future. And the bravest living today will be battered down by these things tomorrow. How good to know that in the shambles One is looking for a few usable items that can be salvaged so that tears of joy may flow again. Jesus always went about searching, and He looked until He had found that which had been lost.

When the last human hope has gone out, Jesus Christ will come through the darkness and make it glow with the brightness of the morning.

PRAYER: *Lord Jesus, You left the ninety and nine and came after the one that was lost. May Your searching power take hold of our whole being so that everything that was lost by sin may be recovered at Calvary. Perfect us anew in all the graces of Your truth. Amen.*

■ **SEPTEMBER 8**

Of every tree of the garden thou mayest freely eat: but of the tree of the knowledge of good and evil, thou shalt not eat of it: for in the day that thou eatest thereof thou shalt surely die.
(Gen. 2:16-17)

One day God planted a beautiful Garden eastward in Eden and grew in it every tree that was good for food. Then He placed in it the man He had formed, to tend it and keep it. After a while He made a helper for Adam, and they stood in innocence and unashamed before a holy God. Thus states the Genesis account of man's early relationship to God.

Now we hear God speaking again. This time it is to Joshua, and He told him to speak to the children of Israel to appoint to themselves cities of refuge, where the innocent would be able to flee for protection from the avenger.

In between these two accounts there opens a great, black shadow in the middle of God's beautiful creation. Sin has marred the Garden home, and man has been thrown out to face a world of unharnessed sin. God comes on the scene and drops an armload of justice in the pathway of the pursuer and sets forth the ministry of love and mercy operating in this hateful scenario of sin.

Today we can take heart, for the God who walked with the innocent in the Garden has covered that innocence with His protection of justice. A spirit of integrity pervades the entire story of God. It was God who conceived the city of refuge to make the most and best of His people and to give them a new chance.

Here is the heart of the gospel, for at last He set up the Cross and said, "This is all that I can do!" For while God provides for the sinner, He also provides for the innocent!

Even as the flaming sword was flashing death at the gate of the Garden, love had already begun to write, "Come unto me, all ye that labour and are heavy laden, and I will give you rest" (Matt. 11:28).

PRAYER: *O God, You never did tell us that the Christian life would be an easy way! Often we do not realize the deep trouble we have been in until we have been delivered and found refuge in the great heart of Your redeeming love. What greater refuge has ever been provided than the promise, "Lo, I am with you alway, even unto the end of the world." Keep us ever in Your protective care. In Jesus' name. Amen.*

SEPTEMBER 9 ■

O death, where is thy sting? O grave, where is thy victory? . . . But thanks be to God, which giveth us the victory through our Lord Jesus Christ.
(1 Cor. 15:55, 57)

In the eulogy this morning at the funeral of a very influential person, the speaker noted, "We must all go down to a common grave." My mind leaped back in time to the emperors, kings, rulers, presidents, and philanthropists who had walked a wide road and stood tall in their day. Now they have all joined the "world-crowd," and a green mound marks their resting-place.

This law is universal and has been written by the finger of God as indelibly as though etched in stone on the mountain. Influence and power succumbed to their decree, but at last all are found in the multitude that cannot be numbered. There comes a moment when all distinctions are mingled and all differences forgotten, and all take their places in the pile of clay.

What might appear as a divine judgment upon the human race can be turned into a means of grace and a source of hope. God knows our frame, and He remembers that we are dust; but it is He who will judge with an infinite wisdom that measures every life that has come into the world.

The heart of Christianity for all people is to know God, the Judge, the Fountain, and the Spring of all things. There is more to life than merely to be born, to live, and then to "sleep with our fathers and be buried with them." The greater law says, "If any man be in Christ, he is a new creature" (2 Cor. 5:17). Here the common grave is not the end, for we may grow in Christ forever, constantly going out after God and never exhausting His grace, yet ever increasing in our capacity to receive it.

"O death, where is thy sting? O grave, where is thy victory?"

PRAYER: *O God, our hearts would be full of fear when we think about death if You had not told us its true meaning. By being in Christ, we shall die into a greater life. We do not die into darkness and extinction, but we die into light and immortality. Our fear is no longer in the grave, for we triumph in our Lord's victory, and we rise again in His resurrection. In His name. Amen.*

■ SEPTEMBER 10

Whoso offereth praise glorifieth me: and to him that ordereth his conversation aright will I shew the salvation of God.
(Ps. 50:23)

God must keep a special book to record all the promises people make to Him at the point of despair and death. Out of the foxholes of life have come great bargaining with God for extension of days and times of peace. Many have cried and prayed and wrestled with God as circumstances condensed life into its bitterest moment.

Sometimes God hears the cry and grants the petition. Sometimes God allows us to have our own way in prayer. Sometimes we have been permitted in wrestling with God to rise as the conqueror. Sometimes God sends us quails in the desert and allows the water to gush from the rock when we cry out in selfish and ignorant prayer.

It is well that we should pray. It is normal to reach out to God in the crises of life. The danger is that we hold on to the problem even while we are making the petition. We forget about the ever-working grace of God and the continual miracle of the Holy Spirit operating in the lives of His people. The glory and the mystery of the Cross is "I am crucified with Christ . . . I live by the faith of the Son of God, who loved me, and gave himself for me" (Gal. 2:20).

It takes God a long time to make Christians out of some of us and to get us to that place where we can honestly say, "Not my will, but thine, be done" (Luke 22:42). And when He does answer some great need, we are slow in saying, "This is God's hand at work. This is God's miracle. I owe to Him the good things of this day!"

A mighty prayer, the tender violence that storms the throne of God and brings down grace, love, and healing but does not own the Giver makes hell rejoice while heaven mourns.

PRAYER: *O God, we are grateful to know that Christ is praying for us in the very act of Your answering our petitions. Your Holy Spirit intercedes in a speech we could never utter. May we ever be willing to receive Your answers as Your gift, and make our hearts rich in praise, rejoicing in the triumph of Calvary. In Jesus' name. Amen.*

SEPTEMBER 11

Behold, as the eyes of servants look unto the hand of their masters . . . ; so our eyes wait upon the Lord our God, until that he have mercy upon us.
(Ps. 123:2)

The question was asked in Sunday School this morning by an honest seeker after God. Life for this person had not been normal. Alcohol had been the downfall, and violence had stolen the few shreds of happiness left in the home. Living alone in a small apartment with her two children, unable to work, she was reaching out for hope that she was sure was not reachable. The question: "If God is a God of love, why does He not show himself more clearly than He does? Why can't I find Him?"

Then comes a greater question, "How far does God manifest himself, and when does He do it?" How easy it becomes for us to dictate to God in matters concerning our own welfare! How easy for us to write the program for God and to appoint the way for the Almighty.

God has never been able to reveal much of himself to the heart that is not prepared to receive Him. "How can I find God?" is the cry. "How can I get to your heart?" is the response. When we begin to set up standards, lay down rules, and map out paths for the movement of heaven, God remains silent to the soul.

Our position before the Almighty is as a dependent. I have nothing that does not bear His signature. The very fact of our dependence should lead us to be careful how we measure the place God can assume in our lives.

Our little day is too short to know the full mystery of God. We can find God if we come with an open heart, saying, "Speak, Lord; for thy servant heareth" (1 Sam. 3:9). When we remain dependent upon Him for the revelation, He will become our God and Source of strength.

PRAYER: *O God, Your knowledge of us is beyond our understanding. You know our needs, our ambition, our desire, our hope, and You know our hearts and our prayers. Help us not just to come to You in our selfishness when the bottom drops out of life. Draw us near to the Cross, where with an open heart we will receive Your forgiveness and grace. In Jesus' name. Amen.*

■ **SEPTEMBER 12**

Then when Mary was come where Jesus was, and saw him, she fell down at his feet, saying unto him, Lord, if thou hadst been here, my brother had not died.
(John 11:32)

Much of our life is based on that conditional factor, "if." "If it does not rain." "If everything goes well." "If you do, then I can." And on and on we lay our plans, wrap them tightly in negative possibilities, and neatly tie them with a security knot, "if." It has come to be a keyword indicative of our thinking and philosophies of life. But the word is not new, for it was used by Jesus and the disciples as well as the chief priests and the Pharisees.

The "if" of ignorance was used in accusation by Martha and Mary, "If thou hadst been here . . ." (vv. 21, 32). Then they sat down with Jesus, and He revealed to them some aspects of himself that He might well have revealed to a vast audience. They were trying to believe that death and Jesus cannot be in the same chamber together, so they had to believe that He was late and all was lost.

They could not believe that Jesus never comes too late. Nor could they believe that the black, grim servant who visits thousands of homes every day is not something wholly apart from God. Death is not an enemy that takes advantage of Jesus' absence, but in a mysterious way it is a servant of the court of heaven.

That little "if" follows life to the end, for if Jesus is present, there can be no death. "I am the Resurrection and the Life; *if* you live and believe in Me, you shall never die" (see John 11:25). If Jesus is in the heart, there can be no death. We need to know that the little child will not die but goes up like a dewdrop called for by the warm sun. We need to know that in the house of the saint death itself becomes a sacrament.

There is that "if" that calls to faith and to heaven and conquers death. "If thou wouldest believe, thou shouldest see the glory of God" (v. 40). We will "know if we follow on to know the Lord" (Hos. 6:3).

PRAYER: *O God, so much of life is conditional upon so many other things that we are lost in the confusion. But we do know that You have conquered death, and if we are "in Christ," we need not fear the terrible enemy. May the vision of our souls be upward, and let our hearts cry out, "How good and gracious is the Lord." In Jesus' name. Amen.*

SEPTEMBER 13 ■

And the King shall answer and say unto them, Verily I say unto you, Inasmuch as ye have done it unto one of the least of these my brethren, ye have done it unto me.
(Matt. 25:40)

I was just a small boy, and I found myself surrounded by men in a lumber camp who had led a rough and tough life. But one of those men put out his hand to me and called me "Partner." He gave me some spruce gum, and he cut a fishing pole and baited my hook with salt pork; and when I pulled in a small perch, he made me feel like it was the biggest event in his life.

At the time I accepted his acts with gratitude in my tender heart, but over the years I have learned that it goes by the name of "kindness." And I have learned that more people hunger for kindness than for bread. Just a gentle word spoken from the heart. One small hint of courtesy. One approach of love. One smile of sympathy and understanding. Hold back your crust of bread, but hold out your hand and say, "Partner."

Not too many people can lift the burden of debt and poverty from the poor and underprivileged. But we can all conduct ourselves as if we would relieve the burden if we could. Kindness brings with it a great, comforting sense of divine nearness, and it creates a heavenly peace in the heart as the companion of suffering. Kindness has an enduring quality, and the more it is used, the greater it becomes.

No person ever becomes so hard that a word of praise, encouragement, or gratitude is not acceptable. A gentle hint of praise, and the dark shadows of defeat are gone. A pat on the back, and a bold step is taken in some difficult venture. A kind word, and courage comes on to defeat an army.

How simple a thing to cut a fishing pole and say, "Go catch 'em, Partner!"

PRAYER: *O God, You are so kind to us that one look is as the morning and the beginning of heaven. Help us to pass it on to that one who looks but does not see and asks but does not find. May the small things that we can do be a support and comfort, and as we are fed by Your kindnesses, may we pass them on. In Jesus' name. Amen.*

SEPTEMBER 14

> Jesus saith unto her, Woman, why weepest thou? whom seekest thou? She, supposing him to be the gardener, saith unto him, Sir, if thou have borne him hence, tell me where thou hast laid him, and I will take him away.
> (John 20:15)

We hear it so often, "I'm at my wit's end. I do not know what to do." And I suppose this is one way of saying that something more is needed in this old world than simply our human ability to meet life's bigger moments. Or it could be a confession that while we were attending to minor details, important matters of life slipped away. And it could be that while life should have glowed with a vibrant faith, it has ended in bitter disappointment.

When we fail to see the divine hand above the human efforts, life becomes a scrambled race and a very disorderly movement. Seldom does it occur to us that God might have had a hand in the outcome; but when we think of it, we are ready to censure and condemn. The problem is that we look for the cruel hand of injustice and close our eyes to the divine beneficent hand working in the shadows. But when His good hand is seen, the whole drama changes as we watch Him bring order out of what has been pure chaos.

Jesus Christ is grander and more alive in our everyday living than we can ever imagine, and we must not see Him only as a theory. His is a divine and infinite life, partaking of our spirit, entering into our thoughts, and making himself part of every move we make. He is not a dead Christ hanging on a crucifix but a vibrant personality standing alive outside the empty tomb, saying, "I am alive for evermore" (Rev. 1:18).

Who has ever seen or known the whole truth of God? Mary could see Him only as the gardener. The disciples listened to Him as a wise man explaining the Scriptures. We see in Him only what we need for the moment.

May the Lord pity our ignorance and show us the true Christ so that our "joy might be full" (John 15:11).

PRAYER: *O God, we place ourselves in Your hands today, not for personal gain but willingly and wisely. We are persuaded that in our limited understanding we cannot know what is best for us. Direct our lives, we pray, as we cast all of our cares upon You. You have told us that we can do this because You love us. In Jesus' name. Amen.*

SEPTEMBER 15 ■

Trust in the Lord with all thine heart; and lean not unto thine own understanding. In all thy ways acknowledge him, and he shall direct thy paths.
(Prov. 3:5-6)

According to the reports in the Bible, God does not seem to have much room for halfheartedness. The church that was neither hot nor cold was not acceptable to the Christ of God. The person who is not all bad or all good, whose days are made up of cloud and glory, and is as a fountain that can send out both sweet water and bitter, has a difficult time getting God's approval.

God insists on knowing the state of a person's heart. He wants to know its greatest desire and its purpose for every area of living. And He expects a firm and positive answer, for the answer determines the relationship with heaven.

To be sure, God's people are called upon to grow, to advance, to become wiser and stronger every day. He wants us to have a heart that is filled with the divine fire, sanctified and permeated by the Holy Ghost. He knows the struggles of the heart that is bound by the double-mindedness of Satan. And it is in the determination of the heart from which He makes His judgment.

Life is made up of two opposing forces. Paul knew it and testified to its effect on his life when he was under the bondage of the flesh. God never makes provision for anyone to fall before the opposition. His challenge is to stand firm for truth. Be strong in the battle. At every point the touch of God is there to encourage His people onward.

If we go to church and sing hymns on Sunday, we should still have a song in our heart in the marketplace on Monday. When we testify to God's grace on Wednesday, the abundant supply must be sufficient for Thursday also.

He can take the instability of the double-minded person and make all his ways an acknowledgment of His grace and power.

PRAYER: *Take charge of our whole life, O God, and keep it without condemnation into Your eternity. Help us so that the enemy will have no charge over us, but may our present and future be under the control of heaven. Speak to us those tender words that will make us live forevermore. In Jesus' name. Amen.*

■ SEPTEMBER 16

The kingdom of heaven is like to a grain of mustard seed, which a man took, and sowed in his field... but when it is grown... becometh a tree.
(Matt. 13:31-32)

Jesus said that the kingdom of heaven was like a grain of mustard seed, and He proceeded to outline the qualities of the seed. We have taken it from there and majored on the greatness of the little kernel, but we have forgotten the real issue: the kingdom of heaven. Jesus was always trying to lead us heavenward, while we have labored to keep our minds on earth.

When Peter talked about our growing in grace, he was speaking about the mustard seeds of growth in the kingdom of heaven. Who can understand the mysteriousness of growth? You cannot see it from moment to moment, but when God's earth, sun, rain, light, wind, and germ are thrown in motion, the whole thing works together to express in something beautiful the purpose of the Creator.

Jesus was saying, "My heavenly kingdom is just like that." How silently and invisibly the saint of God grows to the full expression of God's purpose when the spiritual elements combine under the sunshine of His love!

Jesus did love the birds, and He did care about their roosting places; but He was saying, "How much more will the kingdom of heaven provide a place for you to 'come and lodge.'" And His call was to the Church! Men, women, children, the outcast, the helpless, the homeless, the prodigal, the wanderer, the seeker after righteousness—come and find an open hand, an open heart, and an open hearth in the Church! Be drawn by the glow of its love until you have come into God's sanctuary of truth.

The seed of the kingdom of heaven has been planted, and it is growing and expanding; and someday we shall see it as it is and say, "This is none other than the work of God!"

PRAYER: *We thank You, O God, that You let us see beyond the narrow lines of time. We cannot tell what we see, or what we are; but by Your touch our souls are enlarged and enriched, and we know it was the touch of heaven. Give us the mustard seed touch so that we might be of great usefulness in Your kingdom. In Jesus' name. Amen.*

SEPTEMBER 17 ■

> And without controversy great is the mystery of godliness: God was manifest in the flesh, justified in the Spirit, seen of angels, preached unto the Gentiles, believed on in the world, received up into glory.
> (1 Tim. 3:16)

Just six words, "God was manifest in the flesh." But on these words hangs the mystery of the Godhead. When we want to know what God is, what He does, what He thinks, what He wishes, and how He governs His world, we have to look at Jesus Christ. Jesus Christ is a revelation of God. He is God manifest in the flesh. When we have looked upon Jesus, we have looked upon God.

We look at the God of the Old Testament, and we think of Him in terms of thunder, rolling clouds, a loud voice, and trumpets. In Jesus we see a different phase of God. We see One who is never so great as when He is stooping over someone who needs His care. We see One who is not content that there are 99 in the fold. It is the one that is not there that makes His heart break. We see no longer the God of the ivory throne but a father-mother-heart responding to every cry of need.

When Jesus looks on a city and weeps over it, He is God manifest in the flesh. He associated himself with sinners. He went into their homes with them and ate and drank with them. He brought around Him the deaf, the dumb, the blind, and the lepers, and He healed them. A Christ with tears in His eyes, a heart broken in sorrow, a crown of thorns on His head, and a heavy wooden Cross on His back—this is God manifest in the flesh!

To us today, He is no less God when He causes the thunder to roll or orders the storm to be quiet as when He takes a little child up in His arms and blesses him.

Here is the very beauty and glory of the manifestation! Hidden in the omnipotence of God is the tenderness of love!

PRAYER: *O God, it is a joy to know that You are on the throne and that Your judgments are true and righteous altogether. Help us to know that all that is deepest and truest in our life is found in Jesus Christ, the Manifestation of the Father. We live and move and have our being in Your wondrous ways. In Jesus' name. Amen.*

SEPTEMBER 18

There was a man of the Pharisees, named Nicodemus, a ruler of the Jews ... Jesus answered and said unto him, Verily, verily, I say unto thee, Except a man be born again, he cannot see the kingdom of God.
(John 3:1, 3)

God has always seemed to accomplish His greatest work with one person. The people in Jerusalem were united as one and in one place when the Holy Spirit came upon them in power. It was a Nicodemus, a Lazarus, a widow, a blind man, and a prodigal son through whom Jesus showed His greatest power in love and concern. He never counted the mobs by number, and He easily singled out the man in the sycamore tree to teach another lesson.

After all, need is an individual thing, and God has always been able to single it out for special attention. One person may be fighting battles every day in the week, and no other person in the routine of living may know about it. Our safety may be in fellowship, but the balm for the healing is applied in those personal moments alone with God.

People develop along the lines of simplicity. All the pomp and robes are thrown aside, along with the gold trimmings and relics of power, to lay bare the deeper needs of the soul. One of the great revelations given to us is that "God is a Spirit: and they that worship him must worship him in spirit and in truth" (John 4:24). A person is never more alone than when He bows before God in worshipful prayer.

The greatest words of encouragement ever spoken were, "To day shalt thou be with me in paradise" (Luke 23:43). And they were not spoken to the mob that was watching Him die. They were spoken to the lone sufferer who died beside the Master on the Cross.

The humblest, the most vile, through the Blood of the everlasting covenant and the mystery of the Cross, is a single name written in the book of heaven by God!

PRAYER: *O God, You come to Your people in all their circumstances of loneliness and pain and weakness. Help us to make the most of opportunities to help and to heal and also to be alone with You. May the Holy Spirit himself be a comfort to all who need the balm of Your blessing. In Jesus' name. Amen.*

SEPTEMBER 19

And the publican, standing afar off, would not lift up so much as his eyes unto heaven, but smote upon his breast, saying, God be merciful to me a sinner.
(Luke 18:13)

There never have been steps taken in a downward direction or toward evil or in any backward form without the action being covered with an excuse. The excuse is given in a sincerity adequate to cover any opposition. Justification for the act seems to have been satisfied if an action of equal magnitude can be found in one of high standing in the church or in the community.

"I am better than a lot of people who call themselves Christians" is a cliché that has been overworked by the devil. And the excuse is usually followed by further justification: "I do the best I can, live by the Golden Rule, and trust in the mercy of God." But finding salvation in the mercy of God is falling short of the mark and must be extended to the confession, "God be merciful to me a sinner."

God's mercy is found in Bethlehem, in Gethsemane, and on Calvary in the dying Son of God, and it is too sacred a thing with which to trifle. To live a life of sin and to crucify God's Son afresh every day and still hope to call upon His mercy in the final hour is a travesty against the goodness of God.

We live today in His mercy; every morning we should hallow the day with the prayer, "God be merciful to me a sinner," and every night we recover from our feeble attempts toward goodness and lay our life before Him with the cry, "God be merciful to me a sinner." The mercy of God is found in the life, the ministry, the death, the resurrection, and the whole of salvation through Jesus Christ.

Our justification is found, not in the excuses we make but in His invitation, "Come . . ." When we empty ourselves of ourselves, we can understand and accept this invitation.

PRAYER: *Gracious Father, we come to You as the God of mercy as well as the God of judgment. We pray for pardoning mercy, lest we come at the last before Your judgment. God be merciful to us and save us in the hour of temptation, and deliver us from the enemy of our souls as Your Spirit lifts up a standard against him. This we ask in Jesus' name. Amen.*

SEPTEMBER 20

Why art thou cast down, O my soul? and why art thou disquieted within me? hope thou in God: for I shall yet praise him, who is the health of my countenance, and my God.
(Ps. 42:11)

A long time ago I read a statement that went something like this: "Nothing is ever as good as we hope, but it is never as bad as we fear." Even though things did not turn out as we wanted them to, cheer up, they could have been worse! There are events we cannot control and sorrows for which we have no healing. But every night has its turning toward the morning, and behind every black cloud there is a shining sun!

God's Book assures us that He has the power to turn every curse into a blessing, and the ultimate triumph of every victorious one is found in His care. Under the most difficult circumstance we can bring ourselves face-to-face with the eternal God, where hope is renewed and purpose is filled with meaning.

How much is lost in life by not turning to God! Those who have laid the foundation for our Christian faith looked up when they saw the Almighty, and they put out their hand to touch the hem of His garment. The curses that have been breathed upon the human race by hell may be turned into a blessing by the great and good power of the Holy Spirit of God.

The Psalmist's song answered its own question, "Why art thou cast down, O my soul? . . . hope thou in God." He saw that God's blessing is the only abiding support, and any blessing short of the divine was not worth having. He knew that it was possible to be lifted above all fear and be encouraged in the Spirit of God, who will transform life into something worth living.

Our faith tells us that the tragedy of Eden fades away, Calvary is clothed in beauty, and our worst day can be our best in the power of God's redeeming love.

PRAYER: *We thank You, O God, for all Christian hope and confidence. We need this in the dark times, on cloudy days, and when the sun is shut out. This hope tells us how great is Your love, how tender Your pity, and that You can do that exceeding abundantly when our faith begins to fade. Keep us strong in this faith. In Jesus' name. Amen.*

SEPTEMBER 21

Yea, though I walk through the valley of the shadow of death, I will fear no evil: for thou art with me; thy rod and thy staff they comfort me.
(Ps. 23:4)

A wonderful book to read is by the person who knows all the problems of society, can speak all the beautiful words of the counseling chamber, and cites models of behavior for every crisis of life. Yet the same person can be a disadvantage when sorrow and personal suffering have come into the home or in the life of an individual.

There are moments that call for a reading of the book through tears out of infinite sorrow and brokenness. Those who have never been in the valley of the shadow of death may astound us with their wisdom and awe us with their knowledge, but only sorrow can speak to sorrow with a voice that understands, for only sorrow could have written the words that are needed.

When the light has gone out, and darkness prevails; when summer has ended, and the cold blast of winter is upon us; when the birds have gone, and the flowers have faded; when the laughter has ceased, and sorrow has taken its place at the table—*then* we want comfort and understanding from someone who has walked through the valley.

We can find all of these things in God's Book, and out of His broken heart He can read to us in a language we can know and understand. It has the noblest words for our sorrow, and the purest music for our joy. It has the balm for our needs with a touch impossible to find in any other book. Here there is a sharing of sorrow, for the human and the Divine find common ground.

Sorrow opens the heart's door, so that no man can shut it; and it keeps the door open, so that all may enter who need comfort, quietness, peace, and hope.

PRAYER: *O God, You know what life is to each one of Your children. Sometimes it is a great cloud filled with terror, and sometimes it is a bright summer day filled with music. In whatever state You find us, let Your sanctifying blessing fall on us, so that we may be comforted by the One who knew sorrow in order to bring salvation to a dying world. In His name. Amen.*

■ SEPTEMBER 22

And they told him, that Jesus of Nazareth passeth by. And he cried, saying, Jesus, thou son of David, have mercy on me.
(Luke 18:37-38)

Sometimes when I read the Bible, it appears that Jesus just happened to be in certain places at the time of crisis; and since He was there, He performed His acts of mercy. When Jesus happened to pass by, He saw a man, He heard a cry, He felt the touch of a hand—He met the need! But when I ask the question again, "Why did Jesus pass this way?" I hear another answer, "Love is always where the need is the greatest."

Jesus Christ has always made it His business to find out who needs Him. He stands at the door and knocks. He sits at the well and waits. He walks along the seashore and listens. He never forces himself upon anyone, but He graciously makes His presence felt, and in a thousand ways He sends the message that He is there.

There is a note of sadness running through the Gospels, pointing up a weak spot in humanity. The people rushed to see what the Master was doing rather than listen to what He was saying. They would have cared nothing about Him if He had not done mighty things in their midst. As long as He was a curiosity, they mobbed Him and asked questions; but when He went to worship, He went alone.

He knew that His message would reach some, and He told them about himself. He declared himself to be the Light of the World, the Bread sent down from heaven, and the Savior of all men. He told them about His suffering. He knew that without the Cross nothing could cleanse the stain of sin from the heart.

Whether it just happened, or whether it was planned that way, one thing I know: that Jesus came by, and "whereas I was blind, now I see" (John 9:25)!

PRAYER: *We thank You, Lord Jesus, that one day You passed by and stopped and gave us hope. Every day You come to our world with new revelation, new hope, and new helpfulness. You who walked with Your people to Emmaus and talked on the mount with Moses, reveal to us some of those things concerning yourself so that our hearts may burn within because of Your love. Amen.*

SEPTEMBER 23

But ye are not in the flesh, but in the Spirit, if so be that the Spirit of God dwell in you. Now if any man have not the Spirit of Christ, he is none of his.
(Rom. 8:9)

I saw the power of God at work in the life of a young man. Strong drink had controlled his life, and he was on his way to an alcoholic's grave. But a caring pastor stood in the way and brought him and his family under the influence of a loving and forgiving God.

On his furlough from the mission field he was introduced to the congregation as one in whom "the Spirit of Christ dwelt in all His fullness." The introduction was sincere, and the response from the audience was positive. It was not a case of bringing Christ down to a human level, but the power of Omnipotence transforming a man into what God wanted him to become.

Christ's true relationship to the human family is in His own words, "Whosoever shall do the will of my Father which is in heaven" (Matt. 12:50). It can include the one caught in the master web of sin. Every sinner can enter into the fellowship of heaven and be empowered by the Spirit of Christ.

The Spirit of Christ! In the final analysis is not this the standard by which all life and thought will be judged? If one fails here, it doesn't matter where else one might succeed. The demand goes straight to the mark, and the Bible allows no other way. "If any man have not the Spirit of Christ, he is none of his."

The Spirit of Christ means meekness, gentleness, kindness, sympathy, and forgiveness. But that is not all. Love is the greatest characteristic of the Son of God. Love means everything, and it will never be changed. The writer might have said, "If any man have not love, he is none of his."

Whatever the day might ask, let it find its answer in a Spirit of Love.

PRAYER: *Almighty God, we pray that You will send upon this old world a renewal of Your pardoning love and grace. Lift every opposing load of guilt and send that liberating ray of love through the dark gloom of lives that are in despair. This is Your miracle. Our world needs love. In Jesus' name. Amen.*

■ **SEPTEMBER 24**

When his disciples heard it, they were exceedingly amazed, saying, Who then can be saved?
(Matt. 19:25)

When the disciples looked on the negatives while they listened to the teachings of Jesus, their reaction was, "Who then can be saved?" And in a real sense the matter of salvation is a conundrum, for who can know the mind of God? To look at salvation from the human standpoint has elicited the question, "How can these things be?" (John 3:9).

Only God could tell us that it is impossible to come to Christ in any sense of acceptance except through one gate. And the gate of acceptance, assurance, and forgiveness is known in heaven and on earth as the Cross. When they asked about the numbers being saved, Christ remained silent; but He challenged them to "strive to enter in at the strait gate" (Luke 13:24).

"Who then can be saved?" It troubled those early believers, and it has been a source of theological conflict ever since. The standards of judgment set up by the disciples crumbled before the Man on the Cross when He said to the dying sinner, "To day shalt thou be with me in paradise" (Luke 23:43). Jesus Christ will shut out no one that He can bring in, and at the last final day He will be the Judge.

The greatest mark of salvation is the spirit of love, which the disciples had not yet captured. Love makes room for a friend, a neighbor, an enemy—another. Love begins with little and ends with much more. Love can never exhaust God, for it works on the bank account of heaven. Love does not discriminate, but it says, "Brother, take my hand!" Love says, "Set another place at the table!"

The salvation of God that fills the soul with love says we must go and tell everybody all over the world. The greater question becomes, "Who then can be saved and not share it?" This is the salvation of Christ in action!

PRAYER: *Your ministry toward us, O God, is a ministry of salvation. You are always seeking those whom You may turn toward yourself. You give the glorious liberty of Your salvation to the captive, and You set the prisoner free. Let Your Holy Spirit baptize us with fire from above and show us more of Your great salvation. In Jesus' name. Amen.*

SEPTEMBER 25

Again, the kingdom of heaven is like unto treasure hid in a field; the which when a man hath found, he hideth, and for joy thereof goeth and selleth all that he hath, and buyeth that field.
(Matt. 13:44)

It was Sunday morning, and the congregation was singing with great enthusiasm and from varying years of experience, "He's forgiven my transgressions; / He has cleansed my heart from sin." The presence of God was very near in the service.

A young lady and her little boy had taken their seat near the front of the church. She was shaken by the song as God spoke to the need of her soul. A transformed person, she arose from the altar and testified, "He's forgiven my transgressions . . . I never knew before this morning that it could be possible."

How very much like the parable of Jesus: "The kingdom of heaven is like unto treasure hid in a field." One of God's continual surprises! He is always doing "exceeding abundantly above all that we ask or think" (Eph. 3:20). It makes the old passages of the Bible glow with new meaning, and all the promises come alive with a deeper significance.

People have searched for meaning in areas other than in Jesus Christ, but since the star glittered over Bethlehem, no other man has risen to claim "the heathen for [an] inheritance, and the uttermost parts of the earth for [a] possession" (Ps. 2:8). The love of Jesus Christ knocks at every door and says, "If any man will" be my disciple, "let him deny himself, and take up his cross, and follow me" (Matt. 16:24).

The way of Jesus Christ is the way of forgiveness, love, peace, and joy in the Spirit. It delights in the creation of new life and new relationships, and makes the yoke easy and the burden light.

Only through Him can a young mother testify, "He's forgiven . . . I never knew . . . it could be possible."

PRAYER: *O God, how grateful we are to know that Your forgiveness covers all our sins through love. Go beyond all our hopes and in the abundance of pardon give us assurance again that sin is swallowed up in the victory of the Cross. Show us that here is the beginning of a new life. In Jesus' name. Amen.*

SEPTEMBER 26

> My kingdom is not of this world: if my kingdom were of this world, then would my servants fight, that I should not be delivered to the Jews: but now is my kingdom not from hence.
> (John 18:36)

We stood at the manger with the shepherds and worshiped the Babe. We saw Him in the Temple and listened while He answered the questions of the priests with the wisdom of the Eternal. We heard His Sermon. We saw His miracles. We were amazed at His parables and stood in awe as the blind, the leper, and the deaf took their place in society. We thought He had come to stay with us forever, and we were glad.

He who had come to bear witness of the truth was standing as a criminal before Herod and Pilate. Society had taken Him as an imposter, and they mocked His Kingship with their robe and thorny crown. The peacefulness of Him who had come to bring peace excited the amazement of those who were to condemn Him. And He added to their perplexity by saying to Pilate, "My kingdom is not of this world."

In a deeper sense than we knew, He was speaking for all of His followers, for the watchword of the Christian is, "Here have we no continuing city" (Heb. 13:14). The express purpose of the Son of God was to seek and to save the lost. When we understand our duty toward God, we will discover our greatest mission to be the salvation of souls. In bringing men to the Cross, we are also saying to Pilate, "My kingdom is not of this world."

Witness the martyr, who "endured, as seeing him who is invisible" (Heb. 11:27). Every one who was bound to the stake or torn to bits by savage beasts was a proclamation to the fact of citizenship in a heavenly kingdom.

TESTIMONY. In word: "This world is but a dressing room for eternity." In song: "This world is not my home, I'm just a-passin' through." In affirmation: "My kingdom is not of this world."

PRAYER: *O God, You came into our world, and You have touched our lives, opened heaven to our vision, and given us eternity in exchange for time. This old world is not our home, for here we have no continuing city. Help us to think on these greater things as we journey on toward that city made possible to us by the Cross. In Jesus' name. Amen.*

SEPTEMBER 27 ∎

The Lord is not slack concerning his promise, as some men count slackness; but is longsuffering to us-ward, not willing that any should perish, but that all should come to repentance.
(2 Pet. 3:9)

It would seem that if we had the opportunity of running heaven and its relationship to earth, we would speed up the process of operation. Probably one of the most vigorous bits of praying from this side of heaven has been to urge God to hurry up in His part of the scheme. It often seems that God is very slow.

Well, we call it slow! God calls it "long-suffering, patient, forbearing, and kind."

When we substitute His words for ours and understand more about the One who is in charge, our perspective is greatly altered. Then we see that the ways of God are expanding rather than diminishing. And the closer we get to Him the more we see that what we thought was slowness was really loving and calculating mercy and hope.

It is good that God is in control, for slowness is a term of time, and these terms are unknown in the actions of God. We forget that "one day is with the Lord as a thousand years, and a thousand years as one day" (2 Pet. 3:8). And before we can take over heaven and run His universe, we must also assume His providence. We can never understand eternity through the medium of time.

"Not slow . . . but long-suffering!" God could have crushed us in our sin and thrown away the pieces, but He didn't. He could have slain our enemies when we called upon Him in despair, but He didn't. He could have allowed His suffering Son to come down from the Cross, but He didn't.

He says to our world, "I will meet you with long-suffering!" Now we understand His ways better!

PRAYER: *O God, how wonderfully patient You are with us. How tender in mercy! How loving in kindness! Our hearts are filled with thanksgiving when You accommodate Your omnipotence to our weakness. Then we can become more than conquerors. Every day through the mystery of Your long-suffering we live. We thank You in Jesus' name. Amen.*

SEPTEMBER 28

**If ye continue in my word, then are ye
my disciples indeed; and ye shall
know the truth, and the truth
shall make you free.**
(John 8:31-32)

The expression "I never let books interfere with my education" has been used in jest and as a cover-up for failure. But there is much truth hiding here, for the inquiring mind goes beyond the two book covers, and research goes into the hidden areas of knowledge. The darkest periods in the world have been the times when men's minds have been closed to truth.

Jesus Christ never hinders a person from searching areas of truth for himself. His greatest complaint was that people have ears to hear, but they do not hear; they have eyes, but they do not see. Jesus has never been afraid of being put up beside any area of investigation and wants to be with us in our searching for the best.

Ask questions. Knock on doors. Insist on answers. Be enthusiastic in your search for truth. God will always respond!

God turns His back on indifference. He pays no attention to insincere prayer. His face is turned away from the lips that give praise while the heart pours out condemnation. He has no time for the one who seeks divine favor for his own gratification. But verbalize doubts, and He will stand with you until all questions have been resolved in truth.

Since God made man, He meant to save him and bring him through his most difficult time. God never gives up until He finds the case utterly hopeless. He is always willing to be compared and have honest questions asked and have himself tested by an honest heart.

Don't throw away God's Book in your search for a true education. It will lead you into all truth!

PRAYER: *Enable us, O God, by the ministry of Your Holy Spirit, to know the truth. You are always revealing something to the human mind when we are able to accept it. Touch every point of our lives, give us that outreach over all lesser things, and help us to stand in the truths of eternity. In Jesus' name. Amen.*

SEPTEMBER 29 ■
Rest in the Lord, and wait patiently for him: fret not thyself because of him who prospereth in his way, because of the man who bringeth wicked devices to pass.
(Ps. 37:7)

Recently I had occasion to counsel with a man who had come under deep depression. He recounted in tears an experience with his superior at his work. He said, "This man will belittle you, insult you, and browbeat you until you are ready to break. Then he judges you on your reactions at the breaking point and makes his report." His moment of surrender to pressure was recorded as his real character and the true quality of his soul. And on this record his reputation and advancement in the company stood.

How differently God looks upon those whom He has to judge! To God every person who is trying to do good adds something to the store of heaven's riches. Every life that is well lived makes its contribution to the work of the Kingdom.

When a person is down, it is very difficult to make him see that there is acceptance for him anywhere. When our prayers cannot leave our tongues, it is easy to believe that God does not hear any prayer. We read everything in terms of the shadows and doubts we throw upon them. And in the moment when the enemy has beaten us down to the breaking point, he records our Christianity and tells us that we have failed.

The glorious part of God's way is that He is writing all the time. But when we are at our weakest moment, He puts the pen aside. He looks at the storm and the cloud and the battle. He sees a soul of eternity in the spirit of the Cross and says, "I am in this thing with you."

Our advancement in His kingdom does not stand on our record alone but on His mercy and love.

PRAYER: *You show us, O God, how to be strong, and You have promised to give us wisdom for our need. You bring us up out of the difficult places and out of entanglements where there is not human deliverance. You ask for no more in return than that our lives will be great answers of obedience. At the Cross we leave all our petitions. In Jesus' name. Amen.*

SEPTEMBER 30

O death, where is thy sting? O grave, where is thy victory? ... But thanks be to God, which giveth us the victory through our Lord Jesus Christ.
(1 Cor. 15:55, 57)

Life's greatest unanswered question is held in one small word, "Why?" No pastor has ever lived who has not been threatened with it in details grim with hatred, grasping for an answer. The name of God has been abused, the love of God has been denied, and the grace of God has been spurned for lack of an adequate reason for some occurrence for which God has been given the full blame.

Mary and Martha might just as well have said, "Why did our brother, whom You claimed to love so well, have to die?" "If You really loved him, why did You let him die?" The accusation is still being heard in the home, in the hospitals, at the bedside, and at the cemetery today. And the caring pastor is expected to supply an adequate reply.

Earth and heaven never came so close together as in the reply of the Master, "This sickness is not unto death, but for the glory of God, that the Son of God might be glorified thereby" (John 11:4). He who knows the secret of God, who holds that secret in His own right hand, and who can whisper to us amid all the suffering and loss, says, "God intends it to work out in your life a higher purpose and a nobler strength. Hold steady. Let God complete His work!"

Jesus Christ will not turn away from any harsh accusation from a broken heart. He does want to come into the room with understanding and into the heart with comfort. He does want to lift the soul from the darkness that has settled in upon it. And He will satisfy the necessities of the spirit.

Do we dare to believe that when we say, "Dead," God is saying, "Born." This must be our faith!

PRAYER: *O God, Your Word gives assurance to the aching heart, "Blessed are the dead which die in the Lord." Help us to know that death does not mean darkness and extinction, but for the one who has saving faith in Christ, it is light and immortality. May we triumph in His victory and rise again in His resurrection. May we all see death from the glory side of Calvary. In Jesus' name. Amen.*

OCTOBER 1 ■

He that hath my commandments, and keepeth them, he it is that loveth me: and he that loveth me shall be loved of my Father, and I will love him, and will manifest myself to him.
(John 14:21)

One day when my brother and I were quite young, we decided to tie some poles together so that we could reach up and touch the blue sky overhead. It all looked so simple! But we never quite made it, for the closer we got, the farther away it seemed to get. This disturbed me very much, because I knew that God was up there. If I couldn't reach the sky with a pole, how would I ever be able to reach God!

One day I learned that God is not a far-off and unreachable Being. I discovered that we are temples of the Holy Ghost and can have fellowship with heaven and be partakers of the divine nature. I learned that it is possible to have our feet planted in the dust of this earth and have our hearts hidden in the sanctuary of God. I learned that love is the faculty by which we apprehend God and without which we can never reach the sky.

We can throw away the poles and our human efforts, for Jesus said, "He that loveth me . . . I will love him, and will manifest myself to him." Love has been set up as the condition for divine fellowship. Christianity does not destroy that inner human desire to reach up to where God is, but it gives us a better direction. Finding God becomes quite a new endeavor when the heart is renewed in Christ's love.

This takes a wider view of things and associates us with that which is infinite and absolute. Here the human and the Divine make contact: God reveals himself to the heart.

I have learned that love is a constant going out after God, and Calvary has put heaven within our reach. We can have sweet and ample access to the very heart of God.

PRAYER: *O God, Your love is a continual astonishment to us! You look upon all things from eternity, while we are bound by the chains of time. Help us to reach up and find that love that never doubts, that love that hopes forever, and that love in which the midnight is as the noonday. May we cling to that hope that will never die. In Jesus' name. Amen.*

■ **OCTOBER 2**

> And when Jesus saw that he answered discreetly, he said unto him, Thou art not far from the kingdom of God. And no man after that durst ask him any question.
> (Mark 12:34)

Today I visited in the hospital with an elderly lady whose mind was full of questions but whose attention span allowed no answers. She had been an alert person with keen insight, sharp-witted and always ready with a friendly repartee. Now she had reached a point where inquiry and attitude did not correspond. She was like a weary traveler unable to understand directions for moving on. But her "Amen" was sharp and confident as we prayed together at her bedside. The answer to the greatest question had already been confirmed.

How understanding God is to His people in the crisis experiences of life! He does not turn anyone out into a pathless world. Up the mountain, across the desert, or through the rose garden, He leads His people ever onward.

On the slate of her life was only one word that mattered—God. God was at the beginning of every enterprise, was in the morning of every endeavor, and had first place in every decision. This had brought a beauty all its own to her old age. Hers was a strength that would not be worn out, and her goal was "an house not made with hands, eternal in the heavens" (2 Cor. 5:1). What mattered the small questions that needed no reply?

The soul never asks little questions. When Jesus Christ touched the human mind, it was always to call it up to some high questioning: "What think ye of Christ?" (Matt. 22:42). "Who is my neighbour?" (Luke 10:29). "When saw we thee an hungred . . . ?" (Matt. 25:37, 44). "What is truth?" (John 18:38). Every question served to lift the mind above the world and to assure us that it is possible to know God.

God meets us where we are and leads us on according to our capacity to travel. I think He listens to our questions that need no answers!

PRAYER: *O God, we cannot seem to understand life. We live one day at a time, and we live by faith in Your omniscience. Work out Your immeasurable purposes in all the darkness and disciplines and unfathomable areas of our lives. We find meaning and hope here in You. In Jesus' name. Amen.*

OCTOBER 3 ■

Verily I say unto you, Inasmuch as ye have done it unto one of the least of these my brethren, ye have done it unto me.
(Matt. 25:40)

A wave of protest swept through the congregation when the news broke that the church board had voted to sponsor a Korean family. This meant that they would be brought here and would be given a home, food, clothing, opportunity for an education, and employment until they could be on their own. They came and began to settle into their new life-style. That is, until they left in the night with another group that had been working in the background for this takeover.

The negative voice of "I told you so" rang up and down the aisles, and the church board was reminded of the grave error in judgment, the terrible waste of money, and the gullibility of those who had been "taken in."

But wait just a minute! Doesn't the Bible say, "We then that are strong ought to bear the infirmities of the weak" (Rom. 15:1)? And if we are under the impression that the work of the church does not come in under this test, we are under an impression that is false.

There should be nothing in our world more practical, more ready to help and lift to a new level than our Christianity. It should go into the marketplace, into family living, into every hole and corner, including other countries, and search out ways to help. And the Bible sees nothing unreasonable in the expectation.

The people in the dark corners of our world are not seeking a philosophical religion, nor are they reaching out to some selfish, sophisticated organization to make sport of their destitution. But they are looking for a gentle spirit that does not like their tears and is willing to put out a hand to help drive them away.

Our Korean family may never find God, as we had hoped, but the church held out its hand when they cried for help!

PRAYER: *O God, we pray that You will remember those little ones who are cold and hungry and cannot tell anyone about their need. We pray for all those who are living one day at a time, hoping that food and clothing will be supplied tomorrow. May they read in our desire to help the sweet love of God, which makes possible our outstretched hand. In Jesus' name. Amen.*

OCTOBER 4

That their hearts might be comforted, being knit together in love, and unto all riches of the full assurance of understanding.
(Col. 2:2)

What a slogan for a church! "This church is 'knit together in love.'" This ought to be commonplace and should not awaken attention, for God's love always knits together. Alas, experience contradicts theory, and instead of encountering a commonplace, we are face-to-face with a miracle. For only a miracle of God can make it so.

Paul knew human nature as no other man, and he was fully aware of the effect of sin to destroy. He knew that the day was still with us when the priest would pass the wounded man and the Levite would cross the street to avoid confrontation with the need of a brother. And he knew that it would require the work of the Almighty to bring people together in love. He knew it would take a miracle of God.

He knew that this unity in love is possible. And he knew that it must be love out of a heart that has undergone the cleansing of the Holy Spirit of God. This is the only love that can endure the changing climates of life. This is the only love that "bears all things . . . endures all things" (1 Cor. 13:7, NKJV). This is the only love that does not discriminate and does not turn its back on need.

The church is nothing without love. God's love is not a mere sentiment; it is Christ abiding within. There is mystery and majesty and a self-sacrificing passion in it and about it that establishes itself beyond a doubt. Tragic is the church that is not possessed with this kind of love.

No power on earth can "knit together" like God's love. And it is forever.

PRAYER: *Create in our hearts, O God, Your perfect love. Give us that love that never doubts, that hopes forever, and to which there is no ending. May it be a great love, beginning at the Cross and made greater by the constant inspiration of the Holy Spirit. May it be a love that will never let us go. In Jesus' name. Amen.*

OCTOBER 5 ■

I delight to do thy will, O my God: yea, thy law is within my heart.
(Ps. 40:8)

God's laws were made to obey. Very simple when you consider this in its basic concept! If we could capture the full meaning of the decree, we would have in our hands the mystery that has shaped the whole history of the world.

God places no compulsion on obedience or on worship. A person can turn his back on God and treat the Almighty with indifference. God has not allowed himself the power to bend the human mind, the human heart, or the human will. He begins by seeking the consent of the individual. This is God's limitation of himself toward mankind. He only asks for obedience; He does not demand it!

A holy person in God's sight is an obedient person; one living in the spirit of obedience. God is looking for people who willingly accept obedience to Him as their manner of living. To deny the law of God in our lives is to take away the bricks and the stones on which our foundation is built.

There is a danger, however, in being under a strict adherence to the law of God. This leads one to strive for incidentals, divide up laws, and emphasize particular commandments until the soul becomes adjusted to externals, and the whole spirit becomes more anxious to do than to be.

When we read God's law in the light of His grace, we see a new principle. No longer a burden or a mere commandment, nothing can be easier, more delightful, and in accord with the heart than to obey God. It is then that His yoke becomes easy and His burden becomes light.

There is a delight in doing the will of God!

PRAYER: *Help us to know, O God, that we have no law in ourselves. We are Your creation. We are under Your authority, and if we would live victoriously, we must live obediently. Let the joy of obedience enter into our hearts like a singing angel sent down from heaven. In Jesus' name. Amen.*

OCTOBER 6

For the Lord seeth not as man seeth; for man looketh on the outward appearance, but the Lord looketh on the heart.
(1 Sam. 16:7)

She was an old lady who lived alone in a two-room, tar-papered shack on the back road. She walked with a cane and moved from chair to table and from sink to stove in great pain. Her little place was immaculate, and she greeted her visitors with a hearty laugh as she gave them encouragement for the day. The melody of her song is still clear as she sang, "The toils of the road will seem nothing, / When I get to the end of the way."

No, she wasn't a theologian, and she could not have discussed many religious ideas. She had scant knowledge of the Bible, for she had never learned to read. She was simply practicing here on earth something she intended to carry with her to heaven. And she kept on singing it and living it without knowing it, and every day she was experiencing it.

The important part of this kind of living is that which does not change. It is the spirit of trust and the spirit of faith. It is given by God for the purpose of meeting a particular set of circumstances, and it works, and it does not need a name. It is part of the very being of God.

How often we miss the important issue and see the trappings for the real thing; the temporal looks so big we miss the eternal. It is of not much consequence whether we die in a tar-papered shack on the back road or in the king's palace. It does not really matter if we live in daily pain or never experience a headache all of our days. The important thing is obedience to the divine will and to seek first the kingdom of God.

God reads the prayers that are written upon the heart, and that makes the present worthwhile.

PRAYER: *Almighty God, help us not to think of the troubles we have to pass through, for You make the joy of victory greater because of the hard places. Trouble is but for a moment, yet it achieves for us an exceeding and eternal weight of glory. May our faith overcome our fears and make heaven our goal as we continue on the journey. In Jesus' name. Amen.*

OCTOBER 7 ■

Except the Lord build the house, they labour in vain that build it: except the Lord keep the city, the watchman waketh but in vain.
(Ps. 127:1)

Recently I visited a church on Sunday morning with an overflow congregation, a large Sunday School, and a fairly new building. The thing that made it so special was a memory. I remember having been in Sunday School in the old building with seven people in attendance and listening to a deacon's proposal to close the place down because "we're wasting our time and money." But in those intervening years a miracle had happened.

To understand the greatness of a miracle, one must be familiar with the circumstances that preceded the event. Is this not so in every circumstance of life when only those who have been through the famine can appreciate the feast? The sun is more beautiful to that one who has seen clouds pile upon clouds, adding darkness to darkness.

Let there be no place where sorrow can find a soothing psalm; let affliction find no supporting sympathy in its darkest hour; let the broken heart try to mend without a shred of sympathy or a teardrop of support; let the Sabbath Day become a common day when our people know it as a day of toil and amusement—call all of this deprivation together and then form your estimate of the value of religious privilege.

Now let's go to church on Sunday morning in our well-regulated Christian community. We have Bibles, teachers, and music; our offering plates are full; and our people come in fine dress and vehicle. Only in the absence of this affluence can we know what estimate to place on these things we take for granted.

The miracle is the greatest to the one who has known the empty pews.

PRAYER: *We look upon our salvation, O God, and we say, Herein is the miracle of the Cross. This miracle becomes greater as we stand before You as redeemed sinners. Help us never to forget the condition from which You rescued us. For all the sin and night and death from which we were rescued, we give You praise. In Jesus' name. Amen.*

OCTOBER 8

Come unto me, all ye that labour and are heavy laden, and I will give you rest. . . . and ye shall find rest unto your souls.
(Matt. 11:28-29)

Wherever Jesus went, He attracted crowds of people. Every person who followed Him must have had a reason for being there. It seems harsh to say that they followed Him just for the loaves and the fishes. Standards cannot be set up by which people are judged as to their endeavor to get to where the Master is speaking.

My heart cannot reach out to Him in the same measure as that of any other person on earth. Whatever reason one has for following Christ is sufficient. When we begin to compare our Christs, we are also beginning to grade one's Christian experience. I have heard the tone of His voice; or, I have seen the flash of His glory; or, He has spoken to my need. Actually, I am following Him—this personal testimony as to Omnipotence is sufficient regarding individual conviction of the power of Christ.

Great harm comes to the church when we begin to set up one kind of experience against another. Many have been antagonized and brought down to defeat because some well-meaning saint has tried to run the experience of unstable followers in the mold of their own Christianity. It is saying that if your experience does not accord with mine, then yours is wrong.

Jesus came to a dying world to save it. Now the burden has been left to His followers. I wonder if He isn't saying, "Testify out of your own experience, out of your own knowledge of Me, and through the power of the Holy Spirit in your own life. Make it personal. It is all that I expect you to do."

Away with the disharmony that has hindered the church! Let each person live on his own ground and testify to his own experience. And let every other person in the church have his!

PRAYER: *We thank You, O God, for all the varied experiences that You have led us through since we began to follow You. You have kept us in our tears and led us in good places. You know the yearning of each individual heart, and You supply according to that need. In You may we experience the fullness of grace. In Jesus' name. Amen.*

OCTOBER 9

The eyes of the Lord are upon the righteous, and his ears are open unto their cry. The face of the Lord is against them that do evil, to cut off the remembrance of them from the ear.
(Ps. 34:15-16)

Responsibility is a term that confronts everyone who comes into this world. It is one of the first lessons a child learns as he listens to, "No, no, mustn't touch!" and the glittering thing is snatched from his hand. As the plot of life thickens and the "No, no's" attach themselves to more intricate things, the problem of responsibility increases. It is important that we deal with this problem that has come to live with us for the rest of our lives.

The Bible is very clear in its teaching, and it deals in direct terms to every individual. It says, "Every one of us shall give account of himself to God" (Rom. 14:12). I am responsible to God—this is the revelation of His plan in its application to my personal daily life. God brings it all down to me—a personal soul, a personal consciousness, and a personal will. And it is mine! And if I go wrong here, I am wrong in my relationship to all eternal values.

Is it wrong to suggest that responsibility is the security of the Church? It can never be held together by corrupt individualism, where disregard is given to everything that God calls holy, and the rights of others are looked upon with disdain. Whatever is not backed by God's purpose and regulated by individual responsibility is a compromise and will end up in defeat for the cause of Jesus Christ and His Church.

Today I must know a real, genuine sense of responsibility in the sight of God, and I must be myself. And my individualism must weave in and out with that of every other person I meet. This is the divine plan and the unity of God's purpose.

And it always brings us by Calvary, for responsibility brings us back to the Cross. Here also is peace and gladness.

PRAYER: *You have made us, O God, and we are Your children. Show us our responsibility to You so that every breath we take may become our strength. Turn our weakness into strength, our ignorance into wisdom, and our responsibilities into blessed opportunities; and give us peace because of Calvary. In Jesus' name. Amen.*

OCTOBER 10

What time I am afraid, I will trust in thee. In God I will praise his word, in God I have put my trust; I will not fear what flesh can do unto me.
(Ps. 56:3-4)

We associate the idea of being a Christian with the idea of enjoyment, pleasure, and the complete fulfillment of all that is good. And much of this is true, for it is a deliverance from the power of sin and all the bad things that it represents. Certainly when God comes into a life, He sets that person apart to where all the blessings of heaven are available.

But the call to Christian service is a call to battle. It is not just a conflict of man with man but also a mighty eternal conflict between right and wrong. And the enemy is the enemy of God who is working in daily ministration to overturn the Church. The cross of Jesus Christ is a testimony of this enmity toward God, and the raging battle is against all that heaven represents.

Christ was called the Prince of Peace and still is today! But He is against every bad thing, everything that is false and insincere, and everything that is not founded on eternal truth. He has never met evil without doing battle with it, and He has never accepted sin for the pleasure of the moment. For every follower of the Man of the Cross a similar determination must get hold of the heart.

Jesus Christ wins, not by the sword and the sound of the battle, but by love, tears, tenderness, patience, peace, and mercy, which endure forever. And this warfare can be explained only by the language of love.

The prayer that continually falls from many lips is that life will go smoothly, with no testing, no thorns in the flesh, and no difficulties. God's answers always humble our petition by His promise of an overabundance of grace. Then it is better to have wrestled, so that we might know the power of Christ.

PRAYER: *O God, may we take on Your whole armor so that we may be able to withstand the evil of the day. May we march in step with Your grace so that we may be able to tread down all our spiritual foes. There is no other way provided to gain victory and heaven. In Jesus' name. Amen.*

OCTOBER 11 ■

And the angel said unto them, Fear not: for, behold, I bring you good tidings of great joy, which shall be to all people.
(Luke 2:10)

Normally I don't pay too much heed to messages found in fortune cookies. Recently a friend showed me one he was carefully guarding, awaiting the day of its fulfillment. It says, "Good news will come to you from far away." Something deep inside of me responded, "No greater news could ever come than has already come."

The greatest news to come to our world did not come in this century or under circumstances familiar to our time. It does contain principles that have nothing to do with time, and it anticipates no contender for replacement. However, it can be read in light of our present day, and it stands tall in company with anything that our age can produce.

The Good News came in company with the angels' song, bringing peace and goodwill to all people on earth. He came as a Babe in the manger, grew to manhood, and moved about with love in His heart until hatred nailed Him to the Cross. He came as the Hope and Light of the prophet's vision and lived among His people as the Prince of Peace. His claim to divinity was rejected, and in agony on the Cross He was belittled and mocked. The cold intellectualism of His day said, "I find no fault in this man" (Luke 23:4), yet they spurned His message of peace.

Twenty centuries have gone by, and the Good News is still at work. Amid the tumult of conflicting teaching it says, "Seek ye first the kingdom of God, and his righteousness; and all these things shall be added unto you" (Matt. 6:33).

The Good News from afar has come, and it says, "Behold the Lamb of God, which taketh away the sin of the world" (John 1:29).

PRAYER: *O God, we give You thanks for all the good news and gospel light and hope You send to us. Make our lives to be true expressions of Your gospel as we live it out in our little day. Sustain us by Your mighty power and keep us every day as we seek our place in Your kingdom. In Jesus' name. Amen.*

■ OCTOBER 12

And let us not be weary in well doing: for in due season we shall reap, if we faint not.
(Gal. 6:9)

Some friends of mine moved into a new house this summer. The home is beautifully surrounded by trees hiding it away in peaceful seclusion. A winding driveway meanders through a green lawn to a double garage at the back. But fall came and the leaves fell from the maples and elms, giving a new perspective from the inside looking out.

The lady explained in delight, "With the leaves gone I looked out the window this morning, and I saw the mountain." One of God's special blessings hit my soul as I listened: "The leaves fell off, and I saw the mountain."

There are troubles in life whose shadows seem as long as life itself. How many joys have been dampened during the past season! How many glad laughs have been a cloak over an aching heart! How many cheerful greetings have been a beating of the air! How many smiles have been a mask drawn over despair! How many days have been approached with great fear because the shades of uncertainty have been pulled over the sunshine of the morning!

Hold steady; the leaves will fall off, and a new vision of God will come through. "They that wait upon the Lord shall renew their strength; they shall mount up with wings as eagles; they shall run, and not be weary; and they shall walk, and not faint" (Isa. 40:31). If no sparrow falls to the ground without God knowing about it, He surely will not forsake His nobler creation. At the moment of peril He brings us to the higher places above the infinite dangers that beset.

When words fail, and prayers return to mock, and the days are hidden in darkness, hold steady. The leaves will fall off, and God will let you see the mountain!

PRAYER: *O God, we give You praise for Your patient endurance and long-suffering with us. You could have cut us off in the midst of our days, but You have spared us and renewed our opportunities. Your answers have been greater than our questions. You have shown us the mountain and given us peace. Clear our vision and lead us ever onward. In Jesus' name. Amen.*

OCTOBER 13 ■

When thou prayest, enter into thy closet, and when thou hast shut thy door, pray to thy Father which is in secret; and thy Father which seeth in secret shall reward thee openly.
(Matt. 6:6)

This week I read a book on the scientific approach to prayer. It contained many diagrams, charts, and graphs to show how prayer works through the psyche in bringing man within reach of another power.

It said in part, "Prayer expresses a deep desire that suprasensory power be invoked to ameliorate certain distressful situations, both objective and subjective. . . . By reason of man's conception of Deity as a cosmic, personlike power, man believes that intercommunication is possible."

I am not sure that I understood much of what I was reading, and it did not seem to move me any closer to heaven.

This week I read another Book, and it spoke about prayer. The Author told us how we should pray. He told us to say: "Our Father which art in heaven, Hallowed be thy name. Thy kingdom come. Thy will be done in earth, as it is in heaven. Give us this day our daily bread. And forgive us our debts, as we forgive our debtors. And lead us not into temptation, but deliver us from evil: For thine is the kingdom, and the power, and the glory, for ever. Amen" (Matt. 6:9-13).

Here is God's greatest expression of himself to His people, and it is not separated from life. I cannot surprise God by intellectual ability, but I can come to Him from the necessity of my soul. From this prayer I learned that the more God is needed in my life, the more He is there to help.

The depth of this prayer was hidden in the simplicity that I felt I could understand. But even when I thought I had understood it all, I discovered a depth as deep as Divinity and as lofty as the revelation of God.

This prayer opened heaven to my soul this week!

PRAYER: *O God, we are glad that when we pray, we can touch the Son of God, who loved us and gave himself for us. Give us power in our praying so that we may be more than conquerors when we come before the throne. May each prayer be the preparation for greater fellowship. In Jesus' name. Amen.*

OCTOBER 14

I go to prepare a place for you. And if I go and prepare a place for you, I will come again, and receive you unto myself; that where I am, there ye may be also.
(John 14:2-3)

Can anything touch the innermost depths of the heart of God's people like the words of Jesus, "I go to prepare a place for you"? I, your Lord and Master, am going away to get a place ready for you.

This is the Son of God speaking, and the statements carry with them the authority of eternity. But isn't this in keeping with the divine condescension that marked the ministry of our Lord here on earth? Wherever He was, He was girding himself with the towel to do the servant's work.

He is always doing something for those who believe in Him and love Him. There is a beautiful necessity of love permeating every task of His hand and every concern of His heart. Jesus Christ is always thinking of us. He is always caring for us. He is always going out in the full extent of His love for us.

Some things that Jesus did while He was with His people carried only temporary significance. But when we hear Him talk about the place He is going to prepare for the believers, we have the idea of a continuous, enduring, and never-ending fellowship.

Somehow I sense that Jesus looked over all the worlds His hands had made, and now He is saying, "I am going to do the greatest deed of all. I am going to get a place ready for those whom I have bought with My blood and glorified by My Spirit."

What greater blessing awaits any person than to be in that number to hear, "Come, ye blessed of my Father, inherit the kingdom prepared for you"—by the Son of God (Matt. 25:34)!

I want to be in that number!

PRAYER: *How we thank You, O God, for the hope of heaven and the promise of the One who has gone to prepare it for His people. You have promised Your people a prepared place. We live here in anticipation of that city whose Builder and Maker is God. Make us ready to enter, in Jesus' name. Amen.*

OCTOBER 15 ■

But God forbid that I should glory, save in the cross of our Lord Jesus Christ, by whom the world is crucified unto me, and I unto the world.
(Gal. 6:14)

Up in our attic when I was a boy was an old trunk filled with clippings, postcards, and items that the family had hoarded over the years. Hidden among these keepsakes was a picture of the destruction of a city, showing everything in shambles including a church building. But standing tall and unscathed in the midst of everything was the Cross in all of its shining glory. Written beneath it were these words, "In the cross of Christ I glory, / Tow'ring o'er the wrecks of time."

On rainy days, when my mother would let us up in the attic to play, I would always go to the old trunk. Here I would see God, Jesus Christ, the Church, the mystery of the Cross, and the fact of redemption hidden away there. It all came together in a dust-covered painting. It is still a fact in our world today that everything has value only in its relationship to the Cross. The Cross measures all things, determines all things, and, in a keener sense than we can know, rules all things.

The Cross! The answer to human sin. The mind can hardly take it in. That God should die, make an atonement of himself, through weakness find the way to power, and through agony find the way to rest and peace! This is the way of the Lord, and it is seen only in the cross of Jesus Christ.

Hasn't God always chosen "the foolish things of the world to confound the wise" (1 Cor. 1:27)? The apostle would bypass the wise, the mighty, and the noble and see nothing but Christ and the sacrifice on the Cross. He refused to allow anything to overshadow the place of the Cross in his daily encounters.

After these many years I still go back to the old trunk. "In the cross of Christ I glory, / Tow'ring o'er the wrecks of time."

PRAYER: *We thank You, O God, that the cross of Jesus Christ is still standing among us. Here we come for cleansing, for healing, and for strength. For Your promise is that in Christ You will freely give us all things. Here is our hope and our salvation. In Jesus' name. Amen.*

OCTOBER 16

And they were offended in him. But Jesus said unto them, A prophet is not without honour, save in his own country, and in his own house.
(Matt. 13:57)

When religious instruction was allowed in the public schools, I was teaching a grade six class on the life of Christ. One day I asked for a definition of a miracle and received this answer. "Sir, it is sum'thin' that jist about can't happen." I have never found a better answer. Almost impossible, but it happens!

There are many things in life that are "jist about" impossible. We call them incredible. We say it cannot be true, and our whole being rises up against the report. The *Titanic* was to sail the seas forever because she was unsinkable—but she sank on her maiden voyage. How many years was the great Maginot Line, along the eastern border of France, held up as an impenetrable defense against the German enemy—but it fell. How often gaiety has turned into mourning, and crowns have fallen from the heads of the mighty, and that which was held to be permanent collapses before our eyes. The genius of the great dies, and the days of their influence become a memory.

Still in the realm of the impossible, who would have believed that the Son of a carpenter could save a world? Do we not know His mother and father and His family? Where did He get His wisdom and ability? This Fellow has always been in our neighborhood. We watched Him grow up. Him, forgive sin? Impossible! But He did.

There is something about Him that we can't deny. He says He will have the heathen for His inheritance and the uttermost parts of the earth for His possession. And He meant it! And He did!

"And he shall reign for ever and ever" (Rev. 11:15). Hallelujah! Impossible? No! It is a miracle of God. I believe!

PRAYER: *We look upon our salvation, O God, and we say, Herein is the miracle of the Cross and the triumph of the Holy Spirit. While the world cries, "Impossible," we put ourselves in Your hands for the miracle of pardon performed in the act of atonement at the Cross. Here the penitent find pardon, and the pardoned find peace. We believe! In Jesus' name. Amen.*

OCTOBER 17 ■

Then Simon Peter answered him, Lord, to whom shall we go? thou hast the words of eternal life.
(John 6:68)

There is probably not a living believer in Jesus Christ who has not at some time or other been tempted to "chuck it all" and give up. If this has not been your experience, hold steady. The old enemy is on his way with a load of doubt and defeat.

When you are tempted to give up your religious faith, the question naturally follows, "Now what? What will I replace it with?" What are the alternatives to a living faith in God?

When we give up our faith in God, we naturally close our Bible. What has the enemy given us in its place? He has never spoken to us about the problems facing the soul. He has never written any words of comfort for the human heart. He has never given us any light on the dark questions that haunt and defy life. He never comes to us to encourage, to listen, to lift, or to say, "I care." He has never told us about the Cross, the Resurrection, or death!

The Bible says, "God is our refuge and strength, a very present help in trouble" (Ps. 46:1). The enemy walks away and says, "When you are in trouble, dry your own tears."

The Bible says, "Come unto me, all ye that labour and are heavy laden, and I will give you rest" (Matt. 11:28). The enemy says, "Your weariness is your own problem; keep going!"

The Bible says, "Repent and be forgiven" (see Acts 2:38). The enemy says, "Who needs it? You're as good as anyone else."

Jesus says, "In my Father's house are many mansions . . . I go to prepare a place for you" (John 14:2). The enemy says, "Die and go to the grave; that is the end of it all."

Peter faced the problem and expressed it for all of us before Jesus: "To whom shall we go? thou hast the words of eternal life" (John 6:68).

I needed that! You might, too, someday!

PRAYER: *O God, we know the mystery of doubt, for its purpose is to draw us away from You. When our tendency is to doubt, come to us with Your love and meet us each day at the Cross, where grace is greater than our sin. In Jesus' name. Amen.*

■ OCTOBER 18

> **For ye shall go out with joy, and be led forth with peace: ... all the trees of the field shall clap their hands.**
> **(Isa. 55:12)**

HAPPINESS IS! All the storm clouds are blown away, the sky is blue, the sun is bright overhead, and the breeze rustles in harmony with nature in the trees. And all is well!

There are days in the Christian life that by their very darkness cast shadows on the providence of God. But there are also days so full of bright sunshine and high joy that the dark days remain only in memory, and the soul is tempted to doubt their existence.

We know that all of these times must be blended into a whole, for they are the stuff of which life is made. We must remember that the year is not all summer, nor is it all winter, and only when all of the seasons are taken in their entirety can the year be rightly judged.

The quest of the human heart is for happiness. The heart cries out when the storm clouds cover the sun and hope mingles with despair. Sometimes there will be no answer left but prayer. But if that prayer is complete surrender of the heart to the Lord, then the testimony of the Psalmist can be shared: "Thou hast put gladness in my heart, more than in the time that their corn and their wine increased" (Ps. 4:7).

We are not carried away by the night, and darkness cannot hide the face of God from His people. God's deliverance is always associated with light, and happiness in the soul is God's promise to that one "that walketh not in the counsel of the ungodly" (Ps. 1:1).

The good man has more happiness in despair than the bad man has in all his happiness. There is no despair that can dry up the springs of happiness in the soul of God's people.

HAPPINESS IS! God's peace in the sunshine or in the storm.

PRAYER: *You speak to us, O God, about a happy life that is a marvelous union of the human and the divine. You have shown us that there is no real happiness that does not owe its beauty to the sunshine of heaven. Make us full of Your happiness and ready to do Your will. In Jesus' name. Amen.*

OCTOBER 19

Not that I speak in respect of want: for I have learned, in whatsoever state I am, therewith to be content. . . . I can do all things through Christ which strengtheneth me.
(Phil. 4:11, 13)

How very simple Jesus made the call to His disciples: "Follow me!" It was not a call to worship or to some religious devotion, nor did He outline a life of toil, sacrifice, and death. The call was simply: "Leave what you are doing and come!"

His call has not changed much over the years. However, God has never addressed a call to any human soul that did not involve loss of some kind when viewed from the human standpoint. And one thing is always associated with His call—sacrifice.

Moses was called at tremendous sacrifice, but he counted it a greater honor to follow God than to enjoy the pleasures of sin with all the riches of Egypt at his disposal.

Simon and Andrew left their profitable fishing business and never looked back or asked any questions when Jesus gave the call, "Come!"

Look at Paul's standing in his day; but the call on the Damascus road sent him on a journey of stonings, shipwrecks, imprisonments, and death. Yet he rejoiced that he should be counted worthy!

God's greatest people have heard the call but have never recognized the sacrifice. "He has given to me much more than I have ever been able to give to Him," has been their testimony. They heard the voice but never knew or felt any misgiving in their hearts, and never asked, "What is in it for me?"

God gave John a glimpse into eternity where he saw multiplied millions, battle-scarred and worn, who had obeyed the call and had overcome by the blood of the Lamb, but they heard God say, "Well done!"

His "Well done" outshines any sacrifices in our obedience to His call, "Come."

PRAYER: *Every hour of our lives, O God, has brought its own miracle, every moment has seen some display of divine providence, and every action has been conscious of the still, small Voice calling us to some higher plane of living. Give us what our hearts need, and make our days glad with the beauty of Your grace. In Jesus' name. Amen.*

■ OCTOBER 20

I know, O Lord, that thy judgments are right, and that thou in faithfulness hast afflicted me.
(Ps. 119:75)

There is a dark side of life, and there is a bright side. Some people live in the gloom, while some seem to be able to dwell where the sun shines the brightest. Some people see only the giants, while others see "a land flowing with milk and honey."

Life runs a very narrow path between the two extremes. One side is very dark and full of despair and terror that lives in the night. The other side is bright and filled with the sunshine of hope, where the flowers bloom and the day knows no shadows. Rare is the life that has not seen the dark side of the road with its sorrow and torment of the soul.

God has not placed an impenetrable hedge to guard against the dark and the terrible. But the greatest words from heaven and the most tender message from the heart of God have come when the sky has darkened and clouds have covered the morning sun. God often lowers His voice to a whisper when the heartbroken look to Him through the dimness of tears.

Jeremiah lived on the edge of gloom but was not able to shut out the goodness of God. Seeing "affliction by the rod of his wrath," he recognized that it was only by "the Lord's mercies that we are not consumed" (Lam. 3:1, 22). Again, while his prayers were being "shut . . . out" of heaven, he saw the goodness of the Lord "to the soul that seeketh him" (vv. 8, 25). The Psalmist was caught in this mystery and concludes, "It is good for me that I have been afflicted; that I might learn thy statutes" (119:71).

Divine discipline? The rod and mercy mingled together bringing us closer to the heart of God! There is no contradiction between discipline and blessing when mercy belongs to God.

PRAYER: *O God, we have passed under some hard discipline and gone through some strange circumstances. We have learned that Your rod is a rod of love, and it is held by the Hand of mercy. Through it all we thank You for the hope and gladness we have received from doing Your will. Show us that it all has meaning and purpose. In Jesus' name. Amen.*

OCTOBER 21 ■

Charity suffereth long, and is kind; charity envieth not; charity vaunteth not itself, is not puffed up.
(1 Cor. 13:4)

The last baseball for the World Series had just crossed the plate, and the hand of the umpire indicated that it was a strike. The game was over! The winning pitcher was surrounded by his fellow players, and the media moved in to announce the highlights. One reporter questioned him about his slump in the third inning, after which he sat in the dugout with head bowed. Recognizing that "this is not a religious broadcast," he responded, "I was singing hymns to myself to gain composure," and he proceeded to give God thanks for giving him the strength to finish the game.

Of course the reporter did not respond very well to this comment but proceeded to major on the athletic ability that went into the game. But it pointed out the fact that there is a place for God in all varied aspects of life. And such a simple thing as bowing one's head in the crisis and singing a hymn can put a national TV network in turmoil. It also proves that love can go where fear has never dared to venture!

Love can make great prayers, and it can sing in the crisis, while fear contents itself with a sigh and moves to the back of the stage. Love gives boldness, courage, and confidence, while fear turns off the microphones. Love stands seven days a week, it keeps no time schedule, and it dares to go where the action is the greatest. Love dares to bow its head in the crowd and sing, "Jesus loves me! this I know, / For the Bible tells me so." How very incapable the world is in handling the testimony of love!

God will not keep back anything from His people that will minister to the development of the soul. He wants us to grow in truth and grace and love until the game is over!

PRAYER: *O God, when we are overcome by a great fear, we pray that You will reveal Your love to us. Give us that love that never doubts, that hopes forever, and in which there is no midnight. Every morning and every evening may Your love and compassion be new to us, and every day give us that love that conquers fear. In Jesus' name. Amen.*

OCTOBER 22

> If I take the wings of the morning, and dwell in the uttermost parts of the sea; even there shall thy hand lead me, and thy right hand shall hold me.
> (Ps. 139:9-10)

"I saw God this morning" is not an uncommon expression by those whose religious sensitivity runs deep. Yet those outside this comprehension look with suspicion on the person who would be so bold as to make the pronouncement. When a person says he has seen heaven opened, has seen a vision of God, and has felt in his heart the calm of an infinite peace, the world places him under suspicion.

We do not have to lock up our visions of God in the Bible and leave them with the prophets. We, too, can believe God, glimpse the Divine Presence, and have indications and proofs of God's nearness. The voice of God cannot be mistaken. It changes lives and turns the commonplace into a heaven. And God is always revealing himself to His people every morning!

The need of every age is a spiritual renewal when we have greater visions of life, higher conceptions of morality, a deeper sensitivity to sin, and a greater vision of the holiness of God. We are in danger of falling under the benumbing influence of those who would vehemently deny the possibility and say, "There is no God" (Pss. 14:1; 53:1).

Ezekiel said, "The heavens were opened, and I saw visions of God" (1:1). He believed somewhere in this vast universe, beyond his comprehension, is an everlasting Father. God forbid that we should forfeit this spiritual position due to unbelief and an unbelieving world.

Herein is the authority of the child of God to reach out and touch His mighty arm and have the companionship of His presence even in our present world.

PRAYER: *How we thank You, O God, for that still, small Voice that speaks to us day after day. Show yourself to us each day, not in the unbearable splendor of Your glory, but in the tenderness of Your providence and the goodness of Your daily blessings. Walk with us each day so that we might find peace in our souls and a purpose in every step. In Jesus' name. Amen.*

OCTOBER 23 ■

The steps of a good man are ordered by the Lord: and he delighteth in his way. Though he fall, he shall not be utterly cast down: for the Lord upholdeth him with his hand.
(Ps. 37:23-24)

It was a dark, foggy night, and I was traveling on a route that should have taken me to the Canadian border. When time failed to bring me to the expected destination, I checked the road map. I was on the right road, but a wrinkle in the map had blurred the way—I was going in the wrong direction! Checking the road map was a tribute to the ones who had numbered the highways and marked out all the places toward my destination.

The devil would like to steal all the road maps, fill them with wrinkles, remove all the warnings of hazards, and place safety markers on all the washed-out bridges and highways. He would like to place his little tricks on everything to lead the traveler astray. He knows that God's Road Map has made the way so plain that even the most ignorant can find it.

God never leaves a road half finished, nor will He leave the traveler stranded. To be sure, it may take many detours and lead through many valleys, up long and hard hills, and even through lions' dens. Sometimes a misjudgment in direction may take place. But God will never permit anyone to walk it alone. Our confidence and our joy is that He who has begun a good work in us will continue it until the day of completion.

Christianity has been chained in all the prisons men have ever built. It has been thrown into all the fiery furnaces men could light. It has been under every attack that Satan could devise. Every device that the enemy could conjure up has been placed in her way to lead her offtrack.

A tribute to the love of God is the Blood-marked pathway that takes us in the right direction to eternity, and it leads through Calvary!

PRAYER: *All of the way belongs to You, O God! Help us to accept it even when it goes through the churchyard and the desert or across the river and up the steep hills. Give us that faith to know that the way is regulated by the wisdom and companionship of our Heavenly Father. In Jesus' name. Amen.*

OCTOBER 24

> O Lord God of my salvation, I have cried day and night before thee: let my prayer come before thee: incline thine ear unto my cry.
> (Ps. 88:1-2)

When my grandmother prayed, she would often say to God, "We know that no prayer that has ever ascended on high has ever been lost." In my childhood mind I would picture big piles of prayers stacked all over heaven. Some were too late to be answered. Some were impossible for God to handle. Some I hoped He would put in the pile and forget. Then I saw a special pile that belonged to Grandmother, because she prayed in such a way that I just knew God could not ignore them.

This childhood picture has never really been resolved! What has become of the prayers of the ages? Did the prayers of the great saints go for nothing? Did they perish on the way somewhere between heaven and earth? Prayers so complete in their range, so masterful in expression, so sympathetic in tone and spirit, and so full of faith surely can't be lost.

God said to Solomon, "I have heard your prayer and your supplication that you have made before Me" (1 Kings 9:3, NKJV). And He promised an answer. And isn't the answer of one prayer the guarantee of another? The thing that we want in prayer is a response that touches human life at every point and fills it according to its capacity with love and help that can only come from heaven. God never underanswers, but out of the secret storehouse of His grace He surprises us with His overabundance of blessing.

Maybe God does have piles of prayers in heaven, but He has told us to keep on praying. The prayer may not be eloquent. It might be selfish sometimes. It might not always be offered in the right spirit. But if it is lifted up to heaven from an honest heart, it is in His pile to be answered.

PRAYER: *O God, we know that You anticipate our prayers. The infinite answer of Your love is sometimes uttered upon earth even before our prayer is heard in heaven. Give us power in our praying. Make us to be more than conquerors when we come before the throne to make our supplication before You. In Jesus' name. Amen.*

OCTOBER 25

Confess your faults one to another, and pray one for another, that ye may be healed. The effectual fervent prayer of a righteous man availeth much.
(James 5:16)

The influence of good people has always gone a long way in shaping our world. The good things enjoyed in every generation are because good people have fought and died for a cause.

God has saved the earth time and again because of righteous people. He would have spared the cities of the plains if Abraham could have found 10 praying souls. He blessed the house of Potiphar because Joseph's influence permeated the palace. The ardent prayers of Moses acted as a shield between God's judgment and Israel. For Paul's sake God spared a ship on the pounding seas.

We must bear in mind that God's moral law has not changed with the ages, and He is still in control of His world. God is still the almighty One, the great Lawgiver. Who knows how many lives have been spared because of the prayers of the righteous and the godly character of saints in our time!

The value that God places on righteousness is unchangeable, and His people do play a very important role. Consider some of the great names that God has honored.

"Noah found grace in the eyes of the Lord. . . . Noah was a just man . . . and Noah walked with God" (Gen. 6:8-9).

Daniel was a man "greatly beloved" (9:23; 10:11, 19), and his conduct attracted the attention of heaven.

Job was "one that feareth God, and escheweth evil" (1:8; 2:3; see 1:1)—a character good enough for God to display as His example before the powers of darkness.

Who can understand the mystery of godliness and its influence? We do know that when God's people pray, they can move the hand of God.

PRAYER: *O God, we thank You for the godly influence of those who have gone before us. They have put forth their trembling hand and have stayed Your hand. Make us like the Master, so that the quality of our influence will count for the kingdom of God. In Jesus' name. Amen.*

■ OCTOBER 26

In a moment, in the twinkling of an eye, at the last trump: for the trumpet shall sound, and the dead shall be raised incorruptible, and we shall be changed.
(1 Cor. 15:52)

The Bible tells us that Jesus Christ came into the world to save sinners, yet people asked questions about things quite unrelated to salvation. Paul was called to be a missionary to the Gentiles, and he was faced with many of the great questions in his day. People are still concerned about questions that have little to do with the salvation of the world.

Paul was as much concerned with questions about death as he was about those related to living, and he does not allow much of a separation between the two. Christ is risen, therefore death is destroyed, and he risks everything on the power of the Resurrection.

To every great question that confronts the apostle, he begins with Christ, continues with Christ, and ends with Christ. His thesis is that if there is no Cross and no Resurrection, there is no preaching, there is no faith, there is no gospel, and there is no possibility to gain heaven. Jesus Christ was the glory of all hope and the immortality of all true life. If the question in his day could not be run through this format, it was not worth his time.

All of the questions concerning birth, life, old age, death, burial, resurrection, heaven, and immortality all stand together. These things are all part of a system of progress, and dying is not a finishing day. His conclusion is, "If in this life only we have hope in Christ, we are of all men most miserable" (v. 19).

He sees that the entire spectrum of questions in the human race is in the hands of God. If we can lay hold on this truth, the awesomeness of the problems of life and death pass from us, the grave holds no fear, and the greatest questions have already been resolved at Calvary.

PRAYER: *O God, we understand so little of this life of ours! Our trust is in You, the living God, working out Your immeasurable purposes in all areas of life. The only power that can reach out and give us an answer to the impossible questions of life is the gospel of Jesus Christ. May we rest all of our anxieties in Your keeping. In Jesus' name. Amen.*

OCTOBER 27 ■

But if we walk in the light, as he is in the light, we have fellowship one with another, and the blood of Jesus Christ his Son cleanseth us from all sin.
(1 John 1:7)

"Walking in the light" has always been an expression used in testimony by God's people in their effort to do and go according to the will of God. However, this expression is not new, for Jesus urged His followers to "walk while ye have the light, lest darkness come upon you" (John 12:35). It indicates opportunity, advantage, and that "up and at it" challenge while it is day.

In a sense there is no tomorrow in Christian service, for the challenge is for the "now." The idea is to make the most of God's morning, for as the day wears on, the shadows lengthen, and darkness creeps in to cover the way. Jesus is simply saying, "Here is encouragement, here is a warning, here is an urgency—darkness is coming!"

Could this not apply to the morning days of your human existence? Remember how easy it was to memorize verses of Scripture, and you never forgot those lessons learned in Sunday School? "Store the memory," says Jesus, "while it is fresh and young." The little Sunday School hymn will come back to you again and again. Your earliest prayers will revive within you, and in old age you will relive those precious moments in God's Word.

Christ is the Light of the World. You should make every effort to walk in His company. Walk while you have Christ. Take every opportunity to study Him. Take every opportunity to serve Him by all the good things you can do. What better preparation for the dark shadows of death than walking now with the Light of the World!

When we walk in the light, we do not have to fear the darkness of sin that separates from God.

PRAYER: *Eternal Father, may the light of Your presence shine in our hearts brighter than the noonday sun. We thank You for Jesus, who is the Light of all worlds, the Light of all ages, and in Him there is no darkness at all. We would stand in that light that outshines every shadow and makes the heart clean. In His name. Amen.*

OCTOBER 28

> **In those days came John the Baptist, preaching in the wilderness of Judaea, and saying, Repent ye: for the kingdom of heaven is at hand.**
> (Matt. 3:1-2)

In God's Hall of Fame there must be a special niche for John the Baptist. Matthew, Mark, and Luke will surely have a place there, for they trace out the history of the human side of Jesus. Make room for John the Evangelist, as he opens heaven and reveals the glory of the Son of God from on high. But in what could have been the Baptist's great claim to fame, he simply said, "I am nothing, but there is One coming after me, and I want to tell you about Him" (see John 1:15-18).

While he was preaching about Jesus, a man was sent to him with the question, "Who are you anyway?" And the people would have accepted whatever answer he might have given. He could have given a hint as to the Messiahship, but he said, "I am not the Christ" (John 1:21). Here he could have risen from a nomad in the desert to a place of kingship in the palace. But he said, "The One you seek is coming after me" (see v. 27).

John knew that the moment he took what did not belong to him, he would lose power with God and eventually with the people. He could have said, "I am the Christ," and would have won a moment's victory. But at the bend of the road he would meet humiliation and defeat.

John does not even claim kinship to "that prophet" but is happy with his part in the drama: "I am the voice of one crying in the wilderness" (John 1:21, 23). How simple an answer! "I am a voice—sent to prepare the way for Him who is great!" Then came the beautiful climax of his speech: "There standeth one among you . . . he it is" (vv. 26-27)!

He knew that to have seen everything but the Christ of God is to have seen everything in life but the one thing worth seeing. He wanted to tell the people about Him!

PRAYER: *Have mercy on us, O God, so that we may humble ourselves before You in our smallness and unworthiness. Bring us to that moment when our petitions are answered in all the fullness of the possibilities of Your grace. Draw so near to Christ that we will say, "Truly this Man must be the Son of God." In His name. Amen.*

OCTOBER 29

But we preach Christ crucified, unto the Jews a stumblingblock, and unto the Greeks foolishness; but unto them which are called ... Christ the power of God.
(1 Cor. 1:23-24)

Once when I was a very small child, my stepfather took the whole family to a revival meeting one night in a local church. His conclusion to the whole scene, and especially to the altar service, was, "It's all a big pack of foolishness." I did not know if his pronouncement was the result of conviction, or if it depicted his honest feeling about the church.

Over the years I have learned that the things of God are discernible only as the Spirit of God reveals them to a prepared heart. "If our gospel be hid, it is hid to them that are lost" (2 Cor. 4:3). If the mind and heart contend that the problem lies in the Church, even in God's people, they have been blinded to the revelation of God. "But the natural man receiveth not the things of the Spirit of God: for they are foolishness unto him" (1 Cor. 2:14).

There will always be people in the world to whom the Church with all its ministries is a "pack of foolishness." They do not have the spiritual faculty to take hold of the secrets of God. But "out of the mouth of babes and sucklings" God said He would ordain praise (Ps. 8:2; Matt. 21:16).

God has said that the one who would press on to know the truth would find it. And He promised a growing place in His grace for all seeking people. No child of God should ever demean the place given to him but should seek to grow by constant fellowship and communion with his God. He never ceases to talk to the child-heart that cries out in the dark midnight, "Speak, Lord; for thy servant heareth" (1 Sam. 3:9, see 10).

I know, for I also heard my stepfather pray and testify that it was a "pack of foolishness" only to the one who was fighting against God.

PRAYER: *O God, we pray that You will keep us in tune with heaven the few days You have given to us here on earth. Save us from the folly of anxiety and the bondage of despair. Take us out of the foolishness of our own littleness and give us a vision of Your eternity by which all things are measured. In Jesus' name. Amen.*

■ OCTOBER 30

My times are in thy hand: deliver me from the hand of mine enemies, and from them that persecute me.
(Ps. 31:15)

Impossible! Thanksgiving Day in America has not arrived, yet today there were beginnings of Christmas in the stores. From Christmas to Christmas as a child seemed to be a whole life, an immeasurable quantity, and a thing too distant to anticipate. Now one Christmas is barely gone before preparation for another has begun. It simply drives home the point that time rushes madly onward with little regard for one's readiness.

In spite of the pace and the changing times, there is a wonderful sense of comfort and security for one whose gaze is on the eternal. God help us not to advance beyond the child spirit that can still see the sweet tranquillity of life and the calmness of heart as we advance on the journey.

How wonderful to be able to move in the Spirit of the Lord! We can rise in the morning in His strength. We can lie down at night with a clean heart and God's blessing. We can find resting-places and fountains of fresh water for the heat of the day and abundant grace for everything placed in our way. Yea, we can live and move and have our being in God, and every word, thought, and action can bear the blessing of heaven.

The triumph of the journey is found in simple obedience to God. To obey is to live and to march and to be. To look every morning for the marching orders of the day is to march in the spirit of peace and joy. However, to have no marching orders, no living God, and no trust in heaven means Christmas may as well come in October, for the spirit is already lost!

Only that one who knows the Spirit of Christ can be a happy traveler on the journey, and time no longer intimidates.

PRAYER: *Almighty God, we are caught up in the pressure of time, which is so very short. It is that out of which our life is made and for which we must give an account. Without Your eternity mingled with our time, our sight would lead to despair. With You, O God, may our hearts find rest like a Sabbath calm. In Jesus' name. Amen.*

OCTOBER 31

And I say also unto thee, That thou art Peter, and upon this rock I will build my church; and the gates of hell shall not prevail against it.
(Matt. 16:18)

One of the most powerful statements in the Bible is found in the words of Jesus, "I will build my church." Powerful because of the One who said it, but more powerful because He did say it. The Church has gone through periods of corruption, been shaken to its very foundation, and been divided into a thousand pieces. But it still stands secure today.

The subtle threat that the enemy has forced against the Church has been the misplacement of emphasis. How Satan loves to divide the Church of God! Rising from the altar rail in my church where we had just concluded the local ministerial meeting, one pastor said to me, "The saddest day in my church was when they removed the mourner's bench." The trick of the enemy is to find out the principal things in the church and then proceed to destroy them.

The strength of the Church has been its steadfastness and stability when the urgency has been to live upon a basis of compromise. Paul's argument was that he refused to have it any other way. He has Christ put in His right place and at the heart of things. Paul and Apollos are nothing, but Jesus Christ is everything.

The central theme of the Church must not change, and it must be drawn around the Cross. Every conflict must be settled by the spirit of the Cross. And when people meet here, they will see very little of themselves but very much of him whose death made the meeting place possible.

The church is nothing that is not begun, continued, and ended in the Christ of Calvary.

PRAYER: *This is Your Church, O God. You established it a long time ago and told the enemy that it would stand forever. Its purpose is that through it the world's people may obtain peace and that God's people would experience life of praise. Help us to do our share to make it so. In Jesus' name. Amen.*

NOVEMBER 1

Blessed is every one that feareth the Lord; that walketh in his ways. . . . it shall be well with thee.
(Ps. 128:1-2)

A day has been designated in the calendar as All Saints' Day. How do we know who qualifies for the celebration? For if you think you are a saint, chances are that you are not one. If, in your humility, you think you don't qualify, your commitment falls short in the failure of your identification.

Some housewives post a motto over the sink, piled high with dirty dishes, bemoaning the fact that they cannot find the time to be a saint. But in spite of persecution and martyrdom Paul found saints even in Caesar's household.

Today we honor posterity and those who have borne the burden of their day and "came out of great tribulation, and have washed their robes, and made them white in the blood of the Lamb" (Rev. 7:14), and stand tall in the ranks of the Redeemed.

Sainthood is not a mere sentiment or idea, and it cannot coexist with a selfish spirit. It cannot disregard sin, and it has a deep regard for others.

Sainthood is more than an inspiration. It is a power and purpose found in the soul, an expectation of the whole resources of God, and a giving out of all that it receives. It watches for the secret of the Lord, and it is moved by communication with the Almighty.

Sainthood comes to the meek, the merciful, the pure in heart, and the peace-loving. It is spiritual greatness and worth that is honored by Divinity and accepted in heaven.

Sainthood is still attainable, for no generation is to be the perpetual custodian of God's truth, and no one can claim all of God as a private possession. God is still in the business of making saints.

Toward this goal we all can say with Paul, "Not as though I had already attained . . . I press toward the mark" (Phil. 3:12, 14).

PRAYER: *Holy Father, make us saints in the household of faith, we pray, so that we might be true representatives of the Master. Help us so that our lives may be rooted and grounded in the truth in which the saints have lived in Your kingdom. Make it so today. In Jesus' name. Amen.*

NOVEMBER 2 ■

And they that know thy name will put their trust in thee: for thou, Lord, hast not forsaken them that seek thee.
(Ps. 9:10)

The Bible declares, and experience backs up, the certainty of our relationship with God. It says, "I know whom I have believed, and am persuaded that he is able to keep that which I have committed unto him against that day" (2 Tim. 1:12). I am persuaded. I am resigned. I know.

The "I know" to the man or woman of God is not so much a matter of independent genius as it is a contentment within the bounds of resignation. We do not have to say, "I think," "I hope," "I imagine," or "it may be so," for our faith comes with a definite "I know," and it covers all the demands of doubt.

The religion of complete resignation is a tremendous religion, for it is based on a Person. He was born in Bethlehem; He proclaimed himself to be the Son of Man, the Son of God; He looked upon the entire human race with tears in His eyes; He tasted death for every person; He died, the just for the unjust, that He might bring us to God; He was crucified, He died and was buried, and on the third day He arose again, and now He is in heaven; He is our Advocate before the throne; He still bears the wounds of Calvary; and His love is still my claim to certainty.

In an age of materialism and doubt, when the stock market crash makes the rich man ragged and the wealthy without worth, we can have our treasure in a surety that knows no collapse. We do not have to grab for that which passes away or build a philosophy with a "maybe" foundation.

Jesus Christ is our Surety. It is an answer with personality. "Truly this Man is the Son of God" (see Mark 15:39), and I can know Him.

PRAYER: *Lord Jesus Christ, we accept Your will as complete and final. We would know the fellowship of Your suffering so that afterward we might know the power of Your Resurrection. May we also know the unity of the Spirit of God and the sweetness of the bond of peace. Amen.*

NOVEMBER 3

> **O Jerusalem, Jerusalem ... how often would I have gathered thy children together, as a hen doth gather her brood under her wings, and ye would not!**
> (Luke 13:34)

In a recent counseling session a lady was pouring out her grief in tears of anxiety that she could not control. In the process of probing and defining the hurt, she looked up and said, "I am shedding more tears over my problems than I am over God's pain. Do you think I cause Him to suffer?" I tried to find the answer for her in our commitment rather than in our pain.

We are of this earth and are rooted here in our humanity, and it's easy for every action to be charged with our own welfare. We forget that we have the divine treasure in an earthen vessel. When darkness, anxiety, disappointment, and weakness overtake us, we give in to our impatience and are broken by the burden of guilt. God stands alone in His holy place and weeps and says to us, "How oft would I have carried your load, but you chose to do it alone."

God has made us and not we ourselves. He knows what we can bear. He assures us that He is full of loving-kindness and tender mercy. We are called to acceptance, obedience, and surrender to the divine will. How pleased He must be when we act within the bounds of His love and purpose for us.

In such a temper God can deal with us and take our hurt, failures, and shortcomings and speak to us in the language of our understanding. Indeed, He suffers when we weep alone!

He humbled himself and took on the form of a servant and became obedient unto death. His suffering! And this truth must touch our lives at every point, granting to our pain an answer of ease and to our cry an answer of contentment.

God's heart is broken when I stand alone and cry!

PRAYER: *O God, our hearts respond in warmth when we know that as a father pitieth His children, so the Lord pitieth them that fear Him. You have given us the strength to fulfill our task, and when we have been stricken with grief, Your healing balm has been applied in abundance. Thank You in Jesus' name. Amen.*

NOVEMBER 4

Stand ye in the ways, and see, and ask for the old paths, where is the good way, and walk therein, and ye shall find rest for your souls.
(Jer. 6:16)

Sometime between midnight and morning I got lost in the maze of one-way streets and byways in New York City. On very unfamiliar highways I was carried along with the traffic, and asking for direction was impossible. After hours of frustration and going around in circles, a familiar sign and arrow appeared, leading out of the tangled web of trafficways on to my destination and home.

The incident would hardly be worth the telling were it confined to its own little area of concern. It is typical of happenings repeated every day in some life where the maze of highways is leading in the wrong direction and without purpose.

Life is more than groping one's way aimlessly along crowded streets or trying to get out of an entanglement of unknown highways alone. Unrest and dreams will plague like enemies in the night if we look at life as a game in which there is no control, and for which we can find no direction.

Life is a divine plan. The hairs of our heads are all numbered. Not a sparrow falls without our Heavenly Father knowing it. Our troubles are reckoned, and our tears are counted. The valleys on the road are leveled by the hand of God, and every climb up the steep, rocky cliff is part of the divine purpose. With every temptation God will make a way of escape. Every trial has its own purpose and its own outcome, for our Heavenly Father is in control.

It is not in our human ability to recover from this way on our own, for the journey tends to destruction. Christianity stands at the crossroads, pointing out the road of God and directing men along it to salvation, companionship, and heaven.

PRAYER: *Lead us, O God, in Your way, and the end will be rest. Keep us until the end, and may we not get lost on the wrong road. When life's journey is done, may we stand, through the power of Calvary, among those who are arrayed in white garments. In Jesus' name. Amen.*

NOVEMBER 5

> **For in the time of trouble he shall hide me in his pavilion: in the secret of his tabernacle shall he hide me; he shall set me up upon a rock.**
> (Ps. 27:5)

Life is full of vexing problems and mysteries, and in our misunderstanding we call them contradictions. Often we take a gloomy view of situations in which we find ourselves, for we can see no way through.

We said, "This is the end of everything"; then we discovered that in God's timing it was merely the beginning.

We said, "The raging storm will surely sweep us away"; but it died out before it reached us.

We said, "The agony is more than we can bear"; but God sent strength that made us wonders even to ourselves.

We said, "The way is too dark, and we are all alone"; then we heard a voice telling us that it is the Lord's doing, and we found it marvelous in our own eyes.

We said, "We will never live through the trials and terrors of this day"; then we saw God tear the impossible to bits and throw the fragments into the sneering face of defeat.

God is always giving us an alternative to defeat and whispers to us, "I will show you a better way." He does not waste the benefits of heaven on anyone, and His alternative is a mark of His confidence. He knows our situation, and He knows the need by which we are moved, even if we cannot speak it to Him in words.

He is pleased when we are living out our lives in the simplicity of faith. Then we will know that if things fall upon us suddenly, His grace will be equal to the surprise, and the healing that follows the hurt will be a miracle.

His intention is that this good work He begins in us will continue until the day of redemption and completion.

PRAYER: *We cast ourselves into Your hands, O God, not daring to utter one petition lest we offend the great purposes You have for us. In the contradiction of our human spirit settle upon our minds and hearts the constancy of the Spirit of God. Make us partakers of Your purity. In Jesus' name. Amen.*

NOVEMBER 6 ■

In the day of my trouble I will call upon thee: for thou wilt answer me.
(Ps. 86:7)

Today I watched a telephone operator work the calls coming through a very complicated switchboard. This involved disgruntled customers as well as information unrelated to any outgoing connection. It was at the end of the day, and as she moved away from the board, she remarked, "Oh, this gets so frustrating!"

Tonight I heard someone ask the question, "Have you prayed about it?" My reaction was, "Another call through God's switchboard—I wonder if He ever gets frustrated."

Our life is a continual cry to Him, and His lines are besieged with millions of prayers every day. We are always in want and reaching for something more than what we have. The similarity ends there, for God's phone system welcomes every call.

God always has more to give, more light to shed, and greater revelations to disclose if we call His number. Our yearning after Him will receive a continual answer according to the necessity.

"Call upon me in the day of trouble: I will deliver thee, and thou shalt glorify me" (Ps. 50:15).

"For thou, Lord, art good, and ready to forgive; and plenteous in mercy unto all them that call upon thee" (Ps. 86:5).

"Call unto me, and I will answer thee, and shew thee great and mighty things" (Jer. 33:3).

God's line is also open for words of praise. The language of prayer that expresses itself in supplication can also express thanksgiving. When our words are too poor for heavenly praise, He hears the unspoken language of the heart.

You may call anytime, for God's line is never busy, and He never gets frustrated!

PRAYER: *Gracious Father, our poor words, half dumb and trembling through and through with a throb of conscious weakness, are caught up and presented before Your throne by a power beyond our comprehension. Surely this is the work of the Holy Spirit. May we calmly listen to Your answers. In Jesus' name. Amen.*

NOVEMBER 7

Every man according as he purposeth in his heart, so let him give; not grudgingly, or of necessity: for God loveth a cheerful giver.
(2 Cor. 9:7)

It was an amusing sight in a home mission pastorate to see an elderly gentleman follow the usher down the aisle to get his change from the nickel he had dropped in the offering plate. On the other hand Jesus praised the widow who had given her last two mites in the offering and asked for nothing in return.

The difference could be that one was given grudgingly, while the other was an offering of love. God does not despise what is little and insignificant because it is little and insignificant. He turns the water into a gift of wine, and He looks upon the mite as a nugget of gold.

We are bringing the biggest things in our world to Him when we give Him our hearts, our minds, our wills, and our love. His concern is that when we say we have given all, we may have kept back part of the gift. God wants the entire sacrifice, withholding nothing, a holy offering unto the Lord. The significance and size are matters of consequence only in terms of our honesty and willingness to give.

God has made us wonders to ourselves and mysteries that have no answer in time. He has filled us with longings that cannot be explained by mortal tongue. And He has made us so that our hope and trust are in Him, and our expectation has its basis in heaven.

The teachings of Jesus are anticipated in this master plan, and He made His point very clear to all of us: "He that findeth his life shall lose it: and he that loseth his life for my sake shall find it" (Matt. 10:39).

The spirit of sacrifice that pleases God takes nothing back from the offering plate.

PRAYER: *Almighty God, we are pleased to leave everything on Your altar this day, praying that You will accept the gift in its entirety. You have accepted our weakness and allowed our ignorance to challenge the revelation of Your wisdom. Accept us in the miracle of Your love and providence. In Jesus' name. Amen.*

NOVEMBER 8 ■

That it might be fulfilled which was spoken by Esaias the prophet, saying, Himself took our infirmities, and bare our sicknesses.
(Matt. 8:17)

Today I visited a hospital—a place where the sick come to get well. On my way through I encountered a man with a bag of electrical tools. I saw another one rolling a scrub bucket down the hallway with a mop, and another walked past with a plunger in his hand.

The place was astir with people pushing linen carts, emptying trash baskets, and carrying trays. Behind the desks secretaries were busy at their tasks, as nurses moved quietly in and out of the rooms. The intercom kept repeating, "Dr. S., call 2-2-4 . . . Dr. S., call 2-2-4."

I had always thought of hospitals in terms of operating rooms, pill bottles, stethoscopes, and people in white coats ministering in a healing capacity. How wonderful the lessons God sends, for too often we fail to grasp the idea of divine existence in more mundane activities. I saw a chain of cooperation linked together with a chain of commitment hooked on to the infinite healing power of God.

There is a mystery in the handiwork of God that we can never touch, and it points to a concern beyond our shortsightedness. And there follows an acknowledgment of His concern with every area of ministering to the sick. You will never find human conduct treated with divine unconcern, and even the most menial task in doing good is acknowledging another place for God.

I felt I was in the presence of God, for the work of these people was also the work of God in order to make sick people well.

PRAYER: *Almighty God, help us see that Your healing presence overflows all things. Everything is open before Your eyes, and Your presence prevails in every circumstance. You bring the heart out of darkness and give it the joy of light. How glorious to know that as long as You are, we shall be. In Jesus' name. Amen.*

NOVEMBER 9

> Cause me to hear thy lovingkindness in the morning; for in thee do I trust: cause me to know the way wherein I should walk; for I lift up my soul unto thee.
> (Ps. 143:8)

One week two men were drowned while on a hunting expedition. It did not make big headlines, but it was a startling event to me nonetheless. Had there not been a change in plans, two of my friends and I would have been in the boat that hit a submerged snag and went to the bottom of the flowage.

The natural thing was to thank God that our lives had been spared; this we did. At the same time we were confronted with the inevitable question of God's protective plan. Why were we spared while two other people lost their lives? When put in terms of answers, the simplicity of God's plan suddenly becomes very profound.

And as I search for an answer within my own genius, I meet His response: "The answer is not in you, it is in God." If I do not leave the problem there, I enter into a game with Divinity for the purpose of putting the Almighty to the test.

In the paradox of life, when the heart hurts, even while it is rejoicing, I must know that Providence is not a matter of testing or even asking questions. It is a matter of trusting God, knowing that He does all things according to the wisdom of eternity.

Out of this comes the only satisfying answer I can find. In the divine meaning of life God's purpose is hidden in His love and wisdom. The message then becomes clear to keep my heart from any accusation that leaves an open door for the enemy.

I have to say, even though I cannot know what I am saying, "God does all things well."

PRAYER: *Your ways, O God, are beyond our wisdom. We were born yesterday, yet in our folly we walk as if we owned today. Give us guidance as an insight that shall save us from many a dangerous journey, and keep us in Your peace. In Jesus' name. Amen.*

NOVEMBER 10

In God have I put my trust: I will not be afraid what man can do unto me. Thy vows are upon me, O God: I will render praises unto thee.
(Ps. 56:11-12)

The Psalmist posed the troubled question and was quick to provide a reply: "Why art thou cast down, O my soul? ... hope in God: for I shall yet praise him" (43:5). Hope and praise go hand in hand in the problems of the soul.

For every tone of hope in the human heart our songs should follow in full praise. Too often we are cast down when pain and suffering, disappointment and sorrow, grief and bereavement move in on us unexpectedly. In times like these we need some word from God to touch our lives and to bring back hope, but too often we leave it there and forget to follow with our praise.

Our danger is that because we are of this earth, and we hold it so high, it blocks out any view of the future. We set time against eternity, earth against heaven, and the body against the soul. The enemy of our souls blinds us with comforting lies of satisfaction of the immediate and applies a false balance to the providences that make up our lives here and now.

Our hope needs to extend into the mystery of the Shekinah glory and the deeper mysteries of its peace. This brings the omnipotence of heaven to bear upon our burdens and pains of the passing hour. We need to reply to such good news with new hearts filled with thanksgiving.

If we let the Word of God go from us, our hope is also gone, and the name of God has no more meaning for us. How delightful to have this hope and sing the praises of God, knowing we are in His hands and are guided by His infinite control.

Deeper than all the depths we have fathomed and higher than all the heights we have scaled is this relationship with God.

PRAYER: *We thank You, O God, for Christian hope and confidence, and for Your voice that speaks to us from above. This hope tells us how great is Your love to us, how tender Your mercy, and how precious the dew of Your tears. Through this hope our hearts are filled with thanksgiving. In Jesus' name. Amen.*

■ **NOVEMBER 11**

For I reckon that the sufferings of this present time are not worthy to be compared with the glory which shall be revealed in us.
(Rom. 8:18)

"Lest we forget"—Flanders fields, Iwo Jima, Vietnam! Unnumbered thousands have fallen in death on war-ridden soil to protect lands and loved ones from the forces of greed and from enemy invasion. Prayers of thanksgiving for their supreme sacrifice comes out today from the silent chambers of our hearts. All the fading glory is called back, and all the patterns of high virtue and noble piety are remembered. Their memory becomes as a flower blown through the quiet air, leaving a fragrance for all to receive and be glad.

These memories must not be blotted out of our history. Death has put life on the throne, and sacrifice has made way for freedom. And we hold the memories close, for they tell us what is meant by giving, yet retaining all the mystery of the sacrifice.

"Lest we forget"—Gethsemane, Calvary, the Cross! Equally based upon a distinct history with significance universal both to time and place. Here is freedom coming out of sacrifice, power coming out of weakness, and light coming out of darkness. Our freedom has been bought with a price, and we belong to the Buyer and are admonished to glorify Him in our body and spirit.

Today we offer to Him the sacrifice of thanksgiving, for here is the place where our salvation is founded and where our heaven begins. The Cross is the battlefield of suffering and shame, which He endured so that we might triumph with Him in the glory of the Resurrection. Here Blood was shed for the cleansing of our sins!

We must remember! "Lest we forget."

PRAYER: *We thank You, O God, for the security that comes to us through men who have gone down into the deep valley of death so valiantly. We thank You for those who have sung the martyr's song in the deep places, and for the Cross that makes our sacrifice so sacred. We thank You that there is victory in the death of every saint, and defeat for the powers of evil. In Jesus' name. Amen.*

NOVEMBER 12 ■

For in him we live, and move, and have our being; . . . For we are also his offspring.
(Acts 17:28)

A man whom I have listed as a saint in my special book of memories always used to pray, "O God, You know the way that I take." I never really knew what he meant, but I was satisfied to leave the secret with him and God. Of a much deeper concern has been, "How can I know the way of God that He wants *me* to take?"

God has placed us in a great mystery of life with thoughts, ideas, and actions moving in the direction of eternity. His hand of omnipotence is over and above all. To look at ourselves is to take a view of our littleness and frailty as we stand in relation to Him. When we watch the wonder-working hand of God, we see how His way is crowned with perfectness.

We were born in the mystery of His power. We are kept in the mystery of His providence. We are saved by the mystery of His grace. We do not know our beginning, nor can we know the ending of our ways. We live each dying moment of the present in the strength that is given to us by God.

But He makes us to know Him through the mystery of the God-man, Jesus Christ. Because His heart is moved toward us with all the tenderness of love, our life is not cut off. We live and move and have our being in Him because His compassions fail not. He does not see our littleness nor our shortcomings. He sees our value and paid the ransom for our redemption. In this great mystery of heaven is my way hidden with God. And I abide in Him for its revelation.

My concern is, "O God, let me continue to follow in Your ways."

PRAYER: *O God, You are the God of our life. It is hidden with Christ in You. Without Him we can do nothing, but in Him we can do all things through the strength that He gives to us. This is the Lord's doings, and we are satisfied with His ways. In Jesus' name. Amen.*

NOVEMBER 13

Commit thy way unto the Lord; trust also in him; and he shall bring it to pass.
(Ps. 37:5)

"Don't Fence Me In" was the popular song in its day. But it was more than a song. It was the expression of a desire to be unleashed, unhampered, and let go. The message soon became the norm in living, where no fence was high enough or strong enough to hold the demanding spirit of the age.

"I want to do my own thing." "I don't want any ties, restrictions, or guidelines." "I am going to do what I want to do." "I am not going to be hampered by anyone's rules." The age will be its own judge, and society will have to account for its own harvest. But our poor human race does need a more substantial utterance to accommodate the outrage of any generation.

We are obstinate creatures. We love to have our own way. We think our wisdom is quite divine. By stinging disappointments we have discovered that the road we thought led to liberty actually led to death. We lifted our arms, thinking they were the mighty oak, only to find they were mere willow saplings. We said, "Don't fence me in," for I can run and know no weariness, but at the end we lay down in distress. We called it experience, for we were afraid to use its truer form. And with every self-willed decision we moved farther away from the reach of rescue.

Wondrous have been the ways of God to every age! We need to live under His rules. They are the best because they are His. He knows the end from the beginning and has already reviewed every step of the long road ahead. We cannot lose our place in His order of things without letting go of our character, for there is no meaning without Him.

We are nothing without God; but we can do all things through Christ who strengthens us.

PRAYER: *O God, show us something of the wonders of Your way. Keep us in silence before You and from interfering with the course of Your providence. Help us to say from a heart of sincerity, "God's way is the best for us!" In Jesus' name. Amen.*

NOVEMBER 14 ■

The fool hath said in his heart,
There is no God.
(Ps. 14:1)

There was a time in my life when doubt pulled out all the stops and draped a black cloud over every ray of hope that tried to shine through into my heart. I doubted the existence of God, and I knew there could be no love in the heart of any Divine Being for any creature of this earth.

My life was a rhythm of despair played in a minor key, sending a troubled melody into the depths of my soul. Heaven was a faraway dream, and any identification with God was a mockery.

But a message of love and concern was being written by an unknown Writer on the pages of my aching heart, and I did not know it. Love was working with all the sufficiency of grace that my soul would allow. One day I became a partaker of that "righteousness which is of God by faith" (Phil. 3:9).

Then came the touch of forgiveness, and the next move was out of the doldrums of despair into the sunshine of hope—from darkness into light. In order to complete the work of redemption, I looked up through tears and said, "I believe."

In my ministry I have seen the inexhaustible patience of God in the battle for a soul, and I never knew Him to draw back in the conflict. How beautiful that concern, communion, and the consummation, the result of which is sonship, liberty, and heaven!

Christianity does not want to envelop me in darkness and doubt or shut me up in my prison of hatred and scorn. Christ was sent "to turn [men] from darkness to light" (Acts 26:18). And who can measure the distance?

PRAYER: *O God, how many times in our struggle through life there break forth in words and arguments doubts greater than our capacity of faith can handle. Their purpose is to draw us away from You and to create for us a bleak wilderness through which we can find no safe journey. Help us to do away with all doubts at the center of our lives so that the circumference will be radiant with Your glory. Amen.*

■ **NOVEMBER 15**

Blessed be the Lord, who daily loadeth us with benefits, even the God of our salvation.
(Ps. 68:19)

It is usually sung as a blessing, and a note of sadness always comes out of the words, "God be with you till we meet again." I keep wanting to ask, "And when we meet again, is God's task completed?" God be with you *only* until we meet again! The joy of being a Christian is that the tabernacle of God is with men on earth now and even in the company of our closest friends. The greatest promise in human experience is, "I will never leave you nor forsake you" (Heb. 13:5, NKJV).

We want to see God every day—and walk with Him and talk with Him and tell Him all about our troubles, and hear His reply every day. Our hearts are stubborn, our eyes are blind, and our minds stray in all directions. We need One to speak to us the right words, in the right tone, at the right moment. We need One to speak to the aching heart in that still, small Voice that only the aching heart can hear. We need Him to be near us so that we can reach out and touch Him at any time.

We need One to be in our life all the time, shaping it and giving meaning to the morning and purpose in the dark hours of the night. We need God's Word living in us, giving light to our understanding, leading us into deeper truths every day.

We need One to help us bear life's burdens when our little strength gives way. We need Someone to dry our tears when they make us sensitive only to our own suffering.

Today we need divine wisdom that will enable us to do God's will on earth. There can be no temporary lapse in the need. In reckoning up the times of our life, we can never complete the equation without the omnipresent God.

We need Him as our Redemption, our living Gospel, and our healing Balm—and we need these every day!

PRAYER: *Visit us afresh each day, O God, for it would be dark and dreary without a visitation of Your presence to enlighten the way before us. Give us the strength and courage for each task we face. Strengthen each day with the faith that will prepare us for the next, and we shall be satisfied. In Jesus' name. Amen.*

NOVEMBER 16

> For I acknowledge my transgressions . . . Purge me with hyssop, and I shall be clean: wash me, and I shall be whiter than snow.
> **(Ps. 51:3, 7)**

There is a progression in Christian experience, and even though the whole movement points to a definite time, it is preceded by an act of readiness. If we really purpose in our hearts to go all the way with God, it can never be an accomplished fact until preparations have been made.

There is a cartoon of a little boy sitting under an apple tree with pockets still loaded with the sour apples that were giving him terrific cramps. The caption reads, "Repentance does not begin until the pockets are empty."

One Sunday morning we sang the same message but with different words, "Break down ev'ry idol, cast out ev'ry foe," and in the next verse, "I give up myself, and whatever I know." Preparation. NOW. After the fact. "Wash me and I shall be whiter than snow." Accomplishment!

"If thou bring thy gift to the altar, and there rememberest that thy brother hath aught against thee . . . go . . . and then come and offer thy gift" (Matt. 5:23-24). Now God will meet you in the act of acceptance and accomplishment.

In every area of Christian living God has made the outpouring of His blessing dependent on our commitment. We may keep back part of the consecrated price, but the loss will be ours rather than His. On the other hand, He never allows us to obey without results that far outstrip our greatest imagination (1 Cor. 2:9).

"*Now* wash me and I shall be whiter than snow" (italics added). The case lies between the soul and God in the mysterious communion under the Blood that flows from Calvary. It is here that the conflict is resolved and the bargain is sealed.

"The Blood is applied; I am whiter than snow."

PRAYER: *O God, we yield ourselves to You: body, soul, and spirit; our flesh, our will, our supreme desires; and all the energies of the soul and helplessness of our lives. They are Yours, and only You know their possibilities. Now purge us and make us clean. In Jesus' name. Amen.*

■ **NOVEMBER 17**

> **Enter ye in at the strait gate ... because strait is the gate, and narrow is the way, which leadeth unto life, and few there be that find it.**
> (Matt. 7:13-14)

"Give me an *A!*" Rather an interesting topic for a sermon! A professor friend told me that he had used it in his weekend preaching mission. Dealing with students every day, he was accustomed to being called upon for higher grades, even when the qualifications for excellence had fallen far short of the mark.

A little boy said to his father, "Daddy, when I grow up, I want to be a pilot." The father asked, "How are you doing in math?" The boy dropped his head and confessed, "Not so good!" How easily we support visions of grandeur while the homework is still unfinished on the desk.

Balaam had his eyes on the big *A*, but his epitaph read that he "loved the wages of unrighteousness" (2 Pet. 2:15); he tried ways to break the law and still be justified in God's records. He tried to make "the best of both worlds," but he perished by the sword. The story of Balaam occurs every day.

The New Testament teaching given to us by Jesus is, "He that entereth not by the door of the sheepfold, but climbeth up some other way, the same is a thief and a robber" (John 10:1). If our supreme purpose in life is to try to find an easy way through, then we cannot please God, even if we sing hymns all day, donate all our goods to feed the poor, and give our bodies to be burned.

The Christian position is that God's demand is for excellence. Faithfulness is the homework, and His "Well done," the highest grade in the Kingdom, is the reward.

You want to be great in the Kingdom? "How are you doing in math?"

PRAYER: *Dwell within us, O God, and do not let us walk alone. Help us to be loyal, honest, wise, and patient, going through the solicitudes of life with cheerfulness and joy in the Lord. Show us that in Your time we shall know Your purpose and in the end hear Your "Well done" if we have been faithful in all things. In Jesus' name. Amen.*

NOVEMBER 18 ■

The Lord is my shepherd; I shall not want. He maketh me to lie down in green pastures: he leadeth me beside the still waters.
(Ps. 23:1-2)

We had been fighting fires until a heavy rain came and did in one day what we had been unable to accomplish in one week. After walking many miles, exhausted, hungry, thirsty, dirty from soot, and blistered from burns, we came to a shady knoll beside a gurgling brook. One of the weary fighters held his tin cup of cold water toward heaven and said, "Thank You, God, for a quiet resting-place." Many details of that experience have faded with the time, but over the years I have had many occasions to raise my cup in thanksgiving and say, "Thank You, God, for a quiet resting-place."

We thank God for the varied experiences of life because they show how that in comparison our weariness is not worth the utterance, for the blessing far outstrips the burdens. After we linger in prayer, thinking that God is not there and our searching leaves disappointment, we should not be discouraged, for often the lingering finds its own answer. When we are surrounded by fire and are sore from the blisters, we should keep in mind that God is not far away. The abiding idea is the certainty that the almighty One still keeps everything in place. And He who keeps everything else in place is able to take care of my poor little life. How much of God's healing balm we forfeit in our forgetfulness and move on past the gurgling brook.

Be assured that God is working out His plan, and any effort on our part to hold back His hand is to thwart His purpose for our well-being.

May God help us to walk on with courage and watch for the resting-place and the cup of cold water!

PRAYER: *We come to You, O God, to find rest, for we get so weary. Replenish our strength, for our power has gone from us. Let our necessity be our plea and our triumph be found in Your wisdom. We need that rest of soul understood only in relation to eternity. In Jesus' name. Amen.*

■ **NOVEMBER 19**

We spend our years as a tale that is told. The days of our years are threescore years and ten.
(Ps. 90:9-10)

The days slip by so silently, one by one, as they merge into years that vanish. We cannot lay a hand on that which is gone to bring it back, nor can we walk back over the road again, being aware of the dangers. Little by little our strength lessens, and we become bowed down and aged. The dreams of youth fade into the visions of the old man.

We reach heavenward and ask God to "teach us to number our days, that we may apply our hearts unto wisdom" (Ps. 90:12). While we are yet counting them, they fly by. One year has hardly begun before it has withered away and died. As the beginning and ending of each day has less significance, we would redeem them with the fullness of love that knows no break in a sacred continuity. And as heaven's gates come closer and our time merges into eternity, the cloak of youth is gradually thrown off as the soul is being clothed with the garments of glory.

Old age reviews more tenderly, and repeats often, the wells in the wilderness, refreshing streams in the stony places, bitter experiences that time alone has made sweet, and the dark nights that have been filled with stars.

We see ourselves as God's responsibility and own Him as the Creator and our Father, and in His almightiness we find rest. Our greatest desire is to be deeper in His nature, more mellow in feeling, more tender in sympathy, larger in charity, and more like the Master in all the beauty of His inimitable perfection.

At the last we would have men take knowledge of us that we had been with Jesus—and had learned from Him.

PRAYER: *We stand today, O God, in Your goodness, which has been with us down through the years, even to old age. Beyond that goodness we have no foothold, no hope, and no light. In the spirit of Your care may youthfulness of spirit be our lifelong blessing as we move on toward heaven. In Jesus' name. Amen.*

NOVEMBER 20 ■

The Lord knoweth the days of the upright: and their inheritance shall be for ever.
(Ps. 37:18)

A professor, trying to lessen the homesickness of a student from a country where trees were scarce, remarked, "Wait until you see the New England foliage this fall." In embarrassment the new arrival asked a fellow student, "What did she mean by 'New England foliage'?" But after seeing what God had done to the leaves with His frosty paintbrush, he responded, "I feel like the queen of Sheba—'the half was not told me'" (1 Kings 10:7). Change!

After Jesus had anointed the eyes of the blind man and caused him to see, his testimony to all time was, "One thing I know, that, whereas I was blind, now I see" (John 9:25). Change!

Whether it was the artistic touch of God in nature or the physical touch of the Master in healing, they were both talking about change. Everything in our world is changing every day. We are born, and we grow old; and the new generation forgets, and new paths are made for new feet—repeated in kind in another generation.

Change carries with it much uncertainty and unloads it upon us, so that we fear what will happen tomorrow. Often it is grief and pain; often it speaks to our helplessness. The little baby moves on to maturity, the old man totters in infirmity, the healthy give way in suffering, and the house crumbles to dust; and all of life is engulfed in the narrow stream of death and forgetfulness.

These mysteries we cannot penetrate; but the great paradox of the Christian faith is that it brings delight, for we know we are moving heavenward. We live on with Him who is eternal through the storm and the change by His grace that never fails.

He has not yet revealed the half to us, but He speaks a truth that stands forever!

PRAYER: *O God, You have filled our life with a variety of circumstances. You have placed us in the midst of change, but nothing happens to us that Your eyes have not foreseen. We thank You that You are the Changeless One in our changing world. Amen.*

■ NOVEMBER 21

But when he saw the multitudes, he was moved with compassion on them, because they fainted, and were scattered abroad, as sheep having no shepherd.
(Matt. 9:36)

When Jesus looked out on the world in which He came to live, He was moved with compassion. In fact, compassion was the keyword of the holiest life ever to move among the people of this earth. There are no parallels in our lives that will enable us to grasp the full meaning of this ministry of the Man of God.

The life of Jesus Christ was not merely a life of genius or a display of power. It was a life of love, a story of compassion, and an exemplification of the most tender aspects of the mercy of the Father. But the master word that governed His speech and controlled His actions was compassion.

When He looked on the milling masses of humanity about Him, He was moved with compassion. Out of a breaking heart and in tears He says, "How often would I have gathered thy children together, even as a hen gathereth her chickens under her wings . . . !" (Matt. 23:37). But if He could have taken any other view, He would not have been the Savior of the World!

All the power of the human mind fails in its grasp of His tenderness. The mind goes dumb when we try to conceive of one who is willing to take upon himself the pain, the feebleness, the poverty, and the anguish of those who suffer most. He bore our sins to the Cross, carried our iniquities, took our infirmities, and sustained our afflictions. The writer of Hebrews says, "We have not an high priest which cannot be touched with the feeling of our infirmities" (4:15), but He knows our testings and temptations—He is the Son of God! Herein is the mystery and our confidence: We can tell Him everything as if He knew nothing about us.

Here is also our resting-place: We can recognize Christ's relationship to our need, for out of a heart of compassion He understands, and He still loves us.

PRAYER: *Almighty God, we pray that You will make us as little children upon whom You always had great compassion. We must know this relationship in our search for a larger and clearer vision of the Savior of our world. In our weakness we need to know Your strength. In Jesus' name. Amen.*

NOVEMBER 22

O God, thou art my God; early will I seek thee: my soul thirsteth for thee, my flesh longeth for thee in a dry and thirsty land, where no water is.
(Ps. 63:1)

The old, straight-backed chair sat in the corner of the pastor's study. The varnish was worn from the side posts, and the back crossbar was ugly from the lack of paint. For weeks I had looked in scorn at this unsightly piece of furniture until one morning a group met there to pray. As I knelt before this chair, my hands fell on the worn sidepieces, and my forehead nestled on the back crossbar that was bare of paint, and my tears mingled with the stains on the seat. This old, ugly chair, the place of combat where battles had been fought and victories won, now became more beautiful than Solomon in all his glory. I was kneeling before the throne of grace. Surely God had been here, and I knew it not! So near was I at that moment to heaven that I could almost hear the Almighty asking, "What is your petition? What is your request?" I was in the presence of the Divine!

Often our hearts ache for something not born of time, and our desires long for that which cannot be satisfied with the mundane. We reach for something in our dark surroundings. We listen in order to hear a familiar stirring. We look as if we might see some gentle moving of God's presence. Our whole nature arises as if in response to a heavenly light.

God comes to us in His own way, and for one moment the revelation may strike us dumb, and our eyes open to see His glory. These are experiences that deliver us from the custody of space and time and bring us into the presence of God, where the poverty of the soul is lost in the unsearchable riches of His glory.

Just an old, ugly, straight-backed chair. A symbol pointing toward heaven. The touch of God made the difference.

PRAYER: *O God, grant to us sweet communion and words that only the heart can discern and apply. Gather us in Your care and whisper Your love in ways that we will know that God is speaking to our individual needs. To this mystery we come for rest and security. In Jesus' name. Amen.*

NOVEMBER 23

> **I will speak of the glorious honour of thy majesty, and of thy wondrous works. . . . and I will declare thy greatness.**
> (Ps. 145:5-6)

Where I grew up, when a young person announced a call to the ministry, he was right away put on display to determine the wisdom of God on the decision. When my turn came to exhibit my genius, I announced my text: "They have . . . hewed them out cisterns, broken cisterns, that can hold no water" (Jer. 2:13). The cisterns did break, and all my great ideas ran down the drain. After fumbling for what seemed an eternity, I sat down. One dear saint said, "Amen," but the majority shared my conviction that God had made a major misjudgment in this call.

The lady who had said, "Amen," shook my hand and said, "God bless you. He has called you, but be careful what you do with it." In my confusion I did not know how to respond, but a burden seemed to lift.

Out of that experience I learned that we must be careful how we interfere with that which we did not create. We are not at liberty to add to the mind of God, nor are we free to take away from it. The very heart of God is encompassed in the call. We are dealing with His highest thoughts, His most supreme concern, and an eternal honor.

The danger is that we take our failure of action as God's mistaken judgment and put our rejection on an equal plane with His thought. God's call consecrates whatever bit of humanity it is graciously bestowed upon. And unless it is offered back to Him in sacrifice at the foot of the Cross and sanctified by the spiritual meaning of Christ's offering, it is, indeed, in vain.

Solomon laid down a principle that underlies the true calling of God. "The house which I build is great" (2 Chron. 2:5). He could have said, "The call of God to build is great, for great is the God who called. And great is the love of God that the call represents. And great are they who accept it."

PRAYER: *Help us, O God, to live worthy of the call wherewith You have called us. We pray for triumph in the time of shadow, so that both the darkness and the light shall be full of God, and that we shall recognize His footsteps and follow them. In Jesus' name. Amen.*

NOVEMBER 24 ■

I will hear what God the Lord will speak: for he will speak peace unto his people, and to his saints ... Surely his salvation is nigh them that fear him.
(Ps. 85:8-9)

A very dear friend of mine was buried this week. He had served God faithfully and spent the greater part of his life in the pastoral ministry. His dear widow was consoled with the fact that she would be with him someday.

Someday! Afterward! The word had a mocking sound, for it had overtones of a time that never comes and was used to squeeze out consolation for the moment. "Someday" lies beyond the vision and the range of the grasping need for today.

In our Christian experience we become acquainted with the word and accept it, for Jesus made much of the idea in His ministry. But this dear, brokenhearted mother needed some comfort through which she could view eternity—*now!*

We cannot understand God's work, and there are times when we must not be caught in the confusion of having to find a reason. We accept God's will. We are inspired by His ways. We love Him for His greater love. But when the thorns are sharp, and the valleys suddenly become dark with shadows, and we stagger under a mighty blow, we need some gentle assurance from heaven to meet the need now.

God does not disappoint us. If we are laid aside, and if we are stripped from things we love, and if death takes away the loved ones, He gives assurance, "Let not your heart be troubled, neither let it be afraid" (John 14:27).

Now we can hide ourselves in Christ and find a refuge in Him. For today, "Death is swallowed up in victory. O death, where is thy sting? O grave, where is thy victory?" (1 Cor. 15:54-55).

And our afterward is swallowed up in His peace, which He gives for the present. Thanks be to God for this victory!

PRAYER: *Hear us, O God, when we pray, and keep us from being afraid of death. Abide with us until the nighttime is past and the morning breaks in its eternal glory. May the vision of our soul be upward, and let our hearts ever cry out, "How good and gracious is the Lord!" In Jesus' name. Amen.*

■ **NOVEMBER 25**

> **Then Joseph commanded to fill their sacks with corn, and to restore every man's money into his sack, and to give them provision for the way.**
> (Gen. 42:25)

There is an ugly word in our language, born out of bitterness, and held by an iron grip of selfishness. The word is *resentment*. It shows up in a thousand different ways—peevishness, anger, retaliation, grudges, meanness, and on and on. When a person has been insulted or offended, or has been neglected or snubbed, the bandage of resentment is applied to the sore.

We need to read again the beautiful story of Joseph who had been betrayed by his loved ones, sold into slavery, imprisoned, and forgotten. Well, almost! They meet again! He is a ruler now. He is in a position to get even. How sweet is revenge! An eye for an eye! But the record for the ages is that Joseph "turned himself about from them, and wept" (Gen. 42:24). Vengeance and resentment give way to gentleness and forgiveness.

Nothing but the Holy Spirit of God can bring a person to the point of answering the memory of meanness with the tears of forgiveness. And the interesting thing is that the tears did not show up in the presence of his brothers—he went to his secret chambers and wept. Here is the place that knew him best and, no doubt, was the place where the resentment was resolved. The secret experiences of life have most meaning and lasting value in the place where the battle was won.

Christianity does not teach us to be insensitive and indifferent to the pressures of life. But it does enable us to take the larger view in the long process God has for us.

There is a moral principle that allows for justice. There is a higher morality that calls for forgiveness and tears. God be our Helper to choose the higher!

PRAYER: *Spare us, O God, from resentment and anger and vain conceit, and give us a peaceful life in harmony with the Spirit of God. Bind us to the Cross and give us hope, and fill us with a forgiving spirit that comes from the heart of the Man of Calvary. In Jesus' name. Amen.*

NOVEMBER 26 ■

Is my hand shortened at all, that it cannot redeem? or have I no power to deliver? behold, at my rebuke I dry up the sea, I make the rivers a wilderness.
(Isa. 50:2)

An acquaintance of our family, in facing failure, always hid behind the expression, "Had I a-know'd, never would I a- . . ." and proceeded to place blame and absolve himself of any guilt.

It is sad to see any endeavor fail because of certain unknown conditions. Maybe that is why God makes himself known to us so clearly. "Hast thou not known? hast thou not heard, that the everlasting God, the Lord . . . fainteth not, neither is weary? there is no searching of his understanding" (Isa. 40:28). He shows himself to us in all the grandeur of His divine nature. It comes to us as a question in anticipation of an affirmation, so there can be no protest at the point of failure.

These terms are applicable to God in all relationships, for there is no moment when He ceases to give. His strength is never exhausted. This is the language of the universe. He knows the strong and the weak and the condition of every circumstance.

For some reason we carry on in our own might as if we had the power to remove mountains and beat the embattled hosts of hell. When we come to defeat and cry to Him, "Save me, Lord, or I perish," He looks down and says, "Did you not know? Have you not heard . . . ?"

When David met his difficulties, he reasoned from the lion and the bear to the uncircumcised Philistine and let the enemy know that he was coming to the battle in the name of the Lord. When our faith fails, we faint, and on the ground that we should occupy as a conqueror, we lie a victim with excuses.

Remember that God will not allow us to be tried above that which we are to bear (1 Cor. 10:13). Have you not known? Have you not heard?

PRAYER: *Almighty God, You are always thinking about Your people. Your power over us and in us and through us is beyond our grasp to imagine, but You are there! Who can set himself against the power of heaven? Answer the petition of our weakness in the fullness of Your strength. In Jesus' name. Amen.*

■ **NOVEMBER 27**

Truly my soul waiteth upon God ... He only is my rock and my salvation; he is my defence; I shall not be greatly moved.
(Ps. 62:1-2)

One of the old songs we used to hear at church went, "Take this old world, but give me Jesus. / I won't turn back. I won't turn back." Many situations come up in our lives where choices have to be made, and there is a tendency to look deep into the best of both sides of the issue.

After seeing God work in the darkness, being conscious of His hand in the midst of affliction, and living in the sanctuary of His love, the matter of Providence becomes firmly settled.

It is out of the question to give in to the brokenheartedness, difficulties, and uncertainties of this old world. There is nothing so impossible to the imagination of the one who has been there as the denial of God's goodness and love. Even this day has been crowned with His wonders. We accept His miracles without question and as part of living. Our Christian confidence and hope is that even the last great enemy, which becomes more real as the years are encompassed by the past, has been conquered. This miracle has been completed in the resurrection of Jesus Christ.

His love has been a daily resource, and it has covered and sustained the whole range of life. It encourages, inspires, keeps, and confirms to know that there can be but one choice that is right. The Lord gives as He pleases, and sometimes we look at our little and don't see much. But when we look at the little within the possibilities of God's much, we see the miracle. This is the miracle of choice through the Holy Spirit of God.

If I had the choice to make today, I would ask God for a clean heart, a right spirit, an obedient will, and an unquestioning faith. "Take this old world, but give me Jesus!"

PRAYER: *Be very near, O God, with guidance and understanding to those who are about to make choices for their lives. Be the Lamp, we pray, as well as the Spirit inspiring their hearts to do Your will. Work out in every heart a concern and love that can be used to inspire all humanity. In Jesus' name. Amen.*

NOVEMBER 28 ■

Let us come before his presence with thanksgiving, and make a joyful noise unto him with psalms. For the Lord is a great God, and a great King above all gods.
(Ps. 95:2-3)

What do I have to be thankful for today? Browning's song of love would respond, "Let me count the ways." The little boy in the classroom gives an obvious answer, "I'm thankful that I ain't a turkey." Words of thanksgiving fill the mouths of many today because their hearts are filled with gratitude for the great and wondrous things of God over the past year.

Whenever we awake to look upon another bright morning, we have grounds for rejoicing. While the body may be burdened with pain, and life may be deep in want, God has sustained with a ministry of mercy and love. Guilt has received His answer of forgiveness. The Cross has stood over this year as the Healer of the heart. And in times of deepest despair, beside the beds of suffering and the graves of grief the sweet ministry of hope has been present.

We can be thankful if God has continued our health, strength, mind, and hope within the normal limits of our day. If our friends have stood by us, and we have been able to walk the ways of freedom and breathe the air of liberty, we can give Him thanks. If families have been reunited or held together and are living under the fullness of His love, we can give thanks.

God knows every one of us—our backgrounds, our difficulties, our temptations, and our temperaments. And after knowing all that, we can be thankful that He is still our God.

Oh, that we had the silvery sound of the trumpet and the powerful tones of thunder to shout His goodness! For in our littleness and infirmities we are caught up in great thanksgiving that our farewells here on earth suggest a reunion in heaven.

Our greatest Thanksgiving Day!

PRAYER: *Almighty God, our hearts are alive with thankfulness, and our spirits are lifted up as on wings of eagles. You have looked upon us in love with bounty and store. We stand with heads bowed in thanksgiving and praise, and we ask that we may appreciate Your goodness. In Jesus' name. Amen.*

NOVEMBER 29

> I go to prepare a place for you. And if I go and prepare a place for you, I will come again, and receive you unto myself; that where I am, there ye may be also.
> (John 14:2-3)

Jesus told us that He was going away to prepare a place for His people. The saints have rejoiced in their journey as they marched toward that place whose Builder and Maker is God. Jesus also reminded us that the way to His prepared place was narrow, and that there would be other inviting ways that would lead to destruction.

Often we see a shorter way that is green and soft with hedges, rich in blossom, and musical with song. But we soon discover that the direction leads away from God. Sometimes our road is all gates and bridges, and walled-in ways with wilderness and hill, all without hospitality. Often it goes through the churchyard and across wide rivers. But we hear a comforting voice urging us onward, assuring us that it is the long mileage that ends in the brightest land. And our faith tells us that this way is regulated by the wisdom and understanding of the infinite Father.

How wonderful that God did not choose to show us all the road at one time. He knows we are not capable of understanding, nor competent to judge, how little or much He ordained to manifest himself along the way.

Each part of the way is marked with its shortcomings and overcomings. The urge is to write the patterns of God and point out the way for the Almighty. Sometimes His wisdom is in question, yet He spares us and leads us on.

The experience of the long traveler is to be assured of God's purpose and God's will. The one who continues will discover that every mile toward the city will be a way of light and comfort—and heaven!

PRAYER: *O God, show us something of the wonders of Your way, we pray. Keep us from interfering with the course of Your providence when we cannot understand the meaning. Help us to say from a heart of deep sincerity, "God's way is the best way!" In Jesus' name. Amen.*

NOVEMBER 30

Nevertheless the foundation of God standeth sure, having this seal, The Lord knoweth them that are his.
(2 Tim. 2:19)

Behind the Christian bookstore where I had gone for supplies were huge cables disappearing into the heavy fog of the morning. On the ground were mighty cement blocks embedded in the rocky earth, to which were firmly attached one end of the cables. What I could not see was the fog-enshrouded 500-foot radio tower that was being supported by the cables. Through fog, wind, tempest, and storm the tower stands because it is held by a power greater than the force that would topple it.

A marvelous thing is this as we reflect upon our lives through the medium of God's protective care. The word to Judah in the day of battle was, "Believe in the Lord your God, so shall ye be established" (2 Chron. 20:20). One of the great factors of faith that we find difficult to accept is that we can throw the responsibility for our defense upon God. The New Testament counterpart is given to us in 1 Pet. 5:7, "Casting all your care upon him; for he careth for you." Too many times we fight and lose the battle, condemn ourselves, and worry over the loss, while God stands on the sidelines and says to us, "I could have done it for you."

God's power is accommodated to the condition of our willingness to throw ourselves upon His mercy. The greatest battles that we will have to face today will be those in our relationship to eternity. The devil's army is vast in number, and his power against us is strong. But so great is the power of God that in the most extreme peril of the day we can count on Him for victory.

One of the things we must never drop out of our calculations is God's omnipotence, to which the cables of our life can be firmly secured.

PRAYER: *We place ourselves in Your hands, O God, and would remain there for the few days we have left. There we feel a sense of security, and there our souls fall into sweet peace. In the presence of Your power we will rest in the assurance of Calvary. In Jesus' name. Amen.*

■ **DECEMBER 1**

> **Father, if thou be willing, remove this cup from me: nevertheless not my will, but thine, be done.**
> **(Luke 22:42)**

The Christmas rush for shoppers was not yet in full swing, but the anticipation of the season was in the air. The choices had not been reduced to leftovers, and the shelves were still full of options. A mother and wee daughter were in serious debate over a purchase, which seemed to have been decided in favor of the grown-up. I walked past just in time to hear the final appeal from the losing side, "Mommy, Mommy, maybe if you think about it, you'll change your mind." As far as I could determine, a decision had been made that was not going to change.

There probably comes into every life demands without which we see no sure way of survival. We spend days and nights in search of solid reason and conclude with, "God, it has to be this way." Often out of the bitterness and anguish of souls two wills become involved, and there is pleading with God against what He knows is best for us.

God is always leading us onward, and the road is through Gethsemane—our "Thy will be done" experience (Matt. 26:42). Could we but see it, the walk is a short one. There is, indeed, the night of prayer, the cruel cross with its nails and spear, the temporary burial; but God's final purpose is the resurrection to immortality and hope.

His purpose is that we should take our sorrows as the beginning of our joy, for His denials are not places of defeat. How human it is to look at the gloom and miss the greater visions of glory for which God is preparing us. The spirit of the Master was to endure the Cross, despise the shame, and look ahead to the glory yet to be revealed.

God has thought it over, and this is the way it is!

PRAYER: *Almighty God, we would do everything according to Your will. We look to You for the answer and pray that You will entrust us with Your commandment. You have worked in us by Your grace, and we have no will but Your will. Confirm this in us with Your smile of acceptance. In Jesus' name. Amen.*

DECEMBER 2 ■

This is my comfort in my affliction: for thy word hath quickened me.
(Ps. 119:50)

A catalog came in the mail with a label bearing my name. It was advertising for sale such things as: a long-handled shoehorn, arch supports, compartmentalized pillboxes, belts designed for abdominal protrusion, folding canes, and special rails for the bathtub. There were many more novelties to mock the present crisis and to remind one of the fast movement of life.

Vanity and pomp are no protection against the rigors of time, and neither reason nor objection can stand in the way. It is useless to look on human life and point out its inferiorities or its advantages. God has set everyone in his place, and each one of us must accept the appointment. The folding cane and the pillbox can be mere reminders of the direction of the eternal fulfillment.

To be sure, my catalog is aware of the difficulties that beset the human frame, but it fails in its offering of grace and comfort also necessary in the process. We are never at liberty to stop, and we cannot go back. The journey is ever onward, and life offers little compensation. We may become wise by our failures and grow through our disappointments, but only God knows the length of the journey and its needs.

In our march in God's time we must bury the pride for the reality and look to the uplifted Son of God. The look of the soul must be toward God for healing. The load of guilt is removed through an expression of trust. Pain and shame and sorrow and affliction can find relief through the meaning of the Cross. We must not separate ourselves from these things.

Lay aside the catalog of reminders of time. We must know the words of Christ, "I am come that they might have life, and that they might have it more abundantly" (John 10:10).

PRAYER: *O God, You have placed us here in time but reminded us that our bodies are temples of the Holy Ghost. Help us to understand Your purposes, and that death comes to Your people with a blessing in its hand. In our moving toward eternity, may we keep our vision heavenward. In Jesus' name. Amen.*

DECEMBER 3

From the end of the earth will I cry unto thee, when my heart is overwhelmed: lead me to the rock that is higher than I.
(Ps. 61:2)

We had just left Logan Airport and had gained flight altitude when the pilot announced that in a few minutes we would be passing over New York City. Then it happened: We were looking down on a very tiny section in the panorama spread before our eyes. One passenger remarked to the stewardess, "How can such a small speck have so many people and so many problems?" Her immediate response was, "Sir, the higher you go, the smaller things seem to be." How could she ever know the wisdom of that statement, which was accepted as mere words?

We are part of a fierce and rebellious humanity, and in our strength and ingenuity we spend our days. We pass our time working out purposes upon which we place our values. Yet our greatest achievements mock us, and in our best efforts we merely weave a fabric full of shortcomings. In this there is a deep and tragic mystery, for life reaches out for something more than it has yet been able to achieve.

God has always had a way of bringing order out of our confusion. His call has always been to a higher plane and the heavenly vision. The song of the overcomer is still, "Lord, lift me up and let me stand, / By faith, on heaven's tableland." The place for life's stronger emphasis must be in things that recognize God's plane of action.

This higher view is a way of trust, love, and faith; and it rests in the knowledge that I am a child of the ever-living and ever-loving Father. And I can live and move and have my being in Him.

Under the pressures of life and the bonds of our shortcomings there is a call of assurance; "The higher you go, the smaller these things are going to be!"

PRAYER: *O God, we thank You today for the place of vision and the higher plane of Your concern. Help us to know how very near the earth is to heaven. While we work in our little space in time, our hearts long for that fuller liberty and the greater service. May we ever have the upward vision that leads us on to eternity. In Jesus' name. Amen.*

DECEMBER 4 ■

The way of the Lord is strength to the upright: but destruction shall be to the workers of iniquity.
(Prov. 10:29)

The late Oswald J. Smith, speaking to a group of ministers on prayer, said, "I seem to get closer to God when I'm alone in my study, walking back and forth across the room." One minister remarked that in his private devotions he often lays flat on his back, looking straight up into the heavens. Another said, "When I pray, I like to climb to the top of the highest hill to find audience with God in the heavens."

Is there an appointed way to God? Jesus Christ is the only living Way to the Father. Whatever the posture, we can enter only by Him; there are no other doors. And every person can come this way with a new hope, for a new beginning, or for a renewal of faith and purpose.

God never withholds goodness from His people but maintains His open-window policy in pouring down upon us all the stores of His grace that we can handle. Even the answers to our petitions have their relevance in heaven, for they are inspired by the Spirit of God. Our highest thoughts and greatest actions are the Lord's doings when our trust is in the Spirit of God.

Our prayer times are training times when God leads us in His way by His Spirit. He opens our understanding to His will and enables us to follow the course of His discipline. He gives us assurance for our fears and quiets our anxiety with His peace. He knows our personal needs and answers with replies larger than our asking. When the heart hurts, He applies His balm and attends to the healing. He fits our whole life with just what we need.

Whether we are walking, kneeling, or standing, He answers the prayer of the sincere heart when we come by the way of the Cross—Christ's way.

PRAYER: *All the way belongs to You, O God! How varied, yet how simple! Every day we see the wonders of Your way, and we walk in it, for it is best. Help us to move on only by Your direction and through the ministry of the Holy Spirit, and when it is most difficult, may Your presence be nearest. In Jesus' name. Amen.*

■ **DECEMBER 5**

Jesus saith unto him, I am the way, the truth, and the life: no man cometh unto the Father, but by me.
(John 14:6)

"What is truth?" (John 18:38). This question has been the struggle of great minds in an effort to find some degree of certainty.

He who has declared himself to be the Way, the Truth, and the Life has been revealed to us. To Him we would respond, "How great, O Christ, is Thy truth!" We cannot understand it all, but in Jesus Christ we have found what we can lay hold on with our minds and our hearts. We would be content to sit at the feet of Truth and listen to all the wisdom of His sacred mind.

In this Truth we see the Lamb of God, who takes away the sin of the world. With all our pain of sin and suffering we would look to Him as Redeemer and Deliverer.

In this Truth we would see the Cross, and in it we would see all the love of God for a dying world. And we would see this love in all of its infinite tenderness. In His cross is pardon. In His cross is peace.

In this Truth we find our keeping. We do not know what is best for us, nor can we know the way we should take, for the roads are many, and often the going is very rough. We begin at the point of weak faith and move forward under the guidance of the Holy Spirit. Here we develop our faith life, and in it we find contentment.

In the Truth we find satisfaction at the end of the journey. When our lives are behind us, and our infirmities keep us from undertaking mighty works, the Lord sends His tender Gospels of comfort to enrich the Christian experience.

What is Truth? It is the miracle of God. It is the wonder of life. It is the revelation of light. It is Christ in us, the hope of glory! (See Col. 1:27.)

"Hallelujah! I have found Him!"

PRAYER: *Preserve us, O God, in the love of truth and in the comfort of the peace that it brings. May Your truth dwell in us, touching every point of our lives, making us glad in the midst of sorrow, and giving us an outreach over all things in all the circumstances of life. In Jesus' name. Amen.*

DECEMBER 6 ■

Great peace have they which love thy law: and nothing shall offend them.
(Ps. 119:165)

A few years ago our driving laws were changed, and we were told that we had to lower our maximum speed on the highway. It's a law that our guns must be registered, our houses have to comply with certain standards, and in snow country parking is allowed only on designated areas. Many of the laws cause inconveniences, but all are enacted for our overall good, though they come under criticism when our freedom is hampered.

Laws have always been with us, and the Psalmist talks to us about God's method of control as "wondrous things out of thy law" (Ps. 119:18).

He speaks about the law of the Lord enlightening the eyes, guiding the simple, and converting the soul (Psalm 19), and making a heaven on earth.

On our journey from the cradle to the grave we follow precepts and live by principles; therefore, we should seek the way that is going to get us successfully through. The wise writer told us to inquire the way to the palaces of wisdom and discover the dwelling place of understanding.

Life is a way that we can neither understand nor control. Around every bend in the road we become victims of cruel and startling surprises. The man in *Pilgrim's Progress* learned from the lion in the way and discovered the wolf set in his way to keep him on the right path. A warning and a guiding principle is equal to our safe journey.

Christians today would be established in the truth of God, enclosed in the will of God, live under the touch of the tender mercy of God, and say at the end of the way that the "judgments" of God "are good" (Ps. 119:39).

PRAYER: *Open our eyes, O God, that we may see wondrous things out of Your law. You have told us that it is perfect and that it enlightens the eyes and guides the simple. Help us to know more about Your law and the messages that it holds for Your people. In Jesus' name. Amen.*

■ DECEMBER 7

Justice and judgment are the habitation of thy throne: mercy and truth shall go before thy face. Blessed is the people that know the joyful sound.
(Ps. 89:14-15)

The Old Testament reports battles, bloodshed, and devastation as enemies are overthrown and cities are established. In our own time we have lived through destruction, world conflicts, and the sacrifice of innocent human beings. It has caused nations to look within to see what they really are and to spare no searching in an effort to find the decay that needs healing.

Coming from the nation to the individual, it is often trouble that impels one to take that inward look. We are turned to heaven by pain and the harsh places of life, and sickness brings our minds closer to the things of God. All of this has meaning in it, for it is our defense, our security, and proof that we are not our own.

We find within a hunger that earth cannot satisfy and a thirst that the rivers of time can never slake. This is our immortality and proof of our filial relationship to Him. Our God is near every attempt to reach upward, and He holds in contempt anything that would draw us downward.

Our expectation is never disappointed, for while we are crying out to Him, He is proving by some touch that He has recognized the need. We can never be out there in front of God. Before our thoughts are shaped into purpose, He is waiting at the altar.

How often our insecurity speaks and our conclusions are drawn in ignorance. We cannot put our meaning into words, and we often receive the message in darkness that God would have delivered to us at midday.

The battle trumpet is God's. Yesterday belongs to Him. Amid the tumult and terror His voice finds a way to the heart. God is still in control.

PRAYER: *O God, it is the battlefield and the enemy of the soul that gives us our right to pray. Help our arm not to be shortened, and may we march in step, so that by the grace of God we can tread down every enemy. There is no other way to victory and to heaven. We pray in Jesus' name. Amen.*

DECEMBER 8

Six days shalt thou labour, and do all thy work: but the seventh day is the sabbath of the Lord thy God.
(Exod. 20:9-10)

A little boy was eager to engage in activities that ran contrary to standards the family had laid down for Sabbath observance. In trying to resolve this big problem, the father put his arm around his son and said, "This is God's day, and He wants us to keep it holy. How you do that must be your decision to make in your relationship with God." A deep regard for this special day was implanted that remains uppermost in the life-style of this young man today.

The Lord's Day. What a day it can be in the life of God's people. A quiet, solemn time, always lifting itself toward the heavens where God made it. His smile is its light, and His love is the seal and the guarantee of His peace upon those who deign to keep it holy.

It is the Day of Resurrection! It calls us back from the defeat of death and the open grave. It speaks of life and immortality, of incorporation and heavenly triumph. It is here that all meanness and hatred lose their power. Here the holiness of Christ shines with a radiance above the brightness of the sun. It is Christ's day, the gospel day, the triumph day. It is a time above all other times. It is God's holy day!

On His Sabbath we walk in God's light and grace and truth and love. We stand before Him in reverent humility and live under the ministration of the Holy Spirit.

It is a day the universe is too small to contain. A bit of God comes down to gild a moment of time, and for its expanded glory we shall want the immeasurable arena of eternal duration.

O God, help us to keep it holy as You are holy!

PRAYER: *We thank You, O God, for the Sabbath Day! It is a day of triumph. Through Your Sabbath we pray that You will bind us to the Cross with closer bonds. May we feel its nearness and be subdued by its mystery and inspired by the great sacrifice. Help us to find hope and confidence in Your triumphant day! In Jesus' name. Amen.*

■ **DECEMBER 9**

But he knoweth the way that I take: when he hath tried me, I shall come forth as gold.
(Job 23:10)

An early impression that still lingers in memory is an old saint of God singing with great gusto, "His pow'r can make you what you *want* to be." And I liked what I heard until I discovered His power could make you "what you *ought* to be." This changed everything; it lessened my enthusiasm for God, and acceptance turned into rejection.

Power belongs to God, and we have nothing to say to it; but we look in anticipation to His wisdom, for He knows the way we should take. Not until we have experienced the assurance of forgiveness can we know the power that works in us for good.

His power works in our weakness. Paul's assurance was, "My grace is sufficient for thee: for my strength is made perfect in [your] weakness" (2 Cor. 12:9). It was not Paul's "want" but God's "ought" that brought him to the place where he could make a final commitment.

"Most gladly therefore will I rather glory" (v. 9).

"I take pleasure in infirmities" (v. 10).

"When I am weak, then am I strong" (v. 10).

It is through this experience that our questions are concealed in our commitment. Our "want" for His "ought."

No longer do we present God with a long list of our daily needs, for He has already supplied His sufficiency. And He will withhold no good thing from His people. And He will never thrust His great power against us to batter or to bruise.

We are the people of His hand and the sheep of His pasture, redeemed with His blood and bought with an infinite price, and today we can stand among the angels of heaven—in God's will.

Indeed, we can say, "'Twas best for Him to have His way"!

PRAYER: *O God, we pray that You will show us the wonders of Your ways. Keep us in silent expectation before You, and keep us from interfering with the course of Your providence. Help us to say from a heart of sincerity, "God's way is best!" In Jesus' name. Amen.*

DECEMBER 10 ■

Many are the afflictions of the righteous: but the Lord delivereth him out of them all.
(Ps. 34:19)

The fascinating feature and sales appeal of many leading magazines and printed materials is the nutshell theme, "When all hope was gone—survival." The darker the picture and the more extreme the peril, the greater the appeal. The human mind finds satisfaction in the collapse of hostility and eagerly supports the victor.

Every day holds the possibilities for defeat and shipwreck. We are all sailing on the sea of life and cannot tell where the dangers are hidden. Sometimes the nights are dark, the wind howls, and no voice can be heard above its roar, and we are driven on toward despair.

Sometimes the sun shines, the waters become smooth, and the wind is a balmy breeze. We take heart again, sing a song of joy, and look with hope toward the sunset.

Again the darkness and the black night comes like an infinite burden upon our lives too small to carry it. Fear comes upon us, and we are torn by forces with no strength for control. Life seems to hold within itself only space for trouble.

But this is not all—we sail on! Out of peril, "when all hope was gone," God sent His Son. Survival! The meaning of love and grace was revealed at the Cross with redemption and peace as God's supreme purpose.

This is the victory of faith. This is the triumph of God's people. This is the miracle of grace. This is God's way. He does not delight in our being shipwrecked but wants to shape the ruin of our lives into lighthouses among the shoals.

When hope was gone, Jesus came. It made the difference!

PRAYER: *O God, help us not to think of the troubles we have had to pass through, for the joy of Your victory has been greater because of Your enduring presence. Trouble is but for a moment, but it produces an exceeding great and eternal weight of glory. Give us Your joy and peace. In Jesus' name. Amen.*

DECEMBER 11

Now faith is the substance of things hoped for, the evidence of things not seen.
(Heb. 11:1)

Out of great sorrow and a bleak outlook for the days ahead, a lady testified to a group of senior citizens a few days ago, "God's timing is never wrong, and He does everything in order." It takes a lot of faith to stand in this kind of commitment and trust God for the uncertain future when the bottom drops out of everything!

To believe that God sets everything in order and that there is not a word in our mouth or thought in our heart that He does not know is to defeat the greatest enemy of the soul at any age. To believe in the minuteness of His care without being able to understand it all is to possess the Hebrews faith that looks for the city whose Builder and Maker is God.

There are things in the Christian life that have no explanation outside the realm of faith. Often one does not speak about them, for only the heart can answer them, and it alone knows that we dare not walk outside the counsel of God.

In Christian experience God's name is on everything. It is written in the universe, in the great and the small, in the frail and the enduring, in the mighty and the lowly. It controls the powerful, but it is also available to the weak. His name shone above the manger and hung in superscription on the Cross. He used our humanity and infused in it the mystery of eternity.

The great discovery of old age is that God does not lead through the decades to let one down in the crisis times of life. His purpose that satisfies and unites in youth will not throw one down into destruction in old age but runs on to His completion in time.

This morning the lady raised her hand in witness to the reality of her testimony when the soloist sang, "Earth has no sorrow that Heav'n cannot heal."

PRAYER: *We thank You, O God, for the strength that comes to our faith through Your saints who have walked through the valley so valiantly. They have sung in the deep places the song of the redeemed. Surely here is defeat for the rulers of evil and those who prefer to live in darkness. Give us Your comfort through the peace they have received. In Jesus' name. Amen.*

DECEMBER 12

The Lord is my shepherd; I shall not want.
(Ps. 23:1)

When the Psalmist was at work with his pen, I wonder if he knew he was writing to the ages.

What I am today I might not be tomorrow. The quality of life that surrounds me today just might not be the conditions that marked my yesterday. In every mood or changing condition the Psalmist seemed to have anticipated the deeper meanings of life, which relate to God and to eternity.

Often he speaks as a friend and reaches out a hand in defense and says, "Know that the Lord hath set apart him that is godly for himself . . . Stand in awe, and sin not: commune with your own heart . . . Offer the sacrifices of righteousness, and put your trust in the Lord" (4:3-5). He is saying, "Hold steady, friend! I know exactly where you are coming from!"

Often we cry in pain and anguish as if God had turned His face from us. The Psalmist says, "I have been there, too, and one time I said to God, 'How long wilt thou forget me, O Lord? for ever? how long wilt thou hide thy face from me? . . . lighten mine eyes, lest I sleep the sleep of death'" (13:1, 3).

Then the shadow of the Cross falls across the script, and he agrees that no man can stand under the pressures of the guilt of his yesterdays. He says that God has made a way of escape from the past, and he says that he cried to Him, "Purge me . . . and I shall be clean: wash me, and I shall be whiter than snow. . . . Create in me a clean heart, O God" (51:7, 10).

Often God gathers us in His arms while the blessings of peace and hope roll in waves of victory. And the Psalmist says, "Yes, I have been there too; and He prepares a table before me in the presence of my enemies, anoints my head with oil, and pours out blessings until my cup runs over and I can't hold any more."

I need all of this from a necessity for which I have no words to explain.

PRAYER: *O God, You always know the things we need. We do not have to plead with You, because Your love has already anticipated all our want. We need You above all other needs. Amen.*

■ DECEMBER 13

Thy word is a lamp unto my feet, and a light unto my path.
(Ps. 119:105)

It is the Universal Book of God—the best-selling book in all the world, but the least understood by the masses. It is read for information, debate, inspiration, devotion, wisdom, as literature, and for religious instruction.

The Book was written by God, and He is the One who can tell what it means. It is a Book written on human life: the chapters are events; the sentences are happenings marking each day; and the words come out of human experience. All wisdom is here; all justice is here; all love is here. The law of God is here. The cross of Christ, the gate that opens into heaven, is here.

It contains books within the Book, some describing the living Church. It shows men how to be better and out of failure that tends to evil makes them want to be right. For lives broken down in disappointment and despair it cheers by promise and solace. It is a light, a lamp, a tender comfort, a standard by which our shortcomings are measured, and an encouragement by which all our efforts are inspired. It is an answer to every temptation, a refuge in every storm, a place of security and confidence in the uproars of life.

Through its pages Jesus Christ makes himself real, and beginning with Moses and the prophets He expounds to us things concerning himself until our hearts burn within us even while we read. The miracle of the Cross and the triumph of the Holy Spirit climax the Book as we are drawn on day by day even until we ascend the high hill of heaven and see what is meant by God's eternal day.

It is God's Book, written by God for people everywhere.

PRAYER: *We thank You, Lord, in this evil day for the Book of God. There we see Your redeeming plan unfold in love before helpless humanity in sin's darkest moment. We long for a greater knowledge of Your love given to us here. Help us to stay close to the Book lest we lose our way. In Jesus' name. Amen.*

DECEMBER 14 ■

**But thou, O Lord, art a God full of compassion,
and gracious, longsuffering, and
plenteous in mercy and truth.**
(Ps. 86:15)

So full of questions! So full of uncertainties! So full of inadequacies! So full of inconsistencies! So full of fear! So human!

Our humanity is sticking out all over us. How difficult to understand and obey the call that God has addressed to the human soul. We wonder at His patience.

When we grow in wisdom, we grow in our inability to apply it, and ignorance becomes our genius. But God's patience is increased with our failures and is greater than our need. We are conquered by His goodness, and His love hides us from His angry judgment.

The great revelation of himself comes to the waiting heart through His mighty Word, sharper than a sword but softer than the dew. It comes with a whisper that cannot be imitated, nor can it be mistaken. It comes as a still, small voice: now of reason, now of encouragement, now of persuasion. But it comes hiding in itself all the thunder and judgment that went before. His infinity is suppressed in one still, small, tender voice of love.

His revelation lays a grip upon us and binds us in servitude that we cannot resist. It is everything that can cheer, satisfy, and delight. It brings contentment to the soul, and it comes with a touch as gentle as the morning. This we can know in Christ the Son, the Alpha and the Omega—God over all.

Our enemies are hidden in His forgiveness. Our humanity is hidden in the Divine. Our weakness is hidden in His patience.

It is a long way from darkness to light, weakness to strength, from the depths of sin to the highest attainment of grace. But all of this is ours when we are linked to God's eternity.

PRAYER: *O God, we are so inexperienced in all the deeper mysteries of life. At the end of the day our record is one of blundering. Have patience with us in our ignorance and give to us that measure of Your grace that will give us a better tomorrow. In Jesus' name. Amen.*

DECEMBER 15

And she brought forth her firstborn son, and wrapped him in swaddling clothes, and laid him in a manger; because there was no room for them in the inn.
(Luke 2:7)

We are rapidly moving into the Christmas season with the horrendous expenditures and maddening rush for things. Grotesque characterizations trying to depict goodwill are as sham as the cloak under which they take refuge. The clang of the golden till announces the violence of human nature in its effort not to be outdone in the economy of the day. In the puzzlement of trying to understand the vanity in the competition, the heart cries out, "Is this what Christmas is all about?"

Somewhere we learned that Christmas was about a little Baby born in a manger. He came from God to do good in our world and bring salvation to the hearts of people everywhere. He was to be born anew in our spirits as the Christ of love, the Seal and the Glory of our life.

Somewhere we learned that our hearts were made for Him and that we were meant to live in Him and have Him live in us. He was to be the Root of all things, and in Him we would have growth and hope and bear fruit for His glory.

Somewhere we learned that His birth was closely related to His death on the Cross, and in the Cross we would be bound together in a noble fellowship. And while we lingered at the Cross, we would see the crown, and the angel of God would liberate us from the sting of death.

The clanging of bells and the raucous outcry of the money changers and the emotions of selfishness tend to harden the hearts for which this moment came to soften.

In this season of the year, if our world is not reaching out to touch the hem of His garment to be made whole, we do trust that it may touch the swaddling clothes of the Child and worship Him there.

PRAYER: *Help us, O God, to stop in the midst of our worldly pursuits and maddening rush that we might bow our knees at the manger of Bethlehem. Help us to pour out our praise and renew our commitment before the majesty of heaven's Gift to us—the Christ of Christmas. In His name. Amen.*

DECEMBER 16

Who can understand his errors? cleanse thou me from secret faults. Keep back thy servant also from presumptuous sins.
(Ps. 19:12-13)

Of all the shortcomings of human nature the most universal and never ending is the unique ability to make mistakes. It is very easy to make a mistake. It is very difficult to recover from the blunder. But if we were all turned away as delegates for glory because of our errors, heaven would have to close its doors or look elsewhere for its saints.

Probably our biggest mistake is the manner in which we handle the error. Often people do not accept them, but then they lose heart and go down in defeat under a spirit of condemnation. The next step is carelessness and disregard, and the helpers out of the dilemma are few. Sometimes people recognize the error, make amends, and carry on. Even here, while many will be on hand to assess the damage, few stay on to help in the mending.

It has often been said that we learn by our mistakes, but many are they who meet defeat in their first failure. Not because of the error, but because of the onlooker.

There is a sense in which God is not dependent upon me, nor does my devotion make Him what He is. He could do without me, and He does not have to be concerned with my blunders. But that is not the God of the Bible, nor is it the Christian view. We should never get the idea that God is not affected when we make a mistake.

If defeat comes from discouragement, then victory is assured if we are able to stand hand in hand with God in the dilemma. Surely if He watches the falling of the sparrow and numbers the hairs of our head, He can be counted on for fuller disclosures when our salvation is on the line.

His grace is greater than the blunders, and His blood covers the stain of sin.

PRAYER: *Pity us, O God, in our weaknesses and do not hold our shortcomings and blunders against us. Hear us in these things that weigh heavily upon our hearts. If we have omitted anything from our devotion, You will not omit it from Your love. May the miracle of Your grace triumph over all our errors. In Jesus' name. Amen.*

■ **DECEMBER 17**

> **But seek ye first the kingdom of God, and his righteousness: and all these things shall be added unto you.**
> **(Matt. 6:33)**

A little boy in our Sunday School Christmas program was being coached in his recitation by his teacher. He stopped, waved his hand in protest, and announced, "Leave me alone; I can do it all by myself." Early in life we assert our independence, and nowhere is it as important as in our personal relationship with God.

How soon in life we come face-to-face with those things that tend to baffle, disappoint, and confound us. In our attempt to justify our independence we become confused with the answers that are placed upon these things for us. Sooner or later we come upon these eternal values and the idea of a personal God, which must be resolved for ourselves and by ourselves.

The whole tone of the ministry of Jesus Christ was concerned with decisions in this regard. He said we should seek first the kingdom of God and His righteousness, and everything else would find its proper place in relation to it. We must find our own place in relation to eternity before we can find our place in other areas of life.

Moses spent time in the presence of God, waiting for the divine purpose to be fulfilled in his life; and when he came down from the mountain, his face shone with the glory of heaven.

Daniel did not grope about or hesitate but came swiftly to the point, for he had made an earlier choice, and now he stated his own testimony to the fact: "My God hath sent his angel, and hath shut the lions' mouths" (Dan. 6:22).

There is no other way. "I must do it all by myself." It has to be a personal decision for God and the things of eternal value.

PRAYER: *O God, we believe that a personal encounter with Jesus Christ is the greatest matter in our personal salvation. Through each encounter may we be drawn onward to the things that are full of God and therefore full of heaven. And make us strong in Jesus' name. Amen.*

DECEMBER 18 ■

To give light to them that sit in darkness and in the shadow of death, to guide our feet into the way of peace.
(Luke 1:79)

Early one morning I heard a news commentator remark, "There has been a total collapse of human goodness in our world." The words were prompted by a deep sense of frustration over the preparations for Christmas and the confused meaning that is capturing our society. The gist of his report was despair, and he allowed no room for a possible return to the manger or for the ministry of the Babe of Bethlehem.

Jesus himself came into a world of moral degradation and faced human nature that was before Him. He became one of us so that He might review with us the ABCs of righteousness. And He did not throw the whole alphabet at us all at once. Nor did He chastise the slow learner. He is always asking us, "Where can you begin?" and proceeds to lead us onward, little by little, to a point where we can feel secure.

How differently each of us say the alphabet! How differently we interpret His Word! How closely some of us stick to the letter and never dare to move off into God's vast sea of truth. He loves to place us under the ministry of the Holy Spirit to "grow in grace and in the knowledge of our Lord and Saviour Jesus Christ" (2 Pet. 3:18). He loves to see us branch out in a love that sees God and touches Him in a manner for which there is no alphabet or even words to describe.

In a large department store that afternoon I stood in the middle of a milling crowd of frustrated shoppers. And I sang in my heart the words of "Away in a Manger" as the music from the loudspeaker filled the air: "Be near me, Lord Jesus . . . And love me, I pray."

I am sure others sang it too. He is still teaching us!

PRAYER: *We thank You, O God, for growth in grace, and for the visions of the Christ child that grow brighter every day. You give us a vision of Your enduring love toward all people on earth. Our patience and love is needed when we see how long is Your seedtime. Help us to see it as You see it. In Jesus' name. Amen.*

DECEMBER 19

And thou shalt call his name JESUS.
(Matt. 1:21)

Isaiah said, "And his name shall be called Wonderful, Counsellor, The mighty God, The everlasting Father, The Prince of Peace" (Isa. 9:6). Jesus said, "Whatsoever ye shall ask of the Father in my name, he may give it you" (John 15:16).

That name puts all power in heaven and earth at our disposal, yet it seems we are ever asking and not receiving. Here comes the temptation to doubt without looking on the grander side and examining the reasons. In proportion to our asking in His name, in the pure meaning of the command and the holiness of heaven, will the response of Divinity be ours? For His name is honesty, integrity, selflessness, tenderness, purity, and love.

The whole purpose of God toward His people is love, and He takes no delight in seeing us in anxiety, in distress, in darkness, and in disappointment. His love expresses His eternity, but He will not bow down to our selfish will or even to our genius.

No soul that waits upon Him in trembling faith and reverent love will be disappointed. For when we are lifted up above all that is mean in earth and time, we will know the answer of the Divine. When we come in the name that is above every name, we will not be sent away empty.

God knows exactly where we stand before Him, and He has written down the answer to every problem we encounter. He tells us that the things He has prepared for us are larger than our highest imagination.

The demand of heaven is faith out of a pure heart. The response is that as the heavens are high above the earth, so is God's generosity above our asking, and it is all in Jesus' name!

PRAYER: *We come to You, O God, in that name that is above every name. There we would sing our psalms and breathe our thanksgivings and speak our desires. We know that there is no redeeming help within ourselves and that our all is in God through the precious name of Jesus. Amen.*

DECEMBER 20 ■

Then Joseph her husband, being a just man, and not willing to make her a publick example, was minded to put her away privily.
(Matt. 1:19)

What did that first Christmas mean to Joseph, the man who was to become the husband of Mary?

Customs were rigid in his day, penalties were severe, and retribution accepted no moderation. Into this society Joseph was espoused to a young girl who was found to be "with child" (Matt. 1:18). As he was about to remove her from public condemnation, an angel of the Lord said to him, "Fear not . . . for that which is conceived in her is of the Holy Ghost" (v. 20). Here was weakness in confrontation with strength, and there is always a point of supremacy.

When something of an extraordinary nature occurs in our society, it is easy to point the finger of accusation. And the angel of God does not always come in the night with a solution for the crisis. We begin to measure heights, examine doctrines, and build ideals to support judgment. This was Joseph's day too, but the angel brought quietness and created peace for the troubled soul.

In times like these we long for One who can rule and guide and bless and say to the accusers, "He that is without sin among you, let him first cast a stone at her" (John 8:7). Anyone can judge and condemn and sit upon the judgment seat and pronounce upon others the judgment worthy of the deed. Our day, as well as Joseph's, needs the angel voice to declare the truth.

Joseph was able to take the larger view, for he knew the language of the Divine, and the emotions of the human spirit were in touch with heaven. He was not far from the manger.

Joseph's angel is still able to speak to our dilemma through the mystery of that manger.

PRAYER: *Life, O God, is not easy in a world that is full of unrighteousness and corruption. How often we meet with rebuff and feel the sting of Satan's power! Put life back together again and show us that it is a temple not made with hands—it is the Lord's doing. You do all things well. In Jesus' name. Amen.*

DECEMBER 21

And Mary said, My soul doth magnify the Lord, and my spirit hath rejoiced in God my Saviour.
(Luke 1:46-47)

What did the first Christmas mean to Mary, the wife of Joseph and the mother of Jesus?

In the Magnificat, Mary expresses her joy in one of the most noble songs in any language. Her subject is a Savior, and the song is a hymn of faith. It is the fullest expression of challenge and prophetic knowledge in a pledge with God. A Savior is to be born. And Mary is the handmaiden chosen of God.

To Mary this event was the realization of a long-awaited hope. The prophets had been talking about it, and now Mary hears it directly from heaven. "Fear not, Mary . . . thou shalt . . . bring forth a son, and shalt call his name JESUS" (Luke 1:30-31). Through her this promise was to become a reality.

It meant the rejuvenation of a weary soul. "My spirit hath rejoiced in God." She could not understand the way that God was working through her, but how sweetly she accepts and is able to sing of the wonders of His favor. We know little about the surrounding events, but the hope is revealed in a Light to the world.

Here was the revelation of a loving God. Now comes the greatest mystery of all times—the manifestation of that love in person. This was not a miracle measurable in time, but Mary knew it as a miracle of truth and divine love for all ages. That first Christmas meant that the Desire of all nations had come (Hag. 2:7), and that the long-awaited Savior would be born into this world.

God's miracle did not find its completion at Bethlehem. He is still being born in hearts every day in hope and in revelation in God's extension of time.

PRAYER: *In the gift of Your Son, O God, we have our confidence and brightest hope. It brings thanksgiving for all the possibilities of grace and the mystery of communication with the eternal God. It has come down from heaven and is the crown of the gospel. Help us to abide in this hope. In Jesus' name. Amen.*

DECEMBER 22

And she brought forth her firstborn son, and wrapped him in swaddling clothes, and laid him in a manger; because there was no room for them in the inn.
(Luke 2:7)

What did that first Christmas mean to the innkeeper who turned away the Holy Family?

The Romans were ruling the world with tyranny. The Jew was looking for the promised Messiah. A proclamation came from Caesar Augustus that all the world should be taxed. Joseph, with his wife, Mary, being great with child, came to Bethlehem in response to the decree.

In the land where hospitality was duty, there was no room for the weary travelers. When the innkeeper opened the door, he saw a drab-robed peasant girl from Nazareth with her carpenter husband and a tired donkey covered with dust. He shook his head and said, "We have no room."

He shut the door on God's condescension. He who had been the Creator, graced heaven with His presence, and filled it with His love came seeking an entrance in a world under the awful tyranny of sin. But He was shut out.

The innkeeper shut the door on God's love. Love never did an injustice to any man but sweat drops of blood to defeat the enemy so that man might find redemption. He shut out Love that had come from heaven to win men and save them from sin and judgment.

He shut the door on God himself. God came to the door, but He found rejection. The innkeeper could not have known the meaning of it all, and there is no way to explain it outside the secrets that relate to God and His eternity.

Surely there is a mystery in this prophetic circumstance—no room, no joy, no light, no salvation. The burning agony of rejection haunts our tinseled, Christ-less Christmas today. No room for Him in our inn.

PRAYER: *O Jesus, You were rejected, despised, and disbelieved. You came as a tiny Babe, and they turned You away. You were the Son of God, and they crucified You. Your words touched every heart, and they mocked Your sincerity. Come to our hearts today, we pray—the door is open. Amen.*

DECEMBER 23

And there were in the same country shepherds abiding in the field, keeping watch over their flock by night.
(Luke 2:8)

What did the first Christmas mean to the shepherds in the fields, keeping watch over their flocks?

It was business as usual. The inn was crowded; relatives visited and entertained; questions were asked, and bargains were sealed; watchmen were at their gates, and the Temple was crowded; shepherds were busy in their field, thinking in terms of gain. The thoughts of a Messiah lingered far in the background.

Then it happened! "The angel of the Lord came upon them" (Luke 2:9) and made an announcement to those shepherds, and the heavenly choir came into the world with singing. God's glory shone in their midst, touching them with a bit of heaven, and bringing courage and hope to their night.

The shepherds discovered that God moves in unexpected ways. The Messiah would be a manger child, and to accept that would be to contradict their own conscience and the expectations of the chief priests.

The faithfulness of God was the message that lit the evening sky that night. "Let us now go . . . and see" (v. 15). These words may go for less than their real value because of their very simplicity. But it is, nonetheless, the thing that has turned men from darkness to the light of God's redemption.

When they saw it, they were satisfied. They saw love and thoughtfulness commingled, one of the immeasurable findings of the gospel with its counterpart in Paul's proclamation, "Behold, I shew you a mystery" (1 Cor. 15:51). And here Christianity makes its greatest offer.

God is always breaking into the routine of duty, revealing himself to us in unexpected ways. We can plan, but God rules, and He is too big to be channeled.

PRAYER: *You have made great provisions for us, O God, in Your plan of redemption, but You have hidden Your secrets from us to be revealed in eternity. Lead us on to the accomplishment of Your divine purpose, and help us keep our eyes on heaven. In Jesus' name. Amen.*

DECEMBER 24 ■

Now when Jesus was born in Bethlehem of Judaea in the days of Herod the king, behold, there came wise men from the east to Jerusalem.
(Matt. 2:1)

What did the first Christmas mean to the wise men who came from the east?

Who were they? How many were in the group? How did they know? How did they couple the star with the birth of Christ? They came to worship and found where He was, and being satisfied, they returned to their own country.

They saw the star and came—but they came to Jerusalem. Cold reasoning is in danger of leaving out the significant part of the mission of God. Much is lost when we are narrow and unsympathetic and search for the answers in our own imagination. The star leads to Bethlehem—God's answer.

Following the star, they found the Christ child, opened their treasures, and presented gifts. No man could have invented Christmas and the spirit of giving. This is from heaven. It is a spirit that transcends philosophy, astronomy, and human reasoning, for it is a revelation that can only come from God.

Having seen and given, they departed for home a different way; their direction was altered. These decisions are God's miracles. These impulses are heaven-born. This is the Lord's doing. They might have turned wholly to their own understanding and followed the demands of Herod. They neither began nor did they end the journey in their own wisdom; the star was from above.

The manger can be our starting place. As we stand at the manger-cradle, we also stand at the Cross, for they merge into one. The Incarnation leads to the Atonement.

We would come to Bethlehem and see—and return to be.

PRAYER: *Great meeting places have been recorded in Your Word, O God, where Your revelation has altered the course of lives. Give us these Bethlehem experiences, we pray, and may each one show us those things that are full of divine truths and, therefore, full of heaven. In Jesus' name. Amen.*

■ **DECEMBER 25**

> Behold, a virgin shall be with child, and shall bring forth a son, and they shall call his name Emmanuel, which being interpreted is, God with us.
> (Matt. 1:23)

What did that first Christmas mean to the world into which the long-awaited Messiah had come?

In the first place human history took on a new departure. There came into the world a Man different from any other man—a Savior and a Redeemer. He came by a miraculous conception and was born under unusual circumstances. His name was to be called "JESUS: for he shall save his people from their sins" (Matt. 1:21). He lived in time for a few years and then returned to heaven before the eyes of His followers.

In no sense can He be spoken of as a purely historical character, for He is the Contemporary of all ages. He is living as certainly upon earth today as He ever lived in Nazareth. He is the Man of today, and there is not a man beside Him. If you go to the grave to look for Him, you will find an angel there who says, "He is not here: for he is risen" (Matt. 28:6). And the perpetual miracle of truth extends from the manger to the Cross and on to the tomb.

The Son of Man came to our world in working clothes. The lame, the blind, the leper, and the sick reached out to Him as He passed by. The Cross holds in its arms the spirit of His sacrifice and echoes His last words to the ages, "It is finished" (John 19:30).

He had come before—a nameless Presence, a wrestling Angel, a Cloud by day, a Fire by night, and in a thousand other ways. But He has come now in His incarnation to Bethlehem and to a depraved and dying world. We can never get all the meaning of His life, but His coming is suited to the needs of all generations. Hallelujah!

Only the word *Hallelujah!* can express the joy of the grateful soul who has seen His star!

PRAYER: *O God, we thank You for Jesus Christ, Your Son, the Gift of Your love and the Seal of Your grace and the redeeming Glory for a sin-sick world. Through this blessed season may Your glory be revealed in us. Make us fit to share the great mystery of the manger. In Jesus' name. Amen.*

DECEMBER 26 ∎

Verily I say unto you, That this poor widow hath cast more in, than all they which have cast into the treasury ... she of her want did cast in all that she had, even all her living.
(Mark 12:43-44)

It was Christmas Eve, and the service was rich with organ and cello music depicting the birth of the Christ child. The pastor's message followed, "After Gold, Frankincense, and Myrrh, What's Left?" He answered his own question by citing the story of the widow who placed all she had in her offering to God.

The next day a 10-year-old boy gave me a bag of cookies for a Christmas present with the apology, "Grandpa, I made them myself." Every indication was that there was a lot of "myself" in the present, which made it so precious.

After the gifts of gold, frankincense, and myrrh, what is left? Myself. And is not that what Christmas is all about? God gave himself to us. Can I give any greater gift to Him than myself? Here in a moment in time a whole revelation is condensed into a single incident, and eternity stands back at the wonder of it all!

There is a mysterious quality in life, the giving of oneself, a tender independence that assures relationship with eternal values. And as far as God is concerned, all other phases of life are secondary. Civilization is continually changing in its demands, educational values change, and even theological positions may be altered. But one must never interfere with the eternal quality of the God relationship that asks for the ultimate in devotion.

The Magi came with their gifts, the widow came with her gift, and we have spent centuries measuring the act with our reckoning. But Jesus turns upside down all our favorite calculations and rules of reckoning and mystifies us with His way of understanding. He singles out the poor widow to confound our reasoning.

After gold, frankincense, and myrrh, what's left? The widow's mite? My bag of cookies—I made them myself? Myself!

PRAYER: *O God, You are always giving; we are always asking and receiving. You so loved the world that You gave—gave Your only begotten Son—gave yourself! You gave Your all. How amazing! This is the miracle of love. Our love is in our giving. Our all! In Jesus' name. Amen.*

■ **DECEMBER 27**

> **The heavens are thine, the earth also is thine: as for the world and the fulness thereof, thou hast founded them.**
> (Ps. 89:11)

Can anything be more out of place than a lighthouse on a rocky ledge in a calm sea on a bright and sunny day? It is much like a parent giving a warning lecture on the evils of the day to a child at a Sunday School picnic. Absurd illustration? Probably not!

Sooner or later the stormy night falls, and the bright beam that flashes out over the wild waves is welcome. This goes very deep into the meaning of life's discipline. Life exhorts us to be prepared for the crisis, expect the unexpected, and be sure of the uncertain.

God is always correcting, chastening, training, and educating us for the changing tides and times of our lives. Life is not a heap of unconnected events, nor is it a blind and impersonal chance presiding over us. God marks off special periods in which He places the limits of our endurance. But along with each period is His caring, guiding, eternal love.

God has promised to walk with us through the storm and the mysteries of life and show us somewhat of the meaning. Even if we never know the reason for this discipline, we shall be strengthened and comforted in His way.

We see great tumult, and we are afraid. We see the mighty billows rolling toward our poor little vessel, and we cannot tell why the angry waves. We see the darkened skies and the flashing lightning, and we are deafened by the sound of the wind. We are utterly without strength against the enemy.

All is well, for in the storm and in the darkest night God's lighthouse sends its flashing beam and says, "I care!"

PRAYER: *Stand by us, O God, and let the light from Your lighthouse shine upon the mysteries of our life. Lead us past every temptation and rocky shoal and lead us safely to heaven. We rest in Your care and continual guidance. In Jesus' name. Amen.*

DECEMBER 28

And ye shall know the truth, and the truth shall make you free.
(John 8:32)

Again we sang the Christmas hope that "the wrong shall fail, the right prevail" in the eternal conflict between good and evil. Right against wrong. Faithfulness against disloyalty. God and Satan. The prayer of hope against the cry of distress. God's Elijah challenging the Ahabs of the devil.

Whenever we encounter the conflicts of life that evil has imposed, we stagger under burdens too great to carry. God is always reaching out to touch the vulnerable points of our lives and put them beyond the range of the enemy's grasp.

Truth has always been a challenge to false religions and wickedness in any form. Moses challenged the sorcerers of Egypt. Elijah challenged the priests of Baal. Jesus challenged the religious system of His day. Today Christianity speaks to the agonies of falsehood that tortures the human heart.

What answers do sinfulness, dishonesty, and wrong have for us? What do they say to our world? Where are the souls that sin has released from the torment of remorse? Where are the mourners whose tears sin has dried up? Where are the graves that sin has promised a happy resurrection?

Millions stand today to praise the Spirit of truth. Jesus singled out Moses and Elijah for conversation on the Mount. The valley is full of those who proclaim that in Christ they have found the joy of pardon. Souls with thanksgiving will say that the spirit of Elijah has rekindled the lamps that the fierce winds of Ahab had blown out.

This is the strength and glory of truth: Living witnesses will ever claim its power and testify to its sufficiency. Truth will prevail "with peace on earth, goodwill to men."

PRAYER: *O God, speak to us some comfortable words out of the great heart of heaven and leave us not without that token of love that we need so badly. We would know more fully the riches of Your truth. What is truth? Who can tell what is hidden within the walls of this great mystery? Take us there, we pray. In Jesus' name. Amen.*

■ **DECEMBER 29**

> **And many resorted unto him, and said, John did no miracle: but all things that John spake of this man were true.**
> **(John 10:41)**

No first sentence is adequate to introduce the person of Jesus Christ, because the subject grows while truth is lost in imgination, and the pen goes dry before the half can ever be told. John's observation was that the world itself would not hold all the books that could be written about his Lord (21:25). All that has ever been thought of in prayer, or dreamed of in poetry, is a mere suspicion of His humanity and a brief vision of His divinity.

Matthew had his own way of looking at the life of Jesus; Mark observed a great many things unseen by others; Luke heard the whisperings of the heart, throbbing and sighing in the battle against sin; John's insight was concerned with the soul of the Master. But in every attempt they were unable to overtake the Christ except in brief lines of some of the things He said and did. These have become our whole library, and in it we have tried to condense the wisdom and love of God in the life of Jesus Christ.

We have followed Him from Bethlehem to Calvary, and we have captured so very little of what He brought down from heaven. Every sentence was a sermon, every word was a gem of wisdom, and every thought was clothed with the glory of eternity. Little children listened in amazement, women wondered at the glorious words from His lips, and the leaders were threatened by His demands. The whole world agreed that "never man spake like this man" (John 7:46). He declared himself to be "the way, the truth, and the life" (14:6), and His entire ministry was a sharing of His deity with our humanity.

No person can stand beside Him, for He stands beyond the range of insight. We reach Him by way of His own sacrifice—the Cross. This is a great mystery, yet it says to each one, "Come unto me . . . I will give you rest" (Matt. 11:28).

PRAYER: *O God, we thank You for Jesus Christ, whom You sent from heaven to be with us. His words are words of life and power. They search the heart and teach Your ways to Your people. May every heart know the joy and the glow of His forgiveness. We would ask for a clearer vision of the Savior of the world. In His name. Amen.*

DECEMBER 30 ■

The Lord will give strength unto his people; the Lord will bless his people with peace.
(Ps. 29:11)

The years always seem to end on a note of sadness, for we use the last few days to look at the horrors that came out of the previous 52 weeks. We look for the 10 most outstanding people, highlight the uglies, and hang crepe on doorknobs of the desolate. We make predictions for the year ahead and then cry, "Peace," when we are certain there will be none. One year from now we will repeat the process.

The problem is that each year we leave out the divine element, which says, "Great peace have they which love thy law" (Ps. 119:165).

"O that thou hadst hearkened to my commandments! then had thy peace been as a river and thy righteousness as the waves of the sea" (Isa. 48:18).

"Peace I leave with you, my peace I give unto you: not as the world giveth, give I unto you. Let not your heart be troubled, neither let it be afraid" (John 14:27).

We keep looking for a quietness that is deceitful and lull ourselves into a slumber that is full of fear. The peace of God that is too deep to be measured eludes us in our search for it in the sensational.

One lady commented this week, "Well, if we can't keep Christ out of Christmas, we should try to keep Him out of politics." Jesus Christ makes himself felt in every sphere of life, and when He moves, the world moves. "He is before all things, and by him all things consist," and by Him all things were made (Col. 1:16-17).

There is a relationship between a Christ who can bring peace to reign, and wars and sorrowful times. The devil has made up his mind he is not going to quit.

But still "all things work together for good," in any year, "to them that love God" (Rom. 8:28).

PRAYER: *Almighty God, You have given great peace to all those who love Your Word. They are blessed with the calm of heaven. How thankful we are that our God is a strong Rock, our Peace in peril, and our Abiding Place while the ages roll. May it ever be so. In Jesus' name. Amen.*

■ **DECEMBER 31**

For the Lord God is a sun and shield: the Lord will give grace and glory: no good thing will he withhold from them that walk uprightly.
(Ps. 84:11)

Rush! Rush! Rush! The pendulum has ticked off the moments of the old year. Our days are but a handful, and we have no guarantee of any great extension of time. But God has given us a portion of His providence this year as we have been able to stop and enjoy the bounty of His love.

We cannot catch and hold the days, nor can we recall the yesterdays to mend. They come in darkness, and they go in darkness. They come to us with hope, and they leave us with memories. Every day is a treasury of moments given to us to spend, for which we must give an account of the outlay.

The old year is now dying, so full of the goodness of its Maker, yet so full of trouble. Sometimes the rod has been heavy, and graves have been dug where we would have least expected them. But God has drawn us closer to the divine meaning of life so that we might find ourselves within the purpose of His love and wisdom.

With the New Year in sight we are able to make better vows and are better able to keep them. With a higher courage and nobler faith in Him we can step out of the old into the new, seeking the right course for our lives.

We would remember the year for the good and thank God for His long-suffering and patience. His love is greater than His judgment, His grace greater than our sin, and His mercy has covered our shortcomings.

The New Year is still in eternity, but He is saying to us, "I will trust you with it."

PRAYER: *O God, we would close out the old year in praise from a grateful heart to a good God. You have done great things for us, whereof we are glad. Many times we were afraid but You sent Your angel to comfort. You have brought us a little closer to heaven. We thank You. In Jesus' name. Amen.*